Ferranti-Packard

Ferranti-Packard

PIONEERS IN CANADIAN
ELECTRICAL MANUFACTURING

NORMAN R. BALL AND JOHN N. VARDALAS

McGILL-QUEEN'S UNIVERSITY PRESS
MONTREAL & KINGSTON · LONDON · BUFFALO

Frontispiece: Ferranti-Packard products contributed to the prosperity of many companies and industries. This 1959 photograph shows a 45-ton capacity direct arc steel melting furnace using a Packard furnace transformer. (Ferranti-Packard Transformers Ltd.)

Design: Peter Moulding
Graphs: Dana Hutton
Index: Philippa Campsie

© Rolls-Royce Industries Canada Inc. 1994
ISBN 0-7735-0983-6

Legal deposit first quarter 1994
Bibliothèque nationale du Québec

Printed in Canada on acid-free paper

Canadian Cataloguing in Publication Data

Ball, Norman R., 1944–
    Ferranti-Packard: pioneers in Canadian electrical manufacturing
    Includes index.
    ISBN 0-7735-0983-6
    1. Ferranti-Packard Transformers Ltd. – History. 2. Electric equipment industry – Canada – History. 3. Electronic industries – Canada – History. I. Vardalas, John N. II. Title.
    HD9697.C334F47 1993   338.7'6213042'0971
    C93-090427-3

This book was typeset by Typo Litho composition inc. in Linotype Sabon.

Contents

Foreword

The past does not come back, but it is not irrelevant; it affects us every day. The more of it we see and understand, the greater our potential for survival and growth.

In times of uncertainty and rapid changes in both technology and the marketplace, knowledge of the past reminds us that we are not strangers to adversity, that we have faced it before and risen above it, and have done so because we are active, not passive. Deeper knowledge of the past also provides another healthy reminder: lest we be too inclined to feel deeply and unalterably in love with our current technology and products, let us remember that technology and product lines are the expressions of something far more valuable – the ability to change. Responsiveness to change is one of the hallmarks of living systems, and the past provides the best laboratory for understanding the dynamics of wise change, the best reminder that change is the key to continuing life.

History books are products of the present and provide only an approximation of the past, but one hopes that the approximation is blessed with wisdom and insight. If there are gaps, critical areas about which we can find too little, let us see them as reminders to record our present achievements more carefully for the future. Ferranti-Packard will not disappear – change, yes; disappear, no – and in the future there will be other histories. Let us think about them now.

History books do not just happen, any more than corporate health or new products just happen. This book owes its existence to the foresight of Wordie Hetherington, P.Eng. and Barry Hercus, P.Eng. Both men are former presidents and chief executive officers of Ferranti-Packard. Proud of Ferranti-Packard's achievements and well aware of its failings, these two men understood the significance of the past in charting the future. They championed the cause of this book. For nearly a century, the men and women of Ferranti-Packard have played important engineering, corporate, and manufacturing roles in the growth of Canada. It is time that the company's story is told.

The early interest of John Vardalas in Ferranti-Packard's pioneering efforts in computers and electronics raised the company's awareness of its own contributions and reminded it how quickly the collective memory fades. When Ferranti-Packard and John began to discuss a book about the company's history, I was asked about becoming senior author. Corporate histories of Canadian engineering and/or manufacturing firms are rare. Thus when the opportunity to explore and relate the history of a company such as Ferranti-Packard arose, I was excited and enthusiastic. The three years that followed are best described as arduous fun.

The first chapter of this book presents the reader with the key technological and economic developments in the nineteenth century that set the stage for widespread electrification, the rise of Canada's electrical industry, and the birth of Ferranti-Packard. The development of alternating current (AC) as a means of transmitting electrical energy over great distances was at the heart of a powerful technological, economic, and social revolution. Ferranti-Packard, as the reader will discover, has its roots in the AC revolution.

Ferranti-Packard represents the confluence of two corporate traditions: Packard Electric and Ferranti Electric. Each company grew out of very different corporate and engineering traditions and mindsets. In chapters 2 through 5, the book traces the histories of these two companies as they tried to steer a profitable course through nearly thirty-five years of major technological, economic, social, and political change in Canada. In chapter 6, the reader discovers how the new post-1945 global trading realities brought the two companies together. The first five chapters examine the development of Packard Electric and Ferranti Canada as competing manufacturers of electrical-power equipment. From chapter 6 on the two companies have merged as Ferranti-Packard. In addition to seeing how two distinct corporate cultures are brought together, chapter 9 describes Ferranti-Packard's pioneering efforts in digital computer and communications systems. It also shows how Canada wrestled with the critical problem of whether to encourage innovative, leading-edge research and manufacturing or ride on the coat-tails of others.

Though John and I are the authors and must assume responsibility for errors and omissions, this corporate history was the work of many hands. We owe a great measure of appreciation to the members of the Ferranti-Packard History Committee; they freely made a double contribution: long and honourable service to the company and keen devotion to bringing Ferranti-Packard's story to light. In total they represent 170 years of service. Their commitment has lived on after retirement, and each gladly contributed time and expertise in many ways. We are deeply grateful to Gordon Helwig, Wordie Hetherington, Ed Love, and Jack Wagstaff.

Others could not serve on the History Committee but shared their knowledge, experience, and insight, and again we are unable to thank everyone but wish to give special thanks to Charlie Begin, Jack Coopman, Dave Durgy, Tom Edmondson, Barry Hercus, Bill Lower, Don Ritchie, Ian Sharp, Don Smart, Frank Squires, Ray Taylor, John Thomson, Bob Veitch, and Burt Wigley. Particular mention should also go to Les Wood, one of the founding members of the Electronics

Division. His contributions have been invaluable in sorting out the complexities of the Electronics Division. We also thank the management of Ferranti-Packard Transformers Ltd, St. Catharines, for continuing support and Pierre Lanouette of Ferranti-Packard Transformers Ltd., Trois-Rivières, for his enthusiasm and rapid responses.

For sharing his extensive knowledge of the history of the Packard Brothers and their early motor cars, I am deeply indebted to Terry Martin of Warren, Ohio. For assistance in locating photographs and generosity in allowing their use, we are indebted to the Packard Museum Association and its president, Wendell F. Lauth, as well as Barbara Wasko of Packard Electric. Many of the photographs in this book are from the Ferranti-Packard Collection in the Ontario Archives, where Katrin Cooper enthusiastically provided quality copies of photographs under sometimes harried circumstances. For use of illustrative material our thanks also to AEG Firmenarchiv, Bell Canada Telephone Historical Collection, Canada Institute for Scientific and Technical Information, Canada Patent Office, Canadian Patent Office Record, City of Toronto Archives, Mrs. Lillian Diggins, Ferranti Family Archives, Ferranti plc Archives, Ferranti-Packard Transformers Ltd., The Illustrated London News Picture Library, Madame Gignac, Barry Hercus, London Electric Supply Corporation, Ed Love, the Museum of Science & Industry, National Archives of Canada, National Library of Canada, National Museum of Science and Technology, Ontario Archives, Ontario Hydro Archives, Oxford University Press, Packard Museum Association, St Catharines Museum, Science Museum, Smithsonian Institution, Ontario Hydro, and Toronto Transit Commission Archives.

Learning and writing about a company that is still succeeding has been a pleasure. That is why, as authors, our deepest debt of gratitude is owed to the many men and women who, for nearly a century, have made Ferranti-Packard and its predecessors the success that it is. We also thank their families, for we know that commitment and dedication do not stop at quitting time.

Of the many who keep going until the work is done, there is one in particular whose support, decisions, understanding, and problem-solving skills kept this project going and smoothed some of the roughest spots. My deepest thanks to Paul Cassar, vice-president, Finance, Rolls-Royce Industries Canada Inc. It is a rare pleasure to work with such a truly fine administrator.

Much of the greatness and resilience of companies flows from those whose names are never known to the authors of books such as this one. I wish I knew everyone but I do not. This book is dedicated to the many who have not been named, a gift from the past to the future.

Norman R. Ball
Centre for Society, Technology and Values
Department of Systems Design Engineering
University of Waterloo

Preface

Packard Electric's "net worth is higher than ours, but they have a rotten old building and plant, and are doing less work than we are, so they have less money involved in stock and debtors, but in spite of these two items, they make more profits than we do and have more cash and investments.

In other words, we must pull up our socks and make our profits commensurate with our better equipment and bigger turnover."

Sir Vincent Ziani de Ferranti, memo to Ferranti Limited management, 1941[1]

Examination of a company over an extended period offers unparalleled opportunities for insight into today's concerns, particularly corporate culture and survival, technology, and successful innovation. While Canada has no shortage of theoreticians or science and industry policy experts, it has alarmingly few studies which explore corporate culture, technology, and how things really worked over the long haul.

For the past three years the authors have had unrestricted access to the corporate records, archival papers, and personnel of Ferranti-Packard, a company tracing its origins back nearly one hundred years. If Ferranti-Packard is typical, Canadian corporate cultures exert widespread influence. Varied and complex, they are capable of changing, but not easily.

Ferranti-Packard Ltd. came into being in 1958, four years after the British firm Ferranti Ltd., much to the pleasure of the company being purchased, increased its holdings to become sole owner of Packard Electric Company Ltd. With the merger of Ferranti Ltd.'s two Canadian subsidiaries, Ferranti Electric and Packard Electric, two very different techno-corporate cultures which had survived as competitors became partners. Ferranti Electric, operating in Canada but rooted in British practice, had to become more open and more respectful of Canadian needs and abilities. Packard Electric, with North American roots, was more attuned to a Canadian or continental vision.

Both companies were respected transformer manufacturers; before the formal merger in 1958 Ferranti Electric had actually built larger transformers than Packard. Both companies had pursued quality but with different attitudes towards technology, perfection, and the marketplace. The Ferranti arm of the new company had grown from the brilliant theoretical, but sometimes financially undisciplined, work of Sebastian Ziani de Ferranti, the founder of Ferranti Ltd. Ferranti was largely a technology-driven company with a near obsessive interest in theory, laboratory work, and creating the best possible technology whether or not it was what the market really wanted. The Packard arm had been started by the Packard brothers, better known today as automobile pioneers. James Ward Packard was an adventurous mechanical engineering graduate, his brother William Doud Packard the rare combination of consummate salesman and disciplined businessman. The company they created was more market driven than Ferranti; it had to be. Packard owner-managers had an almost obsessive fear of debt or loss of control over their relatively small, wholly independent company. They certainly had an intense sense of ownership and involvement. Not surprisingly, the companies weathered hard times differently. As a subsidiary of a larger, well-endowed company, Ferranti Electric dug into its parents' deep pockets. Packard Electric was alone, dependent on its own resources and resourcefulness. But the most significant difference was that Ferranti had started to branch out and explore new fields while Packard stuck to what it knew best.

Differences notwithstanding, the merger of these two very capable and individually successful companies formed a new corporate unit stronger than the sum of its parts. The characteristic mindset associated with those who work with the mature technology of sophisticated, high voltage power equipment was joined with the approach of explorers on the leading edge of developments in computers and electronics. Both companies contributed to survival under one management strategy but it was not always easy. The newly created company had to encompass two different technological trajectories, each driven by distinct patterns of innovation and market forces. One trajectory was the result of mature electrical power technology with long innovation cycles, the other, of emerging computer and electronics technology with short innovation cycles.

During the 1960s the technology and market-driven corporate cultures within Ferranti-Packard pursued excellence, each in its own way. Through its work in computers and electronic display systems, the technology-driven Ferranti culture pursued its future on the frontier of emerging technology. Packard, too, sought a more perfect future, but through innovation within the traditional and more mature electric power industry.

This book shows how two smaller companies adapted and innovated in order to fight for survival beside General Electric and Westinghouse, giants with large R&D budgets. Ferranti and Packard each had its own survival strategy, both before the merger and after.

Packard's early specialization in furnace transformers is an example of a small company identifying and pursuing a highly specialized niche, while Ferranti's inclination was to explore the emerging worlds of computers and electronics. The complete history of Ferranti-Packard provides the opportunity to explore a number of illuminating examples of innovation by small companies in an often unfriendly economic climate. The company's bold pioneering in the development of digital electronic and computer technology – part of Ferranti-Packard's attempt to build an indigenous Canadian computer industry – reveals the drama, precariousness, and excitement of life on the leading edge of technology, where the smaller company often finds itself trying to run with an idea whose development costs quickly outstrip its financial capacity. While there are no universal solutions for survival and growth in this type of situation, there are questions and reminders. We found, for example, that good engineering in the narrow technical sense is not enough to make profits. The Ferranti-Packard story underscores the importance of determining the skill sets and personality traits which a company should look for and cultivate in its engineers. A company is fortunate indeed to have a technically fine engineer with remarkable commercial ability.

Examining the birth and survival of modern industries or corporations inevitably raises questions about the roles of government. The authors believe there is no magic formula to determine the amount and kind of government involvement in business. However, the Ferranti-Packard story highlights some important points that merit the kind of study and understanding that comes only from research covering an extended period of time. It is essential to understand when government action is helping the pursuit of opportunities flowing from change and when it is merely pumping bodily fluids into the clinically dead.

Carefully crafted military and civilian government contracts nurtured Ferranti-Packard's Electronics Division at critical phases. These led to the development of useful products and gave the Electronics Division exploration time when there was no preexisting market to draw upon, such as that available to the Meter and Transformer Divisions, which sold to Canadian utilities. To escape dependence on a then-inadequate Canadian demand for high tech products made in Canada, the Electronics Division tried to become a global player in computer-related technology. This gave the Electronics Division brutal experience of what happens when an inadequate capital base is combined with the inability of a private company to raise large amounts of capital without going public. The ambitions of the Electronics Division revealed just how harmful government can be when it makes policy which is not informed by a systems point of view. The government of Canada created an inherently illogical set of policies that discouraged investment and placed Canadian manufacturers at a government-mandated disadvantage. Inherently confused industrial policy pitted Ferranti-Packard, and other pioneers, against a system which offered industrial development grants to encourage investment and location and then hammered Canadian firms with unfair tax laws. The duty rate that Canadian manufacturers paid on computer parts was almost three times that paid on finished computers manufactured out of country. Moreover, foreign manufacturers or importers paid a far lower rate of federal sales tax than domestic manufacturers because the former paid tax on wholesale price whereas the hapless Canadian manufacturers paid federal sales tax on retail price. There was no excessive whining by business over this problem, but it illustrates the dysfunctional nature of certain aspects of government policy. This book explores this and many other aspects of the relationship between government and industry.

Canadians have long worried about the economic implications of relative scarcity of population in a large land mass. With the fading of dreams such as Winnipeg surpassing Chicago in size and importance, or the population of Canada rivaling that of the United States, thoughts and questions about corporate and business survival became a more important issue. The story of Ferranti-Packard provides a glimpse into the way smaller Canadian electrical manufacturers survived in a North American market dominated by increasingly large integrated manufacturers. It is also the story of a Canadian company operating on an increasingly large or global stage.

A major part of Canada's response to the problem of encouraging industrial growth has been to rely heavily on foreign investment, as distinct from borrowing. The resultant growth of a branch plant economy has caused much agony and troubled thought. It has also produced passionately argued speculative thought and unproven assumptions which have been elevated to the level of religious dogma. Strident voices have portrayed branch plants as the domains of unthinking, conscienceless, subservient toadies at the beck and call of foreign masters. But, given the dominant approaches to Canadian historical research, few have examined the detailed workings of corporations to see what they are and what actually happened. This book offers a micro-study of the relationship between a Canadian enterprise and its foreign parent firm. We could not find the fabled passive Canadian subsidiary. Instead, we found, for example, intense, bitter conflict between parent and subsidiary as Ferranti Canada – Canadian in management and engineering staff – stood up for its own national interests and identity.

Early branch plants represented the beginning of the now dominant trend towards globalization of capital sourcing. Another facet of globalization is the increasing dispersal of raw materials, parts, components, and sub-assemblies which are consumed or contribute to finished products. One part of Canada's entire political economy, that represented by the fur trade, timber, pulp and paper, mining, fisheries, and agriculture, has been rooted in international markets since the seventeenth century. However, it is a somewhat different story in Canadian manufacturing sectors where higher value is added. Some industries have been quite successful in tapping into foreign markets but there have been many barriers.

Many countries have strongly nationalistic electric power equipment sectors. This was particularly true of the United States, where private utilities had a strong unwritten "Buy American" tradition. In 1960 Ferranti-Packard decided to develop an export trade in power transformers aimed primarily at the potentially lucrative U.S. market. The beneficial consequences of that decision illustrate the importance of choosing the right project. Whether in sales, research, new technology applications, or other avenues of improvement, corporations always have more potential pursuits than resources. What is pursued and invested in is thus one of the most important areas of corporate decision making. Ferranti-Packard's decision to enter the American market succeeded because it combined strong sales efforts, competitive technology, a willingness to relocate partially in the chosen market area, and a marketing strategy that presented them in all respects as an American supplier.

Survival is a fundamental requirement if a company is to achieve anything. In one sense it is an ecological problem: finding a niche or place in a particular environment, adapting to change or bringing it about when necessary. Industrial research, development, innovation, and technology transfer are all survival moves. Often they are also lots of fun and there are periods in the Ferranti-Packard history marked by an almost childlike joy in exploring new technology. That is as it should be, but ultimately one must ask when this new technology should start to pay back. Perhaps this is the most difficult of all research and management questions: circumstances change, time frames are never the same, and various species of products have vastly different maturation periods. Making such decisions requires leaders who are able to adapt to changing situations.

The story of Ferranti-Packard, a sophisticated electrical manufacturing company almost one hundred years old, is above all one of change. Today, in a world of seemingly incessant technological change, frequently accompanied by brutal competitive and corporate change, it is easy to think that no one has ever had it so tough, no one faced such uncertainty. But one must be careful; while it is true that the past never repeats itself identically, and no one has had exactly the same problems, there have been earlier periods of the uncertainty, unreasonable expectations, and confusion that are the inevitable products of significant change.[2] In writing about Ferranti-Packard change is always there, the rhythm section, varying in intensity and urgency, but always there. In the final analysis this is a book about how two Canadian manufacturers responded to the challenge of change.

The detailed study of Ferranti-Packard's relationship with change provides the melody that complements the rhythm and provides greater range, variety, and distinctiveness in a corporate and technological record spanning nearly a century of extraordinary change. Ferranti-Packard's story begins in a period of high expectations comparable to those generated in recent decades by the combination of the proliferation of computers and the alluring prospects of superconductivity. Exciting things were happening, promise abounded, along with daunting technical problems. The truly insightful undoubtedly realized, as did one pioneering superconductivity researcher, that "The question is not 'How can we ... do something everyone has wanted to do?' but 'How can we do something that no one has yet imagined?'"[3]

Significant change rarely generates uniform opinion. Historian Reynor Banham labeled the rise of electrical technology "the greatest environmental revolution in human history since the domestication of fire."[4] An observer of the birth of this revolution saw it as the devil's handiwork because electric motors released girls from honest toil and allowed them to wander the streets where they could "fall prey to the will of Satan."[5]

This book is about change in Canadian engineering, technology, and business. Electrical manufacturing helped put Canadians on an even larger stage, and helped break down barriers which isolated. Generally, the more advanced the technology, the earlier isolation either starts to fade or proves harmful.

Canadian literary critics have examined how the garrison, or fortress, mentality and its preoccupation with survival have sometimes blocked fresh thought and new ideas. The theme of survival in Canadian technology and corporations, however, has attracted little attention. The authors are bold enough to hope that, by example, their study will help balance Canada's decidedly lopsided involvement in historical, corporate, and industrial research.

The authors hope this book will help others realize the intellectual benefits of looking beyond narrow, compartmentalized views of the past. Canadians should be justifiably proud of their place in world electrical history. They pursued electricity so avidly that it was said that "electrical thought has become a national habit."[6] Canadians openly faced and tackled fundamental questions, such as "Who should benefit from new technology?" The creation, for example, of the Ontario Hydro Electric Power Commission in 1906 was a bold, controversial answer that attracted global attention and the flattery of both imitation and well-financed campaigns to misinform the public and discredit the organization. But utilities, regulation, and the politics of electricity are only part of the story. While Canadian achievements have been impressive and varied, writing about them has been far too limited. Overall understanding of the course and impact of electrical developments in Canada is unbalanced or incomplete because too little has been said about technology, engineering, manufacturing, and private business.

The convenience electricity made possible was important, but a primary motivation for business leaders and ordinary citizens who pushed for greater access to electric power was that it would be a driver or engine of business and economic prosperity. Electricity would help existing industry survive; more important, it would create new industry. New electrical technology created electrical equipment and capital goods manufacturers. Yet the manufacturers involved in these advances, such as Ferranti-Packard, have attracted scant attention from historians. This book sets the stage and traces the story of a Canadian business and manufacturing institution which grew to maturity from two very different root stocks. In the over three years it took to write about the often turbulent and precarious history of this company and industry, the authors also learned something about some of the business and technological issues troubling Canada today.

The authors are acutely aware that only so much may be achieved in one book, only so many questions answered. There are worthwhile questions – such as those regarding working conditions on the shop floor, or the role of skilled labour in a mid-sized electrical manufacturer – which were beyond what we set out to do. Recognizing this, we worked very closely with officials of Rolls-Royce Industries Canada Inc., the present owners of Ferranti-Packard Transformers Ltd., and the Provincial Archives of Ontario to organize and preserve the Ferranti-Packard Corporate Archives. We hope this book will encourage other historians of business, labour, and technology to delve into the rich Ferranti-Packard collection, now housed in the Provincial Archives of Ontario, to pursue questions this work does not attempt to answer.

An introduction only hints at what is to come. But one of the authors' greatest wishes is that readers will share and understand our fascination with Ferranti-Packard. Above all, we hope we have provided a good read, one which will leave more than a vague memory, for the legacy and lessons of Ferranti-Packard are far from vague and deserve to be remembered.

1 *The Technology that Gave Birth to Ferranti-Packard*

A distinguished historian of architecture once described the rise of electrical technology as "the greatest environmental revolution in human history since the domestication of fire."[1] While the history of fire is as old as humankind, the story of electric power began only in the last century. Electricity is woven so thoroughly into the fabric of our lives that few people can imagine life without it. As a common household commodity, electricity has ceased being an object of wonder, excitement, and mystery. Yet, only 100 years ago the idea of providing every home, office, and industry with electricity was only teetering on the very edge of the possible. Canada's present-day electrical system grew out of the dreams of visionary inventors, the ambitions of daring entrepreneurs, and the talents of highly skilled engineers. Historians have written much about the history of electrification in Canada but said little about the important role that Canadian electrical manufacturers played in building this nation's many electrical systems.

Ferranti-Packard is one of the oldest electrical manufacturers in Canada. For nearly a century, it has designed, produced, and sold transformers and watt-hour meters. Without transformers, the transmission of electrical energy across Canada's vast landscape becomes technically and economically unfeasible. Watt-hour meters provide the technological basis that allows electricity to be bought and sold as a commodity. Though simple in appearance, these meters are extremely precise instruments that measure continuously the amount of power that each user consumes.

Because these two types of device are the products around which Ferranti-Packard's growth has revolved, any history of the company must start with the origins of the transformer and the watt-hour meter. The two technologies, which developed as integral components of large-scale electrification, are based on alternating current (AC). In this chapter, the reader will learn how revolutionary technical change – namely, the rise of alternating current, in Europe and North America, set the stage for creation of Packard Electric Co. Ltd. and Ferranti Electric Ltd. in Canada.

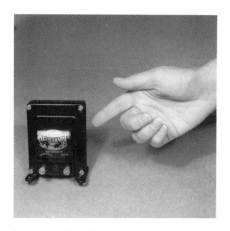

Ferranti-Packard has manufactured transformers in all sizes. The smallest would fit
in a pocket while others, such as the largest,
made in the Toronto plant and photographed 13 November 1972, were bigger than
a house.
(Ferranti-Packard Transformers Ltd. and
Ontario Archives, Ferranti-Packard Collection, neg. 2503–1)

The Birth of Electrical Technology

The interplay of supply and demand has been the central force driving
the development of Canada's electrical system. Under the heading of
supply falls the technology and economic support needed to generate
and distribute electricity. Demand represents society's capacity to
consume electrical energy. Knowledge of what electricity is, how to
produce it, and how to use it has evolved considerably since its discovery in the eighteenth century. In the beginning, progress was slow.
After the discovery of electricity, it took time before anyone could
find any commercial use for it. As it became more readily available,
inventive minds discovered new applications. Commercial opportunities stimulated further improvements in generation and distribution.

The first major break-through in using electrical energy came in
1800, when Alessandro Volta discovered the electro-chemical principles of the battery. Before this time, static electricity was the only
known form of electrical energy. There was very little in the nature of
static electricity that lent itself to practical application. How could
one harness the short, intense discharges associated with it? Volta's
invention, the "Voltaic Pile," replaced the transitory phenomenon
of static electricity with the means to supply a continuous electrical
current.

The first application of Volta's discovery was in the electrolytic

decomposition of compounds. By means of the battery, the British chemist Humphrey Davy was able, in the first decade of the nineteenth century, to isolate hitherto unknown elements, such as potassium, sodium, calcium, magnesium, barium, and strontium.

The first widespread commercial application of the battery, however, arose several decades later, with the perfection of the electric telegraph between 1800 and 1820. Greater demand for this new form of energy spurred improvements in the output, efficiency, and economics of the battery. For many years the battery served as the only source of electrical energy. As electricity became more widespread, two fundamental limitations in the use of the battery became apparent: limited power output and a very short life-time.

In 1831, the English physicist Michael Faraday developed a new and radically different way of producing electrical energy. Through the intermediary of a magnetic field, Faraday's invention transformed mechanical motion into electrical energy, through his discovery of the principle of electromagnetic induction. Whenever a magnetic field moves by a conductor such as wire, or vice versa, an electric current will be induced in the conductor. Faraday's electric generator was crude, but it opened a whole new dimension in the technology and economics of producing electricity. Almost immediately, inventors around the world started designing and building more practical generators, called magneto-electric machines. As long as there was sufficient mechanical energy available, such machines could provide electricity continuously over a very long period.[2]

The electric current made by these new generators behaved very differently from that produced by a battery. Rather than always flowing with the same intensity and in the same direction, it was an "alternating current" (AC). Not only did the voltage continually oscillate in value from zero to a maximum, but the current flow kept changing directions. No one knew what to do with this new type of current. Direct current (DC) flowed in one direction, and the direct, or unidirectional flow of current from batteries had shaped the applications of electricity. The invention of the metallic commutator by William Sturgeon in 1835 let magneto-electric machines produce electricity that was compatible with existing DC requirements for current flow in one direction. Only machines equipped with commutators produced unidirectional current, and the pole, or terminal, that started as positive stayed positive rather than constantly flipping from positive to negative and back.

Development of electric generators remained slow for several decades. By the end of the 1860s, the electric arc light was on the verge of becoming commercially viable, but one obstacle stood in its way. There was no reliable and economically acceptable electric generator powerful enough to illuminate a system of arc lamps. In 1870, the Belgian Zenobe Théophile Gramme, a carpenter by training, developed the first practical dynamo. An immediate commercial success, the Gramme dynamo provided the robust, economical power source needed to launch the electric arc light industry. The resulting growth in demand for arc lighting, in turn, stimulated further innovations in dynamo design.

Although arc lamps produced a brilliant light, they had several drawbacks. The crackling noise of the arc, the smell of ozone, and the intense light made them more suitable for street lighting than for indoor use. Indoor electric lighting became a reality with the invention of the incandescent lamp. Pioneered by Joseph Swan, in England, and Thomas Alva Edison, in the United States, this type of lighting propelled the electrical industry to new commercial heights. With the prospect of such lighting in every home, the market for electric power offered enormous economic potential.

The social impact of the electric light was far-reaching. Electric light became a welcomed replacement to smelly, dangerous gas lighting. Cheap and reliable illumination blurred the eternal rhythm of night and day. The dim glow of candles, oil lamps, and gas lighting had little to offer in this regard. One contemporary novelist described electric light as "radiant electricity" that produced an "immortal transformation of night into day."[3] This may appear to be poetic exaggeration but to the nineteenth-century mind the light bulb was far from mundane. Some saw electric light as a powerful tool to dissipate "moral darkness." As one popular slogan put it: "one electric light is as good as one policeman."[4]

Parallel with development of the electric light came another surprising application for electrical energy. Faraday had shown that mechanical energy could be transformed into electrical energy. Once this discovery had been given practical form, inventors started to experiment with the idea of reversing the process. Could electrical energy be economically converted into mechanical energy? In other words, could the operation of the dynamo be reversed? Gramme's Ring Dynamo proved that the reversal was practical, and the electric motor was born. Initially, powered by batteries, motors had limited application. Before long, "electricians," as electrical engineers were referred to, came to a simple, but far reaching conclusion: dynamos that powered electric lights could also run motors.

In the words of historian Lewis Mumford, the electric motor "effected revolutionary changes in industry."[5] It led to re-evaluation and redesign of the forces of production. The advent of steam power greatly spurred industrial expansion. However, the limitations of steam and mechanical transmission of power became more intolerable as factories and mills grew. Not only was the steam-engine inefficient, but the entire system that was needed to distribute the power became increasingly cumbersome and wasteful as it grew. By the 1880s, the interior of mechanized manufacturing works had become a veritable jungle of pulleys, belts, and shafts.

Individual electric motors installed where power was needed could eliminate the inefficient and sometimes dangerous line-shaft-and-pulley system. Freedom from the restrictions of transmitting power mechanically meant that the factory floor could now be designed on functional grounds to optimize the manufacturing process. Electric power and the electric motor also gave a new lease on life and new opportunities to small shops and manufacturers who could not support a large, expensive steam-engine.

Although the electric motor had a profound effect on industry, the technology did not spread as quickly as some wanted. Manufacturers were reluctant to discard large capital investments made in steam technology. Moreover, some thought the whole process irrational. Why, they asked, use mechanical energy to produce electricity only to get back mechanical energy? They failed to recognize electricity as an easy-to-use medium for transmitting power.

As electric power became more abundant and cheaper, the traditional steam-engine technology gave way to the electric motor. The effects of the new motor as a source of mechanical power went beyond industrial applications and reverberated throughout Western society. This new source of mechanical power prompted a multitude of applications that transformed the material quality of life. Through transportation technology, it gave people greater geographical mobility and offered hope for the ever-growing congestion of inner-city life. With the internal combustion engine for automobiles still several years away, electrical power offered a new framework for urban transportation. The electric train, first developed in Germany, by the Siemens company in 1879 for the Berlin Exhibition, rescued inner-city dwellers: housing no longer had to be concentrated around the factory site. At the close of the nineteenth century, a retrospective editorial in *Electrical Review* observed:

perhaps no agency has had in so short a time so great an effect as has the electric railroad, now in the thirteenth year of its flourishing age ... There is no work conceivable by the most enlightened philanthropy that is more important, both to the future and the present of civilized countries, than the proper housing of urban populations. To spread the city into the country and give every family a chance at the fresh air and daylight is something that the ubiquitous trolley car has already accomplished in many places, and is steadily doing wherever it has been introduced in the greater cities.[6]

The supply of electricity, as represented by dynamo technology, and demand for it, as reflected in the spread of lighting and motors, fed on each other and developed as one organic system. The technical and economic requirements of electric lighting and motors engendered improvements in the generation of electricity. From 1870 to 1890, there was a veritable explosion of innovations in the design of dynamos. By reducing the cost and increasing the accessibility and reliability of electrical service, these innovations stimulated further demand for lighting and motors. Electrical technology elicited considerable social and economic expectations, and consumption of electrical energy started its upward climb.

From the earliest magneto-electric machines to the most advanced dynamos of the 1880s, electrical energy had been generated and used in direct-current form. As the popularity of electrical service grew, it became increasingly costly and more inefficient to transmit required amounts of DC power over ever-greater geographical areas.

The fundamental problem lay in the nature of electrical power, which is calculated as voltage times current. During transmission, some electrical energy is lost in what is called Joule's heating. The amount of loss is proportional to the value of the current squared. Therefore the key to low energy loss, or high efficiency, is transmission at high voltage and low current.

Unfortunately, at the consumer's end it is safer and more practical to use power at low voltage. Therefore the ideal system would have high voltage for transmission and low voltage for consumers. But it was impractical and dangerous to generate electric power at high voltages. The ideal electrical-power system would have: generation at relatively low voltages, transmission over great distances at the highest voltage possible, and delivery to the customer's premises at low voltages.

Decentralized distribution of small DC electric generating stations, each serving a very limited area of the city, appeared at first to be the only means to widespread electrification. Some voices were raised against this approach. In what is today called the "not-in-my-backyard" (NIMBY) syndrome, people objected to having smoky, coal-fired electric generating stations nearby. They wanted power from afar, or at least from another neighbourhood. A fundamental debate

Ferranti-Packard watt-hour meters, such as this on a St Catharines home in 1971, were found all across Canada. Watt-hour meters helped turn electricity into a basic commodity which could be measured and purchased according to the amount used. (Ontario Archives, Ferranti-Packard Collection, neg. 2310)

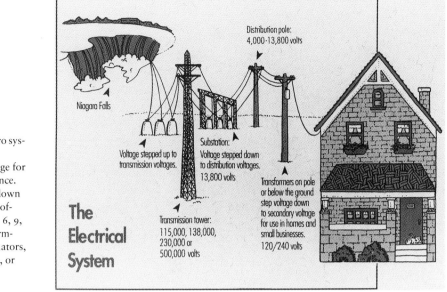

The Electrical System

Niagara Falls

Voltage stepped up to transmission voltages.

Transmission tower: 115,000, 138,000, 230,000 or 500,000 volts

Substation: Voltage stepped down to distribution voltages. 13,800 volts

Distribution pole: 4,000-13,800 volts

Transformers on pole or below the ground step voltage down to secondary voltage for use in homes and small businesses. 120/240 volts

This representation of the Toronto Hydro system illustrates the role of transformers. First they step up from generation voltage for more efficient transmission over a distance. Then they provide successive stepping down for safer delivery. Once in the house or office, voltages may be further reduced to 6, 9, or 12 volts by customer-owned transformers for applications such as pocket calculators, portable computers, dictating machines, or halogen lighting. (Toronto Hydro)

erupted over the best way to move electrical energy from the generator to the customer. Since all the parts of the electric power system are interdependent, the battle over distribution also covered methods of generation and consumption.

Sebastian Ziani de Ferranti and the Need for a New System

The limited service area provided by DC power systems led to proliferation of small generating stations. In Quebec and Ontario, with abundant water-power to drive generators, DC service was relatively easy to provide near the source of water-power. Unfortunately, while most of the hydraulic power potential was in rural areas, the largest potential demand for DC power was in Canada's growing urban areas. If there were no fast-flowing rivers near the city, then dynamos would have to be driven by coal- or wood-burning steam-engines. Many urban dwellers, however, did not relish having their environment dotted with smoky thermal generating stations. Furthermore, in Ontario, the absence of coal reserves made the cost of coal-fired DC generators very unattractive. Canada was not alone in these difficulties: trying to use DC technology to produce large-scale electrification was a problem throughout the industrialized world.

By the 1880s, the need to transmit electrical power over greater distances had become critical. Losses of current and heat accompanying transmission of low-voltage direct current for more than a mile (1,6 km) raised serious economic and technical obstacles. It was wasteful and expensive to generate electricity and then lose it. In addition, low voltage required too much expensive copper wire to transmit the required high currents.

What Are Direct and Alternating Currents?

It is common to liken an electrical current to the flow of water through a pipe. In the latter, the rate of flow is measured by the number of litres per second of water moving past a fixed point. An electrical current, in contrast, is measured in "amperes" and represents the number of electrons per second moving past a fixed point. When a battery or generator produces a current of one ampere, some 6 quintillion (10^{18}) electrons are moving around the circuit every second! Just as the flow of water in a pipe can be converted into useful work, a current of electrons can also be transformed into various forms of energy – for example, the warmth of electric heating, radiant energy of a light bulb, the mechanical energy in a motor, or the energy to drive the digital circuits of a computer. While a difference in pressure causes water to move through a pipe, a difference in "voltage" pushes electrons through a circuit.

The manner in which electrons flow through a circuit falls into two broad categories: direct current (DC) and alternating current (AC). In DC, the electrons always flow in the same direction around the circuit. The magnitude of DC can be constant, as with a battery, or it can waver slightly, as in elaborately wound dynamos. In AC, the direction of the flowing electrons keeps reversing itself periodically. As a consequence, the magnitude of the current varies between a maximum value and zero. To change direction, the current must, for an instant, come to a complete stop. The periodic reversal of current originates from the physics of rotating windings within the generator. The frequency with which AC reverses itself depends on how the generator is designed.

In the early years of electrification, many different frequencies were being advocated as optimal. It took over half a century before 60 cycles/sec became universally accepted as the standard for electric power transmission in North America.

It is current, or the amount of electron flow, rather than voltage that raises the diameter of wire needed. If one is free to raise current or voltage, it is cheaper to transmit a given amount of power by raising voltage and reducing current. The amount of copper wire needed to transmit power over a fixed distance varies inversely as the square of the voltage. Double the voltage, and the amount of copper required drops by a factor of four. Since the cost of copper wiring accounted for a major portion of building an electric power system, higher voltages were economically attractive. The big question – indeed, the major theme of this book – was how to transmit electricity safely and over great distances from generator to consumer.

In 1882, Oskar von Miller, as organizer of an electrical exhibition in Munich, asked the leading French engineer Marcel Deprez to demonstrate the "state of the art" in electrical transmission. Deprez succeeded in transmitting 1.5 kW of DC power over a distance of thirty-five miles (56 km). Despite Deprez's 2,000-volt transmission, high-voltage DC technology faced seemingly insurmountable technical problems. The brushes and commutators of high-voltage dynamos were particularly troublesome. These dynamos also presented considerable risk of electrocution to those working around them. Even if the problems of high-voltage generation had been overcome, electric power could be used only at low voltages. Motors operated at low voltages. Electric lighting, based on Edison's incandescent lamp, was totally incompatible with high-voltage DC.

A new generation of electrical pioneers, such as Sebastian Ziani de Ferranti, quickly pointed out the social and technical drawbacks of DC power systems. In his native Britain, Ferranti saw at first hand how scores, if not hundreds, of little DC electric-light works already dotted the landscape of large cities such as London. It was getting difficult and expensive to place new generating stations in the dense urban areas. Environmental concerns, too, played a major role. In order to reduce pollution, stations had to burn the more expensive anthracite coal. Poor railway development in inner cities gave rise to high transport costs for coal. In Ferranti's view, the future of electrification lay in economies of scale: very large central generating stations located far from the city. "The business of distributing electrical energy," according to Ferranti, "must be done on a large scale to be commercial, and to attain this we must supply a large area, not limited by the exigencies of systems, and we must do this from a site not in the congested heart of a big city, but from a position best suited by its natural advantages to the carrying on of such an undertaking."[7]

Ferranti's family has its roots in the republic of Venice. The founder, Sebastian Ziani, was born in 1102 and, as head of what became the richest and most influential family in the city, was elected doge in 1173. Throughout the Middle Ages, family members held many distinguished positions in the city-states of Italy. Marc Aurelio Ziani added "de Ferranti" to the family name in the early nineteenth century. A distinguished scholar and talented musician, Marc Aurelio

A bold and imaginative engineer, Sebastian Ziani de Ferranti's (1864–1930) inventive and entrepreneurial interests ranged widely. He pioneered the vision of a central electric generating station as well as making important contributions to the development of steam-turbine technology and textile manufacturing equipment. Today he would be regarded as a workaholic, driven far more by the personal need to create and perfect technology than by the pursuit of money. This prolific inventor founded Ferranti Ltd. in England.
(Ferranti Family Archives, Macclesfield, Cheshire, England)

was, in his later years, guitarist for the king in the Belgian court. His grandson, Sebastian Ziani de Ferranti, is one of the principal figures in this book.

Sebastian Ziani de Ferranti was born on 9 April 1864, in England, son of Cesar Ziani de Ferranti and Mme Julie Szczepanowski. Captivated by the new technology of photography, Sebastian's father opened a studio and eventually made photo portraits of some of the most distinguished people of his time. His wife, Julie, had toured Europe as a concert pianist. With the family's long traditions in the arts, Sebastian's talented parents naturally hoped that their son would follow suit. Instead, Sebastian displayed a love of science and machines. To the bewilderment of his mother, he preferred to sketch engines and boilers than study music or paint. Throughout his school days, Sebastian would write to this parents about improvements that he contemplated making to existing machines or about new machines that he had thought up.

At 17, Sebastian Ziani de Ferranti left school hoping to become a manufacturing engineer. With no formal training in engineering, he found it difficult getting a job. However, after persistent and repeated visits to the English offices of Messrs Siemens, he landed a job with this noted electrical firm. Ferranti gained valuable experience while working at Siemens and soon started to invent his own electrical devices. In 1881, Ferranti met Francis Ince, a lawyer and ardent amateur of electrical technology. That fateful meeting changed Ferranti's life. Ince saw the genius in the young man and encouraged him to strike out on his own. He chided Ferranti: "And you mean to tell me you're content to be at Siemens earning 1 [pound] a week! Good God! Ferranti, if you continue at a job like that I'll tell you what will happen. As soon as they discover you've got inventive ability they'll offer you 5 a week and proceed to rob your brains. You'll do the inventing and they'll collect the cash."[8] "Perhaps I'd better get a raise," was Ferranti's naive first reaction.[9] Ince told him, in no uncertain terms, to leave Siemens and go out on his own. Ince took it upon himself to get Ferranti launched in business. In time, their relationship grew beyond the world of commercial and technical affairs. On 24 April 1888, Sebastian married Ince's daughter Gertrude.

In order for Ferranti's central-station concept to compete with the existing DC systems, he needed a technology that would (1) minimize power loss over long-distance transmission lines, (2) offer efficient and reliable generator performance, (3) minimize the amount of copper used, and, most important, (4) provide electrical service conforming to the voltage requirements of the consumer. The concept of centralized electric power systems created an apparently contradictory set of technical requirements: high-current/low-voltage generation, low-current/high-voltage transmission, and low-voltage consumption. Ferranti, along with a small group of electrical pioneers in Europe, realized that alternating current offered the answer to the quest for centralized electrical power systems.

Rediscovery of AC and Birth of the Transformer

The first step in developing an alternative to DC technology was the rediscovery of alternating current (AC). Ironically, the same industry that provoked the rise of DC now became the catalyst for the emergence of AC technology. Soon after its discovery in 1831, AC was relegated to the category of scientifically interesting, but technologically useless.

Early arc lamps, for example, could not function with AC. Every time the current changed directions, the arc would go out. DC arc lamps worked but required costly mechanical regulators. The regulators, which maintained proper separation of the lamp's carbon rods, greatly increased the manufacturing and maintenance costs and thus severely limited widespread commercial development of arc lamps.

In 1876, Paul Jablochkoff, a Russian telegraph engineer, modified the design of the arc lamp in order to do away with the expensive regulators. Instead of having the carbon rods tip to tip in a straight line, Jablochkoff set them side by side at a fixed distance throughout their length, separated by a kaolin clay-based insulator. This simple rearrangement of the rods resulted in substantial savings and greatly expanded the market for arc lighting. Jablochkoff quickly discovered that his invention worked best with AC. Rectification, which earlier had been the key to introducing AC generated current into DC consuming systems, now proved a disadvantage. The rectified current provided by dynamos led to uneven burning; the positive rod wore away much faster than the negative rod. AC ensured even consumption of both carbon rods. Forty-five years after Faraday discovered AC, Jablochkoff's arc lamp established a commercial market for AC. With a market came the first incentive to design and construct large alternators.

While working for Siemens, in England, Ferranti had been toying with a new alternator design. Encouraged by Francis Ince's moral and financial support, Ferranti patented a new alternator in 1882. Backed by Ince, Ferranti and another engineer, Alfred Thompson, formed a company to develop and market this device. As Ferranti was still legally a minor, he needed his father's formal consent before he could enter into the partnership.

The Ferranti alternator patent shared certain elements with an invention patented by Sir William Thomson, later Lord Kelvin. Thomson agreed to accept a royalty arrangement, and the two patents were combined to produce the Ferranti-Thomson alternator. Because of the armature's lightness, it could attain high speeds of 1,000 to 2,000 revolutions per minute (RPM). According to one description, the Ferranti-Thomson machine could generate 10,000 volts and drive several hundred Swan lamps.[10] It outperformed any other generator of comparable size. Ferranti would later use a larger version in the construction of the world's first central power station at Deptford.

In 1882, a French engineer, Lucien Gaulard, and an English business-

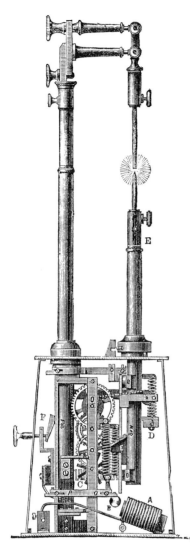

Early arc lamps were temperamental. The light would flicker and go out as the current eroded the carbon electrode sufficiently to make the gap too wide for the electric arc to jump. The carbon electrodes – commonly referred to as carbons – would then need to be reset. One approach to the problem lay in a variety of mechanical clockwork-like devices, such as the Serrin Lamp (above), designed to move one carbon to keep a constant distance between the ends of the carbons being consumed. Jablochkoff (opposite) took a fresh approach, putting the carbons parallel to each other rather than end to end, and his beautifully simple solution revolutionized arc lighting.
(National Museum of Science and Technology, Ottawa)

man, John Dixon Gibbs, filed a patent application in Britain for a system of transmitting electrical power over great distances. The key to their patent resided in a "secondary generator," or, in today's terminology, a transformer – a new interpretation of the existing inductor coil technology. It is the pre-existence of an inductor-coil technology that later allowed opponents to break Gaulard and Gibbs's patent monopoly over the use of transformers. A transformer lowered the high voltage produced by the alternator to match the customer's lower-voltage electric lighting requirements.

Gaulard and Gibbs first demonstrated their system at the Royal Aquarium in London in 1883, but it attracted little attention. They needed a dramatic demonstration to publicize their invention. The opportunity arose in 1884, at the Turin Exposition in Italy. Seizing the moment, the two men managed to transmit 20 kW, at 2,000 volts, over a distance of 40 km (25 miles). There were many technical difficulties and hardships, and they succeeded in making the transmission only just before the exposition closed. Controversy, however, soon arose. The proponents of DC were quick to point out the dangers to humans posed by high-voltage transmission. Unwilling to pay royalties to Gaulard and Gibbs, many within the AC camp were planning to undermine Gaulard and Gibbs's patent claims on the "secondary generator."

The Grosvenor Gallery. In 1884 the first commercial success of the Gaulard and Gibbs system more than compensated for the difficulties encountered at the Turin demonstration. Sir Coutts Lindsay, an English artist of some distinction, had opened the Grosvenor Art Gallery in 1877, on Bond Street in London. Lindsay was dissatisfied with the use of gas lighting in art galleries. Not only was it too dim, but it also exposed paintings to the by-products of burning gas. The radiant light offered by the incandescent lamp allowed works of art to be appreciated in a better setting. In 1882, James Ludovic Lindsay, twenty-sixth Earl of Crawford, served as British commisioner at the Paris Electric Exposition. After seeing the marvel of Edison's incandescent lamp, he convinced his uncle, Sir Coutts, to install a small portable dynamo to light his gallery. Electric lighting immediately caught on as well with the neighbours and soon they were asking the gallery for electricity for lighting.

Seeing a commercial opportunity, Sir Coutts Lindsay decided to expand the sale of electricity with a more ambitious system. In 1884, he launched the AC revolution in England when he contracted Gaulard and Gibbs to install their system in his art gallery. Public demand for electricity was so great that Lindsay's newly expanded system was soon overloaded. Ferranti was called in to advise the gallery on the problem.

Instead of patching up the system, Ferranti made sweeping changes in the system's design. The Siemens alternators were replaced by two 700-hp, 2,400-volt Ferranti machines. Ferranti also made fundamental changes to the Gaulard-Gibbs transformer system, which supplied

When it opened in 1877 the Grosvenor Art Gallery was the height of elegant fashion. Large overhead clerestory lights provided natural sunlight. The gas fixtures shown in this view from *The Illustrated London News* provided additional light, but soot and other combustion byproducts damaged the artwork as well as dirtying the gallery. Electric incandescent lights provided cleaner, brighter, and more uniform illumination: the elegant public face of electricity. (*The Illustrated London News* Picture Library, ILN 5/5/1877, 420)

each consumer with a step-down transformer. The primary windings of all these transformers were connected in series to form a ring. Ferranti chose to connect the primaries in parallel and thus maintain a constant potential across each primary. Ferranti's system was the first to demonstrate the possibilities of parallel connection on a practical scale. A short time later, Westinghouse engineers also concluded that the parallel connection was superior, and it has since become universal practice.

Gaulard and Gibbs saw Ferranti's modifications of their transformers as an infringement on their patents and threatened legal action. Before they could act on their threat, Ferranti went on the attack and petitioned the courts to revoke their original patent. With distinguished lawyers, scientists, and engineers assembled by both sides, a long and controversial court battle ensued. After Ferranti's victory, Gaulard and Gibbs unsuccessfully tried to get the House of Lords to overturn the decision. It is not clear whether the authorities who judged the case understood or appreciated Gaulard and Gibbs's innovations. In the end, revocation of their original patent shattered their dreams of great financial success. The aftermath of the legal battles ruined Gibbs financially. The strain of defending the patent claims took a bigger toll on Gaulard. Left a broken man, he died insane in November 1888 in Paris.

Deptford: The First Large-Scale AC Central Station

Ferranti's success at the Grosvenor Gallery set the stage for his most ambitious project, the Deptford Power Station. The sale of electric power from Grosvenor proved an unqualified success, and demand for power for lighting greatly exceeded supply. Under these conditions Ferranti found little difficulty convincing the directors of the Grosvenor Gallery Co. that the future lay in large central electrical power systems. In 1887, the London Electricity Supply Corp. (LESC) was founded, with subscribed capital of 375,000 pounds sterling. The object of this company was to build an electrical power system, according to Ferranti's design, to supply electrical energy to a large area of London.

Here was an opportunity for Ferranti to design and build a power system that would vindicate his faith in the commercial possibilities of centralized high-voltage AC electrical power systems. In England, Ferranti was practically alone in his advocacy of high-voltage transmission. The engineering establishment thought his scheme foolish, if

The Grosvenor Gallery generating station, as depicted in an 1885 woodcut, presents the more utilitarian and hidden face of electric power. Wires suspended from poles on rooftops ran from the two generators to the elegant gallery. The two largest Siemens single phase 250-kW alternators built to that date supplied 2,500-volt AC current to customers who had a step-down transformer on the premises to reduce the supply to a usable 100 volts.
(London Electric Supply Corporation)

not crazy, and predictions of catastrophe and failure abounded. In the face of such opposition, it took an extraordinarily brave group of financiers to risk considerable amounts of money on the unpopular ideas of a 23-year-old engineer.

Deptford Station was an ambitious and intimidating undertaking, particularly for one man. As little was known about AC power technology, each aspect of the project became a pioneering achievement. Generating plants, transformers, and insulated cables had never been constructed for more than 2,500 volts, and Ferranti undertook to design and oversee the installation of every facet of the project. "The plant included two Ferranti alternators, designed for 5000 volt working and driven by 1250 hp engines, supplying the day-time load; and four Ferranti alternators with 10,000 volt windings each directly coupled to a 10,000 hp steam engine."[11]

The Deptford Station turned out to be more challenging than Ferranti had bargained for. In the midst of this monumental engineering undertaking, with many problems still unsolved, the daring young Ferranti planned to take on the development of an even grander generating station in Canada.

Ferranti Name Comes to Canada

Throughout the 1890s and into the twentieth century, Niagara Falls was the striking symbol of Canada's hydro-electric potential. Its splendour and power symbolized a new era of social, political, and economic progress based on electrical energy. In 1897, at the inauguration of electrical power generation on the American side of Niagara Falls, Nikola Tesla, one of the great electrical engineering minds of the age, proclaimed that Niagara Falls was "a monument worthy of our scientific age, a true monument of enlightenment and peace. It signifies the subjugation of natural forces to the service of man, the discontinuance of barbarous methods, the relieving of millions from want and suffering."[12] Adam Beck, later Sir Adam, also realized the potential of Niagara Falls as a force for social progress, and, in 1902, he declared: "We must deliver power to such an extent that the poorest working man will have electricity in his home."[13] And in 1905, the political implications of hydro-electric power inspired the premier of Ontario, James Whitney, to make the grand, but unrealistic, promise that "the water power of Niagara should be as free as air."[14]

In 1889, few people understood how to convert the awesome power of Niagara Falls into socially and economically useful energy. Ferranti's vision of generating electrical energy in large central stations and then distributing it over great distances by means of high voltages was perfectly in tune with Canadian geographical reality.

While a syndicate of prominent American capitalists was trying to define a technology for the US side of Niagara Falls, Ferranti had already embarked on a well-defined system of electrical power distribution at Deptford.[15] In North America, as elsewhere in the world, contentious and often furious debate raged over the future of electric

It takes backers and customers to further the work of engineer-entrepreneurs. Colleagues and admirers said that Lord Wantage (above), a holder of the much coveted Victoria Cross "deserved another VC" for investing today's equivalent of £7 million in the London Electric Supply Corporation. Sir Coutts Lindsay's (opposite) decision in 1883 to supply electricity to neighbours of his fashionable Grosvernor Gallery led to the founding of the London Electric Supply Corporation and a great boost to the Ferranti name when the twenty-three-year-old engineer was asked to take charge of the ambitious but problem-ridden system. (London Electric Supply Corporation)

power technology. Which would dominate: AC or DC? Colonel Albert Duane Shaw adamantly believed that, at Deptford, Ferranti had proven the technology that would attract the capital to create a very profitable undertaking at Niagara Falls.

We know little of Shaw. A former member of the New York State legislature, he served as US consul to Canada from 1868 to 1878 and to England from 1878 to 1885. He was not a technical man, but he was "known for his valuable consular reports ... on foreign manufactures, and tariff and revenue reform,"[16] which he submitted to the Department of State. With a finger on the pulse of technological development, Shaw's instincts told him that Ferranti's model of electric power distribution had great financial possibilities for Niagara Falls.

How and when Shaw first met Ferranti is not known. Nor is there any evidence to explain how and when he started thinking about generating hydro-electric power at Niagara Falls. Sometime in September 1889, Ferranti and Shaw came to an understanding. If Shaw could obtain a hydro-electric power concession at Niagara Falls from the Canadian Niagara Parks Commission on reasonable terms, then Ferranti would form a syndicate of British capitalists to finance the undertaking. On 16 December 1889, Shaw wrote to Casimir Gzowski, a prominent engineer and first chairman of the Niagara Parks Commission, formally petitioning for rights to the Falls:

A leading electrician ... is in a position to secure the interest of large capitalists in any undertaking he will take the responsibility of recommending, and it was arranged that I should ascertain upon what terms we would secure the right to use the water power, either on the Canadian or American side of Niagara Falls, and that if reasonable terms could be obtained that we would jointly get up a company with the necessary capital to manufacture, by system of which my associate has control, electricity with a view of supplying towns and cities with light and power, and I have the honour to enclose the proposal in that behalf.[17]

In the eyes of the commission, Ferranti's involvement gave Shaw's application the needed credibility, a point overlooked by some Canadian historians.[18]

The commission, Shaw, and Ferranti each approached the proposal from different perspectives. Less interested in the economic role of electrification in the development of Ontario, the commission needed money to ensure that the park would develop into a scenic and unspoiled tourist area. By the mid-1880s, uncontrolled exploitation of the water-power around Niagara Falls had led to an unsightly proliferation of mills. With little coal but an abundance of water-power, Ontario's manufacturers gravitated to sites where hydro-mechanical power was readily and cheaply available. These mills, and the many water diversions that they required, posed a serious threat to the natural beauty of the area.

After considerable public outcry by the "Free Niagara Movement," an international park was created, in 1887, on both the Canadian and

The trial assembly in 1890 of a 10,000 hp steam engine for Ferranti's Deptford Power Station illustrates the massive precision engineering, casting, and machining behind electrical success. For decades Packard engineers and transformer assemblers in St Catharines would dream of a crane such as the large overhead travelling crane on the right.
(Science Museum, London, 31/51)

American sides of the Niagara River. On the Canadian side, the Niagara Parks Commission assumed responsibility for the newly created Queen Victoria Niagara Falls Park. The Ontario government insisted that the park be maintained as a scenic wonder open to all without charge but also that it be financially self-sustaining. Revenues generated by the usual tourist concessions were totally inadequate. Desperate for ways to raise money, the Niagara Parks Commission saw rental fees, for the water rights to the Falls, as an important and guaranteed source of revenue.

Shaw was a shrewd speculator and persuasive promoter adroit at buying and selling options and concessions. Whether his interest in the Falls was short-term speculation or long-term development is difficult to say. Shortly after he negotiated the concession, he skilfully acquired an option to build an electric railway within the park. Dangling the carrot of a British syndicate in front of the commission, he presented the railway as a profitable corollary to the hydro-electric

Sebastian Ziani de Ferranti's fame as an engineer-entrepreneur was greatly increased when his alternator was used at Deptford Station. The workman standing beside the armature which is being lowered into position is a reminder of the massive scale of Victorian technology. (The Museum of Science & Industry, Manchester, England, 2414)

project. Seeing additional dollars flowing into the park's coffers, the commissioners were all too eager to grant Shaw this additional concession. Without any experience in large engineering projects and with little money of his own, Shaw had won two very impressive options from the Niagara Parks Commission.

Ferranti was the man with the technology, the man building Deptford, and the man who had the ear of prominent British capitalists. Though sensitive to the economic implications of the project, Ferranti was a dreamer. In pursuing a vision of greater economic and social well-being through superior technology, he was not unlike other socio-technological revolutionaries of the period. In the words of one British historian, Ferranti, like many of his contemporary electrical power engineers, was part of an intellectual movement of "Fabian-type socialists" whose "optimism and boyish confidence ... abounded in conflict with vested interests, their crusade was marked with great moral fervour ... it is significant that so many of these engineers did speculate about the future, for that is the manner of revolutionaries who imagine that they are 'on the side of the future'."[19] Niagara Falls offered the ideal opportunity to demonstrate convincingly, and on a scale not possible in England, the technical and economic merits of an electrical energy grid based on relatively few large generating stations and high-voltage AC transmission.

Some members of the Niagara Parks Commission were openly skeptical of Shaw's ability to undertake such a project, but Casimir Gzowski, the chairman put his weight behind the proposal. Gzowski was not well versed in the new electrical technology. Nevertheless his engineering background made him the most competent of all the commissioners to judge the merits of the hydro-electric scheme. Moreover, as an eminent engineer with experience and contacts in both private and public sectors, he provided the credibility and stature that the promoters needed.

Born in St Petersburg, Russia, Gzowski had studied military engineering in Russia. In 1830, after taking part in an abortive military coup in Warsaw, Poland, he was captured, imprisoned, and then exiled. After spending eight years in the United States, he came to Canada in 1841 and very quickly distinguished himself as an exceptional engineer and financier. In 1842 he became superintendent of public works in the United Province of Canada. Later, as Gzowski and Co., he completed projects such as the Canadian portion of the St Lawrence and Atlantic Railroad and the Grand Trunk Railway line from Sarnia to Toronto. In 1873, he would cap his career with the International Bridge linking Fort Erie, Ontario, and Buffalo, New York.

But these were all achievements in by-then conventional technology. His foray into advocating leading-edge technology would prove to be a different type of story. Gzowski brought awareness of the economics and dynamics of megaprojects. But as a railroad man and civil engineer entering what was for him a new field he had difficulty assessing information, judging how well things were proceeding and understanding what would be needed.

Getting the concession proved a lot easier than raising the money for the project. Had Ferranti been too optimistic in thinking that capital could be readily obtained for such a major undertaking? In a letter to Shaw, dated 16 January 1890, he confided that some $10 million would be needed to float a company able to complete the project; in 1891, total revenues for the dominion government of Canada were $40 million.

Raising that much money required that potential investors have considerable confidence in the future of AC technology, which only the unqualified success at Deptford could assure. By 1890, however, pressure from critics and disenchanted investors weighed heavily on Ferranti; $6.25 million had been poured into Deptford with no concrete results. Ferranti's wife, Gertrude, later recalled how "on all sides peoples [were] shaking their heads at him and doubting the possibility of his carrying out his promises ... They said that his gigantic scheme was from the first an unsubstantial dream – not thought out and against the teachings of science; that in some peculiar manner he had got men of wealth to believe in him, and that he was spending huge sums of money in the most reckless and haphazard manner, all of which was surely to be lost."[20] With Ferranti's high-voltage AC technology under attack, serious delays in construction, and investors' growing misgivings, Ferranti had his back against the wall. In the words of James Forbes, chairman of the company building Deptford, "[Ferranti] pledged his reputation, his fortune, his labour – day and night – to achieve the result he promised to the directors."[21]

Under such circumstances, Ferranti had little immediate hope of getting people to invest in a scheme even more expensive than Deptford. So in January 1890, be asked Shaw to obtain a further postponement on paying the $50,000 down-payment asked for by the Niagara Parks Commission.[22] No sooner had the commissioners granted this request than Ferranti cabled Shaw for a second delay: "If we can get an extension of the option I do not doubt for a moment but that we will be able to carry the thing through."[23] By late February 1890, investors' uncertainties over Deptford had not changed, yet Ferranti persisted in thinking that he could carry out the Niagara project.

The commissioners were now very worried and became more adamant about receiving the required $50,000, as agreed in the initial offer. Realizing that he was about to lose this important opportunity, Ferranti sought more time. He suggested immediate payment of a modest amount to show good faith, in return for a one-year extension to raise the full deposit. With little money of his own, Ferranti needed a backer; Lord Wantage, younger brother of Sir Coutts Lindsay and a major investor in Deptford, came to the rescue. He agreed to pay $10,000 to the commission if it would extend Ferranti's option until 1 March 1891. Wantage pointed out that "[additional time] will be needed for showing the public what can be done by Mr. Ferranti's mode of conveying electric power."[24]

Wantage had inherited a princely fortune in 1883, after the death of his father-in-law, Lord Overstone. His investment in the Grosvenor Gallery and at Deptford furthered the development of central-station technology. According to Thomas Hughes, historian of electrical technology, "Wantage represented that segment of the British aristocracy which had a history of financing technological change ... Wantage had the financial daring to match the daring of Ferranti's engineering." R.H. Parsons, the engineer and industrialist who pioneered the turbine and was a contemporary, believed that "Lord Wantage's financial courage was comparable to the physical courage that had earned him the Victoria Cross in the Crimean War."[25] This courage and his belief in Ferranti prompted him to put up the non-refundable $10,000 – at a time when the average yearly wage in Canada was about $250.

The personal intervention of a man as notable as Lord Wantage carried a lot of weight with Casimir Gzowski. On 17 March 1890, in a letter to Shaw announcing the Ontario government's acceptance of the extension, Gzowski wrote: "The great ability and talent of the distinguished electrician Mr. Ferranti with the confidence he possesses of noble men of the high standing of Lord Wantage, and the very large expenditure already incurred in works and appliances on a far larger scale than heretofore attempted to solve the still underdeveloped power of transmitting electricity gives the commissioners confidence that the earnest efforts in such competent hands to accomplish this important object will prove successful."[26]

By September 1890, work on the thermal-electric system at Deptford was back on track, and both it and Niagara Falls looked promising. Ferranti reassured Gzowski that successful completion of Deptford was an essential first step on the way to the hydro-electric project at Niagara Falls. In a letter dated 16 September 1890, Ferranti, for the first time, wrote directly to Gzowski:

Our first object was to get our works at Deptford into satisfactory working order transmitting therefrom several thousand horsepower at a distance of 8 to 10 miles, and distributing it for power and light over London ... We have not yet accomplished this in its entirety ... When we have accomplished it, we will have entirely demonstrated not only the possibility of the Niagara enterprise, but that it will also be a good thing commercially. You can no doubt see that this is therefore the first thing to be done in order to give us the necessary means to do Niagara on a sufficiently large scale to make it commercially successful.[27]

One month later, in October 1890, the Deptford Station began transmitting AC electrical energy to London at 5,000 volts. Though Deptford had yet to reach Ferranti's objective of transmission at 10,000 volts, the technology for Niagara Falls was finally being mastered. Then, when everything seemed to be going well, a series of mishaps stole Niagara Falls away from Ferranti. On 15 November 1890 a fire, caused by human error, destroyed the old Grosvenor Gallery Station, which was being used to step down the high-voltage power from Deptford. The entire substation was lost in twenty minutes and cost the London Electric Supply Co. (LESC) dearly. Repairs were carried out with great speed, and service was restored on 1 December 1890.

No sooner had service started again when an improperly repaired transformer at Deptford burned out. In a chain reaction, each burned-out transformer transferred its load to the next, already fully loaded transformer, until all the remaining ones had burned out. It took three months to repair the damage, during which time the LESC lost 75 per cent of its customers to competing DC utilities.[28] The loss left the firm in deep financial trouble.

The station recommenced service in August 1890. On 16 February 1891, regular transmission at 10,000 volts had finally started from Deptford. With capital in short supply, the LESC had to make cutbacks in construction at Deptford. When Ferranti learned that the

LESC would not complete the giant generators as he had originally planned, he clashed with the company's board. It was a tragic and classic confrontation: the engineer's ambitions and dreams striking what others regarded as clear corporate fiscal realities. In a heated discussion with Ferranti, the chairman commented: "you are a very clever man, Mr. Ferranti, but I'm thinking ye're sadly lacking in pre-vision."[29] Ferranti resigned, and the 1891 annual report quietly announced: "the engagement of Mr. de Ferranti has ceased 'by the effluxion of time'."[30] But with his departure, the Deptford Station lost both the vision and the engineering expertise it needed, and by 1898 the LESC had lost $2 million.

The departure also hurt Ferranti. His reputation as an electrician survived the ill-fated Deptford Station, but investors' confidence in similar Ferranti schemes disappeared. Gone were the days when British capitalists had called Ferranti the British Edison. The one-year extension granted by the Niagara Parks Commission, until 1 March 1891, had come and gone, and still there was no indication that any British syndicate was willing to develop Niagara Falls. On reading in the *Times* of London that power had finally been transmitted from Deptford to London at 10,000 volts, Gzowski commented: "the only question now to be solved is whether the English capitalists will be willing to pay up."[31] There was little hope that Ferranti could find any backers to float a new company.

Nevertheless, without advancing additional funds, Shaw squeezed out another year's postponement, until March 1892. Once again the commissioners gambled on the reputations of Ferranti and Wantage. Getting financial support in England for a hydro-electric project in Canada had become hopeless. Yet, on 20 February 1892 Ferranti asked Gzowski, "as a personal favour to your friends over here," for an extension of three months. Ferranti assured Gzowski that if he were given the extension "it is a practical certainty that I will be able to take up the lease and make the first payment of $25,000."[32] Ferranti blamed Shaw for poorly managing the whole affair. Was this letter merely a ploy to buy more time to find a buyer for their option?

Meanwhile, and without Ferranti's knowledge, Shaw was trying to peddle the concession to a powerful American syndicate backed by the financier J.P. Morgan. This was the same group that had won an option to develop the American side of the Falls. As Ferranti and Shaw worked at cross-purposes, on opposite sides of the Atlantic, relations between the two became strained. Ferranti accused Shaw of dealing with the Americans behind his back. Shaw defended himself by claiming that Ferranti had asked him to sell the concession at the best price.

Shaw's negotiations with the Americans were a race against the clock. With the rights about to run out, Shaw would have nothing to sell. Finally, a deal was struck to sell the option for $200,000 to the American syndicate. The commission, however, would not let Shaw sell without Ferranti's consent. With the US syndicate growing impatient and threatening to call off the whole deal, Shaw finally managed

Three-Phase Alternating Current

The rotation of a winding of wire within an alternator's magnetic field produces an alternating current, called single-phase AC. The magnitude and direction of this current resemble a sine wave. If three independent windings are made to turn within a magnetic field, then each winding produces its own separate, single-phase AC. Collectively, the three single-phase currents are called three-phase current.

The technical and economic advantages of three-phase current resulted from the particular way in which the three windings are spaced out around a circle. If the planes of the three windings are arranged 120° apart, then the six transmission wires – one pair from each winding – can be replaced by just three, or four wires. This reduction leads to considerably less use of expensive copper wire in long-distance power transmission.

The advent of three-phase power also helped in the development of a whole class of electric motors. From three-phase transmission, the "end user" can extract either 110-volt, single-phase AC for lighting or 220-volt, three-phase AC to power induction motors.

From the point of view of transformer design, the voltage of three-phase power can be stepped either up or down by means of three separate transformers for each phase or one big transformer to handle the entire three-phase current. In large power transformers, a three-phase transformer occupies less space and costs considerably less than three single-phase transformers of equal capacity.

to get Ferranti's approval. Shaw succeeded in selling the concession, but no one knows the final selling price and how much Ferranti received, if anything at all.

The syndicate had no intention of developing the Canadian side of the Falls but was making a purely pre-emptive strike. As Ferranti had predicted, the American group did nothing more than pay the yearly rental fee. It bought the Canadian option to protect its investment on the American side of the Falls. Had Ferranti got investors to finance a hydro-electric project at Niagara Falls in 1890, there is no doubt that Canada would have been generating power from the Falls long before the Americans. Electrical technology, however, was evolving so rapidly that Ferranti's scheme would have been outmoded before it went into operation. The weakness in Ferranti's technology stemmed from its inability to provide motive power – a practical and economic way to drive electric motors.

Ferranti was not the first to demonstrate the principles of high-voltage transmission of AC. He was, however, the first to design and construct a full-scale central station and distribution system. Deptford provided electrical service for a significant portion of London. Though the forerunner of large, modern central power stations, the Deptford experience did not catch on immediately in England. Neighborhood power stations continued to flourish. As one British historian noted: "Small local stations remained common for decades. Indeed it took Government action, in the form of the Act of 1926 which set up the Grid, to secure anything like general adoption of Ferranti's policy in Britain."[33]

History of the Transformer until 1894

Invented nearly 100 years ago, the transformer has hardly changed at all in its basic structure, but the know-how and materials used to design and build transformers have altered significantly. This situation is analogous to the development of the automobile. The car's basic structure has changed little: an internal combustion engine, transmission system, four wheels, and brakes. Since the first model, however, automotive engineers have learned how to increase dramatically the car's performance-to-weight characteristics. The evolution of transformer design at Ferranti-Packard has been no different. Compared with early designs, today's transformers operate at undreamed of voltages, loads, and efficiencies. The story of these improvements will be brought out in later chapters, but first we shall see how transformer design had crystallized by 1894, when Packard Electric came into being. The early processes of change and design solutions and themes that led to the fundamentals of transformer design would re-emerge in the twentieth century. System functionality and efficiency, manufacturability, and costs, along with government regulation, remain constant concerns.

Early Transformer Design. The principle of induction, which underlies the transformer's operation, had been discovered by Michael Faraday in 1831. In 1848, the German physicist Heinrich Ruhmkorff exploited the Englishman's discovery in order to overcome the voltage limitation of batteries. The resulting induction, or Ruhmkorff, coil consisted of a primary coil winding, of few turns, wound around a cylindrical core. A secondary winding with many turns was then wound directly over the primary coil. A breaker in the primary winding periodically cut off and reconnected the low-voltage DC supply to the primary coil. The resultant movement of the magnetic lines of force across the secondary windings produced a high voltage. The high-voltage sparks generated by the Ruhmkorff coil spurred the advancement of physics. Heinrich Hertz produced the world's first radio waves from such sparks.

In 1878, induction coils found commercial application in Jablochkoff's new arc lamp, or "candle," which worked best with alternating current. Arc lamps were connected in series with the primary windings of induction coils. The rods of each arc lamp were connected to the secondary of each induction coil, while the primaries were all joined in parallel to the alternator. By varying the number of turns and gauge of wire in the secondary windings, Jablochkoff could vary the intensity of the lamp. This system had the added advantage that when a lamp inevitably burned out, only the secondary winding was affected. The circuit feeding current to all the other primaries would continue to function. Jablochkoff used the induction coil as a step-up transformer and as a convenient method to connect up arc lights. Surprisingly, no one thought of reversing the process in the induction coil and using it as a step-down transformer. New perceptions, driven by different imperatives, would be needed before the transformer could be born.

The Gaulard-Gibbs Transformer. Urged on by the need to reconcile high-voltage transmission with low-voltage consumption, Gaulard looked on the existing inductor-coil technology from a new perspective. Why not use the secondary winding to step down a high voltage imparted to the primary? Their insight marked the birth of the distribution transformer.

The Gaulard-Gibbs transformer had two fundamental flaws: poor voltage regulation and an inefficient open-core construction. The design of transformers came to be implicitly and explicitly influenced by regulatory legislation. The peculiar transformer design chosen by Gaulard and Gibbs may well be the first such instance in history. According to the historian Thomas Hughes, many of the inadequacies attributed to Gaulard and Gibbs's design stemmed from their efforts to conform to new British legislation regulating transmission and distribution of electricity.[34]

Gaulard and Gibbs nonetheless launched transformer development. They made the simple observation – simple only in hindsight –

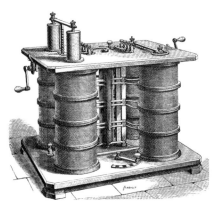

Transformer design changed both quickly and significantly after the appearance of the original Gaulard and Gibbs design, shown here in a woodcut from the 2 March 1883 issue of *Engineering*. Three important needs influenced design: voltage regulation over varying loads, minimizing energy losses in the core, and manufacturability or ease of manufacturing.

To maintain constant voltage over varying loads, transformers were designed to be connected in parallel with constant-voltage generators. While a closed core minimized eddy currents much more effectively than a solid core, there were still significant variations in closed-core geometries. (National Museum of Science and Technology, Ottawa)

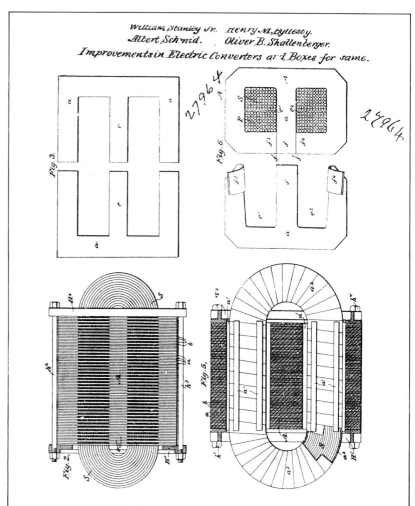

William Stanley Jr.   Henry M. Byllesby.
Albert Schmid.   Oliver B. Shallenberger.
Improvements in Electric Converters and Boxes for same.

The Ferranti transformer with the number 48 written on it is now in the Science Museum, London. It was assembled in 1891 and used in a London Electric Supply Corporation substation. The wound core best exploited the idea of a closed magnetic field but was not well suited to volume manufacturing. The biggest contribution towards manufacturability came from the work of William Stanley and other engineers at Westinghouse, where they completely redesigned the core to reduce manufacturing costs and increase productivity. Using the identical E-shaped metal stampings shown in this 1887 Canadian Patent Application 27,964, the Westinghouse approach constructed a stacked core over which one simply slipped pre-wound copper wire windings. This design led to the modern shell-type transformer. (Science Museum, London, 2854; Canadian Patent Office Record, December 1887)

that the action of a step-up inductor coil could be reversed into a step-down transformer. Gaulard and Gibbs got people thinking in a new direction; their transformer provoked an avalanche of designs.

By the 1890s, the basic elements of the modern-day transformer had taken shape. A theoretical and empirical understanding of the transformer's operation had been firmly established, along with the principles of its manufacture. During the twentieth century, advances in performance, construction, and testing were characterized by close interaction between the competitive realities of the market and the need to operate transformers at higher and higher transmission voltages and with ever-increasing loads.

A Critical Test for AC. Despite the rapid progress in transformer design in the early 1890s, commercial use depended on widespread acceptance of AC power systems. Though a remarkable engineering accomplishment, Ferranti's Deptford Station did not resolve the debate raging over the relative merits of AC and DC systems. Proponents of DC systems, such as Edison, attacked the high-voltage AC systems as a threat to public safety. In an astute public relations move designed to link AC with danger and death, Edison, a DC supporter, suggested that high-voltage electrocution replace hanging as a means of capital punishment. The real attack on AC was directed against the inability of its technology to provide a practical motor for industrial use. Ferranti's single-phase system offered little in this direction.

In 1891, the city of Frankfurt, Germany, announced ambitious plans for large-scale electrification. The proponents of AC and DC systems lobbied intensely. The Frankfurt bids proved to be a critical battle in the history of these two competing technologies. Each group tried to discredit the other. Older companies such as Siemens and Halske refused to consider AC; they were determined to protect their significant investments in DC. For these firms, Frankfurt had become a question of principle. The debate very quickly left the technical arena and entered the political. To settle the issue in the city's best interests, the municipal authorities asked the AC consortium to demonstrate the superiority of its system at Frankfurt's upcoming Electrochemical Exposition. The direction of electrification around the world hung in the balance.

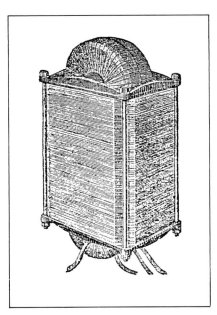

The result was a milestone in electric-power technology. In a collaborative effort, Allgemeine Elektrizitäts-Gesellschaft (AEG) of Berlin and the Swiss mechanical engineering firm Maschinenfabrik Oerlikon transmitted 240 kW of electrical power 177 km (111 miles) from the Lauffen Dam to the site of the Frankfurt Electrochemical Exposition. Never before had anyone generated and transmitted so much power over so great a distance. The transmission reached an astounding 25,000 volts.

The significance of the Frankfurt demonstration lay in its application of the newly invented three-phase electrical system. This type of transmission greatly improved the economic viability and technical capabilities of AC systems. A three-phase power line requires only about half to three-quarters as much copper conducting wire as a single-phase line of the same capacity, voltage, and transmission efficiency. Furthermore, the three-phase system, with its three sets of identical alternating currents separated by 120°, solved the problem of providing a smoothly running AC motor. Now DC proponents could no longer point to the lack of a workable AC motor. Two three-phase alternators, designed by Charles Brown and built by Oerlikon, produced about 4,000 amperes at 50 volts.

With many of the technical objections to AC answered, debate shifted to the economic merits of both systems. The transmission from the Lauffen Dam to Frankfurt revealed convincingly that centralized electrical power systems based on AC were the way of the future. Over sixty years later, George Siemens, a descendant of the family whose company opposed AC, could see it all very clearly: "a veritable revolution broke out in the ranks of the electrical fraternity, and the 25th August, 1891 has for them become a day of remembrance, as it were

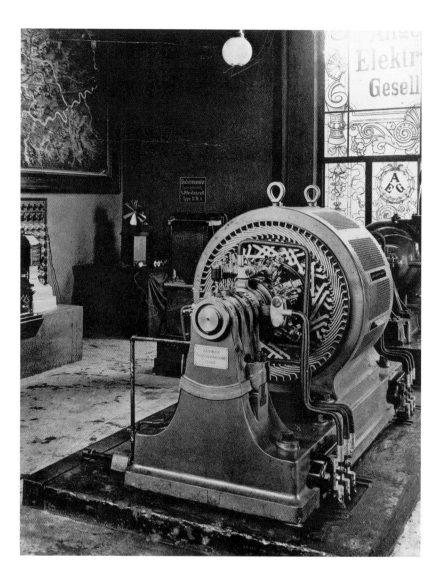

The Frankfurt Electrochemical Exposition of 1891 astounded the electrical world. Oerlikon and AEG designed and built the world's first three-phase transformer. For the first time, a transformer was used to step up voltage prior to transmission. The 14 November 1891 issue of *Electrical Review* pronounced the "multiphase transformer ... one of the cleverest things done for years in electricity" and added that "only gray matter of the finest quality could evolve it."

Three-phase electrical power was the key to devising the practical AC motor known as the induction motor. The 100 hp induction motor shown here in a photograph from the Frankfurt Electrochemical Exposition was designed by Michael von Dolivo-Dobrowolsky and manufactured by AEG. It was part of a brilliant publicity coup to demonstrate that AC power was the way of the future. Hydro-electric power generated at the Lauffen Dam was transmitted over the then great distance of 177 km (111 miles) to this motor where it powered the pump to raise water to the top of the artificial waterfall. Electricity was now truly portable; so, too, was the power of falling water. (AEG Firmenarchiv, Frankfurt)

the storming of the Bastille. The door to a new world had been thrust open and a mighty industrial transformation had begun."[37]

The Watt-Hour Meter: The Cash Register of the Electrical Utility Industry

A watt-hour meter measures the amount of electrical energy consumed over time. Found today by the millions, the ubiquitous watt-hour meter may appear insignificant, but it is the cornerstone of the electrical utilities industry. The revenues of Canada's multi-billion-dollar industry rest squarely on the data gathered from all watt-hour meters placed in homes, apartment buildings, offices, factories, and any other location where electricity is consumed.

The historical development of the meter illustrates how economic, political, and social forces can mould engineering considerations, and

vice versa. The meter was the outcome of asking a fundamental economic question: what is the best way to sell electricity? The technical solution had to take into account the operational and financial requirements of a growing electrical utilities industry while still responding to public expectations and new regulatory legislation. The earliest and most common method of selling electricity was the flat-rate method. Customers were billed a fixed amount based simply on the total number of lights and motors. As the size and complexity of electrical systems grew, the weaknesses of the flat rate became more glaringly apparent. It encouraged wasteful consumption: not paying for the actual power consumed, flat-rate users had no incentive to conserve energy. As a result, the central station ran at nearly full capacity most of the time and could not accommodate new customers without costly capital expansion.

Only metering of consumption would permit large-scale electrifica-

The Ideal Transformer

The alternator generates electrical energy from mechanical energy; the motor converts electrical energy into mechanical energy. The transformer, in contrast, transfers electrical energy between two separate circuits. It has two independent windings – the primary winding, and the secondary winding, which goes to the output circuit. The two windings share a common iron core. Electrical energy is transferred from the primary to the secondary winding via an intermediary magnetic field.

In electric power transmission, the transformer either raises or lowers the voltage of the incoming electrical power. Power, which is measured in watts, is the product of voltage and current. Because the transformer cannot create electrical energy, its operation becomes a trade-off between raising voltage and simultaneously lowering current, or lowering voltage and raising current.

Energy is always lost in the operation of the transformer. "Copper losses" result from the electrical resistance of the primary and secondary windings; "core losses" result from the magnetic properties of the core material. For utility companies, these energy losses, if they are large, translate into significant costs.

The "ideal transformer" is an abstraction in which the transfer of electrical energy between the primary and secondary windings is carried out with 100-per-cent efficiency. Such a transformer experiences no copper or core losses. The main thrust of transformer design since the first transformer was built by Gaulard and Gibbs has been to get as close to the "ideal transformer" as possible, while maintaining an economically competitive design.

Today, transformer efficiencies have risen to 99 per cent. Within the context of energy transfer machines, this is a remarkable achievement. Most of the improvement has arisen from metallurgical advances that have produced core steel material with superior magnetic properties. Furthermore, a real transformer raises complex design issues which do not appear in the ideal case. The physics and engineering of high-voltage insulation, effective cooling systems, and noise reduction become important design considerations.

tion on an efficient, rational, and profitable basis. And yet there was considerable resistance to the concept. Unaccustomed to keeping track of consumption, customers were shocked to see their utility bills climb so high. The meter required new attitudes toward energy consumption. As one owner of an electric light and power plant in Waterloo, Ontario, commented, when he switched to meters:

I find there is an immense waste of power where flat rates are charged and nobody derives any benefit therefrom. By meter rate anyone that wishes to be economical can have all the conveniences, and have reasonable lighting expenses, and those who are anxious to have their premises lighted up well can have it by paying for it. It takes a little time and explanation to get people to understand why they should not be supplied on a flat rate, but any reasonable person can see that no electric light, gas or water plant can afford to have the taps open all day when they are only paid for a couple of hours.[38]

Three classes of meters – electrolytic, motor, and clock – had emerged by the 1890s. With electrolytic meters, one bought electricity literally by the ounce. The weight of zinc deposited on a metal plate by the action of an electrical current represented the amount of energy consumed over a period of time. In motor meters, the total number of revolutions of the meter's armature, in a given period, indicated the energy consumed. Clock meters measured electrical energy used by indicating the time difference between a reference clock and a clock that ran proportionately to the customer's use of electrical current.

Each type of meter had advantages and disadvantages. Technical performance was only one aspect. The sale of electricity and the ensuing growth of the meter business were both premised on the public's belief that meters provided a fair basis for billing. To ensure public confidence in the electrical utilities, John A. Macdonald's Conservative dominion government enacted in 1894 Canada's first laws regulating the electrical industry. The Canadian Electric Light Inspections Act attempted, among other things, to place guidelines on the operation of meters. It required that all meters be directly readable by the customer. In so doing, it effectively killed the electrolytic meter. One electrical expert, however, was outraged at such governmental interference in the meter business. In a widely read Canadian electrical journal, he accused Ottawa of using the public's rights as a smoke-screen to conceal influential monopoly gas interests:

The Edison [chemical] meter has been condemned by a certain class either through ignorance of its principle or prejudice and our Canadian Government have almost seen fit to condemn it – probably not to condemn it, but to curtail the growth of a meter that has no superior and very few equals.

The Government has to raise a revenue, that is settled; the gas companies contribute a certain percentage of that revenue, the electric companies are their greatest competitors, therefore we can readily infer that any little obstacle that can be put in the way by such companies will be done so and it is very common property that this Act was the result of the gas companies.[39]

Quite reasonably, A.A. Dion, general superintendent of the Ottawa Electric Co., stated: "It is necessary to the full success and popularity of the meter system of charging for current, that the meters should be direct reading, in other words that the record of consumption should appear in plain figures on dials available to the consumer, as he has long been accustomed to in gas meters."[40] Others offered similar arguments.

The market wanted a meter that could measure energy consumed in all manner of AC circuits, meet new government standards, and still be cost-effective. The financial success of central generating stations depended on using one measure to sell electricity to all customers, regardless of how the energy was consumed. Use of motors for this purpose posed problems not encountered with electric lighting. Furthermore, the meter's accuracy had to be assured over light loads as well as heavy loads. The cost-effectiveness of the meter would depend on the total expenses associated with its installation, operation, inspection, and maintenance. The meter also had to be tamper-proof – a requirement that tested the ingenuity of meter engineers. Meeting these operational criteria while keeping costs down put considerable pressure on the meter manufacturer.

By 1907, when Ferranti Ltd set up a Canadian agency in Toronto to sell meters, the main lines of the instrument's technology were already well drawn. The induction motor meter, invented by Oliver Shallenberger at Westinghouse in Pittsburgh, in 1888, had emerged as the meter technology for the twentieth century. Working as an induction motor, Shallenberger's meter actually measured ampere-hours, not watt-hours – i.e. total current, not power, used by the consumer. By soon after 1900, several North American companies were manufacturing improved variations of Shallenberger's first meter, and all were now watt-hour meters: Duncan, General Electric, Packard, Scheeffer, Stanley, and Westinghouse.

Canada and the Electrical Revolution

The potential of electrical technology spawned waves of enthusiastic optimism throughout the major industrialized nations. Potential and enthusiasm are one thing, but action is another; not all countries were equally adept at seeing and seizing the opportunities created by electrical advances. Although the Canadian market accepted electrical technology at an early date, the extent of application remained limited. DC technology, in the form of electric lighting and streetcars, had found early acceptance in Canada's largest cities. Large-scale electrification and the high-voltage transmission of electric power over great distances would not start in earnest until the end of the nineteenth century.[41] By the turn of the century, an unprecedented economic boom was launching Canada on the path of massive electrification. Until then, electrical development remained progressive but not very intensive.

As in Europe and the United States, electric lighting started out in Canada as a curiosity as or an advertising gimmick to attract attention. In 1873, R.H. Davis, a provincial cabinet minister, installed one arc lamp in front of his hotel on Main Street in Winnipeg, Manitoba, in order to publicize his establishment. As the only electric light in all western Canada, Davis's lamp must have elicited much discussion. George McConkey installed an arc light in 1879 in front of his ice-cream parlour, on Yonge Street in Toronto, Ontario. People could sit outside on a summer's evening and enjoy their purchases under the dazzling light. Of course, prices went up after dark.

By the 1880s, installation of electric lighting began in earnest. One after another, municipalities across Canada put in street arc lighting. In 1881, a young Englishman named John Joseph Wright started Canada's first electric lighting company in Toronto. He set up Canada's first generator station at the northeast corner of King and Yonge streets. Wright made the generator in the shop of the Firstbrooke Box Factory; he designed his own arc lamps, made the carbons, and copper-plated them himself. Timothy Eaton, founder of the Eaton's department stores, was one of Wright's first customers. In the same year, Ottawa Electric Co. provided several kilometres of arc lighting for the nation's capital. In 1883, Hamilton, Ontario, became the first city to install large-scale street arc lighting. By 1891, Charlottetown, Halifax, Saint John, Montreal, Winnipeg, Calgary, Edmonton, and Victoria all had extensive DC lighting systems.

New ideas and techniques sometimes meet with resistance and

suspicion in Canada, as elsewhere. When Wright built the first Canadian-made motor in 1883, he used it to power a coffee-grinding machine at Timothy Eaton's store: "Wright's grinder was greeted with almost violent opposition as an invention of the Devil. In fact, one minister delivered a sermon in which he strongly denounced the electric motor as an instrument of evil, since it would release girls from honest toil to wander the streets and fall prey to the will of Satan."[42] One day the switch to the coffee-grinder jammed, and the machine could not be turned off and "ground up all the coffee there was at Eaton's – and it still went on grinding. Several stores in the neighborhood fed all their stocks of coffee into the machine but still it could not be stopped. Then at last someone realized how to stop this Frankenstein by cutting the wire."[43] This example of run-away technology surely gave the minister great satisfaction.

Nonetheless, the use of electric energy for motive power found early acceptance in Canada. In 1888 the Barber Paper Mill, in Georgetown, Ontario, became the first mill in North America to use DC electrical power. Barber generated the electricity in a small hydro-electric installation located 1.5 miles (2.4 km) downstream from the mill. In the years to follow, hydro-electric power would become the major stimulus for industrial development in Canada, particularly in Ontario and Quebec.

In the 1890s Canadians realized that future economic development would be impossible without a domestic electrical industry. The country had a great untapped market for electrical technology but little infrastructure to supply it. Improved transportation made domestic markets more open to foreign manufactured goods, and this made it difficult to foster indigenous manufacturing. Development of an adequate manufacturing base in this "leading-edge" technology required substantial foreign investment and access to foreign technology.

In an attempt to harness foreign capital and know-how to the needs of national industrialization, Canada employed a policy of protective tariffs and the power of patent protection legislation. After the Conservative victory in 1878, Sir John A. Macdonald's government set up the "National Policy." The purpose of this strategy was to allow the vulnerable manufacturing sector to grow and prosper under a protective umbrella of high tariffs. As historian Michael Bliss observed recently: "getting American companies to erect Canadian branch plants was of course, a main aim of the National Policy. Politicians hoped the tariff would induce transfers of foreign capital, technology, and expertise to Canada – a policy one journal called 'importing industries instead of products' ... No one thought foreign ownership of factories in Canada was in any way harmful. On the contrary, the 'Canadianization' of American business in this migration was exactly the result the economic nationalists wanted."[44]

As a further inducement to foreign companies to set up manufacturing facilities, patent protection was offered only for products and processes actually manufactured in this country. The Patent Act of 1872 forced American companies to seek Canadian patents if they did

An accurate, easily maintained meter which allowed customers to be charged for the power or electricity they used was one of the essential prerequisites for the widespread use of centrally generated electricity. Before this, customers were charged a simple flat rate based on number of light bulbs or motors rather than actual power used. The *Scientific American* of 8 November 1887 praised the British meter of Professor Forbes (above) because it was "very simple. The electric current passing through the iron conductor creates heat, which sets up a convection current in the air, and this causes the vanes to rotate about the vertical axis and drive the clockwork. The number of revolutions indicated on the dials is ... an exact indication of the number of coulombs or ampere hours which have passed through the conductor." Although praised for accuracy within two or three per cent whether used with alternating or direct current, it was not the way of the future.
(National Museum of Science and Technology, Ottawa)

The modern electric meter industry grew out of Shallenberger's alternating-current meter (opposite). An American invention which added greatly to Westinghouse sales, it used electric current to drive an induction motor which turned the counter dials from which consumption could be read directly.
(Smithsonian Institution, 70509)

not want their inventions pirated. To obtain a patent required a commitment to produce the item within Canada. Patent laws forced companies such as Bell, General Electric, and Westinghouse to set up manufacturing facilities in Canada, and soon there was a proliferation of American branch plants. The National Policy and, perhaps even more significantly, patent legislation fostered the rise of a domestic electrical industry.

There was, however, a dark side to the rapid growth of American branch plants. Tom Naylor, a business historian, argues that government policy during the later nineteenth century rendered the country increasingly dependent on foreign know-how. This dependence, Naylor argues, stifled invention and innovation, particularly in advanced technologies such as electric power. "The greater the success achieved in introducing American technology," Naylor writes, "the poorer became the record of Canadian achievement."[45]

Naylor's views are certainly not universally applicable or accepted by all scholars, and the debate over technological dependence continues. The history of Ferranti-Packard offers good examples of how foreign investment encouraged Canadian innovation.

2 Birth of Packard Electric

Early Years in Canada

Love of the practical dominated Victorian Canada's relationship with science and technology. As a result, the developments that propelled electricity from philosophical curiosity to practical working technology captivated Canadians. Acutely conscious of the limitations of steam- and water-power, and well aware of how unevenly coal was distributed across the country, Canadians anxiously, sometimes naively, searched for new sources of energy and light. They welcomed new technology. The pioneering tradition was alive and, with it, an understanding that land had been cleared, farms created, and industry launched by a combination of adapting technology from elsewhere and creating the rest.[1]

Canada was a nation of immigrants. There were established, stable, "founding families," but most people were on the move, either coming from other countries or simply migrating from one part of Canada to another. The constant ebb and flow of people carried rumours, information about new technology, and faith in what it might achieve. In an age when people were mesmerized by the seemingly unlimited possibilities of new technology, and in a nation inhabited largely by immigrants and itinerants, it was not at all unusual for foreigners – in this case, two brothers from Warren, Ohio – to choose Canada as the place in which to pursue the possibilities of the advanced technology of the day. Electricity and internal-combustion-engine automobiles were on the "leading edge" of late-nineteenth-century technology, and the Packard brothers, James Ward and William Doud, brought to Canada both knowledge and active faith in their potential.

The Search for New Technology

Technological change occurs in many ways, but it is not a random process. It is frequently preceded by perception of a problem, a search

This artist's depiction of the Packard industrial complex is taken from the *St Catharines Standard*, Special Souvenir Number of 1907, which was published to promote Niagara District business and industrial achievement and potential. The entire Packard Electric plant, which covered three acres and employed 300 people plus 7 travelling salesmen, was described as "one of the largest and one of the most important of the factories which have their home in St. Catharines." Geneva Street enters the picture from the left side, while Race Street enters from the bottom right, running in front of the Electric Department building, the former Neelon Mill, to join Geneva Street.

The Welland Canal is visible in the background, and the water power flume runs behind the Neelon Mill building. In cold weather exposed or unheated water-power equipment often freezes solid and will not turn. Clarence Spratt, who became vice president of Sales, joined Packard at the age of sixteen. On cold mornings he and Frank Malloy would break the ice to get things moving again.

The Motor Car Department, with its then up-to-date sawtooth roof and many windows, later became Guaranty Silk and Dye. The Neelon Mill and the Motor Car Department have disappeared. The old house labelled Office at the corner of Bond and Race Streets still exists, as do the other two houses behind it.

(St Catharines Museum, N 3937)

for solutions, and openness to new ideas. In other cases, people are so impressed by the potential benefits and developments that might flow from new technology that they look for ways to use it – they search for appropriate problems.[2] Both scenarios apply to the history of Ferranti-Packard, but, in the years preceding the founding of Packard Electric Co. Ltd. in 1894, public dissatisfaction with existing technology probably played a far greater role than clear understanding of the potential created by new techniques.

The beauty, romance, and undeniable accomplishments of steam technology have clouded its past. Canadian history is filled with affectionate visions of steam-engines: powerful locomotives; gang ploughs breaking acres of virgin prairie soil in a day's work; steam threshing machinery spewing out car loads of golden grain; steamboats crossing oceans, languidly transporting tourists, or furiously racing from one Great Lakes port to another in clouds of dense black smoke.

Immense, beautiful steam-engines stood in the spotlight radiating power that one could see, touch, and feel. Enthusiasts of science quite incorrectly paraded the steam-engine as the offspring of a union between science and technology.[3] But there was a dark side. Numerous boiler explosions left a legacy of death, scalding, and maiming. The steam-engine was also inefficient, inconvenient, polluting, and a fire hazard, but it was the best power source of the day. It was least appropriate for intermittent power because a "head" of steam could not be produced quickly and fuel had to be consumed merely to stay in a

The original Packard Electric office facing Race Street across from the Neelon Mill building. The building, also shown in the artist's depiction opposite, was later added to and is still standing. It is believed that the Packard brothers are included in this photograph. The fine Victorian house to the right is far more elaborate than the 1907 artist's depiction of the Packard site suggests. (Ed Love)

state of readiness. Steam-engines were heavy, and the larger ones were generally more efficient and hence gave a greater return on capital invested. Consequently, factories tended to rely on one or two very large engines connected to machines by a labyrinthine complex of cleverly engineered belts, shafts, and pulleys which encouraged the growth of large, multi-storied factories and mills.

Steam-engines also required prodigious amounts of fuel. In England, that pioneering nation in steam-engine development, coal was plentiful and never far from major industrial centers and users. The situation was different in Canada. Even though some fraud artists duped investors with "salted" coal-mine sites, Ontario and Quebec lacked coal. Steam-engines could use other fuel, and Canada seemed to have plenty of trees but again there were distribution problems. By mid-nineteenth century, major population centres, particularly in Ontario, were suffering from severe energy shortages as wood had to be hauled ever-increasing distances for heating and industrial processes.

With the birth and expansion of a Canadian oil industry in Ontario during the late 1850s and 1860s, petroleum seemed to be the answer to energy needs. But in the nineteenth century, the promise of petroleum as a fuel for heating or transportation went largely unfulfilled.[4]

Until the development and wide use of the internal combustion engine, the lighter fractions of petroleum distillation which constituted gasoline were unwanted and dangerous by-products, often simply dumped into the nearest river or stream. In the absence of adequate carburetion and combustion devices, the heavier fractions could not be burned properly in boilers and were largely failures as sources of steam heat. Petroleum served primarily as a source of lighting fluid and, to a lesser extent, a lubricant. Manufacturers and users of steam-engines sought other fuels, but most of these seemed less desirable in practice than in theory. For example, wheat straw could be burned on farms, but it required a tremendous volume, burned very incompletely, and, even with spark arresters, posed a major fire hazard.

Steam was spectacular and very useful, especially for rail transportation, but water, as a basic source of industrial power, was the great hope for much of Canada. In regions of fast-flowing rivers, often with precipitous waterfalls, rapids, and slopes, settlers eagerly sought "water-powers" – as potential mill sites were known – which then became early town and industrial centres. Turbines made water-power the symbol of energy efficiency. But there were other problems. Dependence on water-power confined industrial growth to stream or river sites which soon became overly crowded. Some places with great potential went untouched because they were too far from other required features such as good transportation networks, markets, and sources of raw materials. If only the energy from water could be made more portable, more evenly distributed.

Numerous interesting technological avenues were tried in an effort to make water-power more transportable or at least strung out over a longer distance. Water that would otherwise drop quickly over a single high waterfall could be rechanneled through longer, more gradually sloping, man-made channels which formed the backbone of linear industrial corridors with numerous water turbine–powered factories or mills. Similarly, the water flowing through navigation canals built around falls or rapids could be diverted to provide power for mills and factories lining the transportation corridor. This was certainly the case with both the Welland Canal and the Lachine Canal. In fact the latter was so successful in promoting industry to tap the excess water-power that industrial users drew too heavily on available water-supplies and hindered shipping because they would not leave enough water to operate the canal locks.

Various mechanical means were tried to transmit the power produced from water. Long rope drives transmitted power from a turbine or water-wheel to factories or mills removed from the watercourse. But such devices were cumbersome, costly, and limited to a range measured in several hundreds of yards. Similar disadvantages applied to systems of reciprocating rods. Compressed air was the most promising medium. In Europe, it had been produced primarily by central steam-engines and then piped throughout commercial or industrial areas. Pioneering efforts in Canada used the power of falling water to produce compressed air for industrial purposes and to provide power for mines. The most famous installation was at Ragged Chutes in northern Ontario, where compressed air transmitted power approximately 8 miles (12.8 km). It was a start, but the distances were severely limited.

Canada's rapidly growing late-nineteenth-century cities also needed better transportation and lighting systems. It is hard to imagine a time when the dream of individually powered vehicles – automobiles – was seen as the saviour for traffic-congested and pollution-fouled cities. But a horse and a carriage moved slowly, took up considerable road space, and required stables. Perhaps worst of all, horses generated and dropped a rather heavy load of organic waste which added to the unpleasant odours of the city, polluted water-supplies, attracted flies, and transmitted disease.

The soaring popularity of the bicycle in the latter decades of the nineteenth century clearly illustrated the need for a reasonably priced, carefully engineered means of individualized transportation which one did not have to feed or sweep up after. However, the bicycle was not an all-weather vehicle, nor was it suitable for long distances or for carrying heavy loads. There was plenty of room for improved urban transportation. Increasingly, entrepreneurs and inventors turned toward two emerging technologies: internal combustion engines and electricity.

Before the advent of electric lighting, Canadian cities, homes, and workplaces were both more dimly lit and far more susceptible to fires from lighting sources. Artificial gas and petroleum-based illuminants met most mid-Victorian lighting needs. Neither type burned cleanly; both required careful tending lest they become very smoky and, at the best of times, left an unpleasant odour. Worse still, they burned with hazardous open flames, and, although the oil lamp was portable, a dropped lamp could spread a thin layer of burning fluid which often defeated the best fire-fighting equipment of the day. In some workplaces, such as flour and certain textile mills, the fine dust particles suspended in the air created a deadly mixture which an open flame or spark could ignite explosively into a catastrophic fireball.

Moreover, as the concentrated power sources of the day created larger and more heavily manned factories and workplaces, the need for improved artificial lighting became even more critical. Similarly, the heavier capital investments and new continuous processes often encouraged, and sometimes necessitated, round-the-clock operations. Greater volumes of trade also strained harbours which would be ice-bound in winter. During the navigation season, loading docks were often taxed beyond capacity, producing dangerous overcrowding. Although the immediate key to the problem was longer hours of work, one could not load ships at night without good lighting.

In the late nineteenth century, industrial nations were seething with frustration and dissatisfaction over the inadequacies of existing power, lighting, and transportation technology. Canada, much more than many other countries, was particularly ripe for change and ready for hot pursuit of the possibilities offered by the new technologies of electricity and the internal combustion engine. But to capitalize on the dissatisfaction and development potential one needed technological pioneers.

The Packard Brothers: Harbingers of the Engineered World

The lives of James Ward Packard and his older brother, William Doud, have an almost mythical story-book quality: long-established roots in the United States merging with the most modern and forward-looking technology which so radically transformed the country around the end of the nineteenth century. The Packards' history in North America begins in Massachusetts, where in 1638 Samuel Packard, an English emigrant, had disembarked from the sailing ship *Diligence*.

In 1825 the promise of prosperity lured William Packard, grandfather of James Ward and William Doud, to the frontier regions of the Western Reserve where he and his wife, Julia, settled at Lordstown, 5 miles (8 km) south of present-day Warren, Ohio. There, between 1828 and 1847, they had nine children before he was lured away once again. This time it was the gold of California, but William Packard found neither gold nor the time or inclination to return to his family in Ohio. The automotive historian Terry Martin observed: "His was a life like many others of that era: the farm, the large family, the desertion of a past for a future filled with promise, the promise unrealized."[5]

Three years before William left for California, his eighteen-year-old son, named after the nearby town of Warren, had started his working career in an iron goods or hardware store in Trumbull, Ohio. A year after his father had been lured by California gold, son Warren owned both the store in which he had been employed and a competing shop.

There followed a series of largely successful ventures, characterized by careful choice of partners, hard work, awareness of opportunities created by new and emerging technology, diversification, and willingness to make solid investments away from home. Warren Packard invested in a variety of enterprises. He and his partners had the first iron-rolling mill in Warren. Lumbering and sawmilling also attracted him. Unprecedented growth in the emerging petroleum industry in nearby Pennsylvania made existing roads inadequate. Suddenly the Titusville and Pithole Plank Road needed three million board feet of planks which Packard and his partners, S.L. Abell and Harmon Austin, supplied over a three-month period. Eventually his lumbering and milling operations extended into Kentucky.

On 20 November 1860, four years after the death of his first wife, Warren Packard married Mary E. Doud. Of their five children, it was the two boys, William Doud Packard, born 3 November 1861, and James Ward Packard, born 5 November 1863, who would make the family name a household word in the early twentieth century. Rarely have the combined interests, strengths, and talents of two brothers been so suited to the needs of an age, or complemented each other so well.

William Doud was the consummate salesman and disciplined businessman. Upon leaving Ohio State University in 1882 he entered his father's hardware store as bookkeeper and salesman. Later he added

James Ward Packard in his steam yacht *Carlotta* on Lake Chautauqua. James, an outgoing, inventive engineer, was general superintendent 1890–91 and president 1891–1903 of the Packard Electric Company in Warren, Ohio, as well as one of the founders of Packard Electric Company and Packard Lamp Co. Ltd. in Canada. His older brother and business partner, William Doud Packard, was a highly disciplined conservative businessman who served with him as secretary-treasurer from 1890 to 1903.
(Packard Museum Association, Warren, Ohio)

the then-coveted skill of telegraphy to his repertoire, operated a hotel, and eventually ran a planing mill as partner in the firm of Warren Packard & Son.

James Ward Packard was cut from different cloth. His strengths and interests lay in things mechanical, not commercial, nor was he initially inclined to the family business in a small town. In 1884, he graduated as a mechanical engineer from Lehigh University in Bethlehem, Pennsylvania, and moved to New York City. Long a great commercial centre, New York was also one of the great centres of exciting electrical development. Pioneer inventor and businessman Thomas Alva Edison had established and shown the workability of his centralized electric lighting system at the Pearl Street station. The battle between arc and incandescent lighting would continue for a few decades, but clearly the latter was most promising for home and office.

Electricity and incandescent lights were "the rage" when James Ward Packard accepted a position with pioneering manufacturer of incandescent lamps Sawyer-Mann Co. In August, he "started in the dynamo room at a dollar a day, but a month later both his wages and his responsibilities were increased when he was made superintendent of the dynamo room, and by November foreman of the mechanical department. Subsequently he applied for the first two of many patents he would obtain during his lifetime – the first for a magnetic circuit and the second for an incandescent lamp bulb, which would later be sold to Westinghouse.[6] Sawyer-Mann would eventually become part of Westinghouse, and undoubtedly Packard could have stayed with

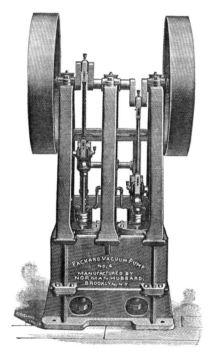

A commanding lead in new technology contributed to Packard Electric's success. The Packard Vacuum Pump was one of the foundations upon which Packard Electric was built. A better vacuum within the incandescent bulb contributed to longer filament life and in 1889 and 1891 J.W. Packard was granted patents for a vacuum pump designed specifically for light-bulb manufacture. By 1891 it was being used by all but one of the light-bulb manufacturers in the United States. The 9 May 1891 issue of the *Electrical Review* from which this is taken described Packard as "an expert in lamp manufacture and an inventor of note."
(National Museum of Science and Technology, Ottawa)

these large enterprises. In 1890, however, the experienced engineer-inventor left New York and returned to Warren, Ohio. To some it might have appeared the road to oblivion, but the Packard brothers had other ideas.

From mid-nineteenth century onward, new technology and innovations spurred North American economic development. Farming continued to be hard work, but, with either steam-engines or horses, it was becoming increasingly mechanized, particularly on the larger farms of the US Midwest.[7] Construction still relied heavily on manpower, but with the added assistance of machines such as steam-powered piledrivers, hoists, elevators, and excavators. Corporate and manufacturing success was becoming more dependent on advanced technological knowledge. There was still room for the skilled tradesman, the ingenious mechanic, but the trend was toward greater and greater reliance on trained professional engineers. Many of the engineers had trained on the job, but the newest wave came from universities. Book learning was often mistrusted and despised in the workplace, and certainly needed tempering on the job, but with the new technologies, it was essential and unbeatable for certain types of problem solving and understanding. Nowhere was this clearer than in electricity and chemistry, glamorous fields in the late 1880s.

Set in the framework of emerging technology and corporate needs and opportunities, the Packard brothers possessed a rare and potentially powerful mixture: proven financial and managerial skills, university training in engineering, and experience and demonstrated ability in new technology. There were other assets and strengths. Throughout his career, James Ward Packard, the engineer, displayed superior ability in attracting and selecting partners – as when in 1890 he asked his brother to become partner in a new electrical enterprise in Warren. James Ward Packard took his big city experience in new technology and brought it home. Here there were valuable allies and contacts. But, most important of all, there was his brother, a known partner with financial and management skills and experience. The new corporate leader of the 1890s still needed the nerve of his predecessor, but it had to be accompanied by finer managerial skills and understanding of marketing, sales, banking, finance, and market trends. Of these, William Doud was a master.

It was more than just another case of "boosterism" and "local boys make good" when the *Warren Tribune* announced of 3 June 1890: "NOW IT'S ASSURED PACKARD ELECTRIC CO., THE NEWEST OF WARREN'S NEW ENTERPRISES." The firm's new buildings, one of brick and one of wood, were rather ordinary. But the products and fitting up were indeed quite novel. They would manufacture "dynamos, lamps, and electrical specialties" with power conveyed to the different machines not by belts or steam pipes, but by electric wires, the motive "power of each machine its own dynamo."[8] A separate motor for each machine was the essence of modernity and efficiency, something newspaper readers expected from "Mr. J. Ward Packard ... not only an eminent electrician, but a mechanical engineer as well."

In 1890 the Packard Electric Company opened new buildings in Warren, Ohio. The false front bearing the company name gave their new quarters a rather impressive air and any fire insurance agent would have liked the roof-mounted water tank. A transformer has been mounted outside one of the second floor windows on the side wall of the main building. Packard Electric, now much larger and a division of General Motors, is still in Warren, Ohio. (Packard Museum Association, Warren, Ohio)

At a time when to be addressed as a mechanical engineer was honour in itself, and electrician more often than not meant electrical engineer, this was high praise indeed.

Two days later, the Packard brothers, and their carefully chosen partners, C.F. Clapp, Jacob Perkins, Juston W. Spangenberg, and M.B. Tayler, drew up the incorporation papers for Packard Electric Company. Tayler and Clapp were local bankers, Perkins a wealthy landowner who had sold the land for its plant to Packard Electric, and Spangenberg a local businessman with experience in partnerships, including a machine shop and foundry which produced sawmills and steam-traction locomotives.

Little is known about the relative financial strengths and contributions of each partner, but in September the new factory was opened on schedule, and the first board meeting was held there on 6 October 1890. The new company was probably both ambitious and short of cash, for on 27 January 1891 the partners decided to form a new corporation. Unable to raise money locally, James Ward Packard successfully called on contacts from his New York days, and The New York & Ohio Company came into being. As with Packard Electric, William Doud Packard was secretary and treasurer, but whereas James had been president of the first company, he was general superintendent of the second, a position in which his talents and interests could be best used. President was John W. Peale, of 1 Broadway, New York; perhaps he had suggested incorporation in West Virginia, with its attendant tax advantages. The new buildings and equipment were rented to the new company, and an addition was made to house Packard Electric.

In only thirteen months, two companies had been created, premises built for both, and – at a time known for indistinct and often muddled corporate lines of reporting and financing – the newly emerging electrical concern had been divided into two separate lines, each representing a different approach to the business. The *Warren City Directory* for 1894 listed both firms at the same address, but Packard Electric was identified as "contractors for Arc and Incandescent Electric Light Plants, Electric Bells, Gas Lighting, Annunciators, Burglar Alarms, Speaking Tubes, Etc." with the added note: "Repairing Promptly Attended To."[9] New York & Ohio was identified simply as "Manufacturers of The Packard High Grade Incandescent Lamp"; an added note reflected the industry's complete lack of uniformity: "Lamps of all Candle Power and Voltage to Fit any Socket."[10]

Separation of specialized manufacturing facilities from the more locally dependent installation and contracting operations allowed for a clearer understanding of where strenghts and profits lay. Predictably, William Doud Packard devoted much of his energies to sales. It is claimed that he visited "every large city from St. Louis to Boston in the 1890s and into the new century to promote Packard products to city-owned and private lighting companies."[11]

As is often the case, corporate records and correspondence have disappeared. William Doud Packard kept a daily diary, but only a few years have survived and the entries are often quite cryptic. Nonetheless, they show an interest in the international marketplace. In late 1898 he was exploring trade with Mexico[12] and selling for export in Argentina.[13] He had also "agreed to make an arrangement with W.B. Tuttle to pay him $25.00 per month for one year – he to travel to Philippines, Japan, China, Java, Corea [sic] and probably India ... Mr. Tuttle is to call at Warren about Jan. 1st for special instruction in re[gard] to lamps and transformers."[14] Early the following year Packard had "decided to send a representative to Europe to look up & establish English trade."[15]

But even earlier the Packards had investigated and travelled to Canada. A listing in the *Montreal City Directory* for 1893–94 indicates that the Packard Lamp Co. Ltd. was sharing premises with the Dominion Electric Manufacturing Co. And in 1893, when the Canadian Association of Stationary Engineers held its fourth annual convention in Montreal, the "Packard Lamp Company Limited" of "96 to 100 King Street" took out a full-page advertisement in the *Souvenir Number*, a special book prepared for the event. It urged delegates to "try our high grade lamp and you will use no other" and claimed that its bulbs were noted for "Efficiency, brilliance, maintenance of candle power, guaranteed for an average life of 800 hours."[16]

Canada Grasps the New Technology

As shown earlier, Canadians were much more than passive observers to the dramatic unfolding of new electrical understanding and technology. Evidence abounds throughout Canadian history to suggest a long and fruitful relationship with technology. Historians who have looked at areas such as cod fishing, fur trading, and early agriculture have all found a respectable level of openness and ingenuity.[17] Nineteenth-century "canal mania" was the first readily visible manifestation of Canada's love affair with large-scale technology. Its legacy of achievement included the Lachine, Rideau, and Welland canals.

Railway mania was even more spectacular. What to the uninitiated may have appeared simply a copy of European technology was actually carefully adapted to suit Canadian conditions. Even the very trackbeds, early trestles, and bridges reflected local conditions and needs. Lambton County's petroleum boom of the late 1850s and the 1860s produced the distinctive Canadian system of drilling, which was used world-wide in petroleum exploration and production. It also coincided with a concerted search for new energy sources which saw a variety of artificial gas plants built – primarily for lighting – as well as widespread use of petroleum-based lighting fluids.

Electricity was pursued with even greater speed and enthusiasm.[18] Very early, Montreal emerged as a key player in that story. When 50,000-volt electric power arrived in Montreal from Shawinigan Falls on 3 February 1903, it was one of the great landmarks in Canadian electrical history.[19] At a distance of 85 miles (137 km), it was not the longest transmission, but it marked the beginning of a pattern that would have great impact on Packard Electric in Canada. Little of the country's best potential hydro-electric power lay near populated industrial centres as it did in Niagara Falls. The Shawinigan Falls area had been of minor economic importance until electric power attracted a number of industries. The electric power was transmitted by what were then considered long-distance lines. Hydro-electric power installations transmitting electricity over increasingly greater distances became the dominant pattern for Canada, particularly in Ontario and Quebec and later in British Columbia.

Signs of Montreal's leadership in electrical matters had emerged before 1903. In 1878, a French-speaking Montrealer, J.A.I. Craig, had given Canada its first demonstration of the recently invented Jablochkoff Candle, a much-improved type of arc lamp. Craig then became a founder of Royal Electric Co. Ltd., which by 1889 was supplying Montreal with electric street lighting and by 1895 had a large factory in the city manufacturing parts for electric generators.[20] In 1891, McGill became one of the few universities in the world that offered a program in electrical engineering.[21] By 1890 Montreal had embarked on rapid industrial growth that would see its population soar from 219,616 in 1891 to 490,504 in 1911. The city would have looked very good to a foreign investor wanting to enter electrical manufacturing in Canada. Arguably the engineering capital of the country, it was leading, or keeping pace with, the rest of the nation in electrical enthusiasm and was home to many other manufacturers and a skilled, willing labour force.

It is not known why the Packards and their partners wanted to manufacture in Canada or why they chose Montreal. The diaries of William Doud Packard reveal an astute businessman who wished to expand outside the United States. Numerous American industrialists and investors had already found in Canada's protective tariffs and patent laws an incentive to locate plants in this country to supply the domestic market and to gain preferential access to the entire British Empire. These advantages were widely advertised by organizations such as the Canadian Manufacturers Association and were common knowledge to many American businessmen. Moreover, the dangers of manufacturing and selling in separate countries and the havoc that could be wrought by changes in tariff policy would have occupied a particularly important place in Packard family lore. The father's 1867 visit to Europe led to a profitable business based on hardware imported from that continent, but it was destroyed almost overnight a few years later when the United States enacted prohibitive tariffs. The decision to manufacture in Canada may have been motivated by a fear of sudden and unpredictable imposition of tariffs which could quickly ruin a business.

The Packards may have seen Canada as an escape from legal problems at home. The history of light-bult manufacture is exceedingly complicated and filled with patent litigation. The move to Montreal coincides with two important points in Packard history: "The Panic of 1893 put a damper on the electric business, and for a while operations were halted because of litigation concerning the Edison patents brought against Packard Electric by the General Electric Company. This lawsuit would be fought until the patents expired, and for the duration James Ward Packard found himself frequently on the road to Cleveland and the courtroom."[22]

Whatever the reasons, by 1893 the Packard Lamp Co. Ltd. was in Montreal with Charles C. Paige as managing director, and it appears not to have imported but to have started making light bulbs right away. An 1893 advertisement for Packard Lamp bulbs claimed that "our 'low volt' is the only one ever successfully made in Canada."[23] But again, another mystery emerges from the pages of the *Montreal City Directory*. As early as 1891 Dominion Electric Manufacturing Co. had been listed at 145 St. James St., with H. Cortland as general manager. When Packard Lamp Co. is listed in 1893, it is at 96–100 King St., the same address given for the Dominion Electric Manufacturing Co. with C. Paige listed as managing director. The same entries continue for 1894–95, but both companies have disappeared with the 1895–96 directory.

Little is known about the history of either company in Montreal. However, letters patent, dated 1 August 1894, were issued incorporating Packard Electric Company Limited, and on 15 February 1895, J.W. Packard, W.D. Packard, H.K. Howry, J.H. Howry, and Alexander Mackenzie met to develop by-laws for the firm. One week later, at a meeting attended by A. Mackenzie, J. Lovell, and J.H. Howry, who held proxy votes for J.W. Packard, W.D. Packard and H.K. Howry, Packard Electric purchased the assets of the Packard Lamp Co. Ltd. and Dominion Electric Manufacturing, which had been owned by J. Packard, W. Packard, H. Howry, and J. Howry. At the

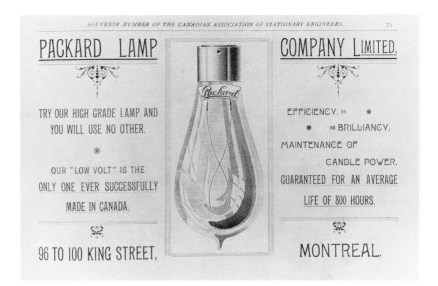

Packard Electric, which was located briefly in Montreal before moving to St Catharines, Ontario, took out a full page ad in the Canadian Association of Stationary Engineers souvenir publication for the 1893 meeting in Montreal. Voltages were not standardized as they are today; "low volt" lamps were for less than 90 volts.
(National Archives of Canada, c 139628)

same meeting, the Packards, the Howrys, J. Lovell, A. Mackenzie, and C. Paige were elected directors. Four months later, on 22 June 1895, the board appointed Charles Paige manager and elected a slate of officers: president, John Howry; vice-president, W.D. Packard; secretary treasurer, H.K. Howry; and general superintendent, J.W. Packard.

The newly reorganized company was also preparing to change its place of business. It had bought the Neelon Mill property in St Catharines, Ontario, for $18,000, of which $5,000 was paid in cash, the remainder in a mortgage held by the Bank of Toronto. In September, Paige resigned from the board and presumably from the company, in which he had held only one share. He was replaced on the board by G. Powell, who became assistant manager when W.D. Packard was elected manager.

On 2 March 1896, the directors passed By-law 18, which relocated the head office from Toronto to St Catharines and the chief place of business from Montreal to St Catharines. This formality recognized changes that had occurred earlier. Despite all the effort that had gone into reorganization, 1895 was still a profitable year. Sales of $35,296.72 were offset by purchases of $19,479.28 and labour costs of $6,790.67, leaving net income of $9,026.77.

Turmoil continued into 1896. The Packard brothers called a shareholders' meeting for 21 November 1896 "for the purpose of removing for cause J. Howry and H. Howry as Directors" and electing replacements for the balance of the term. This was a major blow for the Howrys and the Packards, the original major shareholders. In 1894 each of the four men had held 374 shares valued at $100 per share, for a total of 1,122; there were only five other shareholders, each of these Canadians with one share each. The following year each of the Packards held 499 shares, J.H. Howry also held 499, and H.K. Howry had none. It is not entirely clear what H. Howry had done,

The Welland Canal provided more than transportation: it acted as a magnet, drawing industries to locate along its banks. When Packard came to St Catharines it bought the Neelon Mill site at the corner of Race and Geneva Streets. This was a large industrial complex whose main building, an 80-foot (24 m) by 55-foot (17 m) four-storey stone mill had been built in 1882. The main office building, previously a house, is in the background. Water from the Welland Canal entered the mill via the flume visible in the foreground and generated 300 hp. The Neelon Mill was demolished in the summer of 1965 to make way for two 20-storey apartment buildings which failed to materialize. (Ontario Archives, Ferranti-Packard Collection, AO 799)

but it had involved a stock transfer that the company later disallowed. [24]

Transfers among shareholders continued, and by 1900, although American ownership still dominated, none of the four original American investors – the Packards and the Howrys – remained, nor in fact did the original Canadian investors. Financial control had passed from Warren, Ohio, to Saginaw, Michigan.

In shareholder minute books for 1895, J.H. Howry is identified as a lumberman from Saginaw, Michigan. Both Henry Potter and George Morley were significant shareholders in their own right and as trustees; both were bankers from Saginaw. In addition, the Savings Bank of East Saginaw was from 1898 a major shareholder, as was the

Second National Bank of Saginaw for only one year, 1898. There is also a link between Saginaw and Packard motor cars.

By 1896 James Ward Packard was very enthusiastic about motor cars, and on 16 May 1896 he wrote in his diary: "Engage Cowles to work on motor wagon at $12 per week 8 hrs per day." The expenses were not to be charged to an existing company but to be "divided between Howry, W.D. and J.W.P."[25]

Again, there are no written records to tell why investors from Saginaw would play such a notable role. However, the Packard family had long been investing in the prosperous Michigan lumbering and sawmilling industry. Saginaw had been a lumbering centre, but by the late 1880s the best of the timber in the watersheds leading to Saginaw had been cut and the industry started a period of decline. People who made fortunes in the timber industry were looking further afield. Some entries in W.D. Packard's diaries, such as that on 22 January 1898, are revealing: "the Saginaw stockholders say they are well pleased with the business of the past year."[26] The investors were important, but research, products, and sales were also needed to keep a new electrical manufacturer alive, and, in these, Packard Electric appears to have been doing quite well.

The first Packard Car was made in 1899. The engine had one cylinder and the brakes acted on the transmission rather than on the wheels. As their interest and investments in automobiles grew, the Packards withdrew from electrical manufacturing. (Packard Museum Association, Warren, Ohio)

Products and Research: Corporate Lifeblood

The technological euphoria of the late nineteenth and early twentieth centuries spawned numerous companies and patented inventions; but most went nowhere. The work and legacy of the Packard brothers, in both Canada and the United States, is far from typical. Though their period of financial involvement in Canada was brief, their influence lasted far longer. The independent companies bearing the Packard name in both countries shared two characteristics: careful choice of product lines to prevent resources and efforts from becoming too diffuse and ineffectively marshalled, and commitment to research and the pursuit of up-to-date knowledge.

Concern for "goal-oriented," "product-improving" research characterized James Ward Packard's restless and technologically creative personality and his training as a professional engineer. Long study of his life and numerous business ventures led one historian to conclude: "If there is one keynote to James Ward's career, it is that he was always adamant in securing sufficient provision for testing and design. No matter the endeavour, he was quick to establish laboratories for research work, departments for formulating improvements, experimental rooms for building and testing models. A fascination for original work led him repeatedly into new ventures."[27]

In his commitment to experiment, testing, and improvement, Packard resembled Edison, George Westinghouse, Sebastian Ziani de Ferranti, and the Wright brothers of nearby Dayton, Ohio. Innumerable others shared the same characteristics but are long forgotten, and the bones of their commercial aspirations litter the all-too-full graveyard of broken dreams. To the extent that failure is understood, it often results from choosing inappropriate goals — as with the many inventors and financiers of perpetual-motion machines — or pursuing too many goals. Far too many ingenious mechanics, inventors, and engineers have been so enthused by the thrill of the hunt and the challenge of constantly appearing new trails that they never travelled far enough along any one to ensure success. Had James Ward Packard not had a brother-partner who was a consummate businessman, he, like many inventors, too might have been constantly lured along never-ending new trails which led only to frustration and bitterness.

The Packard brothers, and the firms that they started, chose two areas of emerging technology and then within those found very sensible market niches. Electricity, and then automobiles, both offered numerous possibilities.

Initial concentration on manufacturing light bulbs required sound technical knowledge but was not as capital-intensive as other areas, such as manufacture of generators. Light bulbs were an essential product which offered great scope for quality improvement and economical production techniques. Electric lighting was rapidly reaching toward a mass market. But many bulb-makers had such poor quality control that each bulb had to be individually tested for lighting power and then labelled and sold on the experimentally determined lighting

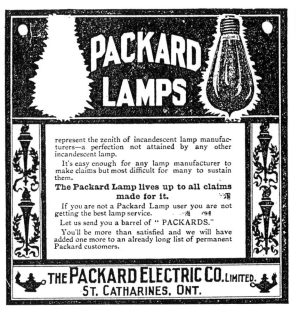

Quality could not be taken for granted with early light bulbs. A 1902 ad (above) in the *Canadian Engineer* claimed that "The Packard Lamp lives up to all claims made for it" and urged readers to "let us send you a barrel of PACKARDS." (National Museum of Science and Technology, Ottawa)

The 1910 letterhead from "The Dominion Electric Co., Renewers of Incandescent Lamps, St Catharines" (above right) shows the most delicate step in replacing burnt-out filaments in vacuum-type bulbs. Formerly owned by Packard Electric, the company had been sold to other owners by 1910. (St Catharines Museum, N 8964)

Manufacturing vacuum incandescent light bulbs such as the one shown opposite was one of the most difficult and delicate of all early electrical-manufacturing operations. (Ontario Archives, Ferranti-Packard Collection, Photo 1054)

As with some high-tech electronics assembly today, women did the work best. The work photos on pages 50–1 were taken in the lamp manufacturing and packing sections of the Neelon's Mill site in St Catharines. Note that the dress of the workers expressed a sense of propriety and pride in their highly skilled work. In two of the photographs the men are talking on the telephone while the women work.

Visible light cords strung from above were a standard feature in homes, offices, and workplaces of the day. Only when buildings were built specifically for electricity did wiring disappear into walls and ceiling. The

capability. Moreover, many bulbs suffered from a rapid decline in light output after a relatively short period of use. Neither of these characteristics was acceptable for mass-market goods, but mass-market acceptance was the key to prosperity.

Shortly after the relocation from Montreal to St Catharines, an article on "The New Packard Lamp Works" in the *Canadian Engineer* reported the results of a very carefully conducted series of tests performed by Professor Thomas of Ohio State University in Columbus, Ohio. He concluded: "Taking economy, maintenance of candle power, and freedom from blackening into account, the results obtained from these lamps are much superior to any heretofore published, and I congratulate you on the excellent showing made."[28] Unlike lamps from other makers, these had a candle-power-versus-time curve that was quite flat, with candle power actually rising over time before settling back to initial power. Two years later, another test of Packard lamps showed the same characteristic. This test, conducted by the superintendent of the Cincinnati Gaslight and Coke Co., moved the editor of the *Electrical Review* to a rare display of mild humour, as he commented that it "shows the Packard product in a very favourable light indeed."[29]

Packard Electric in the United States made incandescent lamps, transformers, fuse boxes, measuring instruments, and cables. But the lamp division was sold to General Electric after 1903 as the incandescent lamp industry became consolidated, with General Electric a leading player. While profitable, the incandescent lamp industry was plagued by costly and incessant patent litigation. This lasted until the reorganization in 1904 of the National Electric Lamp Association, which managed patent rights for incandescent lights and charged

lower photograph was printed from a
cracked glass-plate negative with a piece miss-
ing. All but one of the people are unidentified. Sarah Shannon, wearing a checked dress
with a high white collar, is seated near the
central shaded light fixture over the table.
Miss Shannon worked in the Lamp Department for three years. Later she had her own
bookkeeping and accounting business and
for many years shared a home with city employee Ada McLean. Theirs was not a
rooming house, but when Packard Electric
hired respectable gentlemen from out of
town they might rent rooms there until something more permanent could be found.
When Ed Love and Bob MacKimmie joined
the company in 1950 they lived in the Shannon and McLean home for six months but
took their meals elsewhere.
(Ontario Archives, Ferranti-Packard Collection, AO 1243, AO 1244)

In the final stage of manufacturing vacuum light bulbs, the top was heated in order to attach a glass tube which could be attached to a vacuum pump. After the air was pumped out, the tube was heated close to the bulb, sealed, and detached. This operation left the characteristic nipple on the top of vacuum bulbs. Finished bulbs were wrapped individually in paper and packed in wooden boxes or barrels with shredded wood known as excelsior to absorb shock during shipping. (Ontario Archives, Ferranti-Packard Collection, AO 1240, AO 1241)

The Type G Scheeffer meter is the most historically significant meter in Packard's history. Before the introduction of watt-hour
meters customers could not be billed on the
basis of power actually used. A watt hour,
which is a measure of actual power used, is
measured by a watt-hour meter. Packard originally imported the Type G Scheeffer meter
but began manufacturing it in Canada in
1902, becoming the second company to
manufacture watt-hour meters in Canada. In
1912 the Type G was replaced by the
Packard Type K meter. The great strength of
the Type K, aside from ease of mounting on
a wall or other flat surface, was its extreme accuracy over a very wide range of usage,
from a single one-candle power bulb to
50 per cent overload. This made it popular
with both electric power companies or utilities
and customers, who were confident they
were not being cheated.
(Ontario Archives, Ferranti-Packard Collection, AO 651)

users a royalty.[30] The American Packard Electric became increasingly
dependent on the electrical side of the automobile industry. In the
1930s it became part of General Motors and is now a very large division of GM.

In Canada, Packard Electric continued to manufacture incandescent light bulbs, but at an early date it also diversified so as to include
four additional distinct product areas: instrumentation, particularly
watt-hour meters; arc lamps; transformers; and automobiles.

Instrumentation. The growth of piped water-supplies available on demand for home, office, and industry paralleled that of electric power
for the same markets. Both started on a per-user fee independent of
quantity. Water was available on a flat rate, and early electric lighting
customers paid a fixed rate per installed light bulb. Such a system
made for ease of billing, but inequities were obvious. Equitable pricing based on actual consumption would encourage greater use of electricity. Such a pricing system required an accurate meter to record the
amount of electricity used. The Packard brothers clearly understood
the potential of these non-generating aspects of the electric industry.

Incandescent electric lamps brought the Packards into the Canadian electrical business, but they soon diversified. In the 1890s, the
Canadian Engineer bore the lengthy subtitle *The Canadian Engineer
Metal Trades Review & Electrical Science Review*. Here, in the June
1896 issue, Packard Electric advertised the American-made "Scheeffer Recording Watt Meters,"[31] and it continued to do so in later edi-
tions. In the 1890s Packard did not manufacture the meters. In an
1899 advertisement it was "Sole Agents for Scheeffer Recording Watt
Meters."[32] But by 1902 the situation had changed. Under the headline "The New Type 'G' Scheeffer Recording Watt Meter Is Now
Ready For Delivery," the company announced:

The new type 'G' Scheeffer Recording Watt Meter, which we are now manufacturing in our factory at St. Catharines, Ont., is not only the most accurate meter made but is the most sensitive. It is the only meter we have found
by actual test that will record the current consumed when a single HYLO
lamp is burning on its one candle power filament. Type 'G' is correct on pressure balance so that the meter registers only when the line is in use. Type 'G'
is provided with sealing disc and means of sealing to conform with Government regulations. Type 'G' is the one meter that is satisfactory to both the
central station and to the consumer.[33]

The meter was a relatively compact, light, handsomely designed product easily hung or installed on a wall or other flat surface. But, as
summarized in the ad, its primary advantage was continuing accuracy
of measurement over an extended time period and power range.
"WIDE RANGE — registering from one-half of one per cent. of full load
to overload of fifty per cent. unaffected by any power factor. Perma-
nency of calibration."[34]

Watt-hour meters would continue to be a notable part of the Packard line. By 1902, Packard saw itself as a manufacturer of lamps, transformers, and meters. The change from agent to manufacturer is particularly significant. In a highly competitive, emerging technology it was unreasonable to expect a small company to research and develop on its own a wide range of products, yet both reputation and survival often depended on producing more than one line. Variety reduced vulnerability. One survival strategy was to act as agent for a number of foreign manufactured goods, as Packard had done in the early years with Scheeffer.

Advantageous as it might have been, importing had drawbacks: tariffs, added uncertainty in the chain of supply, plus one more party with which profits had to be shared. The established name from elsewhere, however, did give one access to superior research and development skills in highly specialized areas. Many small Canadian companies were caught in the web of increasing research and development costs as well as competing with emerging giants that had well-known names and what we now call product identification. Under these circumstances, many firms in Canada went from being part-manufacturer, part-agent to agent only. Many were subsequently absorbed by new giants such as Westinghouse or General Electric. By not trying to be all things to all people, Packard was able to retain control of its own destiny as well as increasing its range of manufactured products. These were major accomplishments at a time when innumerable pioneering electrical manufacturers were disappearing, just as would happen many decades later with the computer and microelectronics industries.

Arc Lighting. Historical writing and common recollection often tend to see past developments as occurring more smoothly and inevitably than did contemporary observers. Eventual dominance by the incandescent light and the arc lamp's relegation to very few, highly specialized uses make it easy to misunderstand the process and speed of dominance.

The noise, odour, and intense brightness of arc lamps made them unsuitable for indoor residential and commercial uses. They were, however, well adapted for large factories or warehouses as well as outdoor installations ranging from street lights to docks to sporting facilities. Arc lights required considerable tending, but this drawback was reduced over time as improvements were made. Consequently, although the incandescent lamp had outdistanced the arc lamp by the time the Packard brothers started in Canada, there was still a competitive market influenced by technological improvement and change.

Arc and incandescent lamps coexisted. When "Jas Playfair, of Midland, Ont." bought a generating plant for his steam barge *Hall*, he announced: "Both arc and incandescent lights will be used; the former for lighting the docks at which the steamer is loading."[35] Arc lamps could now run on the same circuits as incandescents. As the *Canadian*

In 1905 Packard Electric was a Canadian
agent for the Jandus Series Alternating Arc
Lighting System manufactured in Cleveland,
Ohio. It is not known when this association
started or how long it lasted. Arc lights are
shown being tested in St Catharines prior
to shipment.
(Ontario Archives, Ferranti-Packard Collection, AO 1246)

Electrical News announced in 1893: "The business of making arc
lamps for incandescent circuits is getting to be a big one in the United
States."[36] It became big in Canada as well.

To keep ahead in a highly competitive realm, the Jandus Electric
Co. of Cleveland, Ohio, developed an enclosed arc lamp much
praised by the electrical press.[37] Its lamps contained a number of innovative features which gave their carbons extra long life – 150 hours
from a single half-inch carbon – noiseless operation, absence of
flicker, ease of adjustment, and, above all, adaptability to the wide variety of circuit types and conditions. As the *Electrical Review* stated,
"these lamps are made for constant potential, constant current, railroad and power circuits, and for alternating circuits."[38] In addition,
the layout and bulb design did away with the undesirable heavy shad-
ows typical of arc lamps. Most important, the outdoor models
featured a waterproof case and terminal wires running through
watertight bushings so that no hood was required; this also gave better, more usable light and led to fewer operational problems.

It is not known when Packard Electric started to sell the Jandus
Series Alternating Arc Lighting System, either in its entirety or in components. Nor is it known if Packard was a manufacturer with rights
to system design use or simply Canadian agent. However, in 1905
Packard published a well-illustrated catalogue for the Jandus system.[39] Once again the Packard name was linked to superior technology.

The Canadian Electrical Exhibition Co. Ltd. held its first annual
show in Montreal in 1907. A detailed report by the *Canadian Electrical News* included mention of the Jandus AC system exhibited by
Packard: "the brightness and steady burning of these arc lamps made
an attractive display, as well as being interesting to all central station
men."[40]

Transformers and Other Products. At the 1907 Electrical Exhibition in Montreal, the Packard display "was one of the most attractive in the hall and was visited by a large number of the electrical fraternity."[41] The visitor got a good idea of the range and diversity of the company's electrical line. Part of the exhibit "consisted of their well-known line of type 'G' recording watt meters, transformers, incandescent lamps and induction motors" including "one of 100 5-horse-power induction motors ordered by the Dominion Government for operating the lock gate mechanisms on the Welland Canal." In addition to the operating Jandus service AC arc lighting system, "The Gyrofan also attracted considerable attention." The report also noted: "The Packard Electric Company are also Canadian representatives of the Crocker-Wheeler Company and the American Instrument Company, and in their exhibit was a full line of American instruments – volt and ammeter of the portable and switchboard types. They had a 65 kw. Crocker-Wheeler generator in operation, besides an 18 inch ventilating fan outfit, and showed other well-known lines of the Crocker-Wheeler Company's manufacture, such as crane motors and small direct current motors."[42]

Packard presented itself at the exhibition as a firm whose product lines were both technologically current and diverse. It displayed a healthy combination of its own manufactures and items for which it was agent. With products for home, commercial, and industrial users, it was not dependent on a single market segment. In addition, there was evidence of Packard's participation in activities in the forefront of technological change. Canada, beginning in Sault Ste Marie, was the world's leader in electrification of canal locks, and on the Welland Canal, Packard supplied induction motors. Transformers attracted

Some Packard transformers stayed in service for over half a century. The three shown here, made in 1900 and 1902, were in service at Morrisburg, Ontario, and continued to give good service until they were removed to make way for the building of the St Lawrence Seaway. Where they once stood is now under water.
(Ontario Archives, Ferranti-Packard Collection, AO 700)

In the photograph above, taken around 1908, distribution transformers – an example of leading-edge electrical technology – are being carried by traditional horse and wagon to the St Catharines railway depot. From there they would be shipped across Canada. In the background the Neelon Mill is on the right, the original office building on the left.
(Ontario Archives, Ferranti-Packard Collection, AO 1247)

James Ward Packard's interest in combining ease of manufacturing with efficient operation was reflected in Canadian patent 49,606 (opposite), granted in 1895 for "certain new and useful improvements in Electrical Converters or Transformers and Enclosed Boxes Therefor." The transformer consisted of two concentric coils of wire with the iron core built up by a series of staggered plates. This produced a snugly assembled core without the need for bolts and fastening devices, providing both a more efficient magnetic circuit and a better transformer and reducing manufacturing costs.
(Canada Patent Office)

little attention, but they were part of the Packard line, and one that would grow in importance after the First World War.

Before 1896, Packard Electric had imported all of the transformers it sold from the Packard Electric Co. in Warren, Ohio. In 1896, it started manufacture in St Catharines. Insulation was one of the principal concerns of transformer manufacturers around the world. In Canada, however, low winter temperatures made insulation both more difficult and more critical, as certain types of insulation developed cracks at low temperatures. Packard in St Catharines paid particular attention to the problem.

Packard engineers were well aware that, once installed, their handiwork was at the mercy of linemen and maintenance men and so designed their transformers to simplify operation. The "fusing device" for making and breaking circuits was designed without the delicate springs of some manufacturers. Packard transformers were easily turned on and off and re-fused without tools. Careful attention to ease of maintenance and reliability was a Packard hallmark, as was careful attention to materials used. In some fields Packard could go beyond the competition, but in others, where the limiting factor was the materials available, it could only equal the best. In a show of modesty that might have seemed out of place in a competitive world, Packard told the *Canadian Engineer*: "we do not claim any higher efficiency than the best transformers on the market, as this has every-

49606

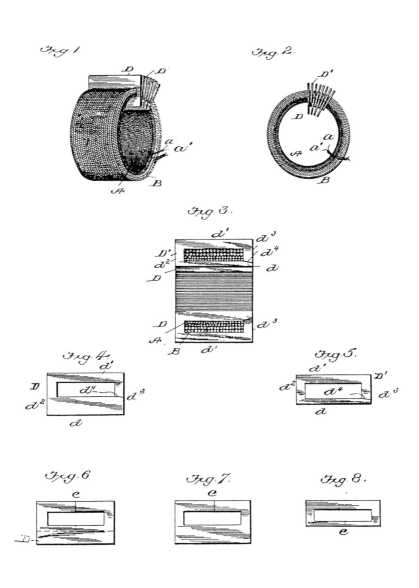

Fig. 1.   Fig. 2.

Fig. 3.

Fig. 4.   Fig. 5.

Fig. 6.   Fig. 7.   Fig. 8.

Washington, D. C.
May 4th 1894.

WITNESSES:

Certified to be the drawing referred
to in the specification hereunto
annexed.

In 1895 James Ward Packard was granted Canadian patent 48,632 for the fuse box, or fusing device, illustrated in the July 1896 issue of *Canadian Engineer*. It was attached to transformers which Packard Electric started manufacturing in St Catharines after doing research on insulating material which would not crack during cold Canadian winters. Because many electrical equipment installers had little formal training, ease of maintenance and installation were important design considerations for Packard products. They claimed a number of such features for their transformer fuse boxes, such as interchangeable plugs designed to "make the lineman's work easy, and this, with the ordinary ... lineman, is an important point." (National Museum of Science and Technology, Ottawa)

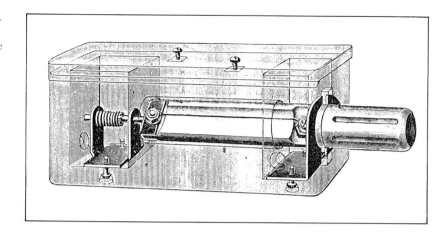

thing to do with the quality of iron used, but we use the best iron that can be obtained.[43]"

Packard Electric continued a tradition of research and improvement in transformers. By 1902 it had a new design on the market, a "shell" type, to replace the older "core" design. The shell type offered "closer regulation than can be obtained with transformers of the 'core' type. In Canada where water power is so cheap and variable, the regulation of a transformer is its most important feature."[44] Again, the combination of design and materials was crucial, allowing closer regulation and reduced core losses by use of a "superior quality of iron ... imported from England." The iron had been tested carefully and found to be "absolutely non-ageing" so as to attain and maintain high efficiency. In addition, special coil insulation prevented "the current jumping from one layer to the layer above or below it." Then, before delivery, all transformers were tested individually.[45] Transformers generate a great deal of heat, and Packard offered customers their choice of oil or air cooling.[46]

Packard made high-quality products but had to sell them in a competitive market. The company had its own sales people, and Packard transformers were found in many places. In 1907, for example, the Ontario Power Co. of Niagara Falls paid $5,000 for "Three (3) 300 K.W. Oil insulated self cooled transformers" to serve the government grain elevator at Port Colborne.[47] Not all jobs were so uneventful. In one letter regarding customer problems with 50-kW transformers, an unnamed Packard engineer writes: "This is another case where the preliminary engineering has been done by the Sales Department and where the information furnished us has not been sufficient to enable us to properly provide for all the conditions."[48] This type of problem seems to have been quite rare, and as Packard transformers were used more and more, their reputation grew accordingly.

The manufacture of transformers was very demanding, and the fact that a small company could keep up with the changes in the field is high tribute. As will be shown in a later chapter, the design and manufacture of transformers underwent many changes during the twentieth century, and only a firm with strong commitment to research as well as quality engineering and manufacturing could keep up with and apply emerging solutions in areas as diverse as increasing overall efficiency, heat exchange and cooling, ageing of materials, insulation behaviour at extreme temperatures, structural integrity as transformers reached unprecedented sizes, and the age-old problems of losses caused by factors such as eddy currents.

Automobiles. Neither the Electrical Exhibition nor much of the subsequent history of Packard Electric hints at a distinctly different early activity: automobile manufacture. The Canadian automobile historians Robert E. Ankli and Fred Frederiksen have noted, with some understatement: "A good deal of confusion had been generated regarding the automotive activities of the Packard Electric Company in St. Catharines, Ontario. Some rather fantastic stories have been printed about this firm, including one which claimed that the first Packard automobile was built in St. Catharines! In fact, no Packard automobiles were ever built by the Packard Electric Company in Canada, but other automobiles were, so the story is worth telling."[49]

The Packard Motor Car Co. of the United States has attracted a great deal of attention from collectors and historians. The Packards' early interest in motor cars, followed by their purchase of one, and the frustration of owning an unreliable vehicle, led to the conviction that they could build a better automobile. In the closing months of 1899 they built a prototype and formed the Ohio Automobile Company. In 1902 the name was changed to Packard Motor Car Co., and it continued to build cars in Detroit for a number of decades.

By 1900, the Packard brothers were no longer shareholders in the Canadian company, Packard Electric, and there is speculation that they sold their shares to raise capital for what bankers considered a very dubious proposition – namely, manufacturing automobiles.[50] Although the brothers had departed, the Canadian firm bearing their

One of the most persistent misconceptions regarding Packard Electric is that it manufactured Packard automobiles in Canada; it did not. The Motor Car Department of Packard Electric in St Catharines manufactured the curved dash Oldsmobile, which had previously been imported into Canada.

Packard Electric manufactured Oldsmobiles from 1905 to 1907. Later the plant manufactured the Reo, named for Ransom E. Olds, founder of Oldsmobile, but in 1913 automobile production came to an end permanently. In the moving assembly line which Henry Ford pioneered in the automobile industry, the workers added parts as the automobile moved along the line. Above we see the typical layout for stationary assembly in which parts are brought to each car being assembled. In order to keep track of what was going where, some parts, such as the axles, appear to have been numbered.
(Ontario Archives, Ferranti-Packard Collection, AO 1234, AO 1235, AO 1236)

name maintained an interest in the emerging technology and a keen eye for new ventures. Given the separate ownership, it is not surprising that the cars manufactured in Canada did not bear the Packard name.

In 1905, Packard Electric began building Oldsmobiles designed by Ransom E. Olds in the newly created Automobile Department of its St Catharines plant, but it discontinued production before the end of 1907. The reason for the short production life was one that would be heard later about American cars. The Oldsmobile, built in St Catharines, was an American design that had become too large and expensive for the Canadian market.[51] In 1920, Oldsmobiles began to be built in Toronto, but there was no connection then with Packard Electric.

In the short period 1905–07, Packard Electric put its imprint on the Canadian automobile industry. The December 1905 issue of *Canadian Machinery*, the foremost journal of its kind, described the factory in St Catharines as "the first plant in Canada to be built and designed for the manufacture of automobiles ... The main feature of interest centering about this department is the machine shop, in which are found of the newest and best designs of machine tools in their particular line; in fact when the installation was made three-

quarters of these tools were the first of their kind in Canada, and in nearly all cases they are special tools bought solely for the special work to be demanded of them."[52]

This was Canada's first production facility designed specifically for automobiles rather than merely adapted from an existing one. Undoubtedly this is why, two years after Oldsmobiles stopped production in the plant, manufacture of Reos began there. The Reo was named after Ransom E. Olds.

On 16 January 1909 the directors of Packard Electric sold part of the firm's real estate holdings – lots 1 through 8 on the north side of Mill Street – plant, and machinery to the Reo Automobile Co. Ltd. of Canada, in return for 890 shares of fully paid-up capital stock in Reo. Packard also agreed to purchase an additional 100 Reo shares at $100 per share for a total cash outlay of $10,000. It appeared to be a favourable deal for both sides. Reo obtained fine manufacturing facilities, and Packard rid itself of unused production capability. On 7 November 1912 the shareholders authorized Packard Electric to sell the Reo shares at the best price obtainable – over $60,000.

On 7 December 1912 it was reported that R.B. Hamilton and J.A. Hamilton had bought the shares. The sale was ratified, but the price not reported. R.B. Hamilton was general manager of the St Catha-

Engines were tested on a stationary test bed.
The vertical pipes seen in the photograph
above were bolted to engines to draw exhaust
fumes out of the building. The sawtooth
roof of the factory represented the most modern design ideas of the time. The vertical
faces of the sawteeth were filled with windows
to bathe the workplace with natural light.
Cars were shipped from the factory by rail in
wooden crates.
(Ontario Archives, Ferranti-Packard
Collection, AO 1238, AO 1231)

rines plant from 1901 to 1918 and holder of 350 Packard shares in
1909. It is often difficult to put transactions and investments such as
these in perspective, but it is clear that automobiles represented a
minor financial interest for Packard Electric, but not for Hamilton,
who had ambitions to control Reo. In 1912, Packard Electric changed
its incorporation from the Dominion Companies' Act to the Ontario
Companies' Act, and the accompanying paper transaction listed the
total value, including assets, holding rights, and credits, at $513,750.

Paradoxically, although Packard Electric was no longer directly
producing automobiles, the Olds connection remained, as did the
firm's influence. Reo had been started by Ransom E. Olds in 1904
after he left the company bearing his name, Olds Motor Works. The
plant purchased by Reo contained the many machine tools that expressed Packard Electric's method of automobile manufacture. At a
time when many cars relied heavily on labour-intensive or shop-fitted
one-of-a-kind parts, Packard emphasized machine tools and standard, interchangeable parts.

Reo's initial production in Canada coincided with booming business and fierce competition. In the late summer of 1912, plant capacity doubled to 1,200 cars per annum. In the same year, a cross-

Canada drive in a Reo by Thomas W. Wilby boosted sales, and his book, *A Motor Tour through Canada*, appeared in 1914 – too late to help. Reo was in financial difficulties and had had to stop Canadian operations in 1913. Large producers, such as Ford, had innovative and cost-cutting manufacturing methods, and Reo too tried to cut costs and increase vehicle performance.

In an era of low-powered engines, weight reduction enhanced performance and reduced running costs. There were, however, few easy ways to reduce weight. Reo's use of a pressed-fibre body from the Chatham Carriage Co. might have revolutionized the industry. Instead, because the panels could not be waterproofed fully, moisture penetration first caused distortion and then disintegration. This was probably the final blow to producing Reos in Canada.

Survival: A Major Achievement

The demise of Reo as an automobile maker underscores one of the unfortunate facts of life for small businesses – namely that they are so vulnerable that one major bad decision can drag a company under. It is realization of this fact that makes survival one of the most significant pre-1914 achievements of Packard Electric Co. Ltd.

When the Canadian Manufacturers Association's *Industrial Canada* surveyed the "Electrical Apparatus" industry in Canada in June 1905, it identified the three largest as Canadian General Electric Co. of Peterborough, Canadian Westinghouse Co. of Hamilton, and Allis-Chalmers-Bullock Ltd. of Montreal.[53] Only the first was more than two years old, but the combined capital of the "big three" exceeded $8.7 million and total employees numbered about 2,500. *Industrial Canada* mentioned as well four "other concerns which are doing a good business," and "Packard Electric manufacturing company of St. Catharines" was one of them. Compared to the big three, Packard Electric was a dwarf; in 1909 it employed only about fifty people. But it was at least healthy and had good prospects. Before the First World War, and even faster afterward, many small firms, similar in size to Packard Electric, either failed or were swallowed by the giants and lost their corporate life and identity.

It is always easier to identify the causes of death than the reasons for continuing life. Nonetheless, the first two decades of Packard Electric give some insight into why it did not join the numerous companies that appeared and then disappeared during the period. During the time of emerging and highly variable technology, corporate life can be short. The limited product lines of Packard Electric could have been its undoing had they been unreliable or uncompetitive. But its products seemed to be reliable and were backed up by their own repair facilities. Packard Electric very wisely offered repairs on the products that it manufactured or sold. Electricity was still very new and mysterious, and customers needed the reassurance that when things went wrong, as they undoubtedly would, they would not be set adrift or left at the mercy of another company.

Research and attention to quality of materials helped Packard Electric achieve a high reputation. From an early date the firm's transformers were noted for insulation that would not deteriorate or underperform in the low temperatures of Canadian winters. In addition to manufacturing its own products carefully, Packard Electric chose wisely the other products that it sold. The Jandus Arc Light System, which it carried but probably did not manufacture, was highly regarded, as were the watt-hour meters which it first carried and later manufactured. Early products had been based on trusted Packard designs from the United States; transformers, for example, were imported from Warren until 1896. By depending on a combination of its own research and development, plus the experience and design of products from other manufacturers which Packard Electric had found reliable before changing from agent to manufacturer, it found itself with unusually high-quality products.

If the way in which the Automobile Department of Packard Electric was equipped reflects the company's approach to modern machinery – and there is no reason to believe otherwise – then the firm continued the Packard brothers' tradition of careful engineering and manufacturing procedures.

3   *Ferranti Arrives in Canada*

Corporate Changes in Ferranti UK and the Canadian Market

In 1894, the Packard brothers came to St Catharines on the eve of an economic transformation. Prior to this, Canada had "languished and even the most sanguine were troubled by forebodings about the success of Confederation."[1] By 1896, a fortuitous conjuncture of international events catapulted Canada from stagnation and depression to unprecedented growth and prosperity. Cheaper transportation, high prices for wheat, and intense world demand suddenly made the main crop of the Canadian prairies the centre of the international market and brought it within the range of profitable exploitation. The availability of millions of acres of homestead land unleashed waves of immigration and migration into Canada's prairies. The one million who, between 1896 and 1913, moved into Manitoba and what soon became Saskatchewan and Alberta transformed vast tracts of virgin prairie into productive land. The amount of land taken up by farming increased seven-fold, and wheat production a hundred-fold.[2]

A prosperous agricultural sector created an immense internal market for Canada's manufacturing sector, particularly Ontario's. The growth of the manufacturing sector was fuelled by the price differential between agricultural exports and domestic manufactured products. Between 1896 and 1913, export prices for agricultural products rose dramatically – by as much as three times the rate for manufactured goods sold at home.[3] Expansion of cities created demand for manufactured products.

Economic prosperity engendered rapid urbanization. In the west, thriving agricultural service centres rose from obscurity into thriving cities. Towns such as Edmonton and Calgary increased their populations nearly ten-fold. In the east, people rushed to the cities in search of the new opportunities created by manufacturing. Writing in 1913, a prominent Canadian political economist described the remarkable expansion of manufacturing activity since 1896 as the "Canadian manufacturer's Golden Age."[4] Prime Minister Sir Wilfrid Laurier was inspired to proclaim that the twentieth century belonged to Canada.

An integral part of this economic prosperity was the soaring demand for electrical energy and the start of mass electrification. In response, there was a phenomenal 850-per-cent increase in Canada's generating capacity, as more and more of the nation's vast hydraulic potential was put into service between 1891 and 1911. Heightened demand for electric power led to new markets for electricity. From 80 rather small DC electric works in 1891, with revenues of $1.1 million, the number of generating stations rose to 266 in 1911, with revenues of $12.9 million.[5] There was a technological shift from DC to AC power systems, and the resultant need for transformers and watt-hour meters grew – enough finally to sustain a domestic electrical manufacturing sector. In two decades, 1891–1911, the value of goods produced by the sector increased by 4,400 per cent. In the same period the value of Canadian manufacturing as a whole rose by only 250 per cent.[6]

The Ferranti name did not enter the story of Canadian electrification until some time after the arrival of the Packard brothers. While Packard Electric Co. Ltd. was busy participating in Canada's "Golden Age of Manufacturing," Sebastian Ziani de Ferranti was trying to rebuild his business prospects after the ill-fated Deptford undertaking. Finding a market niche to match his engineering ambitions proved difficult, particularly when Britain had turned its back on his dream of long-distance, high-voltage AC technology.

The decade from 1894 to 1904 proved tumultuous. After his falling out with Deptford's backers, the LESC, Sebastian Ziani de Ferranti set out on his own. With the problems of Deptford still in the market's memory, his struggle to break into the highly competitive British electrical market was an uphill battle. The collapse in demand for engineering services and a sharp downturn in the electrical market further compounded his difficulties.[7] Ferranti travelled throughout England and the continent trying to raise orders for his troubled company. Gone were the days of affluence. With money in short supply, supporting his parents, wife, and three children proved difficult. To survive, Ferranti had to swallow his pride and accept a modest allowance from his father-in-law.

By 1894 the future of S.Z. Ferranti Ltd. had been starting to look brighter. Two years later, it needed larger manufacturing facilities, and so Ferranti moved operations from the cramped quarters at Charterhouse Square, in London, to a large factory in Hollinwood, Lancashire, near Manchester. In July 1901, a new company, Ferranti Limited, was formed to take over the assets of S.Z. Ferranti Ltd. Like its financially troubled predecessor, it remained a private company in Ferranti's control. Although 60,000 preferred shares, each valued at £1, were sold on the open market, 96 per cent of the common voting stock was alloted to Ferranti.

Ferranti's fiercely individualistic approach created serious liquidity problems for his company. In order to fulfil his ambitious and diverse engineering projects, his company needed a large infusion of capital.

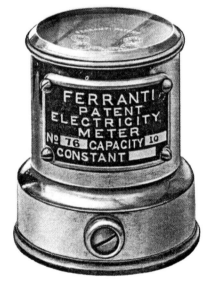

Sebastian Ziani de Ferranti invented the mercury meter in the 1880s to measure consumption of current by individual DC system customers. Ferranti, one of the early influential advocates of AC, fought hard to overthrow DC electrical systems. Ironically, DC kept Ferranti Ltd. alive during its early years. England was slow to change to AC and, during the first decade of the twentieth century, sales of the mercury meter provided Ferranti Ltd.'s most important source of income.
(Ferranti plc Archives, Manchester, UK)

Ferranti, however, stubbornly rejected any such action. Many years earlier, when asked by his father-in-law, Francis Ince, to bring in other investors and create a joint-stock company, Ferranti replied categorically that it would "take all interest out of the work."[8] Maintaining total control of all the firm's affairs was an obsession with Ferranti. To sell any large blocks of voting stock would have compromised this control. After his bitter experience with the LESC, Ferranti did not want any interference from outside investors.

Ferranti's "interest" in the electrical business and his corporate decisions were what we today call technology-driven. Profits were important, but as a means to an end, and they would be sacrificed for loftier engineering goals. As J. Wilson points out in a recent book on Ferranti, the inventor's preoccupation with technical excellence often overrode crucial questions of commercial viability. The Engine Department had run into heavy losses because Ferranti spent "so much time on the design and production of each engine that customers were able to impose harsh penalties for failure to deliver on time."[9]

Ferranti's penchant for innovation and total control became a strong family tradition. For the next seventy years, these principles ruled the family's conduct of business. These attitudes also shaped the development of Ferranti Ltd.'s future Canadian subsidiary.

Ferranti's lofty technical goals were costly to pursue, and without any outside equity, Ferranti Ltd. was heading for financial crisis. In order to raise more working capital, Ferranti took on fixed-interest debentures and large bank overdrafts. In 1903, when his efforts to develop new steam-based prime movers to drive generators produced serious losses, the company's creditors had had enough. In February 1904 a petition was made to the court to liquidate Ferranti Ltd. and receivers were appointed on behalf of the debenture holders.

Shrewd enough to realize that the firm had great promise, if managed soundly, the creditors chose not to sell off the assets. On 27 February 1905 the company was registered under the directorship of chairman A.W. Tait, S.Z. de Ferranti, J.M. Henderson, and A. Whittaker. Terms of the reconstruction saw the first- and second-mortgage debenture stockholders come out relatively unscathed. They received corresponding shares in the new company together with back payments in interest. Preferred shareholders received 50 per cent of their original investment in ordinary shares of the new firm while the ordinary shareholders got nothing. As owner of most of the ordinary shares, Ferranti suffered the biggest losses.

A key element in the reconstruction involved a shift from a technology-driven management, as epitomized by Ferranti himself, to a more hard-nosed approach to financial management. The creditors brought in two highly respected chartered accountants, A. Whittaker and A.W. Tait, as receiver-managers, to restore order to the company's chaotic financial affairs. Tait and Whittaker were now in charge; Ferranti lost all control of his company, though he did retain a seat on the board and a position as technical consultant. The new managers immediately slashed research and development in high-risk product areas such as alternators, steam turbines, and electrically driven textile machinery.

As at Deptford, Ferranti's technological focus clashed head-on with the new, pragmatic directors. His protests over the cuts fell on deaf ears. Frustrated, deeply saddened, and with little else to do, Ferranti pulled totally away from the business that he had created. For the next ten years, he pursued his love of invention. He developed an improved superheating steam turbine for the Vickers company in Sheffield. According to one biographer, Ferranti's superheated turbines "became accepted as the best practise in turbine economy."[10]

Ferranti did not forget the loss of his company. He waited patiently. In 1923, he finally won back control from the accountants and professional businessmen.

With the management and finances of Ferranti Ltd. now on a sound footing, the new general manager, A.B. Anderson, looked for markets to use the occasional excess capacity at the Hollinwood plant. Also an accountant by training, Anderson designed an aggressive effort to establish a sales network throughout Britain and subsidiary marketing companies elsewhere. He travelled abroad extensively, studying markets for their export potential. He believed that Canada had potential: electrification was proceeding vigorously, and there were preferential tariffs.

The first sales agency in Canada, however, was more the result of happenstance. In 1906, Donald Hill, who had worked at the Westminster Electric Co. in London, had decided to move to Canada. Having had dealings with Sebastian Ziani de Ferranti, Hill approached Ferranti Ltd. with an offer to serve as exclusive agent for the firm's watt-hour meters in Canada. Within a year of his arrival, Hill transferred his agent's rights to Toronto Gas & Electric Power and went on to work for the same company as a sales engineer. Unable to sell any watt-hour meters, Toronto Gas & Electric proved totally ineffective as agents; its relationship with Ferranti did not last long. The financial collapse of the Toronto firm in 1907 offered Ferranti Ltd. the welcome opportunity to find a more suitable agent.

During this period, there was one unsolicited sale of Ferranti watt-hour meters in Canada. J.E. Brown, newly appointed municipal electrical engineer for the city of Ottawa, had grown dissatisfied with the uncompetitive stranglehold that American meter manufacturers held over the Canadian market.

In 1907, while reading the British *Electrical Review*, he noticed an advertisement for a Ferranti type B – 5-ampere, 60-cycle, 110-volt, single-phase – watt-hour meter. The price was attractive. Anxious to examine the meter's suitability, Brown placed a small order directly with Ferranti Ltd. In the years that followed, he developed into a steadfast customer of Ferranti products. Seventeen years after Sebastian Ziani de Ferranti's unsuccessful bid to develop the first large-scale AC power station at Niagara Falls, the Ferranti name entered the story of Canadian electrification with a humble order of watt-hour meters.

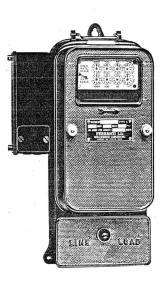

FERRANTI ELECTRICAL COMPANY OF CANADA, LTD.

90, Sherbourne Street, TORONTO.

ALTERNATING CURRENT
TWO-RATE WATT HOUR METERS.

Fig. 1.
Type " C."
Single and Poly-phase Balanced Load.
Sheet Steel Cover.
Supplied with Bottom Terminals only.

Fig. 2.
Type " CT."
Poly-phase Unbalanced Load.
Supplied with Cast Iron Cover
and Bottom Terminals only.

Issued October, 1913. THIS LIST CANCELS PRIOR PUBLICATIONS AND IS SUBJECT TO ALTERATION WITHOUT NOTICE. List A.C.M. 18.

Ferranti Canada started as a sales agent for the parent firm's watt-hour meters manufactured for export to those parts of the British empire where AC dominated. Trade literature, such as this piece issued in October 1913, was an important means of advertising and disseminating technical information. These meters had two sets of dials and a timing device to switch from one to the other. This was used in areas where there were two separate electricity rates depending on whether one was using power at a time of peak load or low load for the system. (Ferranti-Packard Transformers Ltd.)

Ferranti Ltd. decided to focus on the export of meters because this product was crucial to the company's business strategy. Profits from this "bread-and-butter" product line had long sustained the firm's riskier technological endeavours. Tait, Whittaker, and Anderson saw future profitability in the sale of watt-hour meters. Meters also made a very convenient product base from which to penetrate the Canadian market. They were small, easily packaged and shipped, and required minimal installation and after-sale servicing. Furthermore, growing demand for electricity caused by the rapidly expanding Canadian economy created a vast, practically untapped market for the humble electric meter. Every new electricity account – residential, commercial, or industrial – required a meter.

The rise in importance of the watt-hour meter in the affairs of Ferranti Ltd. is one of the great ironies of the British electrical industry. In 1883, when DC technology was unquestioned, Sebastian Ferranti, still only nineteen, invented the mercury motor meter, which became the most successful method of measuring consumption of DC power. He then went on to gamble his professional reputation on AC technology and large-scale electrical generation. Britain did not, however, embrace AC technology the way the rest of the world did. Two decades later, Ferranti Ltd. had become Britain's largest supplier of DC meters.

The dominance of DC technology in Britain led to a split in Ferranti Ltd.'s meter manufacturing business. Up until the First World War, DC meters were made for the domestic market, and AC meters for export. Ferranti had hoped that a basic, or generic design would be good enough for all the "colonies." However, in North America meters made by the likes of Westinghouse and General Electric were changing very quickly. The unchanging Ferranti Ltd. design only reinforced the negative image of Ferranti as a foreign – i.e. non–North American – supplier. To succeed, Ferranti Ltd. would have to commit itself to AC meters.

Royce Family Establishes an Important Ferranti Sales Presence in Canada

Determined to gain a foothold in the expanding Canadian market, Ferranti Ltd.'s general manager, A.B. Anderson, set sail for Canada in 1907. He realized that Ferranti needed better agents in Canada. En route, Anderson learned, in casual conversation, of the Royce family, who lived in Davenport, a small village on the outskirts of Toronto. The Royce brothers – James, Allan, and George – had played an important role in the development of the West Toronto Junction, and they had also built a reputation from their electric railway business.

The Royce name was already known to Anderson, but in a different context. In England, the brothers' first cousin was Henry Royce, who was later knighted. In 1883, the London Electric Light and Power Co. appointed the twenty-year-old Henry Royce as chief electrical engineer for its pioneer scheme to provide Liverpool with electric lighting. In 1884, Royce started an electrical manufacturing firm in Manchester to produce arc lamps, dynamos, and electric cranes. The company continued until 1933 as Royce Ltd.

But like the Packard brothers, Royce soon shifted to another technological revolution. In 1903, disappointed with the mechanical performance of a French 10-hp Decauville motor-car that he had just bought, Royce set out to design a new vehicle. The result was a 10-hp, two-cylinder engineering marvel called the Royce. So impressed was C.S. Rolls, owner of a well-known sales agency for foreign cars, that

The Royce Family in 1901. The early years of Ferranti's business in Canada illustrate that achievement in one area often leads to other opportunities. The Canadian branch of the Royce family played a leading role in the development of the West Toronto Junction area. The Royce brothers, Allan, George, and James, started the Davenport Electric Railway and Light Co. Ltd. in 1890 to encourage settlement in the newly incorporated West Toronto Junction area. Their experience with electrical technology prompted the Ferranti family to ask the Royces to be their agents in Canada. Top row: Lt.-Col. Gilbert Royce, Harold Royce, Allan H. Royce. Bottom row: Col. George Cooper Royce, Allan Royce, Mrs. Allan Royce (née Sarah Jane Gilbert), James Cooper Royce.
(National Library of Canada, NL 18171)

in 1904 he agreed to buy Royce's entire stock. The two men soon entered into partnership and launched the Rolls-Royce Motor Car Co.; James Royce later figured prominently in the development of Rolls-Royce's American operation. In later years, the company also became a leading manufacturer of airplane engines. Today, Rolls-Royce is one of the largest industrial concerns in Britain. In 1989, the family's connection with the Canadian Ferranti company came full circle: Rolls-Royce bought controlling interest in Northern Engineering Industries and became the new owners of Ferranti-Packard.

When the Canadian Pacific Railway announced plans for construction of a major junction near Keele and Dundas streets in Toronto, D.W. Clendenan and J.M. Law were quick to see the real-estate potential of the surrounding land. They bought 240 acres adjacent to the CPR development in 1882, laid it out into building lots, and called the estate the West Toronto Junction. The area is bounded today by Dundas Street on the north, Keele Street on the east, Bloor Street West on the south, and Evelyn Avenue through to Kennedy Park on the west. In June 1887, the village of West Toronto Junction was incorporated, and it comprised all the lands south of the CPR Toronto-London line to Bloor Street West and west to what today is Runnymede Road. In 1888, the village expanded to take in Davenport and Carlton.

Clendenan became the first reeve of West Toronto Junction. With the merger of Davenport into the village, Allan Royce, a barrister, was immediately drawn into local political life and became an alderman. In 1890, electric streetcars replaced Toronto's horse-drawn cars. Royce saw electrical technology as the future in urban transport. He realized that future development of the Junction depended on a good transportation link with Toronto, and so he concluded that his village needed an electric street railway service. Royce lost little time in creating the Davenport Electric Railway and Light Co. Ltd., later renamed the Davenport Street Railway.

In February 1894, an act of Parliament amalgamated the Davenport Street Railway and the City & Suburban Railway into the Toronto Suburban Railway Co. Ltd. Allan Royce became president, and his brother George, general manager. Though not an engineer like his brother James, George Royce had pursued some science courses at the University of Toronto after graduating from the Jarvis Street Collegiate Institute in Toronto.

By the turn of the century, the Toronto Suburban Railway was still a local railway with just some 10 miles (16 km) of track and generating its own DC electric power at 500 volts DC from a steam-driven plant on St Clair Avenue.[11] In 1904, with the idea of extending the line to a full-scale interurban electric railway, the Royces discontinued their small DC generating plant and opted for high-voltage AC power from Niagara Falls. The power was transmitted to Toronto by the Toronto & Niagara Power Co., a concern controlled by Sir William Mackenzie. Before the Royces could implement their planned expansion, "control of the Toronto Suburban Railway passed from the hands of the Royces into those of Sir William Mackenzie. ... Debenture stock was offered in London, England with the purpose of obtaining capital for the extensions."[12] With the Toronto Railway Co. as his financial base, Mackenzie soon took up the challenge of building Canada's second transcontinental railway, the Canadian Northern. It was not a financial success and in 1916 was taken over by the Canadian government to form part of the Canadian National Rail-

The fieldhouse in Toronto's Earlscourt Park, 1924. The park is on the site of the Royce homestead in Davenport. It was donated by the family to the City of Toronto for public enjoyment as a park.
(City of Toronto Archives, OPW 52-1192)

The Davenport Street Railway and the City & Suburban Railway were amalgamated by an act of Parliament in 1894 into the Toronto Suburban Railway, which George Royce managed. In this photograph, taken 12 August 1912, roadbed is being prepared at Keele and Dundas Streets for Toronto Suburban Railway track west to Royce Avenue. Men and horses provided most of the power.
(City of Toronto Archives, Salmon 433)

ways. In 1923, the Toronto Transit Commission (TTC) took over the Toronto Suburban Railway.

Operating the Toronto Suburban Railway gave the Royce family an unparalleled understanding of the Canadian electrical market. Not only did they run an electric railway but they also sold electric power. At various substations, AC power at 13,200 volts from the Toronto & Niagara Power Co. was stepped down and converted to the appropriate DC voltage for streetcar operation. Two of the Toronto Suburban Railway's substations, at Weston and Davenport, also "supplied 2,400 volts, 3-phase AC current as primary for the railway's subsidiary power and for the lighting distribution system which supplied power at 120/240 volts to 2,500 customers in the area from Bloor Street north to Weston, between Dovercourt Road and Lambton."[13]

For Anderson, the Royces' reputation provided an established market presence for Ferranti products. Allan Royce was very receptive to Anderson's business overtures; an agency arrangement seemed very promising. By now a busy and prominent corporate lawyer, Allan Royce could not possibly assume management of an agency, but he persuaded his reluctant brother George to accept.

George Royce located the Ferranti agency headquarters directly above the Toronto Suburban Railway Co.'s office at 22 Dundas Street. Colonel Royce could not manage the daily administration of

Old Toronto Suburban railway car number 5
at Evelyn Crescent at Fairview in 1903.
(City of Toronto Archives, Salmon 164)

both the family streetcar business and the Ferranti agency. He hired
Fred Rowntree, member of a prominent Davenport family, as his
"jack-of-all-trades" assistant, to divide his time equally between the
railway and the agency. Rowntree did everything from sweeping
floors to sales and bookkeeping and eventually rose to become a director of Ferranti Canada.

With only Royce and Rowntree handling promotion and sales of
Ferranti meters for all of Canada, marketing methods were kept very
simple. A sample meter was mailed, on a "sale or return" basis, to
public and private electric utilities across the country. Many of the
initial sales resulted from the Royce family's contacts in the electric
railway business. Like the Toronto Suburban, many of the other electric railways also operated as small electric utilities.

Selling to the large, and potentially more lucrative, municipally
owned utilities proved difficult. These organizations usually placed
their entire meter order only once a year. On those occasions, meter
salesmen from every company would gather, each striving to win the
contract. Salesmen willingly haggled over price, but price was not
always the determining factor. Loyalty to a long-standing supplier
and personal contacts often overrode all other considerations.

The Ferranti Royce Agency appeared to have little chance of competing against the well-entrenched, American-based manufacturers.
Royce needed an experienced and aggressive salesman. The first full-

George Royce hired the young Fred Rowntree as his general office helper in 1907, soon after the agency arrangement between the Royce family and Ferranti Ltd. Rowntree rose within the company and eventually joined Ferranti Canada's Board of Directors. He retired in 1951, 44 years after joining the company.
(Madame Gignac, Penetanguishene, Ontario)

time salesman hired by the agency was Fred Simmons. Rowntree recalled that Simmons "claimed to have come from the city of Kingston and knew the Manager of the Kingston Electric Light Plant, Mr. C.C. Folger. Simmons had high hopes of getting the Kingston business; but for many years ... the only meter we got into Kingston was the original sample meter, as it seems Mr. Folger's friendship with the Canadian General Electric Co. predominated."[14] After a few years, Simmons left to work for Westinghouse.

Simmons's replacement, J.G. Monaghan, had once worked for Ferranti's earlier, short-lived agent, the Toronto Gas & Electric Power Co. He had served as a colonel in the Boer War and had a flair for selling. According to one close associate, "every move [Monaghan] made was that of a well trained soldier, and this, coupled with his immaculate dress, ready Irish humour and ability to force his way into the inner office of the 'big fellows', and knowing how and when to handle liquor commanded great respect for him."[15]

Monaghan was a one-man sales army. In the west, the success of his efforts prompted the opening of a sales office and stock room in Winnipeg, with Monaghan as general manager.

Shortly after Monaghan joined the agency, Royce hired a second salesman with considerable technical knowledge of meters. Joseph Showalter, former employee of a meter company in Fort Wayne, Indiana, came to Canada to start up his own meter business in Peterborough, Ontario. He discovered, at first hand, the difficulty of competing against the large American concerns. No sooner had he set up shop than General Electric threatened legal action. The spectre of a costly patent lawsuit forced Showalter to close down his business.

Sales of Ferranti meters in Canada grew from 4,655 for 1909 to 16,616 for 1912. Annoyed with this success, Canadian Westinghouse

Electric street-railways needed more than tracks. The original Toronto Suburban Railway carhouse on the south side of St Clair Avenue, west of old Weston Road, was a major part of the built environment. Photographed 21 September 1920. The dark lines along the edge of the building, chimney, window, and door openings came from retouching the photograph at an unknown date.
(Toronto Transit Commission Archives, 17056)

lashed out at the Ferranti Agency. In 1912, it circulated to all the utilities a four-page leaflet entitled "26 Knocks against Ferranti Meters." The propaganda campaign served only to stimulate interest in Ferranti products and expand their sale in Canada.

Canadian Westinghouse next took legal action against Ferranti. Arguing that "any measuring device for alternating currents which used a shifting field was covered by their patent,"[16] Westinghouse claimed that the Ferranti type B meter was an infringement on the Westinghouse-owned Shallenberger patent. The strategy was classic: threaten a small company with costly legal battles and it will back down. Such lawsuits were part of a general strategy practised by big American companies to monopolize the Canadian market.

Willing to bear an expensive legal battle, Ferranti Ltd. was not about to be squeezed out of the Canadian market. But Westinghouse fell victim to the same patent law with which it was trying to bully the Royce Agency. According to clause 28 of the 1872 Patent Act:

Every patent ... shall be subject ... to the conditions that such patent and all the rights and privileges therein granted shall cease ... and the patent shall be null and void, at the end of two years from the date thereof unless the patentee, or his assignee or assignees shall, within that period have commenced; and after such commencement continuously carry on in Canada the construction or manufacture of the invention or discovery patented ... at some manufactory or establishment for making or constructing it in Canada, *and that such patent shall be void if after the expiry of twelve months from the granting thereof, the patentee or his assignees or assignees for the whole or a part of his interest in the patent imports, or causes to be imported into Canada, the invention for which the patent is granted.*[17] (Emphasis added)

By making actual manufacture in Canada a prerequisite of patent protection, clause 28 became a powerful tool for Canadian industrial development. Patent protection depended on the condition that a firm not import the product into Canada for a specified period of time. Allan Royce, whose law firm handled the case, asked the Royce Agency's sales people if they knew of any Westinghouse meters sold in Canada with the Pittsburgh nameplate on them. Rowntree recalls vividly how he went about getting such a meter from the electric light plant in Newmarket, Ontario: "Newmarket was a town that would only purchase Westinghouse meters, presumably because some of their members of Council were dyed-in-the-wool Westinghouse followers. They would not allow their superintendent to purchase even a sample Ferranti meter for test purposes but subsequently I found I was able to overcome this difficulty by offering, unknown to his council, two Ferranti meters in exchange for two Westinghouse meters, to enable him, for his own curiosity, to test the Ferranti meter."[18]

Westinghouse dropped its suit when the Ferranti lawyers produced the two Westinghouse meters with Pittsburgh nameplates.

Skirmishes continued, and Ferranti salesmen, especially Monaghan, could not pass up an opportunity to embarrass this competitor. W.A. Coates, who started with the agency as a Ferranti switch-gear specialist, recalled a public dinner thrown by the mayor of Medicine Hat, Alberta:

Monaghan and I had gone to Medicine Hat for the formal competition day in connection with the annual meter contract when all the other competitors were also present. The business took so long that by the time they decided to place the business with Canadian Westinghouse, whose representative was one Duff, the evening trains east and west had both departed and the Mayor invited all of us to have dinner at his expense. It was a cheerful party and, particularly at Gerry Monaghan's end of the table, there was continual merriment. Suddenly he dried up and, as often happens in such circumstances, everybody went silent. Then Gerry leaned forward and, looking in the direction of the Mayor, hiccoughed twice and said "Mishter mayor, I've been thinking". "What have you been thinking, Gerry", replied the Mayor. "I've been thinking that you've dropped the biggest brick of your life – You've placed the business with Duff here and you've only got to change one letter in the name of his company and you've got their trade name – *we sting youse*".[19]

The campaign by other Canadian meter companies to discredit Ferranti products used the fact that Ferranti Ltd. had no manufacturing facilities in Canada. While American producers responded to the Canadian market by building branch plants in Canada, Ferranti Ltd. viewed this country as but a colonial market for its excess capacity. There was some truth to the view that as a foreign firm, Ferranti Ltd. did not have the sensitivity to local market requirements that domestic companies did. If Ferranti Ltd. wanted to compete effectively, it would have to establish itself beyond an agency arrangement.

The British electrical industry was aware of the United Kingdom's weakening competitive position in Canadian markets. In 1906, Canada imported nearly $2,435,000 worth of American electrical equipment, and $85,000 worth of British. Germany was a distant third, with $15,000.[20] In 1907, the British journal *Electrical Review* urged British capitalists in the electrical industry to set up branch plants in Canada. Pointing out the disadvantages of shipping goods across the Atlantic, it claimed:

Experience proves that where this country is in competition with the foreigners for Canadian orders, the most frequent cause of the settlement away from the British house is on the score of delivery. This is a point that cannot be emphasized too strongly. It would seem that ... a Canadian stock or even branch works is essential for the British manufacturer to maintain a continuous profitable business in the Dominion.

From time to time we receive enquiries from readers as to the advisability of the formation of branch factories in Canada. We can here state definitely that in the great majority of cases the establishment of such branches will prove highly successful.[21]

Chiding the "stay-at-home Englishman" for his misconceptions of Canada as a collection of small settlements and camps, the journal portrayed a vast country experiencing considerable growth, with substantial markets opening up everywhere. Waiting for markets to reach a certain size, Ferranti Ltd., like many British firms, took a cautious attitude. In the view of the *Electrical Review*, waiting for markets to grow was "an unreasonable attitude to adopt, and the more one considers the matter in detail the more impossible does it become to justify it."[22] Ferranti Ltd., however, was content to view Canada as a simple export market and initially discouraged any manufacturing capacity there. Eventually competitive realities and persistent Canadian managers made it change its attitude. But this would take many years.

Ferranti's growing sales created a need for more service and technical support in Canada. The long sea voyage from England often resulted in misalignment or damage to meters; only technically trained people could test and readjust the meters. In October 1911, Albert Schofield, brother of R. Schofield, sales manager of Ferranti Ltd., arrived from the parent company's meter-testing department at Hollinwood, England. Some forty years later, Schofield recalled his first impressions: "On being introduced to the 'meter-room' I received quite a shock at the rough and tumbledown state of affairs. ... The rear room upstairs was a dusty place with few seasons deposit of dirt on the windows."[23] After setting up a proper meter-testing room, Schofield immediately set about training a core of technicians to carry out meter testing and adjustments. As sales climbed and additional technical help was sent to Canada, it became apparent that a full-time company was now needed to market Ferranti products on a larger scale.

Birth of Ferranti Electrical Co. of Canada Limited

In 1912, the agency created by the Royce family passed out of existence when the Ferranti Electrical Co. of Canada Ltd. was formed. On paper the new firm was incorporated with capital stock of $250,000, divided into 2,500 shares worth $100 each. In reality, there were only five shareholders, Alan Gilmour, Robert Henderson, John O'Conner, Charles Watson, and Ella Wilson, the original petitioners for incorporation, each of whom had one share. They also served as the board of directors. George Royce remained as general manager. John Dougherty was appointed eastern sales manager, with an office in Montreal, and operations moved to rented space in the Lowes Building at 90 Sherbourne Street in Toronto. At this stage, the Ferranti Electrical Co. of Canada was still an entirely Canadian-owned company.

The decision to expand into a full-fledged electrical trading company reflected Anderson and Royce's belief in the future of the Canadian electrical industry. By 1912, the economic transformation brought about by wheat sales had reached full steam. Canadian de-

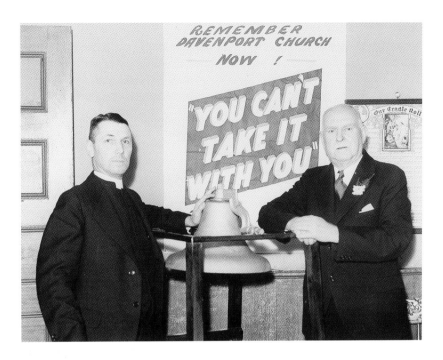

The Royces believed that successful business people should contribute to their community and its institutions. Colonel George Royce maintained his family's close, long-standing connection with Davenport United Church. Royce, shown on the right in this 18 November 1937 photograph, was an active fundraiser for the church.
(City of Toronto Archives, G&M 47794)

mand for electrical energy rose sharply as prosperity, rapid industrialization, and intense urbanization created large markets for electric lighting, heating, transportation, and motive power for industry. Residential and industrial construction grew significantly and, with it, demand for electrical products. The number of incandescent lamps produced in Canada rose from 150,000 in 1894 to 3.25 million in 1914. The rise of motor manufacture was equally dramatic. In 1891 only a hundred or so electric motors were made in Canada; in 1911, 14,826. In short, Canada's enthusiastic embrace of electric power represented a vast untapped market for Ferranti watt-hour meters.

The new Ferranti Electrical Co. of Canada took up the ground and second floors of the Lowes Building. In the front of the ground floor a show room displayed Ferranti products. The back served as the shipping and receiving area. On the second floor, offices were in the front, and meter stores and assembly and testing areas in the back. These new quarters were a substantial improvement over the crowded office above the Toronto Suburban Railway, but they did not impress the newly arrived H. Doughty. Recruited in England by R. Schofield, sales manager of Ferranti Ltd., Doughty passed up an offer as meter superintendent for the city of Hull, in England. Why accept an offer from a "Hole in the Wall," asked Schofield, when Ferranti Electrical in Canada offered far greater prospects? Doughty expected the Canadian facilities to resemble those at Hollinwood. Dismayed at what he saw, Doughty wondered whether Schofield's words "hole in the wall" had not been misdirected.

The equipment in the meter-testing room was far from up to date and was even dangerous. Doughty recalled that the "first test rack was a relic which Albert had used in West Toronto, and was responsible for George Franklin getting an electric shock while testing a 500 volt three phase meter."[23] Franklin received a bad burn, but the consequences could have been more serious had Doughty not been there to pull the switch. It was only after Anderson's second visit, in late 1913, that arrangements were made for modern equipment to be sent from Hollinwood.

Anderson drowned on his return voyage to England in March 1914, when the *Empress of Ireland* collided with a Norwegian freighter and sank in the Gulf of St Lawrence, off Father Point. He had been the driving force behind the pursuit of the Canadian market, and his death was a serious blow.

The Ferranti Electrical Co. of Canada was still functioning as an independent sales agent for Ferranti Ltd. On 3 April 1914, an agreement between Ferranti Ltd. and Ferranti Electrical of Canada gave the latter possession of all of Ferranti Ltd.'s patents and assets in Canada, exclusive use of the Ferranti name, and exclusive and unrestricted access to all Ferranti technology, and it cleared all outstanding debts owed to Ferranti Ltd. The deal cost Ferranti Electrical Co. of Canada $400,000, which was more money than it had. The 2,495 unassigned shares, valued at $100 each, were assigned to Ferranti Ltd., and the rest of the payment was made in cash.[24] With all the capital stock taken up, the shareholders passed, on 12 May 1914, a by-law doubling capital stock to $500,000 – 5,000 shares at $100 each.[25]

By 1912, Ontario's meter market had changed. The Hydro Electric Power Commission of Ontario started buying meters in bulk for resale to municipal utilities. By buying in bulk, at lower prices, the commission could pass substantial savings on to the smaller utilities. This new purchasing arrangement resulted in larger, but fewer, orders for meters. One company would now get the lion's share of the year's orders.

In 1914, Westinghouse got a huge order of 15,000 meters from the commission. Ferranti Ltd. in England decided to fight back by selling below cost. Rowntree later recalled how Ferranti Electrical of Canada

decided to undermine it [the Westinghouse contract] by quoting $6.00 for the 5 amp., single phase meter direct to the small Hydro Municipalities, telling them as a sales argument they could buy in small quantities cheaper than the Hydro Electric Power Commission could buy 15,000 under contract, which was, as I remember $6.15 or possibly $6.25 per meter. This went over big, with the result that the Hydro Electric Commission could only take a fraction of the 15,000 meters on order from the Westinghouse Company. Of course, this $6.00 price was under the cost of the Ferranti meter but after consultation with Hollinwood, it was decided to write off the small loss here against the profit they made on the parts at Hollinwood.[26]

Such a strategy was not without its risks. Canadian Customs, at the instigation of Westinghouse, accused Ferranti Ltd. of dumping and ordered Ferranti Electrical to pay an anti-dumping duty of $13,000 on meters previously imported from Hollinwood. According to Rowntree, "the big companies knew we were importing certain meter parts and assembling them here and they tried to convince the customs officers that we were importing the parts under costs."[27] The anti-dumping levy, introduced in 1904 and amended in 1907, applied to "free as well as dutiable goods, and provided that, if articles of a kind made in Canada were sold for export to Canada at a price less than the ordinary home market price, a special duty equal to the rebate given would be imposed."[28] After appealing to a friend and cabinet minister, the company's solicitor, Allan Royce, was able to get the fine lowered to $1,000, and everyone saved face.

Besides selling meters, Ferranti Electrical also tried to develop a Canadian market for the parent firm's switch-gear and transformer products. At high voltages and power, the simple act of opening a switch under load is risky for both operators and equipment. The problem resides in the dangerous arcs produced across the metal contact points the moment a switch is opened or closed. During his pioneering undertaking at the Deptford Station, Sebastian Ziani de Ferranti became the first person to consider seriously the design of high-voltage switching equipment, or switch-gear. Ferranti pioneered the use of oil in switches as a means of rapidly extinguishing any arcing produced during operation. As high-voltage AC transmission grew in scope, the design and manufacture of switch-gear developed into a sophisticated technology of its own. In order to lend technical support to the sale of Ferranti switch-gear in Canada, George Royce hired W.A. Coates in 1913. Some Ferranti transformers were sold in Canada, but the volume was very small.

Ferranti Ltd.'s top managers saw the Canadian company, from the very outset, as a simple sales outlet for products from the parent firm. As the Ferranti Electrical Co. of Canada started to grow, the subsidiary's management voiced concern over this dependence. Canadians argued that the parent firm did not understand the subtleties of the Canadian market. Pressure started to build within the Canadian company for greater autonomy from England in design and manufacturing. Tait and Whittaker, the principal directors of Ferranti Ltd., resisted giving the Canadian enterprise any mandate for manufacturing meters.

The outbreak of the First World War altered the relationship between parent firm and offspring. Hostilities cut off Canadian access to British goods and gave new impetus to the expansion of manufacturing facilities at Ferranti Electrical. It was during the war that the Canadian branch decided, for the sake of economic survival, to start designing and building its own transformers. Only after the shortages created by the Second World War would it be permitted to design and make its own watt-hour meters. In the next chapter we shall examine the impact of the First World War on the growth of Ferranti Electrical, along with the effects of the post-war boom and the Second World War.

4 *Ferranti Builds a Manufacturing Base in Canada*

From 1914 to 1945, the fortunes of Packard Electric and the Ferranti Electrical Co. of Canada rose and fell to the rhythm of international events. This country could not avoid being pulled into the powerful currents of change sweeping across the world, and the electrical industry experienced a three-decade-long financial roller-coaster ride. The responses of Ferranti and of Packard, as we shall see in the next two chapters, reflected very different corporate cultures.

Companies are like miniature societies, with their own beliefs, values, traditions, and folklore. A corporation's traditions, or "culture," reveal the way it answers such fundamental questions as: who are we? what is our business? what will our business be? and what should our business become? In short, corporate traditions embody an attitude toward doing business. Starting from different limitations, Packard Electric and Ferranti Electrical (hereafter Ferranti Canada) evolved contrasting sets of traditions. These differences manifested themselves in marketing, innovation, productivity, physical and financial resources, and profit requirements.

Canadian Electrical Industry in Doubt

By 1914, Canada's economic miracle was showing signs of imminent collapse. The harsh realities of debt repayment and severely reduced foreign investment quickly replaced the euphoria and optimism that had accompanied Canada's massive foreign borrowing from 1896 to 1912. To meet foreign debt obligations, the economy required structural changes. The cure to Canada's economic ailments promised to be a bitter pill. According to one retrospective view, written some twenty years later, "Adjustment to this situation required the diversion of idle labour and resources into the exporting industries to obtain employment and also to enable the country to meet the interest charges on its external debt. Under normal circumstances, the process would have been slow and painful involving deflation of costs and prices and at least temporary decline in industrial activity – the principal elements of a major depression."[1]

As the economy went, so too did demand for electrical products and the fortunes of Ferranti Canada. A sharp drop in residential and commercial construction reduced demand for watt-hour meters.[2] The infant Ferranti Canada found itself competing with the likes of Canadian General Electric (CGE) and Westinghouse over a much smaller pie. In addition, European producers such as Siemens were trying to unload their excess capacity on the Canadian market. Like Siemens, the British Ferranti Ltd. was an offshore competitor, and Ferranti Canada soon found itself branded as foreign-based by its domestic competitors.

Political turmoil in Europe postponed the depression. In the city of Sarajevo, Bosnia, on 28 June 1914, with a shot "heard around the world," an assassin struck down the Archduke Ferdinand, heir to the Austrian Throne. The same day Austria declared war on Serbia; within weeks, a complex web of bilateral alliances dragged most of the industrialized world into war.

What proved destructive for the European economies became an economic reprieve for Canada. Spared the direct material ravages of war, the country became a major supplier of foodstuffs, munitions, other military equipment, and soldiers. Initially, however, the war further constricted British investment in Canada and intensified the downward trend to depression. It was only after 1915, when Britain's wartime requirements became critical, that Canadian production took off. By 1917 the nation's foreign debt had disappeared, and in the later years of the war, Canada became a lender, financing British purchases of Canadian goods. Increased wartime production also translated into high industrial demand for electricity and a new impetus for the domestic electrical industry.[3]

Ferranti Canada during the War

The early years of the war were tough for Ferranti Canada. All employees took a 25 per cent cut in pay in order to keep the company afloat. George Royce had difficulty even in raising money to cover the rent.[4] Once-profitable western business fell into a slump. To make matters worse, the pillar of Ferranti Canada's western sales efforts, Gerry Monaghan, moved from Winnipeg to California, where his wife's family owned an orange grove. Monaghan, however, could not get the electrical business out of his blood and soon set up a profitable sales agency for the up-and-coming Sangamo meter company.

Within a year of Ferranti Canada's incorporation in 1912, Ferranti Ltd. (hereafter Ferranti UK) decided to ship meter parts to Canada for assembly – a pragmatic answer to the costly damage resulting from shipping. Ferranti Canada was, however, still completely dependent on Britain for all the parts that constituted the Ferranti type C meter. By 1916, the small Canadian operation was, according to

Schofield, accounting for roughly 15 per cent of meter sales in the country.[5] As the war continued, it found the flow of meter parts from the parent firm increasingly unreliable. The war eliminated competition from the likes of Siemens and stimulated Canada's depressed electrical market, but it also cut off the source of meter parts. It underscored how vulnerable the Canadian company had become in its role as a mere importer.

Total reliance on imports soon backfired. Less than a year into the war, Ferranti Canada won a three-year contract to supply the Canadian Electrical Association (CEA) with 25,000 meters per year. Excitement was short-lived: a shortage of parts from England forced Ferranti Canada to pull out of the deal. Lacking the manpower, machinery, and expertise to produce its own meters, the firm had to look for a new source of meters to tide it over for the duration of the war.

Salesman Joe Showalter's acquaintance with the owner of the prominent Duncan Meter Co., in Lafayette, Indiana, resulted in an agency arrangement. As it did for Ferranti UK's meters, Ferranti Canada remained an importer of parts which it assembled in Toronto. Only the source had changed. The sale of some 22,000 Duncan meters during the war had certainly contributed to the firm's survival.[5]

Royce realized that the company could not live exclusively on sales of Duncan meters. Before the war, Ferranti Canada had also sold some of its parent firm's switch-gear and transformers. During the war, however, one never knew which ships would make it through the submarine wolf packs. The city of Winnipeg ordered a three-phase, 1,000-kVA, 12,000-volt Ferranti transformer for the King Street substation. A German submarine sunk the first shipment. After considerable delay, a second shipment finally arrived in Winnipeg. When the transformer was unloaded and inspected, city engineers discovered that it had been flooded with sea water.[6]

Bob Lofvengren had come to Canada in 1911 to develop Ferranti UK's switch-gear business. A year later he left Ferranti Canada for the Toronto engineering firm Chapman and Walker. There he met and became good friends with J.W. Chipperfield, a transformer engineer. In 1915, Chapman and Walker folded, and both Lofvengren and Chipperfield found themselves without work. Lofvengren went back to Royce and was quickly rehired. He suggested that Ferranti Canada design and manufacture its own transformers, and he had just the man in mind. These were difficult times, and Royce was open to any proposal that would bring work and profits. Lofvengren got Chipperfield hired as the company's new and only transformer engineer. Chipperfield stayed with the firm for 32 years, rising to vice-president in 1942.

Designing and building transformers marked a turning-point for Ferranti Canada. The decision to do so met with opposition from Ferranti UK. "It was the idea of the Hollinwood plant at the time," in Rowntree's view, "to do all manufacturing in England and ship same to the 'Colonies' as we were called."[7] Ferranti UK worried that after the war was over the manufacture of transformers would distract the Canadian concern from the sale of Ferranti UK meters.

In the first few years of transformer operations, Ferranti Canada manufactured only very small pole-top transformers. The first one, produced in October 1915, was a single-phase, 60-cycle, 10-kVA model that dropped the voltage down from 2,200 volts to 550. Few of the transformers sold during the war years reached the 50-kVA range, and most were 10 to 20 kVA. By the end of 1915, Royce's company sold twenty-five pole-top transformers. In time, production of them grew into a respectable business as public and private utilities and industrial concerns started to buy from the firm.

Success with pole-top transformers prompted the company to pursue another segment of the small transformer market called instrument transformers. Safe, efficient, and economical operation of an electric generating and transmission network requires installing various meters throughout the system in order to monitor the flow of electrical energy. However, these instruments cannot directly handle the high voltages or currents that they are supposed to measure, and these voltages are very dangerous. Instrument transformers step down current or voltage to a low value that can be economically, conveniently, and safely measured. Current transformers reduce current, and potential transformers reduce voltage. Manufacture of instrument transformers offered the company another relatively low-capital entry point into the transformer market. During the war years, sales to utilities and other meter companies, such as the American-based Lincoln Meter Co., grew into a substantial business. In 1918 the company sold transformers worth $28,397[8] – nearly 27 per cent of its total sales.[9]

The start of transformer manufacturing led to munitions-related work. An inventor by the name of E.J. Brunning, along with F.C. Burnett, proposed fitting copper bands tightly onto cannon shells by means of a transformer.[10] Brunning's shell band heater expanded the copper band by using it as a short-circuited secondary winding in a transformer. The resulting high current heated the band to the point where it glowed cherry-red. At this point the transformer core was opened and the band was removed and then slipped into position over the projectile. As the band cooled, it contracted to produce a very tight fit. Brunning went to Ferranti Canada with his idea and asked Chipperfield to develop and sell an industrial version of his prototype. In June 1916, the company delivered its first shell band heater. By the end of the war, it had sold some seventy to munitions plants.

From War to Depression

On 11 November 1918 the armistice was signed. With a total of thirty million casualties on all sides, the First World War had been one of the most devastating wars the world had ever seen. Canadian veterans returned home eager to build a new life for themselves and their families. After leading the 225th Queen's Own Rifles Battalion

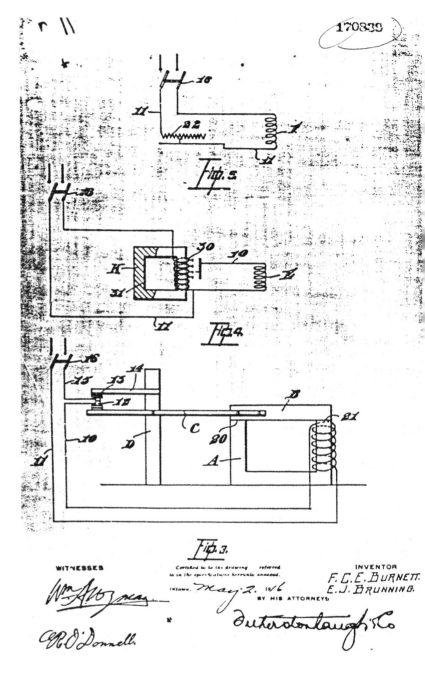

Ferranti Canada made an important contribution to manufacturing war materials during the First World War with the Shell Band Heater, which used transformers to heat copper bands to be fitted to cannon shells. The worn patent submission document of F. Burnett and E. Brunning is the only remaining physical evidence of this important equipment.
(Canada Patent Office, patent, 170,839)

abroad, George Royce returned to his duties as general manager. Fred Rowntree came back with valuable manufacturing experience: after being conscripted, he had been sent to the United States to help James Royce manage the Rolls-Royce production of the Eagle fighter airplane engine in Syracuse, New York.[11] Albert Schofield, Horace Doughty, George Franklin, and Jack Haig returned to meter operations. Before the end of 1919, there were twenty-four people working at Ferranti Canada.

During the war Ferranti meters had lost ground in the Canadian market. The immediate challenge was to recapture the old market share. The war had heightened the ascendancy of American financial power in Canada and accelerated the relative decline of British interests.[12] In the face of competing meter designs, the Ferranti type C had little chance of regaining its pre-war market share. Ferranti UK had introduced the meter in response to the criticisms raised by Schofield and Showalter over the unsuitability of type B for the Canadian market. Type C improved the competitive position of Ferranti meters,[13] but by 1919, it had fallen behind the new competitors' more technically advanced meters.

Once again the Canadian organization lobbied England for a mandate to design and manufacture meters in Canada. Albert Schofield and Showalter argued that Ferranti Canada could better understand the Canadian market than could its parent firm. In Schofield's view, "the common fault of British manufacturers in the past was to follow their laboratory ideas instead of designing to suit the Canadian market, where American practice is followed very closely. To make a success of the Canadian branch factory, we should design and sell what the Canadian user demands."[14]

Ferranti UK saw the Canadian request to design and manufacture

This dramatic advertising portrayal of a watt-hour meter was prepared in the early 1930s. Although it carries the Ferranti Electric Limited nameplate, the parent firm in fact did not allow the Canadian subsidiary to design a meter more suited to Canadian conditions until after the Second World War. (Ontario Archives, Ferranti-Packard Collection, AO 803)

While very rare in Canada, prepayment electrical meters were common in Great Britain. Ferranti Canada assembled, tested, and marketed a model of the British parent firm's prepayment meter. It was used in some pool halls to assure payment for use of the table: each table had its own overhead light and, when the prepayment meter turned it off, playing time was over unless more money was put in the meter. It is not known if these meters were used in rooming houses, as in Britain, to ensure that tenants left no unpaid electricity bills. The brass plate in the upper right reads "Insert 25 cent piece, turn handle slowly one complete revolution in direction of arrow."
(Ontario Archives, Ferranti-Packard Collection, AO 801)

meters as even more threatening than the similar incursion into transformers. The decision took time: unlike transformers, meters were the lifeblood of the parent firm. In 1919, Ferranti Canada finally got the go-ahead to design and build its own meter. Showalter was to design a new meter, the Canadian type S, using as many parts from type C as possible. The company hired George Peters, a meter specialist from Westinghouse, to help design the new meter. Excitement and enthusiasm bubbled at the prospect of designing meters in Canada.

In anticipation of this new manufacturing role, Ferranti Canada left its rented Sherbourne Street offices and bought larger quarters at 26 Noble Street, in Toronto. It also changed its name, in December 1919, to the Ferranti Meter & Transformer Manufacturing Co. Ltd. The new name symbolized electrical equipment built in Canada, by Canadians, for Canadians.[15] After production and sale of only some 2,000 Canadian type S meters, the parent firm decided to design its own "Export" meter, called the type FD, for sale in Canada. The news hit Ferranti Canada like a bomb-shell: there had been no consultation – only the order to cease production. Showalter quit to work for Westinghouse. The export meter met with a lukewarm reception in Canada. Over a decade later, the Canadian company's general man-

ager reminded Ferranti UK's directors that "the reduction in percentage of meter business between 1921 and 1927 in the face of our
utmost sales efforts, reflects the dissatisfaction with the 'FD' Meter,
and recalls to mind the failure of our combined efforts to modify it
and adapt to Canadian conditions."[16] It would not be until the end of
the Second World War that Ferranti Canada would have another opportunity to manufacture a made-in-Canada meter.

Between the First and Second world wars, Ferranti Canada's meter
business fluctuated wildly, as did its overall performance. The ebb
and flow of profit margins reflected the unstable Canadian economy
of the period. As in the past, national cycles of prosperity and depression followed the price fluctuations of resource-based export products. In 1921, a sharp drop in agricultural prices on the world market
severely disrupted transition to a peacetime economy. A 50-per-cent
drop in the price of wheat cut western farmers' purchasing power as
well as demand for Ontario's manufactured products. Once again,
the country was heading for a depression.

From 1918 to 1922, Ferranti Canada's financial performance dete-
riorated substantially. Although the unfavourable economic climate
was no doubt a major factor, serious internal problems underlay the
company's poor results. Morale was at an all-time low, and there
was an absence of leadership. Proud, capable, and ambitious people
working in a subsidiary will invariably seek to promote the interests
of their company over those of the parent firm. Creation of the Transformer Department and efforts to manufacture the type S meter illustrate Ferranti Canada's efforts to assert itself. Last-minute rejection of
the type S demoralized the Meter Department to a man. Increasingly
uninterested in daily operations, Royce could not restore morale and
impose order on the company's activities.

By late 1921, the board of Ferranti UK had become greatly concerned about its Canadian investment and the absence of proper management. Sales manager R. Schofield travelled to Canada to find a
new general manager. Looking for someone knowledgeable about the
domestic market, Schofield contacted the chief engineers of the major
utilities in Ontario and Quebec and asked them if they could recom-
mend someone with whom they had personal dealings. E.T. Brandon,
chief electrical engineer for the Hydro-Electric Power Commission of
Ontario, introduced Schofield to Ashton Bert Cooper.

A new era began for Ferranti Canada in January 1922, when
Cooper was hired as general manager. Born in Bloomfield, Ontario,
on 31 December 1883, Cooper received his bachelor of science degree
from Tufts College, Boston, in 1903. After two years at the General
Electric Test Course, in Schenectady, New York, he got a job as an in-
spector in Westinghouse's East Pittsburgh plant. In 1907, Westinghouse sent newly married Cooper to the jungles of Brazil to help
install hydro-electric equipment in Rio des Lages, which supplied
power to Rio de Janeiro Light and Power. On returning to Canada,
Cooper went to work for Canadian General Electric in Toronto,
where he specialized in commercial transformer engineering. When

Schofield met Cooper in 1922, the latter had been a transformer sales engineer at General Electric for over nine years.

By 1923, Ferranti Canada's losses had turned to profits. In a confidential report to the board of Ferranti UK, R. Schofield wrote: "The striking improvement dates from the appointment of Mr. A.B. Cooper as General Manager. His work during the year has been arduous, primarily because there was much to be done to organize the business for satisfactory progress."[17] Cooper had all the attributes needed to ensure profits in Canada: he was "exceedingly well established" with all the leading utilities and had an "intimate knowledge of the business." Most important, he combined "a good engineering knowledge with a remarkable commercial ability."[18]

In October 1922, for reasons that remain unclear, Royce sold Ferranti Canada to Ferranti UK for $15,000.[19] In exchange, Royce agreed to purchase the Noble Street factory from Ferranti UK for $30,000 and become landlord. In effect, Ferranti Canada's five-year lease with Royce paid off Royce's mortgage. As part of the deal, Royce replaced Tait as president of Ferranti Canada at an annual salary of $2,500 but played only a nominal role, because Ferranti UK had placed "Executive Management" of its subsidiary totally under Cooper's control.

By redesigning the flow of material through the building and introducing new winding lathes, Cooper dramatically increased productivity in the cramped factory. The company, however, could still not keep up with orders. In less than a year after Cooper took over, the factory had reached full capacity. As a result, Ferranti Canada had to turn away considerable business. To squeeze more out of the factory, Cooper resorted to running it three or four nights a week. He knew that when economic conditions picked up, the firm would be hopelessly unprepared to profit from increased demand for transformers. With Canada's economic recovery imminent, Cooper recommended in the fall of 1922 that Ferranti UK "expand [its] manufacturing facilities in Canada, so as to place [the company] in a position to receive consideration next to General Electric and the Canadian Westinghouse Companies."[20]

The time had come for Ferranti UK to decide about the future of its Canadian subsidiary. Would Ferranti Canada remain a mere export arm of Ferranti UK? Or would it become a true domestic manufacturer? Cooper explained to his shareholders in Britain that the future of British manufactured meters in the American-dominated Canadian market was limited. "There is no good to be gained by failing to recognise the fact," Cooper wrote to Schofield,

that among a certain class of Canadians a strong feeling exists of preference for Canadian manufacture, and by the same token in certain directions, there is a feeling that the United States manufacturers are ahead of all other manufacturers in development, and this latter feeling operates to the advantage of those Canadian companies who are affiliated with American concerns, and duplicate or imitate the American designs.

This is an un-British view point and is hard to reconcile with certain conditions, but on the other hand, I think it is a natural feeling and one which must be recognized when you consider the influence which the American technical and trade journals have on the Canadian Engineers and Central Station operators.[21]

A few years earlier, the board of Ferranti UK would have looked on Canadian calls for a greater manufacturing mandate with great trepidation. Tait maintained a very conservative, if not colonial, attitude to his Canadian subsidiary.

A perceptible shift in policy started to emerge by 1922, with the appearance of a new force on Ferranti UK's board. After years of near-total exclusion from management of the company bearing his name, Sebastian Ziani de Ferranti made a dramatic comeback and in 1922 regained control of Ferranti UK. Tait had managed, for ten years, to exclude Ferranti from much of company's business. With the start of the First World War, the British electrical industry went into a tailspin. Managing director A.B. Anderson had perished with the *Empress of Ireland*. Without him, the board had stumbled along, with no clear wartime policy.

Driven by a combination of patriotism and the need to increase sales, S.Z. de Ferranti had recommended to the board that it convert the Hollinwood plant to making shells and fuzes. Despite the board's initial rejection, Ferranti had persisted and in 1915 had finally obtained approval. He had gone out and won substantial government munitions contracts and had solved a host of engineering problems associated with munitions manufacturing.

At war's end, munitions work had left Ferranti UK in its strongest financial position ever, and everyone recognized S.Z. de Ferranti as the architect of this success. In 1918, Arthur Whittaker, a board member, had recommended Ferranti's appointment as technical manager and head of the executive committee. Tait had agreed reluctantly. He still feared S.Z. de Ferranti's technology-driven approach but hoped that Whittaker could keep his inventive spirit in check.[22]

S.Z. de Ferranti had again become the prime moving force behind the company. In recognition of his new role, and after intense pressure from him, the board altered the firm's capital structure. S.Z. and his son, Vincent Z., gained 29 per cent of the total equity – the largest block of stock. With father and son's rise to power came a more ambitious approach to development of the Canadian subsidiary.

In January 1923, V.Z. de Ferranti and R. Schofield made a crucial visit to Canada, to determine the potential of the market, examine the soundness of their investment, and make recommendations about any further investment. "The development of electrical trade in Canada," observed Schofield, "is amazing when compared with Great Britain. Electrical thought has become a national habit. The average rate of expansion is about 15% per annum, and, in fact the progress chart of the Ontario Electric System shows that they are increasing at such a rate that they will double their present output in four years."[23]

Sir Vincent Ziani de Ferranti, the son of Ferranti Ltd. (hereafter Ferranti UK) founder Sebastian, was responsible for making transformers a prominent part of the business during the 1920s.
(Ferranti Family Archives, Macclesfield, Cheshire, England)

On their return to England, the two men recommended that transformers become the pivotal point of Ferranti's approach to Canada.
Schofield observed that with the high volume of transformer business
in Canada, there was "more justification for a Transformer Factory in
Canada than there is in England."[24] The time had come, they argued,
to expand manufacturing facilities in Canada – to improve Ferranti's
prestige in Canada and respond to the aspirations and ambitions
of the staff. Aware of the frustrations that arose from the abortive
type S Canadian meter, Schofield reminded the board that "the staff
under Mr. Cooper's leadership are now very enthusiastic" and added:
"I believe that it will be impossible to retain their enthusiasm and
good work unless they are given the facility for growth and development."[25]

V.Z. de Ferranti's visit to Canada marked the beginning of a special
relationship between him and Cooper. Though Ferranti was destined
by birth to take over the company, in 1923 the two men found themselves in similar circumstances. Both were building their careers at
Ferranti on the transformer. While Cooper was committed to expanding the manufacture of transformers in Canada, V.Z. de Ferranti
wanted to increase the role of the Transformer Department which his
father had given him to manage. As these two men exchanged information and advice on the transformer business, a close professional
bond developed, based on understanding and respect. For nearly
thirty years, until Cooper's death, Cooper would remain V.Z. de
Ferranti's most trusted confidant and friend in Canada.

V.Z. de Ferranti's visit to Toronto contributed to the development
of his own Transformer Department. Canadian economists and historians have often argued that subsidiaries are an excellent vehicle for
acquisition of foreign know-how. The history of Ferranti Canada
does lend ample support to this argument. The flip side to this argument, however, has not received the attention that it deserves. Technological innovation can flow as well from the subsidiary to its parent
firm. Rather than being the passive recipient of such technology, Canadian subsidiaries are often staffed by talented and ambitious people
who are eager to excel, innovate, and distinguish themselves from the
"senior" company. At times the ambitions of subsidiary and parent
will conflict. In some instances, the latter will suppress its subsidiaries' innovations or appropriate the technology. In other cases, it will
encourage innovative initiatives.

Ferranti Canada's story provides eloquent testimony to this two-
way flow. During the First World War, the firm developed its own
pole-top transformer business. The highly competitive domestic market forced it to develop cost-effective design and manufacturing methods. The same market climate for small transformers did not exist in
Britain. As a result, Ferranti UK knew little about making small transformers. After the January 1923 visit to Toronto, Schofield reported
that "Mr. Vincent Ferranti has accumulated a lot of information
on the manufacture of small size transformers which we intend to develop here for export to Dominions other than Canada."[26] Several

years later, in a letter to Cooper, V.Z. de Ferranti acknowledged the contribution of Ferranti Canada in the growth of the parent firm's Transformer Department: "I am well aware that the whole of our small transformer business, which has increased from practically nothing to quite a large business in the last few years, is largely due to what you taught us about the construction of pole type transformers."[27]

Soon after Schofield and V.Z. de Ferranti returned to England in 1923 with their recommendations, Ferranti UK gave Cooper the green light to proceed with his plans for expansion. The first stage involved construction of an extension that would double factory space. Ferranti UK would supply the machinery and working capital. As landlord, Royce agreed to finance construction, with Ferranti Canada agreeing to lease the space on the same basis as the existing building. After formal tenders for construction were in, it became apparent that Royce had greatly underestimated building costs. His efforts to raise the additional money at the banks ran into unexpected difficulties. In a letter to V.Z. de Ferranti, Cooper explained: "[Royce] originally obtained some promise of a loan from one of the banks, but before this loan was consummated the bank situation in Canada took a very serious turn, resulting in the collapse of the Home Bank of Canada and the curtailment of the quick assets of the Standard Bank and Bank of Hamilton, and as a result, all of the banks immediately tightened up on their loans."[28]

S.Z. de Ferranti had agreed to travel to Canada for inauguration of the extension. But one delay after another forced Cooper to keep putting off the visit. The delays were also costing the company valuable new business. Royce's inability to set a construction date visibly irritated Cooper. Royce did finally obtain financing, and the extension was completed in early 1924.

With a new facility in hand, Cooper quickly set about modernizing the company's transformer manufacturing practices. The first important improvement came in the critical area of insulation techniques. The lifetime of a transformer depends on the effectiveness of the insulation used in the windings. In 1825, Joseph Henry, an American physicist, discovered that powerful magnetic fields could be created by closely packing many turns of wire around a piece of iron. The brilliance of Henry's discovery lay in his idea of insulating the conducting turns of wire from one another. From that moment, finding the most effective, durable, and economic insulating material became a central concern of electrical engineering.

A common insulating material used in transformers was some form of paper or cotton material. Impregnating paper with special compounds greatly increased its insulating qualities. Heat, which is produced during the operation of transformers, can damage insulation. If one immerses the windings in oil, the oil then becomes part of a finely balanced heat exchange system that draws potentially harmful heat away from the windings and onto the metal surface of the outer transformer wall. The walls then conduct and radiate the heat into the sur-

Vacuum impregnation of insulating material into all of the space around a transformer's winding eliminated dangerous moisture, which could short circuit the transformer and burn it out. For many years it was a critical step in manufacturing transformers. In this 1927 photograph taken inside Packard's Neelon Mill building in St Catharines, the windings, made of wire insulated with varnish, are being lowered into the vacuum impregnation tanks.
(Ontario Archives, Ferranti-Packard Collection, AO 793)

rounding air. Because the coils are immersed in oil, impregnating compounds had to be developed that were insoluble in oil. Water conducts electricity. At very high voltages, even the smallest traces of water in the wire insulation or the oil can lead to disastrous short circuits, and so moisture is a significant problem.

The impregnating room that Cooper installed assured the highest insulation standards during the transformer's assembly. The core and coils were heated for several hours in a large tank subjected to a high vacuum. While still under a vacuum, the molten impregnating material flowed into the tank, completely covering the core and coils. Then dry air under pressure of 100 lb per square inch was forced into the tank, thus driving the impregnating material deep into every crevice of the windings. The process purged the insulation of moisture and sealed the windings against the later entrance of any moisture. Because the impregnating compound conducts heat well, forcing it into all the dead air spaces greatly facilitated heat removal from the operating transformer.

Promoting transformers made with the vacuum impregnation process opened new business, and the cost of the facilities was quickly recouped. The facilities qualified Ferranti Canada "for a portion of the Toronto Hydro Electric business. It was not long before [the company] received an initial order for 100 − 25 kVA pole types."[29]

Cooper also realized that the company would not go very far if it continued to limit itself to small pole-type transformers. As demand for electrical power climbed, so did transmission and distribution

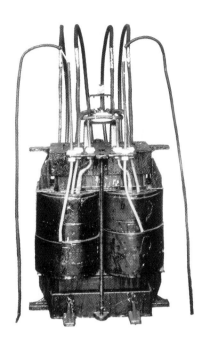

Shortly after the end of the First World War, Ferranti Canada entered the transformer business, manufacturing small pole-top distribution transformers which provided the final voltage reduction to 220 or 110 volts before lines fed power into residences or small businesses. Taken during the 1920s, this photograph shows the inside of a pole-top transformer after impregnation. (Ontario Archives, Ferranti-Packard Collection, AO 814)

voltages and loads. Changing market requirements led to demand for larger transformers. Besides expanding the volume of business, the new extension at Noble Street also permitted manufacture of larger transformers. For the first time, Ferranti Canada could bid for larger substation transformers required by utilities and industry.

Ferranti Canada still lacked the expertise to build larger transformers which required considerably more engineering sophistication. The transformer appears to be nothing more than many turns of conducting wire wrapped around pieces of iron. In reality, an efficient and economical transformer requires the harmonious union of a host of subtle and sophisticated technologies. Important design questions must be answered and then translated into profitable manufacturing procedures. How do insulating materials behave under very high voltages, currents, and temperatures? How does ageing affect the materials constituting a transformer? How do various steel alloys behave under very high magnetic fields? What harmful stresses arise from intense electric and magnetic fields generated deep within the transformer? How can transformers handle the harmful effects of heat? How can the performance-to-cost ratio of transformers be improved? One has to consider as well any technology that will improve the quality and productivity and reduce the costs associated with manufacturing. The larger the transformer, the more complex become the solutions to these problems.

Ferranti Canada closed what is now referred to as the technology gap by availing itself of the parent firm's know-how. In 1926, V.Z. de Ferranti sent two of his transformer designers, Frank Flitcroft and Cliff Caldwell, to Canada. Flitcroft specialized in electrical aspects of design, and Caldwell in mechanical. As a result of Flitcroft's expertise, Ferranti Canada started bidding for the larger and more profitable power transformer business. It often, however, placed bids for contracts that it had little hope of winning and no capacity to build. Cooper believed that bidding for 5,000-kVA transformers improved the company's prestige, which, in turn, created better opportunities for selling smaller power transformers, say at 1,000 kVA.

Under Cooper's able leadership, Ferranti Canada cashed in on the economic recovery of the 1920s. Renewed world demand for Canada's resources produced a sharp reversal in the nation's economy. Between 1922 and 1926 Canada supplied 38 per cent of the world's wheat exports, compared with 12 per cent during 1909–14, and by 1929 wheat made up one-third of the value of Canada's total exports. Once again the miracle of wheat stimulated manufacturing and spurred on consumer and industrial demand for electricity.

Two other, more direct stimuli drove up demand for electricity: mining and forest industries. Advances in metallurgy, mining techniques, and land-based transportation, a well-established technological base in long-distance power transmission, and an abundant supply of hydro-electric power greatly increased the commercial profitability of Canada's distant mining and forest regions. "The exports of pulp and paper and non-ferrous metals rose to 30% of total ex-

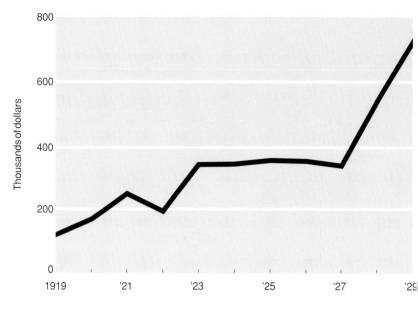

Ferranti Canada transformer and watthour meter sales, 1919-1929

ports in 1929 compared to 19% in 1920."[30] By 1930, the energy-intensive pulp and paper, electro-metallurgical, and electro-chemical industries were consuming nearly 45 per cent of all the electrical power generated in Canada,[31] and were also responsible for a proportionate share of new hydro-electric development.

During the 1920s, electrical energy had, more than ever before, become the lifeblood of industry. The generating output of public utilities leapt by 310 per cent, while new capital investments in electric power installations increased by an astounding 690 per cent.[32] As consumption of electricity soared, so did demand for electrical products. From a low output of $41 million during the 1922 recession, the value of electrical products climbed to $103 million in 1930. Expansion of Canada's electrical distribution system translated into higher demand for transformers.

Although economic prosperity pulled Ferranti Canada along, Cooper's astute management helped create a 400-per-cent increase in business from 1922 to 1930. The entire electrical industry averaged a 275-percent growth rate during the same period. In October 1926, the company changed its name from Ferranti Meter & Transformer Manufacturing Co. Ltd. to the more manageable Ferranti Electric Ltd. We shall continue to refer to it as Ferranti Canada.

Birth of the Radio Department

In 1926, Ferranti Canada extended its transformer business into radio technology. Following V.Z. de Ferranti's visit to Toronto, the

Radio Laboratory was established, in 1926, with a young electrical engineer named John Thomson as head. Thomson was born in Trinidad, the son of missionaries. In 1924, he received his bachelor of applied science in electrical engineering from the University of Toronto. After working several years for General Electric in Schenectady, New York, and then for English Electric, in St Catharines, Ontario, Thomson moved to Ferranti Canada in 1926. His thirst for knowledge led him to obtain a master's degree in 1933 and his PhD in applied mathematics in 1937.

A doctorate made Thomson a rarity in the Canadian electrical manufacturing world of the 1930s. Many of his fellow engineers wondered what he would do when he returned to the practical world of designing transformers. Cooper, however, encouraged Thomson to pursue his studies, at the company's expense. For Cooper, Thomson's PhD was an important investment in the firm's marketing image.[33]

Thomson's love of mathematical abstraction set him apart, and his theoretical understanding of the complexities of transformer design was second to none. Producing numerous technical notes on transformers' operation and design, he became an indispensable source of knowledge for all the company's design engineers. Thomson later rose to become general manager, then president, and finally chairman of the board. To this day, he takes greater pride in his research accomplishments than his corporate achievements. Ask him about his past research work and his eyes light up. You are then quickly led into his office, lined with volumes of mathematical and scientific literature, and shown filing drawers overflowing with his mathematical analyses of various transformer design questions. With such a love of abstract research, Thomson might well have been just as happy in the scholarly environment of a university; it is fortunate for Canadian industrial development that he was with Ferranti.

Throughout the 1920s, radio technology was a public passion that grew commercially in leaps and bounds. From 1925 to 1931, yearly production of radios in Canada grew by 600 per cent. An important component in radio electronics was the audio-frequency transformer. In 1924–25, S.Z. de Ferranti perfected a new transformer design, which improved upon "the low-frequency inter-valve transformer of early valve receiving sets. This resulted in the famous AF3 transformer, which sold all over the world – particularly in the U.S.A. and Canada."[35]

Good reproduction of sound requires amplification with minimum distortion over the broadest audio frequency band-width. Transformer design for electric power systems did not have to consider band-width because power was transmitted at a constant frequency: in those days 25, 50, or 60 cycles per second. Prior to Ferranti's invention, using a transformer to couple vacuum tubes in the radio's audio-amplifier circuits proved unsatisfactory because the transformer's response was not constant over all frequencies. Through careful design of core and windings, Ferranti UK produced an audio frequency transformer with amazingly uniform amplification over the entire

Ferranti UK's audio transformer led both parent firm and Canadian subsidiary into the radio market by selling to radio manufacturers or enthusiasts who either built their own radios or modified commecially produced ones to give better performance and higher-quality sound. Ferranti UK consciously diversified its product mix to reduce their dependence on selling to electric utilities. In England during the 1920s Ferranti UK produced high quality radios with cabinet designs still regarded as classics by designers and art critics. The company also made electric clocks and in the 1930s ventured into television. Ferranti Canada hoped to follow the same path.
(Ferranti-Packard Transformers Ltd.)

Range of 'Cello 75-1000   Range of Tympani 250   Range of Piano 50-3000   Range of Human Voice 75-1000   Range of Violin 200-3500

Note the even amplification of FERRANTI (AF3) Transformer ➤

Note the uneven Curves of 3 Popular American Transformers ➤

Here is how to Purify the Tone of your Radio

NOW you can make reception clear, full and uniform in both high and low tone ranges with this wonderful little instrument.

Did you ever invite your friends to hear your Radio—when the piano selections rattled, and the voice of the high soprano cracked, and you couldn't hear the bass notes of your favorite orchestra?

Its aggravating and disappointing to have such a set—*but it can be remedied*.

Your set needs FERRANTI Transformers. Here is the reason. First, study the curves on the graph above which is divided to show low and high frequencies. The higher the frequency the higher the note. The heavy black line (AF3) is the curve of the FERRANTI

Transformer—level, even amplification at all frequencies. The next three lines represent the frequency curves of three well-known American Transformers—so far from even amplification that you can readily understand why your reception is so unsatisfactory.

Whether you are building a receiver or already possess one, install FERRANTI Transformers. You'll be amazed at the clearer, even tone volume you get. With our detailed direction sheet they are simple to install. If your nearest Radio Dealer is out of them send your dealer's name and $11 for each transformer desired. We will deliver them direct or through your dealer all carriage charges paid.

PRICE $11

FERRANTI ELECTRIC LIMITED
NOBLE STREET, TORONTO

Until the appearance of the Ferranti audio transformer Ferranti Canada's marketing efforts had been aimed at utilities and large industrial users of electrical power. Advertisements such as this, from the *Montreal Gazette* of 19 October 1926, helped attract customers in new markets.
(National Library of Canada, NL 18177)

audio frequency range – a major contribution to truer sound reproduction.

The Ferranti family pursued radio technology with its usual intense fascination with engineering and innovation. Soon afterward, the company became a leader in all aspects of radio design, including exterior appearance. Development of the radio business, however, was far more than a quest for technological novelty. Sebastian and Vincent de Ferranti felt that their company had become dangerously dependent on one market – public utilities – and wanted to expand into design and manufacture of electrical consumer goods. Sebastian had long advocated a society based on widespread use of electrical home appliances.

As early as 1912–14, Ferranti UK had produced a range of electric heaters, cookers, and irons, but the war put a damper on this. However, in 1927, sale of consumer products increased dramatically with introduction of the parabolic reflector heater; an electric clock and other appliances such as water heaters soon followed. As Vincent explained to Cooper, "We feel here the absolute necessity of getting half our turnover from the selling of articles bought by the public in contra-distinction to articles sold on the public tender. We feel that to make any business reasonably secure that this sort of thing is necessary."[36] The sale of radios and electrical appliances finally brought the Ferranti name to the general public's attention.

Over the years, the Ferranti family's concern for expanding the product base and the strong emphasis on technology fed on each other and pushed the company into diverse advanced technologies. This approach greatly influenced Ferranti Canada's engineers and managers. Ferranti UK would often coax an only-too-willing Ferranti Canada to embark on new activities, as in the introduction of the audio transformer.

By 1931, V.Z. de Ferranti was contemplating manufacture of electric clocks and radio sets in Canada.[37] The initial strategy was to produce the audio frequency transformer in Britain and sell it in North America through Ferranti Canada. The market was limited to other radio manufacturers and hobbyists, but the former had too much invested in their own designs and the transformer thus became a specialty for performance-hungry hobbyists, who made their own radios, from scratch or kits, or modified off-the-shelf radios.

Providing no more than 2 to 3 per cent of the company's total sales and gross profits, the Radio Department never developed into a substantial money maker. Nonetheless, the sale of audio frequency transformers helped the company's public image. "It must be borne in mind," Rowntree writes, "that it was always an uphill fight to sell the Ferranti name in Canada, because in those early days our big competitors were knocking the name FERRANTI as being foreign. I fully believe the one thing that took the Ferranti name out of this category and converted it almost overnight to a household name was the advertising and sale of the Audio Frequency Transformer."[38]

Manufacturing Roots in Canada

Heady economic times and Cooper's able management catapulted Ferranti Canada into extraordinary growth, spurred on by the remarkable expansion of the transformer business. From 1921 to 1929, transformer output increased seven-fold in dollar value. The uncertainty of the early 1920s now seemed a distant memory. As Schofield later recalled, "a very friendly spirit started to develop amongst the employees. Family picnics were organized every June, and corn roasts in the Fall, and for nearly twenty years the annual Ferranti Staff Dance was a social event of importance in Toronto. The general morale amongst the employees was at a high level. Group life insurance was established for all employees."[39]

In the fall of 1928, with a booming Canadian electrical business showing no signs of slowing down, a bold plan to expand Canadian operations took form in Cooper's mind. "I think," he wrote to V.Z. de Ferranti, "that our next move in Canada should be made with fairly broad vision."[40] Cooper recommended construction of a factory on a site with railway facilities and on enough land to "provide room for logical expansion over a period of twenty years."[41] He thought a new factory a necessity: "It is impossible to stand still in any competitive field, – one must either go forward or backward."[42]

Where to locate the new factory? The company had always wanted to expand its trade with Quebec's largely privately owned utilities. Since existing transformer factories were all located in Ontario, Montreal presented distinct competitive advantages. In the end, Cooper concluded: "we are very firmly established in the Ontario market and it would seem suicidal to sacrifice this connection for the possible improvement in our Quebec business."[43] Cooper believed as well that potential demand for meters and transformers lay in Ontario and western Canada.

It was necessary to expand output in order to keep up with anticipated growth in demand. Further, pressure to expand the geographic scale of electrification and to increase the load-carrying capacity of electric power lines made Canadian utilities think of higher transmission voltages. Transmission voltages had grown enormously in just over three decades: 11,000 volts at Batiscan River in 1895; 50,000 volts at Shawinigan Falls in 1903; 60,000 volts at Niagara Falls in 1906; 100,000 volts in 1911; 110,000 volts in 1924; 220,000 volts at Paugan Falls, Quebec, by Gatineau Power in 1928; and 260,000 by Ontario Hydro in 1930.[44]

Gatineau Power's 220-kV Paugan Falls Station of 1928 represented a great leap forward. Using power from it, the Leaside Transformer Station in Toronto became Canada's first 220,000-volt substation.[45] With such dramatic advances in technology, the power and voltage ratings of all classes of transformers climbed. In response, the Dominion Bureau of Statistics redefined its method of classifying transformers. Up to 1929, a power rating of 50 kVA had been used to separate distribution transformers from power transformers. In 1930 the separation was moved up to 200 kVA.

Cooper felt that Ferranti Canada had to establish itself as a serious manufacturer of power transformers, but he knew that it could never produce the extremely large transformers that Canadian General

In the mid-1920s, Ferranti UK decided to pursue the market in the very large power transformers needed to handle the ever-climbing transmission voltages utilities were demanding to make long-distance transmission of electrical power more efficient and thus more profitable. To gain needed design knowledge, Ferranti UK conducted research on the behaviour of conductors and insulators under extremely high voltages. In 1925 Ferranti's High Voltage Laboratory produced Britain's first one-million-volt spark.
(Ontario Archives, Ferranti-Packard Collection, AO 1278)

Electric and Westinghouse were building. Rather, his goal was to target a less ambitious range of power transformers, even there technical and manufacturing requirements were continually being pushed up. If the firm's capacity were to keep pace with the ever-expanding limits of transformer technology, a modern factory was imperative. The manufacture and testing of larger transformers required a great deal of space, very high ceilings, and powerful cranes to lift and move heavy components and transformers.

Cooper's proposal for a new factory coincided with the parent firm's break-through into the power transformer business. In 1926, the British government created the Central Electricity Generating Board to oversee construction of a national electric power grid. Thirty-six years after S.Z. de Ferranti had passionately argued for a system of central power stations, work started on what would eventually become a 4,500-km (2794 mi) network of overhead high-voltage transmission lines linking all of Britain into a common grid.

It was not until 1926 that England finally decided to develop a national high-voltage AC power grid. Ferranti UK research paid off when it received the contract to build the largest power tranformers in the British power grid. In the photograph, a 132,000-volt transformer is being pulled to its point of installation. The national power grid contract work lasted from 1926 to 1932 and the parent firm's substantial profits on this project played a crucial role in keeping Ferranti Canada afloat during the Depression of the 1930s.
(Ontario Archives, Ferranti-Packard Collection AO 1273)

Ferranti UK got the order to supply the largest share of the grid's big 132-kV transformers. It also built the grid's largest three-phase units of 75,000 kVA. This work for the grid was very profitable and established the company as a world leader in power transformer design. In the euphoria of this success, Sebastian and Vincent de Ferranti were quite receptive to Cooper's idea.

Ferranti Canada could not finance a new factory entirely from its profits. Initially, Ferranti UK assumed that its contribution would not exceed $150,000 of the estimated total cost of $250,000. On 11 January 1929, the British board – of which S.Z. de Ferranti was now a member – authorized Cooper to "negotiate the purchase of not more than 15 acres of land east of the railway tracks, being part of the Tretheway Farm, in the Township of York, the said land to be purchased subject to the approval of Ferranti Limited, at a price of $4,000 per acre."[46]

In Canada, vast hydraulic reserves and greater distances between generating sites and consumers drove transmission voltages up far faster than in Britain. The Leaside substation in Toronto was Canada's first 220,000-volt substation. Workmen pose on 15 August 1928 as the transformer core is lowered into its tank at Leaside. Ferranti Canada did significant development work in pole-top transformers. However, if it were to compete in the upper end of the Canadian power transformer market it would need to acquire high voltage technology from the parent firm. Two-way technology transfer was an important, but sometimes controversial, part of the relationship between Ferranti Canada and Ferranti UK.
(Ontario Hydro Archives, 20599)

After the land was bought, and tenders were received, cost estimates started to climb. The British board became uneasy. Fearful that concern over mounting costs would set back construction, Cooper argued that he could cover the increased costs from the next year's profits. V.Z. de Ferranti found Cooper's financing scheme too risky because it did not leave an adequate margin of safety. He wanted to delay the project so that it could be done properly. In a letter to Cooper on 2 July 1929 he explained:

I quite agree with you that conditions may appear favourable in Canada, and I always agree with you that it is very important to get going on a bigger scale. On the other, I do not wish to get started in a manner which is at all inadequate. I am very much afraid that with the proposed amount of money, we should be seriously handicapped and might in fact get into a very difficult position.

I think that it will probably be necessary for us to provide from over here $300,000 which is in excess of 50% of what I arranged to put in the business. I then think, notwithstanding the profits, which I hope you would have available, that you might still have to get finance from your bank to at first provide the extra working capital which will be necessary for the increased business.

... I feel that it is better to delay our start for a few months and then make sure of making a thoroughly good start than to go at once and take the risks of a set back later on.[47]

By the fall of 1929, financing had been arranged and construction started. When the 70,000-sq.-ft (6503 sq. m.) factory opened in April 1930, it had only a 30-ton crane, even though the 400-foot runway was designed for a 60-ton crane. Mrs. Florence Cooper used the customary bottle of champagne to launch a transformer, via the crane, on its way to the shipping room.

S.Z. de Ferranti had taken great interest in the new plant and planned to be in Toronto at the official opening. Before the completion of construction, however, he was suddenly taken ill in Switzerland and died in Zurich on 13 January 1930. In honour of the great engineer and founder, the Canadian board erected a plaque at the entrance of the new factory with the following inscription: "THIS FACTORY IS DEDICATED TO THE MEMORY OF SEBASTIAN ZIANI DE FERRANTI, D.SC., F.R.S., ENGINEER, PIONEER AND INVENTOR, BELOVED FOUNDER OF THE COMPANY WHICH BEARS HIS NAME.

Ferranti Canada financed most of the over-$400,000 final cost of the new factory through profits, loans, and an increase in its authorized common stock to $500,000 from $250,000. Ferranti UK bought the entire issue, thus retaining sole ownership. Its willingness to invest heavily in Canada reflected a change in attitude toward its subsidiary. In the field of transformers, Ferranti Canada was finally accepted as its own profit centre. In 1931 V.Z. de Ferranti told the Canadian company that it was now free to pursue its own international marketing strategy and compete in any markets it saw fit.[48]

For decades Ferranti Canada lacked a large
overhead travelling crane such as the one
shown in this 1965 photograph of the north
bay in the Toronto plant. Without such a
crane for moving parts and finished transformers, Ferranti Canada could only dream
of building large transformers.
(Ontario Archives, Ferranti-Packard Collection AO 1526)

New Manufacturing Capacity and No Markets:
The Depression Strikes

The new factory was financed in the expectation of doubled output
and growing profits. The president of Canadian General Electric,
D.C. Durland, boasted that the prosperity experienced by the industry in 1928 and 1929 "was perhaps one of the truest indices of the satisfactory economic position of the Dominion."[49] These were the most
successful years in the histories of Ferranti in Canada and the United
Kingdom, and both boards were naturally caught up in the optimism.

Soon after construction started on the new factory, the economic
bubble enveloping the industrialized world burst. In October 1929,
the stock market on Wall Street crashed, and the world soon fell into
the deepest depression it had ever experienced. It took a year before

the effects hit the electrical capital goods industry. As a result of contracts won in 1929, Ferranti Canada's transformer output continued strongly and reached an all-time high in 1930.

After one year in the new factory, the company's transformer sales plummeted. The collapse of the economy sharply reduced demand for power and, consequently, for transformers and meters. Rapid expansion of the electrical industry during the late 1920s had suddenly left Canada with a huge excess in manufacturing capacity.

Like many other businessmen, Cooper underestimated the severity of the Depression. After a year of heavy losses, he told a shareholders' meeting, on 25 November 1932, that he was "very optimistic that trade would pick up during the calendar year of 1933."[50] But losses in 1933 were nearly double those of 1932. In 1933 alone, net losses were 42 per cent of total sales. With a great deal of money tied up in mortgages and new facilities, Ferranti Canada had a dangerous cashflow problem that threatened to sink the company. It cut salaries and staff in an effort to minimize losses. Radio manufacturing had slumped so much that in 1933 the Radio Department was phased out, six years after its creation.[51] Thanks to business arising from Britain's national grid, Ferranti UK maintained high profits throughout the period 1930–34. Its ability to carry Ferranti Canada's losses helped keep the Canadian company afloat;[52] the amount owed to Ferranti UK grew each year during the Depression.

New Products Evolve During the Depression

As the Depression persisted, a growing feeling of despair filled the industrialized world. "Let's talk of graves, of worms and epitaphs — Let's choose executors and talk of wills,"[53] was the way that one ed-

In 1929, confident that it could manufacture and compete in the large power transformer market, Ferranti Canada started building a much larger facility on Industry Street in Mount Dennis on the northwestern outskirts of Toronto. The onset of the Depression dampened the market and soon money-losing Ferranti Canada had to rely heavily on the parent company to stay solvent. This photograph was taken in 1941 when the plant was much busier.
(City of Toronto Archives, Salmon 1980)

itorial, in an electrical journal, described the situation. Canadians were looking to government for solutions, but government was powerless to influence world markets. Michael Bliss observes:

In Canada it would not have helped to have had Franklin D. Roosevelt and his New Deal to wrestle with the depression; nor would an earlier adoption of the new economics of John Maynard Keynes have made a difference. Canada's was a far more open economy than the United States, highly dependent on international trade.

The Great Depression was not the result of a business foul-up ... Rather it was an international crisis, rooted in the deep dislocations caused by the Great War of 1914–18 and its aftermath ... Businessmen, like everyone else, were caught in the winds of economic turmoil. There was nothing they could do, except try to hold on.[54]

And hold on Ferranti Canada did. Thanks to Cooper's leadership, it faced the hardships of the Depression with courage, determination, and imagination. Its meter business was mediocre, with little future promise, and Cooper's ambitions to build large power transformers found no market opportunity. Despite the Depression, Ferranti Canada pursued product innovation in an attempt to carve out a niche in the economy. Two of the firm's most successful products, surge absorbers and step regulators, resulted from the interplay of the parent firm's know-how and Canadian ingenuity and innovation.

In 1930, the dangers posed by lightning to transformers had not been adequately addressed; costly damage to transformers and disruption of service made lightning protection crucial. In rural areas, exposed distribution transformers were more vulnerable. The standard protection of the day, lightning arrestors, had drawbacks. They were particularly unsuitable in rural areas; they were connected in parallel to the line and offered a more attractive path for the lightning surge to take – namely, away from the transformer and into the

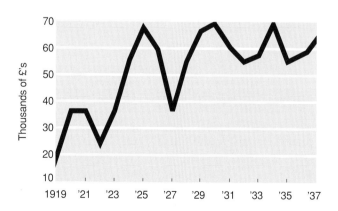

Ferranti Ltd. profits, 1919-1937, in British Pounds

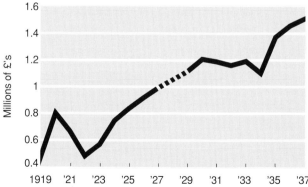

Ferranti Ltd's Total Output of Production, 1919-1937, in British Pounds

As the Depression gathered momentum in 1930, Fred Rowntree (left) and A.B. Cooper, the manager and president of Ferranti Canada, still had a sense of humour. Like so many others, they probably thought prosperity was just around the corner.
(Madame Gignac, Penetanguishene, Ontario)

ground. Because the arrestor diverted dangerous surges to the ground, its effectiveness depended on finding and maintaining low ground resistance. Varying soil conditions, particularly in remote or rocky areas, could increase ground resistance.

In 1930, V.Z. de Ferranti delivered a paper to Britain's Institution of Electrical Engineers advocating a new approach to surge protection, called the surge absorber. Ferranti Canada immediately grasped the significance of this proposal for Canada, and it quickly set about developing an economical and reliable version for North America. After hearing from Ferranti UK's chief design engineer that small surge absorbers could be built cheaply, A. Schofield became "convinced that the best place to put the Surge Absorber was inside the tank of the pole top transformer."[55]

Perfecting a surge absorber that could work inside a transformer required deeper analysis of how and why such a device worked. Dr. John Thomson launched mathematical investigations of the performance of surge absorbers. His research produced several scholarly papers and formed the theoretical and empirical foundation for transformers with built-in surge absorbers. No other manufacturer was putting lightning protection inside the transformer.

The effectiveness of Surge Absorbers, as Thomson's research had proven, lay in their ability to nullify the extremely rapid rise in voltage associated with lightning surges. When lightning strikes a transmission line, a high speed wave of electrical energy travels down the wire. According to Thomson's findings, it was not the amplitude of this wave that caused transformer breakdown, but rather the very steep front of the wave. The voltage associated with the lightning surge would go from zero to its maximum in only a few microseconds, producing stresses in the winding several thousand times greater than that found in normal operation. The surge absorber damped out the harmful steep wave front of the lightning surge.

Getting customers to see lightning protection in terms other than amplitude reduction took time.[56] Ferranti Canada's credibility helped. This is where Cooper thought that Thomson's PhD would come in handy. The firm marketed its new product as "Ferr-Anti-Surge" transformers. During the Depression, the Ontario gold mining industry developed into a major market for this product. The Depression precipitated the collapse of the international gold standard which had previously kept the price of gold fixed. Soon the price of gold started to float higher and higher in the international markets. The Canadian-dollar price of gold rose from $20.67 per fine troy ounce in 1929 to $35.18 in 1938.[57] Gold fever swept northern Ontario, boosting mining development. Even George Royce, president of Ferranti Canada, spent a good deal of his time pursuing gold mining interests there.

By 1936, over 80 per cent of all the gold ore milled in Ontario came from mines equipped with Ferranti Canada transformers. The reputation of the company's surge absorber systems for ruggedness and reliability led to sales across the industry in Ontario and into Quebec. In places such as Red Lake, Porcupine, Kirkland Lake, Larder Lake, and Rouyn, every major mining company had installed Ferranti equipment. Such was the operational success of the surge absorber system in rural areas that, in 1936, the company proudly proclaimed in its sales literature: "No transformer winding protected by Ferranti Surge Absorbers has failed due to lightning in any year."[58]

Ferranti Canada's presence within the mining community led to sale of other products such as "Flame-Proof Mining Type" transformers. The risk of an electric arc igniting an explosive gas, along with the

Transmission lines and transformers need to be protected from lightning strikes. This was particularly difficult in some rural areas where it was difficult to obtain and maintain the low ground-resistance needed for discharge-type lightning arresters. The Ferranti Surge Absorber developed by Ferranti Canada was virtually independent of ground resistance and could be added to existing transformers or incorporated into the design of new transformers. It was instrumental in the company's success in selling transformers in Northern Ontario's booming mining sector during the 1920s and 1930s. In a clever play on words in the Northern Electric Catalogue No.7, 1935, Ferranti advertised them as Ferr-Anti-Surge Transformers. (Bell Canada Telephone Historical Collection, 92-201, negatives 5 and 9)

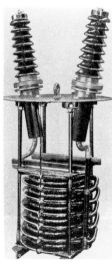

Quality control and testing have long been a major concern of transformer manufacturers. Here Ferranti Canada surge-proof pole-top transformers are pulse tested in the Industry Street plant in Toronto sometime during the 1930s.
(Ontario Archives, Ferranti-Packard Collection, AO 816)

fire hazards of transformer oil, made installation of transformers inside mines of particular concern. Ferranti Canada had developed a distribution transformer whose tank could withstand flames and whose switching system was designed to avoid any arcing in air.

Ferranti Canada continued to expand its role in rural electrification with development of the step-voltage regulator. In 1933 it started investigating production of low-cost, automatic voltage-regulating devices for rural power lines. Efficient operation of lights, electrical appliances, and industrial machinery requires that voltage not vary beyond strict limits. The incandescent light bulb is an example: decrease voltage by a small amount, and intensity drops off considerably; increase it by a small percentage, lifespan is reduced dramatically. Because of the great variations in demand on a power system during a twenty-four-hour period, voltages fluctuate greatly if variations in load or demand are not properly compensated for. By the early 1930s, electric utilities had developed various methods to regu-

Ferranti Canada's development of the Flame Proof Mining Type Distribution Transformer boosted sales in Northern mining areas. These transformers were designed to operate without any electrical sparks or arcing which might ignite explosive dust or gas. They used an oil-immersed switch and, to resist corrosion, the transformer itself was mounted in a flame-proof tank of copper-bearing sheet steel.
(Ontario Archives, Ferranti-Packard Collection, AO 815)

late voltage. Most were applied to the generators and primary distribution lines, with little voltage control being developed for secondary rural lines.

Problems of voltage regulation in rural lines usually resulted from distribution lines running at near capacity. The obvious solution was to upgrade the lines by using larger conductors or to raise the distribution voltage by means of a new substation. Both entailed substantial investments and costly interruptions in service. The economics of rural electrification did not always justify such expenditures, but Ferranti step-voltage regulators offered an inexpensive alternative.

The business of regulators arose out of a proposal brought to Ferranti Canada to develop a "thermal motor" as a means of automatically changing the taps on individual pole-top transformers used in rural areas. The idea was not economically viable. But the research and development experience in thermal motors convinced the company to pursue voltage regulation further. Starting with the astatic relay developed by the parent firm, the Canadian group improved the product and used it to develop an automatic step-voltage regulator suitable for the Canadian rural market. In 1933, it boasted, in its sales literature, of having "supplied the first low-cost automatic voltage boosters in Canada on rural lines."[59]

Throughout the Depression, the sale of surge absorbers and automatic step-voltage regulators increased slowly but steadily, even though the total value of the busines was not very great. By 1937, the Canadian electrical industry started to pick up, and Ferranti Canada showed its first profitable year since the Depression started. In 1937, Ferr-Anti-Surge transformers accounted for nearly 55 per cent of the Ferranti transformers sold. By 1939, 50 per cent of the utility members of the Canadian Electrical Association were using them. The fact that 98 per cent of those sold in 1939 were repeat orders attested to customers' satisfaction.[60]

Sales of automatic step-voltage regulators also increased. However, the real jump there occurred during the Second World War, when large demands on rural lines and restrictions on electrical raw materials made the regulator far cheaper than building additional rural substations. While the war increased demand for regulators because of the expansion of military installations and airports into rural areas, it also led to the demise of the surge absorber. In the interests of conservation, the government ruled that the absorber did not have any priority for allocation of copper.

Pressure to Merge

The climate of the Canadian electrical industry prior to the Depression had been heady. Ferranti Canada, like the rest of the industry, expanded facilities in the expectation of continued growth. The Depression turned expansion into crippling over-capacity and led to pressures to rationalize production through mergers and acquisitions. There is evidence to suggest that, on several occasions, large Canadian

Heavy use of electricity in downtown areas of cities led to an unsightly and often dangerous profusion of overhead wires. One response was to put the delivery system for electric power underground. Underground transformers, also known as subway type transformers, had to be designed to be safe and operational in the event of flooding. In the late 1920s Ferranti Canada started manufacturing its patented "Diving Bell" system to keep transformers watertight in case of flooding. Subsequent designs were less angular.
(Ontario Archives, Ferranti-Packard Collection, AO 813)

and American concerns expressed an interest in acquiring Ferranti Canada. V.Z. de Ferranti, however, made it quite clear that he had no intention of selling his interests in Canada.

On a visit to England in 1935, Mr. Moloney, principal owner of the American Moloney Electric Co., proposed that they merge their Canadian operations. The Canadian electrical market was divided between two classes of manufacturers. The big full-line manufacturers were Canadian Westinghouse, Canadian General Electric, and the English Electric Co. of Canada. Smaller companies – Moloney Electric Co. of Canada, Packard Electric Ltd., and Ferranti Canada – produced a more restricted line of heavy electric equipment, i.e. transformers and meters. Although the Depression sent the entire industry into disarray, its effects were felt most by the smaller companies.

The offer to merge had definitely piqued V.Z. de Ferranti's curiosity. With Moloney's products restricted to pole-top and small power transformers, the merger, at least on paper, promised nearly to double Ferranti's share of the Canadian transformer market. With his own Canadian company having incurred such high losses and running at very high overheads, Ferranti was struck by how well the Moloney Electric Co. of Canada appeared to be weathering the Depression, with lower losses and tight control on overhead.

Cooper saw the prospect of merger as a setback to his own vision of how Ferranti Canada should grow. Though he had a "fair regard" for Moloney's business abilities, he nevertheless saw him as "more of an opportunist than a consistent organizer." He argued that the benefits from a merger were small and did not merit turning over any majority or major minority share of voting stock.[61] Not only were the Moloney losses much higher than stated by its owner, but the low overheads were, in Cooper's mind, a product of a very short-sighted approach to industrial development.[62]

In the wake of the Depression, Cooper's efforts to expand operations had produced considerable overheads. Moloney did no research and development, maintained a minimal engineering department, and thus produced a smaller range of products. Cooper believed in diversity but was unable to tame costs when business was slow. He once admitted that, as result of the Depression, his strategy had produced a company that was "over-organized and over-systematized for the volume of business" that it was doing. Nevertheless, Cooper remained convinced of the soundness of his approach and, in a letter to Ferranti, made it clear that he opposed any mergers with competitors: "The fact that this type of organization and activity has carried us forward into a steadily stronger position with relation not only to the Moloney Company but other independent companies, makes me loath to take a backward step in this respect."[63] The merger never got very far. It is not known whether this was a result of Cooper's objections or resulted from other factors.

A few months later, the possibility of another, far more interesting merger fell into V.Z. de Ferranti's lap. In the summer of 1934, the board of the English Electric Co. fired its president, Mr. Stinson, and general manager, Mr. Ansing. On 1 August 1934, Stinson and Ansing started the Commonwealth Electric Co. Ltd. They then bought an empty factory and set about manufacturing in Welland, Ontario. They raided English Electric and hired the entire engineering staff along with some other senior managers. The entry of another firm further increased excess capacity in the industry. While other companies were trying to maintain some semblance of price stability, Commonwealth started slashing prices in order to gain a foothold in the market. Ferranti, Packard, and Moloney all saw their share of business drop.[64]

English Electric had to rebuild its management and engineering personnel, and in August 1934 the directors hired Andrew Tait as general manager.[65] Tait, previously Montreal sales manager for Packard Electric, was also a major shareholder in that firm. Feeling pressure to expand its capital base, Packard Electric had agreed to merge with English Electric in 1929, and Tait was involved in the negotiations. Both companies had come to terms, but before the documents could be drawn up and signed, the Depression hit and English Electric lost all interest in the merger.

Once Tait had become general manager of English Electric, he offered to sell back his shares in Packard Electric to the small group of shareholders, most of them employees of the company. An informal stock-pooling agreement had meant that shareholders sold only to other members of the pool. Tait, however, found the Packard Electric offer for his shares too low. Frank T. Wyman, president of Packard Electric and major shareholder in the pool, figured that he could just wait Tait out. Tait lost patience and started looking for other buyers.

On hearing of Tait's willingness to sell his shares, Cooper informed V.Z. de Ferranti. Ferranti wanted to purchase controlling interest in Packard Electric. In order to sell his shares, Tait agreed to feel out some of the other Packard shareholders to see if they would also sell to Ferranti. Ferranti was unable to obtain the majority of voting shares but got over one-third of voting common shares. On 3 October 1936, an agreement was signed whereby Tait sold his 4,640 Packard class "A" shares and 11,209 class "B" shares to Ferranti UK for $35,000.[66] Although purchase of the Packard shares by Ferranti Canada had been considered, V.Z. de Ferranti had feared that Canadian utilities would see Packard Electric and Ferranti Canada as a single supplier and, as a result, buy less from each. Consequently, it was thought wiser to buy the shares through Ferranti UK.

Wyman knew nothing of the negotiations until the shares were sold. News of the sale angered Wyman. He considered Ferranti's purchase as a foreign intrusion on Packard's tightly knit family. Wyman was afraid that Ferranti would acquire more of Packard's shares. He lost no time pushing through a new pooling agreement to protect the company from any further Ferranti intrusions: members of the pool were contractually bound to sell only to other members of the pool.

Relations between Wyman and the Ferranti group were cold. Wyman kept Cooper and V.Z. de Ferranti at arm's length from the affairs of Packard Electric and fed them information only on a "need-to-know" basis. As Ferranti UK's proxy, Cooper had the right to attend Packard shareholders' meetings and receive copies of the annual financial statements. These statements were remarkably tight-lipped: a simple balance sheet revealed only total profit or loss.[67]

While V.Z. de Ferranti dreamed of gaining control of Packard Electric and bringing the two together, Wyman repeatedly offered to buy back his shares. On one occasion, he even sent the treasurer, Tom Edmondson, to England to convince Ferranti to sell.[68] In an effort to build stronger ties between Ferranti Canada and Packard Electric during the war, Ferranti suggested to Cooper that the two companies exchange directors. Cooper did not feel that the time was right and recommended that "so long as the war lasts, we should let the Packard dog lie." He added that he "had developed a much improved relationship with the whole Packard organization, and this in all probability can be further improved as the time goes on."[69]

Birth of the X-Ray Division

Keeping a plant operating at full capacity year round is no simple matter. The problem is particularly acute in the watt-hour meter and transformer business, where demand is cyclical. By 1929, Cooper realized that almost-exclusive dependence on one product – pole-top transformers – had left the company especially vulnerable to downturns in the market. Cooper actively pursued diversification but faced many pitfalls it trying to manage this policy. "Technology-driven" product development sometimes led into marginal markets, which spread engineering, manufacturing, and sales resources too thin. Products such as power transformers, regulators, surge protectors, and neon transformers were attempts to lessen dependence on any one product. Cooper even advocated selling non-competing electrical products, such as switches, made by other companies. The parent firm, of course, sold only what it designed and manufactured.

As with Ferranti UK in England, Cooper wanted to diversify beyond the electric power market. By the 1930s, X-ray machines had become an important part of modern medicine. The Victor Co., a subsidiary of Canadian General Electric, had a virtual monopoly on high-voltage X-ray equipment in Canada. With Victor, the sole supplier, setting its own prices, hospitals and doctors welcomed competition.

In 1935, the Winnipeg General Hospital was planning to install a 400-kV X-ray unit. News of this opportunity made its way back to Ferranti UK via the British trade commission in Canada. The company had already supplied 400-kV transformers for the Cancer Free Hospital in London, England. V.Z. de Ferranti suggested that the unit be built in Canada. The British trade commission's reaction to this suggestion was very colonial. The commissioners asked Cooper "if [he]

Ferranti Canada's entry into building medical X-ray units was an attempt to diversify in order to lessen its traditional dependence on the electric utilities market. In 1938 the X-Ray Division launched the *Ferrantigram*, a quarterly newsletter geared primarily to the interests of doctors and hospitals. This 1943 cover for an issue featuring "Heat in Medicine" was designed to be "symbolic of heating by high frequency Radio Waves." (Canada Institute for Scientific and Technical Information, Ottawa)

thought Ferranti Ltd. would make the designs available to some other British manufacturer, so that this equipment could be quoted on for manufacture in England."[70]

Dr. MacMillan, X-ray authority for the Winnipeg General Hospital, was delighted at the prospect of having another Canadian manufacturer of equipment. Dissatisfied with the Victor Co.'s service, he was willing to give Ferranti Canada every consideration. He even offered to supply trained technicians to help develop this class of equipment in Canada. With no experience in X-ray machines, Ferranti Canada's engineers were unsure how to bid on these products.

Cooper wrote to V.Z. de Ferranti: "We are over our heads when we start discussing X-Ray equipment with X-Ray specialists, because we cannot speak their language. In our first contact they asked us questions about the R unit output and details of the filter and valve construction which we could not answer."[71] When Cooper cabled engineers at Ferranti UK for technical information about the Cancer Hospital's X-ray unit, they told him to write to the hospital. Upset at their response, Cooper wrote Ferranti, pointing out that if this important attempt at diversification were to succeed, then Ferranti would have to personally give "instructions to his people to take more than the ordinary interest in Ferranti Canada's requests for information on this type of equipment."[72]

Though Ferranti Canada could build high-voltage X-ray units and had access to the parent firm's technology, it did not have the know-how to market the equipment. If it were to develop X-ray machines into a business it needed people who understood the requirements of the medical profession and the dynamics of the Canadian market.

The Solus X-Ray Co. was one of a handful of firms that hoped to cash in on the growing market for high-voltage units. Created in 1934, it found itself in financial difficulties after two years of operation. Cooper saw Solus as a perfect complement to his own company's electrical manufacturing skills. Solus knew how to sell, and Ferranti Canada, how to build. Cooper acquired Solus's assets and experience in September 1936. He gave the X-ray business to his sales manager, Arnold Brace, to manage. A meter salesman by experience, Brace was thoroughly unfamiliar with the medical market, and his sometimes seemingly autocratic and abrasive nature quickly alienated the entire X-ray staff. Six months later, Cooper was forced to take the

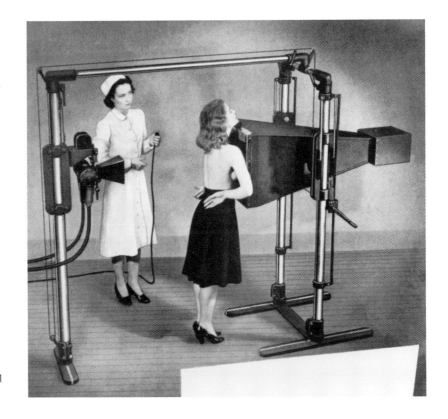

This photograph appared in a 1942 *Ferrantigram* story on Ferranti's new "Photoscope," a high-volume screening device for situations where a large number of people needed a preliminary examination to identify those who needed a full X-ray. As described in the *Ferrantigram*, the "Photoscope produces a miniature Radiograph of remarkable quality at a cost which makes mass savings possible. The Photoscope combines photography and the fluroscope – a camera photographs the image of a special fluoroscopic screen – on small, inexpensive, easily stored 35 mm film. The Photoscope is a single unit, consisting of a light-tight enclosure, carrying the fluroscopic screen at one end and a special camera." Because "speed is an important pre-requisite to making large group surveys," other features aimed at rapid operation. These included an extra cost "exclusive Ferranti feature [–] a fully automatic camera ... to speed up surveys to the almost incredible rate of two hundred examinations per hour." At that time shielding either operator or patient from stray X-rays or low level radiation was not a concern. (Canada Institute for Scientific and Technical Information, Ottawa)

X-ray business away from Brace and create a separate X-Ray Department, with L. Forsyth, former president of Solus, as head.

Buying Solus was a gamble on Cooper's part. Ferranti Canada's performance, though improved from its 1933 low, was still shaky. It was still running a 13.6-per-cent net loss as a proportion of total sales. Cooper sought another market independent of utilities. After three consecutive years of losses in the X-Ray Department, Cooper must surely have had second thoughts about diversification.

Canada's entry into the Second World War changed the fortunes of the X-Ray Department. Ferranti Canada became a major supplier of mobile X-ray units for the Canadian army and also produced "several special X-Ray inspection units for use on the inspection of aircraft castings which were designed for 'continuous batch' operation."[73] With the resulting increase in production, Ferranti Canada cut manufacturing costs and could compete more effectively against the Victor Co. in the sale of X-ray units to doctors' offices, clinics, and hospitals. The X-Ray Department was soon registering impressive revenues and profits, and in November 1944 Canadian Westinghouse signed an agreement to distribute the Ferranti X-ray equipment all across Canada.

The Second World War

Rapid wartime expansion of Canadian industry spurred industrial demand for electrical power. Factories sprang up, seemingly overnight. The nation's electrical distribution systems had to grow in response, and a large number of transformers were needed. From 1939 to 1941, the total value of power and distribution transformers produced in Canada jumped by 384 per cent and 163 per cent, respectively.[74]

The excess capacity of the factory built by Ferranti Canada in 1930 was now put to good use. The Transformer Department was soon humming with activity. Between 1939 and 1941, the value of transformer sales jumped by 183 per cent.[75] In 1941, transformer sales broke the $1-million mark.[76] Even more impressive, the company's net profits rose 423 per cent during the same period.[77] With such profits, the firm could finally pay out dividends to its shareholder, Ferranti Ltd.[78]

Once the electrical infrastructure required by industry had been put in place, demand for transformers diminished. Wartime restrictions on metals prevented certain uses of transformers. The ban on transformers for rural areas and farms badly hurt Ferranti Canada. When the ban was lifted in 1944, the company "was swamped with orders for small rural transformers," but, as Cooper explained at a shareholders' meeting[79]: "Unfortunately, the price ceiling remained at the 1940 level and as a result, these small transformers which normally sold at an extremely small margin of profit, are now, due to increased cost, sold at an actual manufacturing loss. No redress is immediately in sight, and as this type of transformer currently represents an important percentage of our trans-

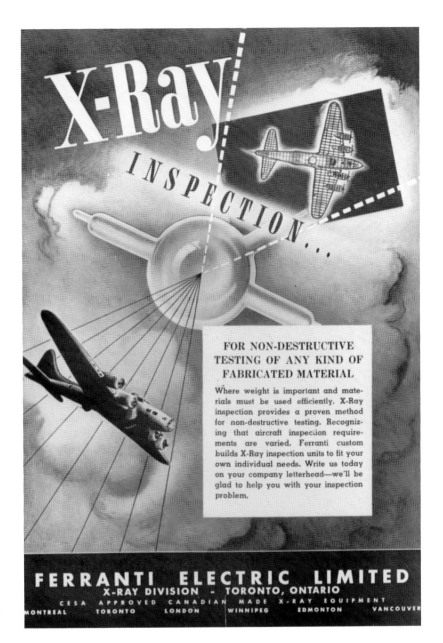

The Second World War provided Ferranti Canada with an opportunity to build and sell many portable medical X-ray field units to the Canadian army. Ferranti Canada also sold much-needed X-ray systems for inspection and non-destructive testing of crucial war materials such as aircraft parts. This system was advertised in the *Ferrantigram*, which, as X-rays found more industrial uses, had expanded its coverage.
(Canada Institute for Scientific and Technical Information, Ottawa)

former business, it seems probable that our current year's operation will be in the red."[80]

The war effort challenged Canadian industry to be flexible, productive, and innovative. Schofield later recalled how Ferranti Canada devoted itself to the wartime needs of Canada and its allies:

The Meter Department made several thousand variable ratio transformers for Radar equipment. On Government contract the Ferranti Company built and supplied special electrical apparatus including control panels for the submarine detection program, transformers, stud welders for ship builders, and

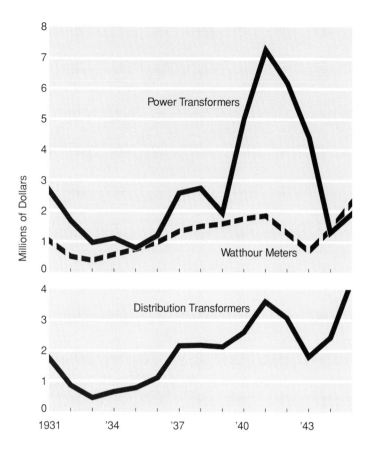

Total Canadian Production of meters, power and distribution transformers, 1931-1945

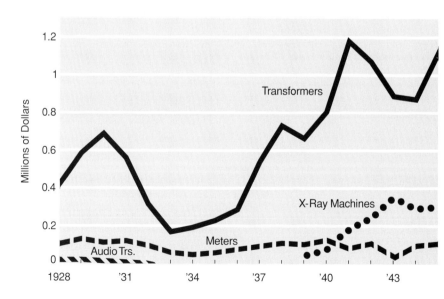

Ferranti Canada's transformer, meters and X-ray sales, 1928-1945

A Canadian sailor operating a Bofors 40 mm anti-aircraft gun during the Second World War. Ferranti Canada first ventured into military manufacture by producing Magslips, which gave the Bofors gun servo-controlled fire, for the British and Canadian navies. (National Archives of Canada, PA 184491)

moving coil regulators for mobile field telephone transmitting stations and selenium rectifier units for mobile telephone exchanges and other similar needs. Shell band heaters of improved design were again manufactured, as their success in the 1914–1918 war was remembered by the manufacturers of projectiles.[81]

Cooper's drive for diversification and the parent firm's technology-driven traditions pushed Ferranti Canada into high-precision ordnance work, an area in which it had no experience. In 1941, the company received a substantial contract from Canada's Department of Munitions and Supply on behalf of the British government to manufacture Magslips – precision instruments vital to the remote-fire-control system of the Bofors 40 mm anti-aircraft gun. The contract, which gave birth to the Ordnance Department, called for production of 1,000 Magslips per month. Ferranti Canada agreed to manage and operate a 30,000-sq-ft (2,760-m²) new, fully equipped manufacturing facility erected on land leased from it and paid for by the Department of Munitions and Supply.

Given its total lack of experience in this line of manufacturing, Ferranti Canada scored a major coup in obtaining this contract. "Magslips were covered by Admiralty specifications and as they had never been made on this continent, doubts were expressed by the Admiralty and other British authorities whether, on account of the precise nature of their construction, they could be manufactured in Canada."[82] Cooper and Chipperfield masterfully convinced government officials in Ottawa that their firm had the requisite skills and staff.

Management, engineers, and workers at Ferranti Canada set about proving how superb Canadian manufacturing skills actually were. By June 1942, production of Magslips had exceeded the agreed-upon rate by 20 per cent. In addition, Ferranti Canada made significant improvements to the Magslips that met with immediate acceptance by the Admiralty. Such acceptance from the notoriously conservative Admiralty was highly unusual. The contract was then extended to 2,000 Magslips per month; this rate, too, was exceeded, and production reached a peak of 2,750 instruments per month. At a time of serious scarcities of material, management reduced production costs to less than half of the original estimate.[83] Such cost reductions were exceedingly rare in military contracts and were an indication of Ferranti Canada's efficient planning, efficient manufacturing, highly productive workers, and talented management.

The success of the Magslip program led to a second military contract, placed in January 1944, to manufacture ARL Plotting Tables for the Royal Canadian Navy. With the Ordnance work, Ferranti Canada established a foothold in the defence business that set the stage for entry into digital electronics.

From their earliest correspondence, in 1922, A.B. Cooper and V.Z. de Ferranti exhibited remarkably similar views on industrial development, the future of the electrical business, and the practice of business in Canada. By the end of the war, Ferranti Ltd.'s corporate traditions of diversification and technology-driven product development had taken firm root in its Canadian subsidiary. Throughout this time, both men had struggled to find an equilibrium between diversification and the needs of both short- and long-term business development. Packard Electric, in contrast, diversified cautiously. While Cooper tried to offset the cyclical nature of the electrical market by spreading the risk over many products and new markets, F.T. Wyman followed the old adage: "Stick to what you know best." Success for Packard Electric was based on aggressive selling, a tight rein on manufacturing costs, a pragmatic approach to product development, and a conservative approach to capital expansion. As a result, the firm generated higher profits, with less capital, than Ferranti Canada. As we shall see in the next two chapters, this disparity in earning power grew in the post-war years and precipitated major restructuring of the two companies.

5 *Packard Electric, 1912–1945*

At the 11th hour of the 11th day of the 11th month of 1918 the Great War, the war to end all wars, ended. Wars stimulate business, but the joys of peace are often tempered by recession, which accompanies the problems of putting the economy and life on a peacetime footing. In Canada and much of the Western world, war was followed by the disappearing businesses of the early 1920s. A few years of prosperity seemed a hollow mockery when the Stock Market Crash of 1929, followed by drought and crop failures, produced the worst depression in Canadian history.

And yet, for all these disasters and portents of failure, there were bright spots in the economy. Rapidly changing technology opened up new opportunities for those who could get beyond mere survival; there were winners during the dark years. Moreover, there were various definitions of winning; for some, it meant simply survival, while for others it meant dramatic growth.

The Opportunities and Costs of War

On 12 November 1912, the directors of Packard Electric Co. Ltd. conducted the last of the formalities to change from dominion to provincial incorporation with R.B. Hamilton as president and general manager. Major corporate changes followed within six weeks; E.F. Seixas resigned as vice-president and relinquished his seat on the board of directors; two other directors, J.B. McAndrew and T.M. McCarron, also resigned.[1] It is not known if these startling changes were the results of dissatisfaction, an unsuccessful palace revolt, or normal attrition. But major changes notwithstanding, R.B. Hamilton, general manager and president, was clearly at the helm.

The directors' meeting of 1 February 1913 resolved to "enter into a contract with R.B. Hamilton to be General Manager of this Company for a period of five years from January late, 1913 upon the terms as to present salary and future increase mentioned in an Agreement dated the 15th day of November between R.B. Hamilton and J.A. Hamilton, of the First Part, and J.H. Baker and A.B. Watson, of the Second Part."[2] Baker and Watson were bankers to Packard Electric.

Soon Hamilton and his colleagues would be manufacturing during wartime. A small producer of electric equipment is less well positioned for contributing to the war effort than industries such as makers of boots, clothing, ships, or automobiles. For Packard Electric, the major event of 1914 seems to have been installation of much-needed automatic sprinklers, indicative of a progressive company.[3]

From December 1915 to December 1917, Packard Electric "did all of the Superintending, and all of the Research and Engineering work connected with the running of the Precision Manufacturing Company Limited."[4] This probably involved some type of war work. Continuing drives to save materials and contribute funds were to characterize both world wars; early in 1916 the firm subscribed $1,000 to the Patriotic Fund.[5]

In October 1916 war news came with far-reaching consequences for Packard Electric. As major shareholder in a private company over which there was no public scrutiny, R.B. Hamilton, general manager and president, must have found it difficult on occasion to separate corporate from personal interests and activities. In a letter of 6 October 1916, Hamilton informed fellow directors about the formation of a new company, a wartime contract, and an infallible system for drawing his salary:

As you know, I have successfully negotiated a large and profitable contract for the manufacture of fuses for our Company and in connection therewith have arranged for an association with an already established fuse-making concern. In order to meet requirements as to factory space, and to avoid complications, it has been decided to handle this fuse contract through a separate company to be known as the Packard Fuse Company, Limited.

As the management of the fuse company will demand the major portion of my time and energies, it is fair that the expenses of the Packard Electric Co. should be reduced thereby and I therefore suggest that in each month in which my joint salaries for the two companies exceed $1250, I will forego a portion of my Packard Electric salary equal to such excess, up to the full amount of such month's salary. In other words, when the Fuse Company gets up to its proposed output, my Packard Electric Company salary will be temporarily entirely discontinued.

It is, however, understood that, as the Fuse business was secured by me for and in the name of the Packard Electric Company, and is being handled through a separate company only for convenience sake, my contract with the Packard Electric Company, dated February 6, 1913, shall apply as to that portion of the Fuse Company's business proportional to the share holding of the Packard Electric Company, such portion being considered equivalent to an equal amount of business transacted by the Packard Electric Company in its own name.

During the early decades of its history Packard Electric manufactured AC electric motors. They were used extensively in the nearby Welland Canal for jobs such as opening lock gates and across Canada in a variety of industrial applications.
(Ontario Archives, Ferranti-Packard Collection, Photo 1621-8)

A Packard employees' picnic at Queenston Heights. Packard took pride in its softball team and a young unidentified lad in front row centre is holding his baseball bat. Slightly behind and to his right, with hands clasped over his knee, is Fred Todd, who became foreman of the Winding Department. The man with the moustache at the left of the front row is believed to be Hugh Malloy, an assembler in the plant. In the second row from the front, the young man with bow tie and dress shirt is Hugh's son, Frank Malloy. Frank become works manager and was known as a very capable but blunt individual. Once he told the young engineer Wordie Hetherington "you are no salesman." Hetherington, who later became president, CEO and chairman of the board, agreed. To Malloy's right is Clarence Spratt, who became vice-president of sales. (Ontario Archives, Ferranti-Packard Collection, AO 697)

I feel that I may congratulate the Directors upon the opportunity now offered our Company, which is by far the most promising of anything we have ever touched.[6]

On the same day, a directors' meeting attended only by R.B. Hamilton, president, J.A. Hamilton, vice-president, J.H. Baker, a banker, and G.C. Rough, secretary treasurer, carried several motions. First, it ratified and confirmed "the agreement entered into between E.B. Cadwell Co. Inc., and the Packard Electric Company, Limited, bearing date October 4, 1916, and having reference to certain contract for the manufacture of No. 101 Fuses, and that the President and Secretary be, and are hereby empowered to sign said agreement on behalf of the Company and to carry out the terms." Packard Electric would borrow $50,000 for purchase of stock in Packard Fuse. Moreover, Baker and Hamilton would represent Packard Electric on the board of Packard Fuse, and Hamilton and Cadwell would be president and vice-president,[7] respectively. Hamilton was clearly at the helm and very well paid: $1,250 per month plus stock dividends and bonus based on sales. One could buy a good new car for less than $1,000.

Packard Fuse prospered. On 8 April 1918, Hamilton wrote to the directors of Packard Electric:

In view of the orders received by the Packard Fuse Company, from the U.S. Government, and the probability of greatly increased business in connection therewith, it seems desirable that I should devote more time to that work than has been possible heretofore, and that other arrangements than at present existing should therefore be made to handle the large transformer business now accessible to this Company. After consultation with members of this Board, as to the best and most practical method of carrying out this plan, I propose:

   1. That I be relieved of the burden of the active management of this Com-

The Packard Electric softball team won the
City and Industrial League Championship
in 1923 by defeating Jordan before a crowd
of 2,500 at Lakeside Park. Packard Electric
had a very active athletic association which
organized a variety of sports and family
events. During the Depression of the 1930s it
turned to assisting needy families.
(Mrs. Lillian Diggins, St Catharines)

pany, and that the General Management be placed in the joint hands of
Mr. G.C. Rough and Mr. F.T. Wyman.

2. That in order to afford them free scope ... I be permitted to resign the
office of president ...

3. That ... during the period of full operation of the Fuse Company, my
entire remuneration will be paid by that Company.

4. That the resolution of the Board relating to the operation and maintenance of my Motor Car be rescinded, as it will no longer be a proper charge
for the Company.

5. That the vacancy in the office of Treasurer be filled by the appointment
of Mr. S.R. Cruikshank to the position of Secretary & Treasurer.[8]

Rough and Wyman would each receive $5,000 per annum plus 1 per
cent of gross sales. At the time of these changes R.B. and J.A. Hamilton owed Packard Electric $38,200.[9]

Packard Fuse, in conjunction with E.B. Cadwell and Canadian
Standard Products, Ltd., continued to obtain government contracts,
but the Hamiltons were drawing further and further away from
Packard Electric. On 22 April 1919, J.A. Hamilton informed the
board that "having sold my stock in the Packard Electric Co. Ltd. I
hereby beg to present my resignation as a Director of said Company
such resignation to take effect immediately."[10] Six months later he

wrote to the firm's bankers that "My brother Ralph B. Hamilton and I are ready to turn over to The Packard Electric Co. Ltd., or to any one the company may name, one hundred (100) shares of the stock of The Gary Safe Co. of Buffalo, and one hundred forty-five (145) shares of the common stock of The Packard Electric Co. Ltd., in consideration of a full release from the Packard Co. to us, and the surrender or cancellation of the various documents now outstanding, evidencing or relating to this indebtedness."[11]

The board, initially thought of relieving the Hamiltons of their joint indebtedness but still trying to collect R.B.'s outstanding debts to the company.[12] However, it was determined after "careful investigation of the financial position of J.A. and R.B. Hamilton ... that the claims of the Company against them were uncollectable, and that their indebtedness to the Company could not be realized in full," and the offer was accepted on 6 November 1919[13].

The repercussions over financial affairs gone sour spread. On 3 January 1920 Secretary Treasurer S.R. Cruikshank wrote Vice-President F.T. Wyman: "As my leave of absence has expired, I herewith tender my resignation as secretary-treasurer of the Packard Electric Co. Limited, the same to take effect at your convenience or when a successor is appointed."[14]

Cruikshank's personal letterhead gave his residence as 133 Geneva Street and his office as Room 4, Packard Electric, and he advertised that he offered "Auditing, Accounting/Bookkeeping Systems Installed/Income Tax Returns Prepared." One wonders how many key executives gave Packard Electric their undivided attention.

Next, George C. Rough resigned as president, effective 31 December 1920. Frank T. Wyman, a professional engineer, assumed the office of president, and W.H. Mandeville, a banker, became vice-president.

Plans, Prospects, and Problems

For the first time since the days of the Packard brothers and their fleeting involvement in Packard Electric Co. Ltd., a professional engineer was at the helm. Frank T. Wyman had been a professor of engineering at the University of Pittsburgh and chief engineer of the Pittsburgh Transformer Co. before joining Packard Electric as chief engineer and then rising to the presidency. C.W. Baker, chief engineer, had extensive experience as an electrical engineer with Westinghouse in both Pittsburgh and Hamilton, Ontario. The two men possessed formidable expertise and experience in design and manufacture of transformers. In addition, Packard had a fine reputation for watt-hour meters for which there would be continuing demand. Other technological and economic factors as well as an important corporate alliance all seemed to point to a bright future. Yet continuing problems would have to be addressed, and the greatest of these were financial.

A 10,000-kVA 25-cycle Packard furnace transformer, photographed 30 November 1917 before the transformer was lowered into its tank, showing the complexity of the parts normally hidden from view. Furnace transformers needed to manufacture special alloy steels were a major part of Packard Electric's war effort. The unidentified employee provides a sense of scale. (Ontario Archives, Ferranti-Packard Collection, AO 808)

Canada in the 1920s

The 1921 census of Canada portrayed a country whose basic industry was agriculture, which employed 38 per cent of the male work-force. Transportation employed 7 per cent, professions 2.9 per cent, mining 1.9 per cent, logging 1.5 per cent, and hunting and fishing 1.1 per cent.[16] But the Canadian economic landscape was changing quickly. Except in the four western provinces, the percentage of labour force involved in agriculture was declining.

Though growing less quickly than pulp and paper, mining and metallurgy had "an even greater impact on the national imagination."[17] The Precambrian Shield, once seen as a formidable obstacle to railways and national development, was now touted as the "northern treasure box" "pulsing with wealth." One promotional piece declared that "Canada would pass through the portals of a great mining era – perhaps the greatest any country in the world has ever known. The nation with mines is the nation that has the whip hand of industry."[18]

In the words of one historian,

when one reviews the statistical dimensions of the new mining boom of the 1920s it is easy to understand this excitement and difficult to avoid succumbing to the superlatives of the stock promoters. ... Between 1921 and 1929 production of silver doubled and that of gold tripled, but nickel, lead, and zinc production quadrupled and copper production was seven times greater in 1929 than in the recession year of 1921. The total value of these six non-ferrous minerals rose without interruption from $41 million in 1921 to $150 million at the end of the decade, and the number of employees involved in producing them increased from 10,000 to 23,000.[19]

The great mining boom that started in the 1920s was not, like many earlier ones, based simply on a single metal such as gold or on one or more new finds which used traditional technology. Instead, "this remarkably rapid expansion came about because of a conjunction of increased demand and improved prospecting, smelting, and refining techniques."[20]

Abundant hydro-electric power, the single most important element in the boom, "could serve as power to run industrial machines and as a cheap source of the energy needed for smelting certain ores."[21] "Almost four times as much electricity was generated in 1930 as in 1921, and every intervening year registered an increase... Canadians could boast that they enjoyed the cheapest power in the world and that only Norway exceeded Canada in per capita generating capacity."[22]

The parallel and interdependent growth in output of industrial hydro-electric power and in mining and metallurgy meant double opportunities for Packard Electric. The firm could offer step-up and step-down transformers for transmission, and it had also identified and become pre-eminent in the specialized market niche of making transformers for electric furnaces.

English industrialist Sir William Siemens – born Karl Wilhelm Sie-

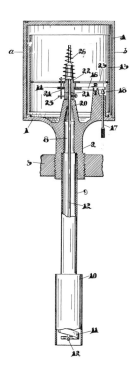

Patent drawing for Canadian Patent 244,397, a Temperature Recording Device invented by Carey W. Baker and assigned to Packard Electric. The drawing is dated 23 January 1922. This indicator would be mounted on the top of a transformer to measure transformer temperatures. Too high a temperature could indicate a transformer malfunction or overload, conditions which could lead to burn out and interruption of service. Ferranti and Packard were fierce competitors in the pole-top distribution-transformer market and it was a measure of the superiority of the Packard Temperature Indicator or Signal that Ferranti offered it to customers. Advertising Leaflet 13A from Ferranti Meter and Transformer Manufacturing Company Ltd. advised customers that "After a careful study and comparisons of various makes of temperatures indicators, this Company [Ferranti] endorses and is prepared to furnish the Packard Temperature Signal on all its standard Pole Type Transformers in size 7 1/2 kVA and above. The Packard Indicator provides at all times a definite indication of the maximum temperature of the transformer. The Signal is so designed that it can be read from the street, and indicates intermediate as well as maximum temperature. We feel that it is the most convenient and helpful device available as a guide to the proper loading of transformers."
(Canada Patent Office)

mens in Germany – constructed the first electric arc furnace in 1879. Sebastian Ziani de Ferranti suggested the induction furnace which became so central in steel metallurgy.[23] Systematic experimentation on the use of electric furnaces for the direct production of pig iron from iron ore had been carried on in Ontario as early as 1905–06 but did not become a major factor until several decades later. In 1930 it was clearly stated that

the electric arc furnace is an important and growing factor in the electrification of the iron, steel and alloy industry. It is being used for turning out superior steel castings, tool and alloy steels, and is designed for use in producing a superlative quality of gray and malleable iron. With the electric arc furnace, all grades of iron and steel which are made in the cupola, crucible, converter, bessemer and open hearth furnaces can be produced in a single electric furnace by means of the melting, refining and superheating processes. This means a saving in labor and material; the result is a better product.[24]

Large quantities of cheap hydro-electric power and suitable transformers also helped revolutionize aluminum production. Because of aluminum's intense affinity for oxygen, production of the pure metal was very costly until introduction of the electrothermal Hall-Heroult process.

Production of steel, and aluminum, and other metallurgical processes, created a great need for specialized transformers capable of handling high amperage, as distinct from distribution transformers, with essentially higher voltage. Packard Electric possessed the expertise, and, equally important, it had the confidence of a major manufacturer of electric metallurgical furnaces, the Volta Manufacturing Co., of nearby Welland, Ontario.

Despite their extremely high efficiency in energy conversion, large transformers generate enormous quantities of heat, so that limiting production and build-up of heat, as well as encouraging its dissipation and monitoring it, affects design and production of transformers.

On 21 July 1922, F.T. Wyman "informed the Shareholders that the Company had patented in Canada, and was already manufacturing a *Transformer Indicating Temperature Signal*, and from the orders and enquiries received, should prove highly profitable when the factory reached its maximum production on same. He also stated that a Patent had been applied for in the United States, and from the Report of the Patent Attorneys – had no doubt of the Patent being granted." Wyman announced as well that "he had opened tentative negotiations with Mr. M.D. Summers of Buffalo, N.Y. who was about to form a company to manufacture the Signals in the United States, and ... strongly recommended that Mr. Summers be granted this contract":[25]

The inventor Carey W. Baker who assigned his patent to Packard Electric Company Limited clearly explained in his patent application that the object of my present invention is to devise an electrical transformer, or other apparatus, to which it is applied, is subjected, and which will also give visible indication of any rise in temperature in the interior of the transformer or apparatus, and the lineman or attendant thus warned should the temperature rise above a predetermined limit. As transformers are usually mounted on poles a considerable distance above ground, an important feature of my invention is the arrangement of the visible signal so that it may be clearly seen from the ground, thus avoiding the necessity of the observer climbing the pole.

Later in the year the directors decided to delay any decision on organizing an American company and agreed to open a patent investment account to represent "the value of certain patents granted the Packard Electric Company Limited, on Transformer Heat Dissipators and Indicating Transformer Temperature Signals."[26] The five-year projection for the Indicating Transformer Temperature Signal in the United States and Canada called for minimum sales of $50,000 per annum, which, with a 10-per-cent royalty, would give that patent alone a healthy value of $25,000 over the five years.

There was also a patent for a transformer Heat Dissipator for which there were already many sales in hand. Wyman reported: "During the year 1922, we have shipped approximately 2100 Transformers, 50% being equipped with our Patented Heat Dissipators. As our total sales will approximate $310,000, 50% would represent the sales due to Heat Dissipators ... Consequently this patent is worth, as a very minimum figure, 2% on $155,000, = $3100 per year, or a total for 5 years of $15,500."[27] By March 1923, further evidence of the value of Packard Electric's patents appeared when the company concluded arrangements with "W.D. Crumpton & Company, New York City, to manufacture and sell the Signals, on a straight royalty basis of 50 cents per Signal."[28]

In his 1918 letter of resignation, R.B. Hamilton had claimed that his departure would afford the new management "free scope in carrying out the plans which have been discussed for the extension of our Transformer and other Electrical business," and he had spoken about "the large Transformer business now accessible to this Company."[29] But many a company has run into trouble during periods of high sales, and Packard Electric appeared to be heading for difficulty.

Chronic Financial Problems

In a very candid letter to shareholders on 19 June 1925, Frank T. Wyman advised that

1924 ... was not very flattering as our net profit was exceedingly small, [but it] ... is really better than would appear at first sight.

In Canada for the past three or four years there has been a great industrial depression, which was worse in 1924 than in any year since before the War.

The wider use of one technology often forces a change in earlier technologies. Greater use of telephone and radio led to increasing dissatisfaction with static caused by electric street-railways whose old-style rectifiers were prone to short circuits, resulting in fluctuating high-frequency voltages which caused phones and radios to pick up static. The 1928 photograph shows a Packard air-core reactor with a mercury-arc rectifier which dampened the static-producing fluctuations. (Ontario Archives, Ferranti-Packard Collection, AO 761)

The interior of the Packard Electric welding shop on Welland Avenue photographed in 1928. This is where transformer tanks were fabricated from sheet steel and pipe. A number of operations were carried on here, including cutting sheet steel on the large cutter or press on the left, bending, gas welding, and spray painting. The long shaft, pulleys, and belts on the left transmitted power from a large motor to individuals machines. Later, as smaller motors became more common and older equipment wore out and was replaced, this kind of power-transmission system was replaced by one electric motor per machine. In this 1928 photograph the man with the suspenders, to the left of the welder, is believed to be Ben Hallett, the welding shop foreman. (Ontario Archives, Ferranti-Packard Collection, AO 754)

Most of this being due to bad governmental conditions, and certainly can be remedied in a short time by a change ...

Furthermore we were faced with another condition, namely, that our transformer prices were not stabilized and we were forced to sell at a price very little above our actual cost in order to obtain business. On meters this has already been remedied and all Companies quote the same price and the profit is excellent, but unfortunately we cannot obtain enough Meter business to carry our Company. We must have Transformer business in order to make the volume sufficient to cover our overhead and give us a profit. We are expecting almost daily that the transformer situation will be remedied and prices stabilized. If this had been done at the beginning of 1924 we would have showed from $50,000.00 to $100,000.00 of clear profit, but until this condition takes place and the general depression of the country is improved we cannot hope to make a very good showing. It means that we have reached the point where all we can do is to mark time until the above conditions are remedied. We really expect that by Fall, the country will become prosperous and ... transformer prices will be stabilized, and the moment that these two events take place, this company is in condition to make an exceedingly handsome profit yearly. We have two excellent lines, namely, Transformers and Meters, and they are well regarded by all of the large buyers in Canada. We have a reputation for our product second to none, and, frankly, we are doing well to hold our own, because there is no doubt the majority of manufacturing companies in Canada have shown a loss during that last two

The back of this photograph, taken 25 November 1929 at Packard Electric in St Catharines, bears the inscription "Annealing ovens for core steel in Transformer Department." Annealing was a very important process. The choice of alloy, manufacturing processes, and annealing before assembly strongly influence transformer performance. Metallurgical advances have greatly increased transformer efficiency. (Ontario Archives, Ferranti-Packard Collection, AO 787)

years. During 1924 we did $450,000.00 worth of business and if the transformer prices had been stabilized and if we had received $600,000.00 worth of business at a reasonable price, we should have cleared $100,000.00[30]

Wyman concluded that "everyone connected with this Company is doing their utmost to get business and make the Company successful. I feel that the Officials, Department Heads, and Salesmen are all to be congratulated on the work that they are doing."

There should be no question as to Wyman's competence and enthusiasm, but perhaps he was being optimistic, perhaps becoming too accustomed to working for a company that appears to have been suffering from chronic financial woes and shortages of cash.

In January 1920, "owing to the very large volume of business on the books, and the ever increasing demand for the products of the Company, it was decided to provide additional working capital to take care of increased production."[31] This was to be achieved not by issuing shares but by increasing indebtedness through five-year notes, but there were far fewer takers than anticipated.[32] In 1921 the company operated at a loss but ceased having to pay "cash on delivery" (COD) for shipments of materials and supplies and started obtaining them "on a thirty to sixty day basis" because it was now meeting supplier's minimum requirement for that privilege – "A/C Receivable exceed the Payables by 52%." In the same year "improved manufacturing methods" and "a slight drop in [costs for] raw materials" meant that the firm was "manufacturing Transformers and Meters at a reduction in cost of approximately 20%."[34]

Midway through 1924 Wyman reported that "some eighteen months ago, your Management adopted a policy of standardizing all our Raw Material, as far as practical. This method reduced our purchasing to the lowest minimum and also brought out merchandise in improved ratio to the amount of our Monthly Sales."[35] He indicated also that "Meter business has been exceptionally good. This department has been operating overtime to keep up with our orders."[36]

There was a small loss in 1925, but midway through 1926 prospects seemed "exceedingly bright, in fact, the factory is literally swamped with work,"[37] and there was a small profit that year.[38] But bonds that the company had issued in 1912 would come due 1 October 1927, and it would have to seek an extension. Early in 1928 Wyman "drew the attention of the Board to the crowded condition of the Company's Head Office, and the lack of conveniences in same,

Packard manufactured and sold transformers in a wide range of sizes and wanted to convey this information visually in advertisements. This late 1920s or early 1930s shot of transformers lined up outside in a storage yard ended up, after retouching (overleaf), as an attractive progression of transformers suitable for use in advertising literature. (Ontario Archives, Ferranti-Packard Collection, AO 772, AO 771)

and stated that an addition to the present office should be arranged for this coming spring in order that the Engineering and Administrative work could be carried out in a more efficient manner."[39]

Business improved, however, and on 2 January 1929 it was agreed that "a 50% bonus on their yearly salary for the year 1928" be given to ten employees, including Wyman, whose salary had already on 9 July 1928 risen from $8,000 to $9,000. The salaries of the others are not known.[40] Business had improved, but such generosity is hard to understand, although it should be noted that all ten of the employees given to 50-per-cent bonus were also shareholders.

Given the chronic financial problems and inadequate facilities of Packard Electric, it is perhaps surprising that early in 1930 the company turned down an offer to sell shares to the public. Wood, Gundy & Co. Ltd. of Toronto had suggested that a new firm be formed with public shares and that Wood Gundy purchase stock worth $300,000, which would allow Packard Electric to retire $100,000 in 7-per-cent notes and provide $200,000 for a sorely needed new building. "After considerable discussion of the proposition," the president was "instructed to write to Messrs. Wood, Gundy & Company, Ltd., declining their offer."[41]

The decision was undoubtedly one of the most revealing and significant made by the directors. Packard Electric needed greater financial resources in the long run, as well as newer facilities. It appears as if the critical issue was independence. The company had long survived against the giants; it had resisted the trend toward merger and had attracted men who valued "going it alone," seemingly at any cost.

Also in 1930, the president received a further raise of $3,000 per annum, and the firm purchased shares and bonds as part of an investment fund for a new building; the following year the company paid dividends."[42] But by 1932 the Depression was making itself felt; Packard Electric lost over $35,000, as compared with a profit of over $34,000 the previous year. Losses continued until 1936.

The company survived the Depression but did not deal with its fundamental financial problems. Excellent products and dedicated employees allowed it to operate, often with ageing equipment, but there was a price to be paid. Packard Electric just was not able to put enough money aside to prepare for the future.

In 1941, V.Z. de Ferranti wrote that "we must pull up our socks and make our profits commensurate with our better equipment and bigger turnover."[43] For years Packard had been pulling its socks up higher and higher; there was now no more room for pulling, and the socks were dangerously thin.

Weathering the Depression

Business must carry on, even when there is a depression. In the spring of 1930, Packard Electric sold 10,000 class B shares to the Power Corp. of Canada, Ltd., for $10,000, with which it then bought "Canadian Bonds, as an investment fund for the proposed new factory building."[44] F.T. Wyman was given a $3,000-per-year raise.

Packard Electric declared dividends in January, March, and June 1931, but on the latter occasion it was recorded that "in consideration of the officers and directors of the Company reducing their salaries, that John H. Baker, John Hutchinson Baker and Blanche K. Baker, waive all rights to a dividend of seventy-five cents (75) per share, declared this day and payable July 2, 1931, on the No Par Class 'A' shares of the Company."[45] Shareholders and directors who had benefited from the good times now put corporate health above personal gain. The same meeting authorized purchase of common stock in Shawinigan Power Co. Ltd., Montreal Light, Heat & Power Co. Ltd., and the Power Corp., to a maximum of $25,000.

As the Depression tightened its grip, Packard Electric went beyond salary reductions and layoffs; it had to spend reserves and defer payment of liabilities. Early in January 1934 the directors decided to issue up to $25,000 of bearer notes to pay off an equal amount in notes maturing 1 May 1934.[46] In April of the same year, it authorized sale of $27,500 of the bonds in the investment account.[47] Customers too were having difficulties. The directors recorded "the acceptance of $8900.00 par value St. John Harbour Commissioners 3% bonds due January 1, 1937 in payment of Accounts Receivable of the Co." They sold the bonds at a discount to raise capital[48].

Better times in 1937 inspired a "10% increase in salary of the President and general staff, effective January 1, 1937,"[49] and a bonus of $2,200 to be distributed among twelve people.[50] The company could once again invest, modestly, in physical additions and improvements. Additions to office and plant cost $9,276.57, and new machinery and equipment $8,650.86, during the year ending 31 December 1937.[51] In 1938 the board approved "purchase of an automatic machine for the meter department at an approximate cost of $4500.00"[52] and spent $9,124.66 on bonds "as an investment for the Company."[53]

In 1939, "Mr. Wyman drew to the attention of the Board that while the salaries of certain senior executives had been adjusted in the past two or three years to compensate in some measure for the drastic reductions made during the depression, the salaries of many junior men had been held in check. He expressed the opinion that as the Company was now in a sound financial condition, attention should be given to adjusting the salaries of these junior men to a more equitable basis. Factory wages should also receive consideration."[54] In October, factory employees got a general 10-per-cent pay increase, and the board approved "the principle of substantial adjustments to the salaries of the junior men, effective for the full year 1939."[55]

Corporate Strengths and Market Niches

As the Canadian Manufacturers Association followed the ravages of the Depression seeking signs of hopes, it reported in January 1934: "A company manufacturing motors and generators states that they reached the bottom of the depression in their business last January and February, when business dwindled to about 15 percent of what would be quite a reasonable capacity for their plant and organization."[56] Unfortunately, no other significant details were given; one does not know whether the unnamed company had overexpanded during the prosperous years nor which market segments it served. Parts of the electrical industry suffered grievously during the Depression, many far worse than Packard Electric.

Cautious expenditures and milking of every ounce of production from existing facilities and equipment had characterized this small-to-medium-sized company in an industry increasingly dominated by giants. This same approach served well during the Depression. Modernization and the quest for greater efficiency were standard engineering responses for many Canadian companies. Although the details of most initiatives have been lost, Packard Electric reported in 1940 that "the development of the new plunger type relay was now perfected and

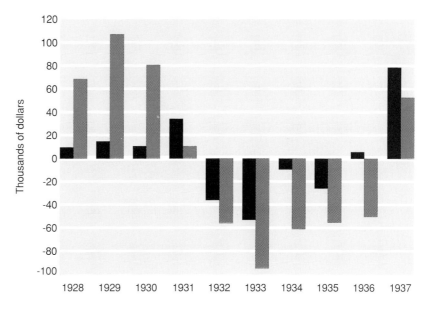

■ Packard Electric ▓ Ferranti Electric, profits and losses, 1928-1937

indicated a production cost of approximately $8.00 factory cost as against $12.50 for the one now being produced."[57] Such a time-consuming development indicates the type of care that helped a small company survive.

Packard Electric benefited as well when others sought efficiency. Much of the January 1936 issue of *Industrial Canada* was devoted to modernization and efficiency as ways to counter the effects of the Depression. The journal pointed out that "modernization is paid for in one way or another whether it is employed or not"[58] and commented that "the advantages of modernization are nowhere more apparent than in the electrical field, the ramifications of which extend throughout the whole of modern industry."[59] While electric welding, including the automatic welding of new all-metal radio tubes, attracted a great deal of attention, the lion's share went to electricity as a source of heat for both heat treatment and melting in electric furnaces. Packard would benefit from some of these changes.

B.J. Coghlin Co., Ltd, a spring manufacturer in Montreal, illustrated modernization that "not only resulted in a better and more uniform product but has also reduced costs." It replaced all of its furnaces with "modern electric or oil-burning furnaces" offering "precise means of controlling temperature," so that one could "produce without guess-work any number of springs of uniform quality to meet any specifications." Such companies were well aware that "two main factors enter into the manufacture of a steel spring: first, the type of steel used and, secondly, the heat treatment given to it." Metallurgical heat treatments were changing radically and rapidly during the 1930s, when astute ob-

The next seven photographs represent the range of people and activities which made Packard Electric such a successful company.

A 3 December 1928 photograph of the Accounting Department reveals an orderly traditional office laid out somewhat like a classroom. Tom Edmondson, then office manager but later president, is at the head of the office looking towards the others. The woman on the right is believed to be Gladys Overholt. The major pieces of office equipment included typewriters, adding machines, cheque-writing machine, ledgers, telephones, and inkwells. A walk-in wall safe is on the right wall. There was no air conditioning and in summer the heat from the overhead lights added to the temperature. Subsequent modernization with higher-wattage indirect lighting made the office even hotter.
(Ontario Archives, Ferranti-Packard Collection, AO 764)

servers realized that "the advance of metallurgical knowledge has changed heat treatment from an art to a science."[60]

Other Canadian companies were switching to electricity for processes that heated but did not melt metals. Thus, for example, Dominion Foundries and Steel Co. Ltd (Dofasco), in Hamilton, Ontario, installed electric annealing furnaces as part of a modernization process aimed at producing a more cost-competitive uniform product. The electric furnace had "new features producing what is known as a bright anneal, and after annealing the silver finish remains. It is the first furnace of its kind installed for tin plate work and working very satisfactorily."[61] Even closer to St. Catharines, Canadian Alloy Steels, Ltd, in Welland, "manufacturers of high speed carbon and alloy tool steels," was making "extensive improvements" in 1934, including "a new two-car type electric annealing furnace ... of the most modern design, having three heating zones, each zone automatically controlled by automatic temperature control equipment."[62]

An early 1930s photograph of the Drafting Department in the upstairs of the original old house office building. With a dirt road outside and no air conditioning, windows were kept open in summer. As a result, drawings and desks seem to have had a permanent coating of dust.

George Murray, who later became works manager – a position which would now be called manufacturing manager – is at the drafting table at the far right. Art Herr, chief draftsman, is in the foreground. Herr was noted for his unwavering attention to punctuality, detail, and precision. Each morning he stood at the door with watch in hand to make sure no one was late. During the worst years of the Depression, when wire suppliers put Packard on a COD basis, Herr rushed to the railway station with cheque in hand when a shipment of wire arrived. (Ontario Archives, Ferranti-Packard Collection, AO 765)

While heat treatment and annealing furnaces increased the need for transformers, even greater scope for change and market inroads came from the steels being produced in increasing quantities.

Automobile manufacturers and component suppliers were hit particularly hard by the Depression, and many went out of business. Those that survived cut back on both employees and investments. Ford Motor Co. of Canada Ltd did the same thing, but when it decided to make its "first major capital investment ... since the beginning of the depression" it was for "a new $425,000 electric furnace foundry." As Wallace B. Campbell, president, explained, "it was necessary because of the inability of the existing electric foundry facilities in Canada to supply the Company's requirements."[63]

The foundry, which opened in May 1935 with one five-ton electric furnace, produced over 450 crankshafts a day for the Ford V-8 engine. Earlier crankshafts had been forged, but these new ones were cast from the steel alloy produced to very exacting specifications in

Working from engineer's specifications the Drafting Department provided fine drawings such as this one, produced in 1926, of a 10,000-kVA 60-cycle transformer. This particular transformer was water cooled, a common practice in the 1920s. Water pumped through pipes drew heat away from the transformer coolant oil more effectively than air. Drawings usually guided those in the plant or on the ship floor, but sometimes were more a record of what had been done. Frank Wyman was a brilliant engineer but Art Herr often found his writing undecipherable. Herr would wait until Wyman's work had been completed, walk into the shop, take measurements, then go back to the drafting office and label the drawing accordingly. (Ferranti-Packard Transformers Ltd.)

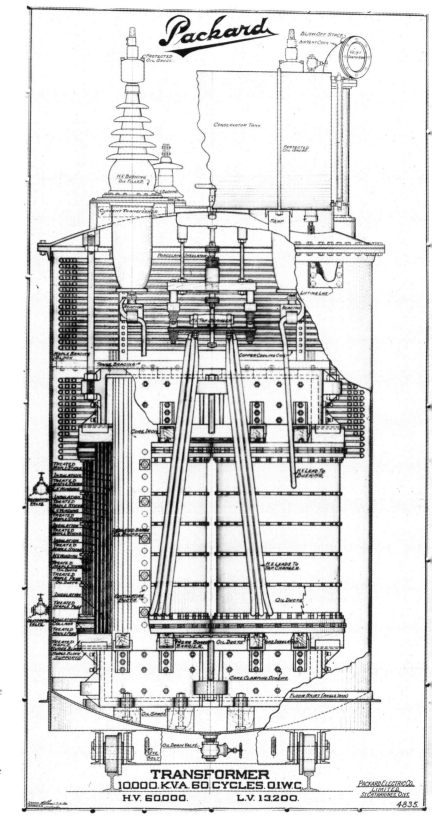

TRANSFORMER
10,000. K.V.A. 60 CYCLES. O.I.W.C.
H.V. 60,000.   L.V. 13,200.

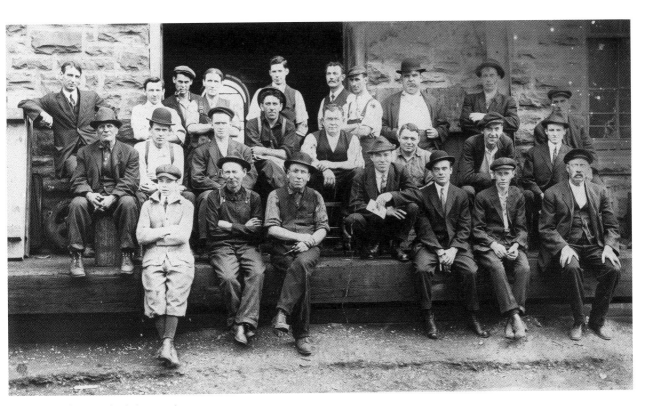

An undated photograph of plant employees outside the Neelon Mill Building in St Catharines. The names of most have been lost but the man third from left smoking a pipe is Art Dean; winder Sid Brennan, wearing a white shirt, is second from the left in the back row. Fifth from left, with a vest and grease-stained shirtsleeve, is Frank Malloy. Men such as these, some of whom were regarded as "characters," were the backbone of the company's reputation for carefully made products.
(Ontario Archives, Ferranti-Packard Collection, AO 696)

the electric furnace. The result was "a better crankshaft ... at a reduced cost." In addition to being stronger, "about a dozen less machining operations are required than with a forged shaft, and only nine pounds of steel is machined off, as against nearly 30 pounds for a forging."[64] In the same year, Ford in Windsor annnounced "enlargement of the recently completed electric furnace foundry which will double its size." The addition, measuring 225 ft by 120 ft, or 69 m by 37 m, would contain a "second automatic electric furnace for making steel" and would be slightly smaller than the first and used "for castings of brake drums and other parts of alloy steel or alloy iron."[65] Other similar installations opened during the Depression. For example, in Orillia a new Canadian firm, Fahralloy Canada, Ltd, manufacturer of stainless steel castings, commenced operations on 25 January 1936 after it had "installed electric furnaces and other equipment" in a "completely remodelled ... old factory formerly used as a lock works."[66]

The breadth of uses to which the new steels were being put was hinted at in a brief article which observed that there were good prospects for Canadian limestones, noted for their hardness, being used more for building purposes because high-speed tool steels and carborundum made them easier to work.[67]

Electricity also became more important in the mining industry. In 1937, 79.7 per cent of Canada's mining industries were electrified; for industry in general the figure stood slightly lower, at 79.2 per

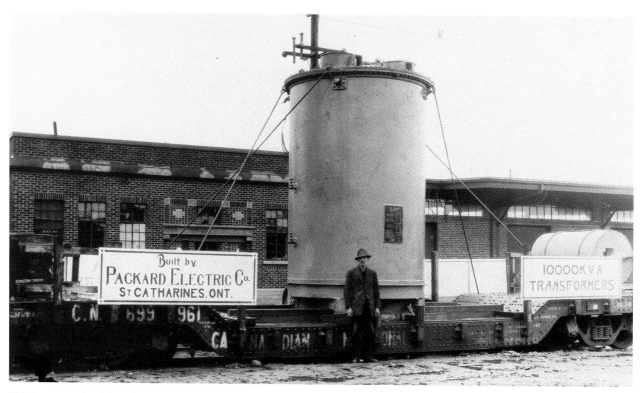

This is an example of the end product of the work of many people. A 10,000-kVA power transformer has been carefully loaded and tied down on a low-boy railway car specially made for carrying heavy equipment, machinery, and oversize loads. Jack Wagstaff, who joined Packard in 1936, remembers that large transformers built in the main plant were taken by special truck to N S & T (Niagara, St Catharines, and Toronto) yards. By that time, N S & T had been bought out by CN. As the truck went along Geneva and Niagara Streets, overhead electric wires had to be pushed up by workmen to clear the transformer. At the yard the transformers were loaded using a hand-powered crane. The workman posing in front of the transformer is believed to be Bill Beck, the watchman. The transformer does not have a pole coming out of the top – that is a hydro pole in the background. This is the type of situation photography books warn against. (Ontario Archives, Ferranti-Packard Collection, AO 798)

cent. In 1923, manufacturing in general had been in the lead, with 61 per cent electrified, whereas mining stood at 57.3 per cent.

Packard Electric had no easy time during the Depression, but its own strengths as well as wider technological developments gave it potential access to healthier market segments than many other Canadian manufacturers. The onset of war would propel Packard even further out of the Depression but would not fundamentally alter its close relationships with the metallurgical industries.

Packard at War: Necessary But Not Glamorous

On 2 October 1939 the directors of Packard Electric decided that employees who enlisted or were called up for active service "on their return shall be given seniority rights for re-employment, and a preference over employees who have joined the Company since September 2, 1939. The Company will endeavour to carry the complete cost of the group Life Insurance of $1000.00 for each employee, until his return, but owing to the excessive extra premium involved for overseas travel, the company reserves the right to modify this position if it is found necessary."[68] Other companies made similar decisions, but it was particularly appropriate for Packard, which was so well known for its family-like atmosphere and sense of responsibility. The meeting of 2 October also voted factory employees a 10-per-cent raise.

By August 1940, the "great increase in war orders" had necessitated expenditure of $5,000 for a new boiler house and equipment, with another $5,000 for a new building to accommodate the Japan (painting) house, printing shop, and advertising office. At the same time the company made its first purchase of Canadian War Bonds.[69] Business, which had been so wanting during the Depression, was now coming in so fast that the president, F.T. Wyman, reminded the directors that "the large increase in business and the difficulty in obtaining experienced help had placed a heavy burden on the staff in general and in his opinion some additional compensation should be made," and it was.[70] In the spring of 1941, an additional $13,996.23 was spent "for special buildings and equipment as approved by the War Contract Depreciation Board," and negotiations had been started for a new factory.[71]

Business kept increasing, but so did living costs, and workers were becoming scarcer, so that raises of between 5 and 10 per cent were necessary to keep employees. Industry was under growing pressure to help finance the war, and in July 1941 Packard bought $50,000 worth of 1941 Victory Loan 3% Bonds,[72] and by October 1943 it had purchased a total of $275,000 in Victory Loan Bonds.[73] It spent $100,000 to extend the office and the plant and to purchase additional equipment under conditions negotiated with the War Contracts Depreciation Board to allow 37.5-per-cent write-off in 1941 and an equal amount in 1942.[74] Such accelerated depreciation helped both government and company. The former saw money invested in war production capability, while accelerated depreciation lessened taxation and effectively freed more of the company's money for expansion, wages, and profits.

Packard Electric's work was not the stuff of headlines. Rather, the direct machinery of war monopolized the headlines, which constantly reminded Canadians about their extraordinary achievements in producing tanks, armoured vehicles, planes, ships, heavy guns, and a host of other products consumed by war. Radio helped keep Canadians informed about the war and the contributions of industry. On 3 April 1941, John R. Read, president of Canadian Westinghouse, Hamilton, spoke on the Tools of War Series broadcast on the CBC National Network. He observed that "behind every phase of the war effort you will find some aspect of the giant Canadian electrical industry."[75]

The electrical industry was one of the cornerstones of home-front production. *Industrial Canada* gave an account of Packard Electric's expanding plant capacity, which would cost $40,000 for a two-storey office 44 ft by 18 ft or 13.4 m by 5.5 m; a two-storey factory addition 100 ft by 30 ft, or 30.5 m by 9.1 m; plus two or three small buildings, as well as $60,000 for equipment. It also noted: "At present, the company's production is devoted almost entirely to transformers for furnishing power to war plants and electric furnaces." That was the heart of the story.[76] The role of Packard Electric, and other similar manufacturers, may be likened to a bridesmaid or a manservant without whom the seemingly more important could not function. The war

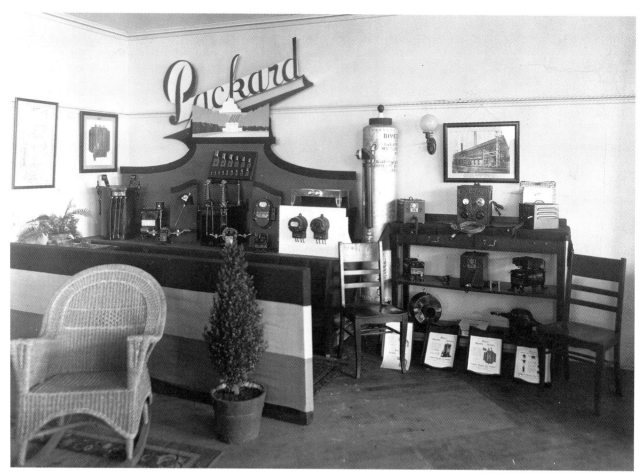

No matter how good they might be, transformers, meters, and other products did not sell themselves. A good sales force, advertising literature, and participation in trade shows, conferences, and conventions were essential. The Packard apparatus display at the 1927 Canadian Electrical Association Convention presented the full Packard line, from small audio transformers, meters, temperature indicators, and small distribution transformers to a drawing and photographs of large transformers.
(Ferranti-Packard Transformers Ltd.)

drew heavily on modern technology, but electricity was crucial to Canada's war contribution, and Packard to the electrical story in Canada.

John Read had pointed out that "the Canadian worker has more electrical energy at his elbow than anybody else in the world, with the exception of the Norwegian. Each Canadian has almost six times more electrical power than the American to help him do his work." Electric power was supplying "over 80 percent of the power used for all purposes in Canada." Since the First World War, production had risen five-fold. The uses to which electricity was put underscored its role as a modern war material. Read touched on the "enormous supplies of power and power equipment ... required in the manufacture of explosives," but added:

Aluminum is a key war metal ... To make aluminum very large amounts of electricity are required. Hitler's successes on the continent of Europe closed off Britain's major source of aluminum. Most of her supplies formerly came from Norway because Norway had great supplies of electric power. For the present time at least, Britain can get no more from that source. In recent months, British housewives have been cheerfully turning in their pots and saucepans to help meet Britain's urgent needs.

But in order to provide Britain with adequate supplies of aluminum, to make absolutely sure she will never want for a single pound of the white metal, a big new aluminum plant is now being constructed.

The plant, at Arvida, Quebec, "represents an investment of about $50,000,000. When completed it will produce enough aluminum every day for the construction of around 130 military aeroplanes." Bringing this project to fruition required prodigious efforts from many sources; "some parts of the Canadian electrical apparatus industry worked twenty-four hours a day to produce electrical conversion equipment, machinery that had never before been made in this country."[77]

Other metals were perceived as equally crucial and dependent on electricity and the electrical-equipment manufacturers. A war-time article titled "Making Specialized Ordnance Steels" stated clearly and succinctly that "under war conditions tool steels are the life blood of

The Packard Electric Co. Ltd. office staff, photographed in front of the main office building, November 1937. Front row, left to right: Cy Hassen, Jerry Disek, Jim MacMillan, Hugh Howes, Art Herr, Clayton Snyder, Tom Edmondson, Frank Wyman, Catharine Monroe, Vi (last name unknown), Helen Garner. Second row, left to right: Jack Wagstaff, Armando Occocupio, Joe Tatarino, Jim Evenden, Wally Thompson, Bert Wigley, John Pidduck, Irving Lorenzen, Norm Service, Bill Flummerfelt, Allan Elderkin, George Murray, Harry Harper. (Ferranti-Packard Transformers Ltd.)

This ad from the 15 August 1945 issue of *Electrical News and Engineering* is a reminder that Packard did more than manufacture transformers for factories and foundries during the Second World War. In addition to instruments for Canadian-built Lancaster bombers, Packard also manufactured the air intakes.
(National Museum of Science and Technology, Ottawa)

production." And this life blood was produced by companies such as Atlas Steel Co., where "melting is accomplished by six electric arc type furnaces – four 30-ton, one 12-ton, and one 6-ton."[78] Hamilton's Steel Company of Canada installed a 70-ton-capacity electric furnace in 1943. The furnace was the largest of its kind in Canada at the time and was expected to produce from 7,000 to 8,000 tons of ingots a month, which would be in addition to the steel already produced in the existing open hearth furnaces.[79] In the same year the Ford Motor Company of Canada made the fourth expansion to its electric foundry since the outbreak of hostilities. The $2,900,000 expansion increased foundry capacity fivefold over pre-war levels so that "all told the foundry will be equipped with 18 large electric steel making furnaces, two iron making furnaces and several smaller induction furnaces."[80]

The strategic importance of electric furnaces reflected back on their makers, and in mid-1942, the "Volta Manufacturing Co. Limited, manufacturer of electric furnaces" in "Welland, Ontario," was reported as "erecting an addition to be used for erection work. The building will be 85 ft. × 50 ft. × 30 ft. [26 by 15.2 by 9.1 m] concrete and steel construction." The addition would "double their capacity and provide employment for 20 more hands."[81] It is often difficult to trace the flow of parts, but in the overall picture of the Canadian electrical industry, Packard Electric supplied crucial components used by others; it was the major, perhaps single, supplier to Volta.

Peace returned in 1945, and in the following year the company hoped for significantly higher transformer sales as soon as post-war strikes and material shortages ended. And at Christmas 1946 there were bonuses, chiefly for key employees whose salaries had been fixed since 1941 as a wartime measure.[82]

The problems and achievements of two world wars, separated by economic depression, had proven that there was a place for a specialized electrical equipment manufacturer dwarfed in size by the giants of the industry, but not in engineering talent, managerial skills, and employees' commitment. But some wondered how much longer Packard Electric could remain an independent entity in an age of ever-rising research and development costs in an increasingly complex industry.

But there was more than wonder and speculation. There was another company with far greater financial resources, a long record of interest, and an underperforming Canadian branch. Moreover, that company knew the details of Packard Electric's much-praised ability to make money under poor conditions. In 1936 Ferranti UK had acquired some of Packard Electric's formerly closely held shares and, with them, the right to financial information.

During the Depression there were only four years when Packard Electric lost money, and by 1937 it was in a position of astounding profitability for the time. Ferranti Canada also suffered during the Depression, but its losses were even greater, despite, or perhaps because of, its newly equipped plant. Vincent Ziani de Ferranti knew what was happening in both companies. Undoubtedly, old longings to acquire control of Packard Electric had been rekindled before 14 July 1941, when he wrote to A.B. Cooper, his Canadian general manager and trusted confidant: "Their net worth is higher than ours, but they have a rotten old building and plant, and are doing less work than we are, so they have less money involved in stock and debtors, but in spite of these two items, they make more profit than we do and have more cash and investments. In other words, we must pull up our socks and make our profits commensurate with our better equipment and bigger turnover."[83]

6   *Ferranti and Packard*

In the preceding chapters we saw how, from the First World War through the Second, Ferranti Canada and Packard Electric tried to establish a secure footing in the Canadian electrical market. As small companies, they both faced, from their earliest days, a common challenge: how to plot a course in a market increasingly dominated by large American-based firms. Though both had to deal with the same national and international market realities, each evolved its own set of management, sales, and engineering strategies.

Packard Electric was a small, independent manufacturer with deep roots in the North American electrical business. Not being the subsidiary of a wealthy parent firm, as were most of its competitors, Packard shaped its corporate decisions by one overriding imperative: "we have to make it alone." That it had survived, even thrived, is clear testimony to its leanness, efficiency, and self-reliance. Lacking direct access to technology from a parent firm, and with limited resources to pursue extensive research and development, it adopted a "market-driven" method for allocating manpower and money for product development. Sticking to what it did best, it developed a very focused approach to engineering, sales, and management.

Ferranti Canada's history, in contrast, reflected the subtle interplay between the parent firm's corporate culture and the Canadian subsidiary's own vision. Ferranti Canada had always looked to the parent firm to finance its expansion programs. Nevertheless, its management pushed for greater marketing and engineering autonomy. In building its own corporate indentity, it inherited Ferranti UK's "technology-driven" philosophy. Under Sebastian Ziani de Ferranti, and later under his son, Vincent, Ferranti UK tackled a wide, often innovative, range of manufacturing activities — electric meters, transformers, textile machinery, radio and television, military research and development, electronics, and even computers after 1945. In the process, it grew into one of Britain's largest technology-driven manufacturers, with thousands of workers and as many corporate departments as it had research interests.

This same product diversification also manifested itself at Ferranti Canada. The parent firm's pursuit of new markets in North America often pushed the Canadian Company into new areas; at other times, product diversification resulted from internal decisions. In 1926, with obvious ambitions to duplicate the parent firm's entry into radio technology, Ferranti Canada added a separate Radio Department to its meter and transformer operations. In 1936, it created the X-Ray Department for production of X-ray equipment. During the war, like its parent firm, it also entered sophisticated ordnance work with creation of its Ordnance Division. And then, shortly after the war, it created the Research Department and became one of the first Canadian companies to pursue electronic digital research – once again paralleling developments in the parent firm. Ferranti Canada's willingness to leap into new engineering and manufacturing areas showed considerable daring and vision, but it also created a real danger of spreading limited management resources and finances too thinly.

Corporate differences notwithstanding, Packard Electric and Ferranti Canada also had some important structural similarities. In terms of size, capital investment, sales, labour force, and product lines, the two resembled each other more than their competitors. They also had a common thread running through their existence – Vincent Ziani de Ferranti, who was knighted in 1960. In 1935, in the midst of the Depression, he managed to acquire a block of Packard Electric stock from a disgruntled shareholder. Ferranti UK's stock purchase was not sufficient to give it controlling interest, but it did give V.Z. de Ferranti access to the firm's inner operations.

As V.Z. de Ferranti followed the growth of Packard Electric through the 1930s and the war years, he became particularly im-

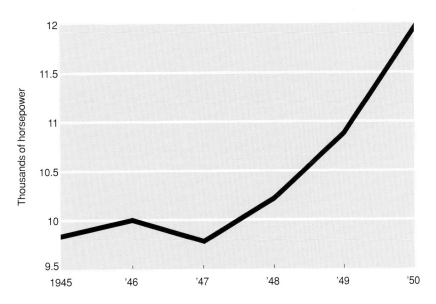

Canada's electric generating capacity, 1945-1950

pressed with the management talents of its president, Tom Edmondson. Trained as an accountant, Edmondson had little understanding of electrical technology but had great business vision and could lead by letting his managers and engineers do what they did best. After the war, de Ferranti tried on numerous occasions to recruit Edmondson as a successor to A.B. Cooper, the president of Ferranti Canada. But Edmondson declined. His deep roots in the St Catharines community, and his strong sense of loyalty would not permit him to go to Toronto and compete against his friends and colleagues at Packard Electric. If de Ferranti wanted Edmondson, he would have to buy Packard Electric.

During the years that followed 1945 a series of events slowly but inexorably pulled Ferranti Canada and Packard Electric together. Four interrelated factors shaped this attraction: (1) the dramatic change in the electrical market brought about by a new Canadian and international economic order; (2) the ability of Ferranti Canada and Packard Electric to respond to these changes; (3) Ferranti UK's fortunes; and (4) the trust and respect between Tom Edmondson and V.Z. de Ferranti.

The Post-War Economic Boom

With the Second World War at an end, a boom in public, consumer, commercial, and industrial spending sent the fortunes of the electrical manufacturing industry soaring. The end of wartime restrictions unleashed a back-log of demand for all things electrical. Demand for electrical consumer products seemed almost insatiable. The massive demobilization of Canadian service personnel pushed residential construction levels to new highs. Production of consumer durable goods, including automobiles, surged ahead to fulfil demand and expectations held in check by depression and war. Cities overhauled and expanded their street lighting. Material prosperity led to construction of many new hospitals and schools as social services expanded. Rural electrification, on hold since the Depression, started in earnest. To meet new demand for goods and services, Canada's industries expanded and modernized. By 1951, manufacturing had more than tripled its spending on new construction.

This activity raised demand for electrical power to unprecedented highs. Within a few years, Canada had the second highest per capita consumption of electricity in the world.[1] By 1947 the electricity-intensive dimension of Canada's post-war growth was severely straining the nation's electric generating capacity, particularly in Ontario. Dr. T.H. Hogg, chairman of the Hydro Electric Power Commission (HEPC) of Ontario, noted in 1946 that "Ontario entered the war with adequate reserves of power. When the war ended we had practically reached the limit of our capacity."[2]

Electric power shortages in Ontario became critical, and blackouts followed. The HEPC was forced to institute a program of energy rationing which caused a great public outcry. Public utilities across the

Shortages of materials, labour, and money during the Second World War sharply curtailed expansion and updating of Canada's electrical-power infrastructure. As a result, some utilities could not keep up with the post-war upsurge in demand for electrical power. In Ontario, brownouts forced Ontario Hydro to restrict certain uses of electrical power. The regulation, here from the 15 November 1947 issue of *Electrical News and Engineering*, appeared in many newspapers and magazines.
(National Museum of Science and Technology, Ottawa)

REGULATIONS

applying to certain uses of

ELECTRICITY IN ONTARIO

WHEREAS the requirements of war production and the scarcity of materials since have restricted the construction of electric power developments;

AND WHEREAS the consumption of electric power has continued to increase at such an accelerated rate since the termination of the war that consumption demand of consumers now serviced, without taking into account pending applications for power, has increased by 25 per centum over the 1945 consumption demand and if the Commission were to carry the reserve of 15 per centum considered provident prior to the war and absorbed in meeting wartime demands, the increase in power requirements would in fact be 40 per centum;

AND WHEREAS the demand upon the Commission for electric power is substantially in excess of its electric power resources, and the Commission is of the opinion that a state of emergency exists and has so declared;

NOW THEREFORE the Commission makes the following regulations:

REGULATIONS MADE BY THE COMMISSION UNDER THE POWER COMMISSION ACT

1. No municipality or municipal commission receiving electrical power from the Commission shall without the written authority of the Commission supply or use or permit to be supplied or used by any person the electrical power or any part thereof for the following purposes:—

   (a) lighting of interior or exterior signs;
   (b) interior or exterior lighting of show windows;
   (c) interior or exterior outline or ornamental lighting;
   (d) interior or exterior lighting for decorative or advertising purposes;
   (e) out-door and flood-lighting for white-ways and for parking lots, used-car lots, service stations and out-door industrial premises above a minimum permissable only between sunset and sunrise, as follows:—
      (i) parking lots and used-car lots, 2 watts per 100 square feet of space only while open for business;
      (ii) service stations, 100 watts per gasoline pump standard, exclusive of lights in pumps, and only while the service station is open for business; and
      (iii) out-door industrial premises, amount necessary for working areas only;
   (f) the operation of air heaters, electric grates or electric boilers used for heating purposes in stores or offices;
   (g) street-lighting between sunrise and sunset;
   (h) lighting of marquees or sidewalk canopies except 2 watts per square foot of floor-space or sidewalk area covered by the marquee or canopy between sunset and sunrise;
   (i) lighting of entrances or exits in excess of 5 watts per foot of width of the entrance or exit; and
   (j) lighting of interiors of business premises after cessation of business with the public except the amount necessary to enable staff to work.

2. These regulations do not apply to,—
   (a) (i) flood-lighting of airports;
      (ii) lighting for police and fire services and protection;
      (iii) lighting required by law; and
      (iv) lighting of direction signs and signs designating the office of a medical practitioner; and
   (b) the use of electricity for interior domestic purposes and in hospitals.

3. No person shall, unless under the written authority of the Commission, take from any municipality or municipal commission any electrical power received from the Commission and use it for the purposes specified in regulation 1.

4. No person shall, unless under the written authority of the Commission, take any electrical power generated or procured by the Commission and use it for the purposes specified in regulation 1.

5. These regulations shall come into force at One o'clock a.m. of the 10th of November, 1947.

If further clarification is required please contact your local Hydro Office.

THE HYDRO-ELECTRIC POWER COMMISSION OF ONTARIO

country embarked on impressive programs of capacity expansion, producing from 1947 a remarkable increase in availability of electric power. After surveying the major utilities across Canada, one electrical journal estimated that approximately $1.6 billion would be spent to expand Canada's power producing capacity over five years.[3] The same journal estimated that an additional 45,000 miles (72,405 km) of electric transmission and distribution would be added to the Canadian power grid over those five years. In Ontario, expenditures for the construction of electric power facilities were second only to road and highway building.[4]

Post-war expansion of Canada's electrical infrastructure presented Ferranti Canada and Packard Electric with wonderful opportunities. The vast number of new electrical services resulting from all the new apartments, homes, businesses, offices, and industries being built needed new watt-hour meters. Feeding power to all these new users required a more extensive distribution network, and hence more distribution transformers. None of this could be done without also expanding the capacity of the primary power transmission system linking the generators to the distant users. This expansion offered both companies their first real opportunity to expand the volume and range of their power transformer businesses.

New Market Opportunities for Meters and Transformers

Watt-hour Meters. Wartime restrictions on new residential construction had severely reduced the sale of meters at Ferranti Canada and Packard Electric. At Ferranti Canada, sales hovered at Depression levels. Post-war construction led to a phenomenal rise in demand: in 1943, Canada produced about 63,000 meters, and in 1949, nearly 600,000!

If there ever was a propitious moment for Ferranti Canada finally to design and sell its own meter, it came in 1945. With the growth of meter production, North American and British meter practices had clearly diverged. Until about 1937, "North American meters were quite similar to their British counterpart, being designed for service indoors, having a separate back cover, and usually using metal front covers. But utilities realized that mounting the meter outdoors would drastically reduce meter reading costs and probably reduce theft by power diversion."[5] Initiated in the United States and introduced to Canada several years later, the outdoor meter caused a revolution in North American meter design. The plug-in–type meter with an all-glass front cover became standard. But the Canadian climate created important technological challenges. Meters had to function uniformly in both very hot and very cold temperatures, and details such as oil-lubrication methods for moving parts had to be redesigned for Canada's cold weather. Outdoor meters also needed better internal corrosion protection, improved weatherproofing, and superior electrical insulation.

Ferranti Canada's dependence on the parent firm's meter designs

Ferranti Electric Advertising Manager Ray Unsworth was also a talented cartoonist who gave Ferranti ads a distinctive humorous touch. This ad appeared in the 1 June 1950 issue of *Electrical News and Engineering*. (National Museum of Science and Technology, Ottawa)

placed it at a serious disadvantage. The pre-war series of Ferranti meters, the FDb, FCb, and FCc, which had been imported from England, never fully met Canadian needs. In 1937, with war looming, Ferranti Canada's executives feared being cut off from their only supply of meter parts. After some discussion, Ferranti UK agreed to transfer meter production and ship the necessary dies and machinery to manufacture the meter in Canada. But war broke out sooner than expected, and British wartime export restrictions ended any hope of shipment. The long-awaited supply of meter manufacturing machinery finally arrived right after the war, and in 1945 Ferranti Canada started to manufacture its own meter.

Ferranti Canada had difficulty marketing its watt-hour meter against the new line being produced by Canadian General Electric. Despite improvements made by its engineers, it was producing an outdated, British-designed product. Sales were buoyed by a booming market, but management knew that it was only a matter of time before their British designed meter fell by the wayside.

Marketing difficulties were compounded by productivity problems. Never having mass-produced meters before, Ferranti Canada had problems getting the required efficiency for its operations. It carried out numerous time-motion studies and instituted incentive programs in an attempt to increase productivity. Even after it increased productivity, meter operations consistently lost money.

After calling for nearly thirty years for more design autonomy, Ferranti Canada finally got permission to design its own watt-hour meter. In 1950, after investing considerable money in retooling, it came out with the Type-FMA and -FMS meters. These were single-phase watt-hour meters equipped with an Alnico V magnet, temperature compensation, and 400-per-cent load compensation, which meant that the meter was accurate even when operating at as much as four times its nominal rating. Meter sales climbed but later flattened. By 1952, the rate of growth of new electrical services in Canada began to taper off.

Packard Electric also saw its own watt-hour meter operation slow during the war. Later, it too was at a disadvantage trying to sell its pre-war Type-A1A and -A1S meters. Robert D. MacKimmie, who joined Packard Electric in 1951 as a meter engineer and became chief engineer, wrote:

The design of these meters was adequate for the time before the war, but manufacture continued into the post-war period where the deficiencies became increasingly apparent. The meters had a very heavy cast iron frame which was expensive to produce, the machining set-up being not too sophisticated, having regard to our small rate of production. The chrome damping magnets were less resistant to demagnetisation due to lightning surges than the new Alnico magnets coming into vogue. Registers depended on oil for low friction, which gave poor light load performance in cold weather. Balance between coils on the three wire meter was poor. The mounting of the separate current element made it difficult to get the required symmetry of air gaps, and cores could shift in transportation causing calibration changes.[6]

Realizing that the firm needed a new meter design to stay competitive, MacKimmie set out to do a systematic study of watt-hour meter technology and Canadian market requirements. Along with Packard's vice-president and general sales manager, Clarence Spratt, he travelled across the country, visiting every major meter shop and speaking to all the principal customers. Based on this survey, Packard Electric produced the B1 meter, which incorporated as many of the survey features as possible. However, as MacKimmie later reflected, "the heavy reliance on survey results meant that we were adopting the most popular features of existing competitive designs that had been introduced before the war. The people surveyed were mostly meter shop personnel and were not aware that GE had already introduced their I50 meter in the U.S. which incorporated many radical innovations."[7]

Two of these new features were magnetic suspension and permanent factory–pre-set power-factor adjustment. The Packard meter could have incorporated similar features. Typical of Packard Electric's caution, management reasoned that its company did not have the market presence to get such novel developments accepted by the typically conservative meter customer. It thought it wiser to wait and let the new designs prove themselves before incorporating them into its product. Not until 1960 were these changes incorporated into the company's meter line.

Distribution Transformers. Ferranti Canada and Packard Electric both found their order books filled as electric utilities started building new distribution lines, as well as overhauling lines neglected during the war. In the four years following the war, the total number of distribution transformers produced in Canada tripled.[8] The rapid rise in demand was accompanied by a new wave of innovations. Offering smaller, lighter, more rugged, and more efficient distribution transformers was as important as proper pricing. Ferranti Canada redesigned its entire line of oil-filled distribution transformers and, with a new type of voltage regulator and self-protected – against lightning surges – pole-top transformer, repeated its pre-war success in rural sales.[9]

In 1953, the firm's engineers came out with the Lock-Wound Core, which reduced the weight of pole-top transformers by 30 per cent and operated at a far smaller exciting current than conventional pole-top transformers. This was achieved by a core wound so as to maximize the magnetic characteristics of the newly available "grain-oriented" steel.

The most significant advance in transformer technology this century occurred in the early 1930s when an American metallurgist, Norman Goss, discovered a process of aligning the magnetic silicon iron crystals in sheet metal along one direction. This new steel revolutionized the transformer's core performance. When a transformer made of this steel was properly assembled, "the saturation improved 50%, the hysteresis losses dropped by a factor of four and the permeability increased fivefold."[10] Smaller transformers implied savings in core steel, in structural and tank steel, and in copper or aluminum winding materials. Pole-top transformers could be more compact and more economical to produce and operate.

Grain-oriented steel did not become commercially viable until 1941. But wartime restrictions limited its use in distribution transformers, and only after the war did it become readily available in Canada. Obtaining its benefits required considerable revisions in the cutting and assembling of cores. One could no longer assemble a core

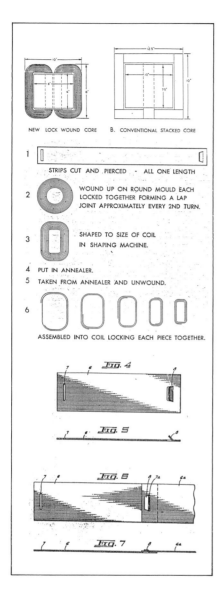

NEW LOCK WOUND CORE   B. CONVENTIONAL STACKED CORE

1   STRIPS CUT AND PIERCED - ALL ONE LENGTH

2   WOUND UP ON ROUND MOULD EACH
LOCKED TOGETHER FORMING A LAP
JOINT APPROXIMATELY EVERY 2ND TURN.

3   SHAPED TO SIZE OF COIL
IN SHAPING MACHINE.

4   PUT IN ANNEALER.

5   TAKEN FROM ANNEALER AND UNWOUND.

6   ASSEMBLED INTO COIL LOCKING EACH PIECE TOGETHER.

FIG. 4

FIG. 5

FIG. 6

FIG. 7

An efficient transformer core allows the magnetic field to flow smoothly without encountering discontinuities in the core material. Stacked cores, assembled by bolting sections together at right angles, have joints whose air-spaces reduce the strength of the magnetic flux, reducing the transformer's efficiency. To overcome this problem, in 1953, Packard Electric developed and successfully marketed the Lock-Wound Transformer. From a manufacturing perspective, success of the Lock-Wound Transformer depended on the development of suitable winding techniques and the invention of the lap-joint by one of Packard Electric's engineers, J.W. Flummerfelt. (*Electrical Digest*, April, 1955, 33, Canada Patent 595,950, Figures 4–7)

from a stack of E-shaped punchings stamped out arbitrarily from sheets of iron.

The ideal way to construct a core with grain-oriented steel is to wind it continuously from one strip of the required width and length. A more practical method is to join up small sheet cuttings – all having the same grain orientation – into one continuous winding. The engineers at Packard Electric found that the conventional "lap-joint" method of joining the cut laminations slipped and produced inconsistent transformer operation. After experimenting with the "lap-joint," the head of Research and Development, J.W. Flummerfelt, came up with a "slot and lip arrangement, with each sheet containing a slot at one end and a lip at the other."[11] The innovation was patented, and everyone had high hopes for this new design.

Future success of the Lock-Wound Core depended on finding a cost-effective method of actually assembling, disassembling, and reassembling the core. Grain-oriented steel brought core design back to the methods of early pioneers, such as Sebastian Ziani de Ferranti. Ferranti's use of iron wire as a core material naturally lent itself to continuously wound cores. The early iron wire-wound cores had been abandoned in favour of the stacked core, developed by William Stanley at Westinghouse, because winding the copper coils around the core did not lend itself to volume manufacturing.

Power Transformers. Until 1948, the value of power transformers produced each year in Canada had never exceeded that of distribution transformers by more than $3–4 million. But in 1948, Canada's utilities, needing to supply larger amounts of electrical energy, expanded their generating and transmission capacity. A central item in the expansion was the power transformer. As technological advances pushed up transmission voltages and increased system power capacities, the associated power transformers became larger, more sophisticated, and very expensive. From 1948 to 1955, the annual value of power transformer production in Canada increased 900 per cent; its 1955 value of $92.5 million was over 4.5 times higher than that for distribution transformers.[12] Both Ferranti Canada and Packard Electric went after the power transformer business.

As far back as 1930, when Ferranti Canada built its new factory on Industry Street in Toronto, A.B. Cooper had wanted to produce power transformers. After 25 years of service, Cooper retired because of poor health in 1947, before he could see his dream realized. He had won the respect and affection of all of the company's employees, and his retirement saddened everyone. At the farewell ceremony, the day in 1930 was recalled when Cooper's wife inaugurated the new factory. A new 30-ton crane had carried the factory's first transformer out to the shipping area after Florence Cooper had launched it with the traditional breaking of a bottle of champagne. At his retirement, Cooper received a motion-picture projector, delivered to him with the same crane, under the control of the man who had operated it in 1930. In recognition of Cooper's great contributions, V.Z. de Ferranti arranged a generous pension, along with emolument as president for as long as Cooper held the office.

Although there was a market for all sizes of power transformers, Ferranti Canada was limited in what it could produce. Unlike the situation with distribution transformers, the design and manufacture of power transformers are a vast and complex undertaking. Because of lack of facilities and experience, Ferranti Canada confined itself to a modest range of power transformers. Charlie Begin, who started with the company in 1947 and rose to be general manager of its Trois-Rivières operation, remembers that the biggest transformer built by the firm in the immediate post-war period was only 5,000 kVA. In 1949, Hydro-Québec ordered four 5,000-kVA, three-phase, 25-cycle transformers, to be installed in the Rouyn-Noranda area.

Despite limitations, the company developed a fair business in power transformers. But the market was calling for larger and larger power transformers. Ferranti Canada found its ability to produce the larger and more profitable transformers limited by its plant – overcrowding, insufficient head room, and the inadequate lifting power of its cranes. Once again the Canadian and British boards would have to consider investing substantial capital for newer and larger manufacturing facilities.

Packard Electric had been designing and building power transformers for considerably longer than Ferranti Canada. Although Packard Electric had developed a well-deserved reputation for its furnace transformers, it still operated under many of the same constraints as Ferranti Canada. It had overcrowded and inadequate facilities and insufficient technical know-how. Technological advances in power transmission required voltage ranges beyond what either company had ever designed. To ensure a profitable share of the market, both companies had to modernize and expand. The methods used by each company are indicative of their differing styles of management.

Packard Electric Expands

F.T. Wyman's frugal approach to capital spending had served the company well, particularly in the late 1940s. By 1950, however, it was apparent to most observers that Packard Electric had to modernize and build new facilities to remain competitive, but Wyman resisted all such plans. With its capital investments in buildings and machinery depreciated by 85 per cent, Packard Electric had to modernize and expand. Growing market opportunities revealed that cramped facilities and old machinery had severely inhibited the company's ability to increase production and sales. A 25-ton crane and limited overhead clearance often blocked the pursuit of contracts. On occasion, engineers had to design a power transformer so that it could fit into the confined workspace of the half-century-old factory.

By late 1950, with Wyman sidelined by failing health, Tom Edmondson assumed a greater role and started to plan for expansion. After four exceptionally profitable years, Edmondson decided that the time

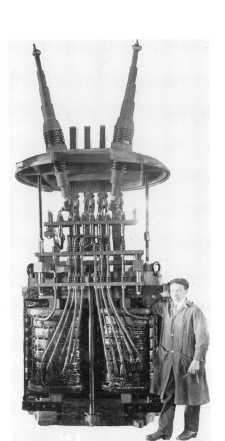

Ferranti Electric had wanted to get into the large power-transformer business since the 1920s, but had very little experience in this area and often looked to its British parent firm for the needed technology transfer. Packard Electric, however, had a long tradition in building power transformers. The power transformer in this photograph was one of six 1,200-kVA, 60-cycle, 60,000- to 100-volt stepdown transformers built in 1914 for Shawinigan Water and Power. Packard Electric invested in this Quebec utility at the height of the Depression. In an era of more formal work dress, skilled workers such as Sid Brennan, who is posed with one of his transformers, regularly wore a shirt and tie covered by a smock coat. (Ferranti-Packard Transformers Ltd.)

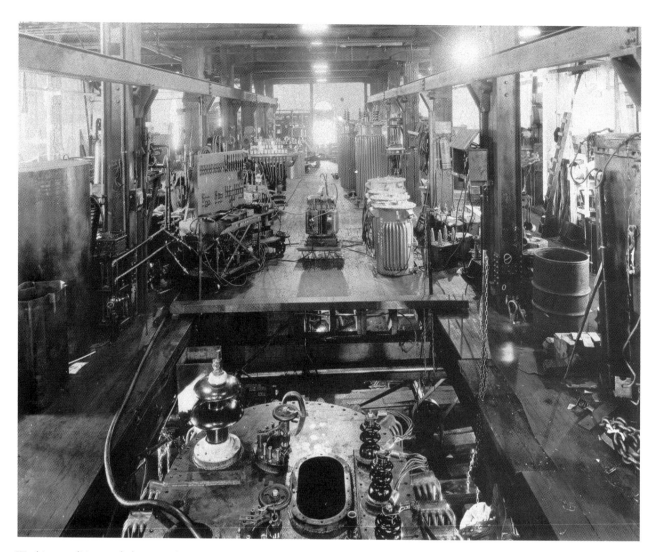

Working conditions and plant capacity changed over time. The photograph above, taken 9 January 1929, shows the "Pit," which had been built beneath the ground floor of the Neelon Mill building to accommodate assembly of larger power transformers. Note that the ceiling and the rails for the overhead travelling crane are relatively low. By the 1950s cramped quarters in the old Neelon Mill and its low crane capacity jeopardized Packard Electrics' ability to pursue the postwar market for large power transformers. (Ontario Archives, Ferranti-Packard Collection, AO 792)

had come to build for the future. In 1951, Packard Electric took the first step of what would be a six-year expansion. Plant No. 2 was built on a 35-acre (14.2-ha) lot in a new industrial area, near the fourth Welland Canal and north of the Queen Elizabeth Way, being developed by the city of St Catharines. In that same year, Edmondson became president and general manager.

In 1954, Packard added a new bay to its No. 2 Plant for research, development, and testing of high-voltage transformers; the addition had new, sophisticated impulse-testing equipment. With the high cost of power transformers, electric power utilities across North America insisted that transformers meet well-defined operational specifications before delivery. New testing technology has been both the cause and effect of utilities' insistence on stringent standards. Most often, economic concerns led utilities to insist on higher operating standards. However, after the war, the public's concern over environmental issues also became a factor. For example, in the 1950s operational noise became a major issue as larger and larger power transformers were installed in residential neighbourhoods. The utilities required manufacturers to test and certify that the transformers did not produce noise above a certain level.

Expanded testing facilities constituted an important part of Packard Electric's strategic plans for power transformer development. Impulse testing had become indispensable for selling power transformers of more than 69,000 volts and established a transformer's ability to withstand lightning surges. Engineers at Packard Electric used impulse testing to ensure that both the windings and the insulation of their transformers could withstand lightning and switching surges at levels equal to or higher than those set by existing standards and specifications. The company's new impulse generator, built by Philips, in Eindhoven, Holland, could generate a 1,400-kV output with a 1.5 × 40–microsecond impulse wave shape. With such sophisticated technology, Packard Electric further increased its credibility in the industry.

Its new manufacturing facilities allowed Packard Electric to ride the tremendous increase in demand for power transformers after 1948. It expanded the scale of production and the capacity and size of its transformers. Its new facilities and products did not go unnoticed in the industry. Articles on its new impulse generator appeared in Canadian trade journals, and it even demonstrated its impulse-testing facilities to the Niagara International Section of the American Institute of Electrical Engineers (AIEE). In a pictorial retrospective, *Electrical Digest* included two Packard products to represent the industry's achievements for 1953: a 30,000-kVA transformer built for Hydro-Québec to use in residential and industrial load service in Montreal's

In 1951, work started on construction of a new plant on the Queen Elizabeth Way in St Catharines. Packard Electric moved from a building near the old Welland Canal to one near the new Welland Canal. (Ferranti-Packard Transformers Ltd.)

west end, and two 16,600-kVA furnace transformers being built for the phosphorus reduction furnace at the Electric Reduction Co. in Buckingham, Quebec. These furnace transformers were then some of the largest furnace transformers ever built in Canada.[13]

Foreign Competition

The record-breaking expansion of Canada's electrical generating and transmitting capacity continued to produce high demand for heavy electrical equipment such as generators, transformers, and switchgear. Post-war prosperity still fuelled heavy demand for electrical appliances and other electrical consumer goods. And yet from 1954 to 1958 a dramatic turn of events shook the Canadian electrical industry and turned post-war buoyancy into apprehension and gloom. After eight years of solid growth, Packard Electric and Ferranti Canada suddenly found themselves struggling to minimize losses at a time when industry and utilities were spending large amounts on power transformers. Ferranti Canada was hit harder, with losses at one point equalling 15 per cent of sales.[14]

The two companies were not alone in their plight. The entire Canadian electrical industry was under siege. In 1955, Kenneth Farmer,

Group photograph of the Packard Electric staff in 1955. The bicycles in the background are inexpensive one-speed coaster-brake models quite unlike the road racers and mountains bikes which are so popular today.
(Ed Love)

After the war, Packard Electric remained a key designer and manufacturer in the specialized market for furnace transformers. This 16,000-kVA furnace transformer was one of two built for the Electric Reduction Co. of Canada, Buckingham, Quebec, for use in a phosphorus-reduction furnace in Varennes, Quebec. John Carrol "Carl" Gray is kneeling inside the transformer tightening a high-voltage connector. In June 1953, *Electrical Digest* featured this transformer in a photo-retrospective of significant events in Canada's electrical industry in 1952. (Ferranti-Packard Transformers Ltd.)

president of the Canadian Electrical Manufacturers Association (CEMA), wrote that "Canada's electrical manufacturers will again be faced with one of the lowest operating profits in the history of the industry."[15]

The low profit rates were distributed unevenly. Hardest hit were the manufacturers of heavy electrical equipment. In 1956, the continued slump manifested itself in a dramatic 75-per-cent drop in the total value of transformers produced in Canada; the value continued to fall for another five years. In 1954 Canadian Westinghouse saw its "net income" drop by 65 per cent, while that of Canadian General Electric (CGE) fell by 35 per cent.[16] The situation prompted H.H. Rogge, president of Canadian Westinghouse, to proclaim that "the electrical industry in Canada was engaged in a struggle to survive."[17]

Why was Canada, the world's second-largest per-capita producer and consumer of electrical power, unable to offer a more profitable electrical market? For the first time, foreign competition had pushed the industry's back to the wall. From 1950 to 1953, the value of imports rose from $116.2 million to $281.7 million – an increase of 140 per cent. While imports made up only 15.4 per cent of the Canadian electrical market in 1948, this figure had grown to 23.7 per cent in 1953.[18]

The increase in foreign competition sparked considerable debate. Who, or what, was to blame? Inefficient Canadian manufacturers? Greedy unions? Insufficient tariff protection? In 1954, the CEMA commissioned Professor F.A. Knox, head of Queen's University's Department of Economic and Political Science, to investigate the problem. The Knox Report (January 1955) dispelled several misconceptions, confirmed what many of the industry's leaders had long suspected, and showed that the challenge of imports was multifaceted.[19]

The report noted a clear geographical split in the origins of imports. American manufacturers were flooding Canada with mass-produced electrical consumer products, while the Europeans, particularly the United Kingdom, Sweden, and Switzerland, were providing an increasing share of Canada's customized heavy electrical equipment, such as large generators and power transformers. Off-shore competition was driving the prices of power transformers down to the point where Canadian companies had to sell at below cost in order to compete.

Getting into the power transformer business entailed considerable capital investments, and one could not simply pull out later. Packard Electric was still carrying the heavy overhead of plant expansion, and Ferranti Canada had already started investing in a large new transformer-manufacturing facility. In 1954 Tom Edmondson wrote a letter to all the company's employees:

I am sorry to say that transformer prices are very bad. Most of the orders this year have been taken at a loss in order to keep our people employed. This, of course, cannot be done for too long. No business can survive unless its operations cover all expenses and provide funds for improvements necessary to keep up with its competition.

On May 19th, we were again faced with a general reduction in power and distribution transformers varying from 3 to 17 per cent and averaging 10 per cent overall. This puts transformer prices back to 1949 values although wages are still 42 per cent higher and materials 23 per cent higher.[20]

Edmondson concluded the letter with the plea: "Each one of us should ask ourself, 'If I was paying for this time or this material, would I consider I was getting full value?'"[21] His strategy was to streamline design and production in an effort to reduce costs. To improve the plant's efficiency, he created a Time Study Department. The Canadian electrical heavy industry, however, required more than just workers' co-operation.

In the late 1950s Packard made a major design change in its furnace transformers. Current flow on the low-voltage side may be in the tens of thousand of amperes. To better accommodate this very large current, Packard Electric moved from copper wire to solid copper bus bars, such as these rising on the left side of this furnace transformer. Wordie Hetherington helped design and sell this successful transformer. Solid bus bars had been available earlier and, almost 40 years after the design change, he recollected that "other than we were accustomed to thinking about wire, I don't know why we didn't change earlier."
(Ferranti-Packard Transformers Ltd.)

While Ferranti Canada struggled with its power transformer operations, Ferranti UK was doing record business in transformers and making very profitable sales to Canada. The most striking example was the ALCAN Kitimat project in British Columbia. In 1951, the Aluminum Co. of Canada (ALCAN) committed $550 million to building the largest hydro-electric project ever financed by private capital in Canada.[22] At a site 350 miles (563 km) north of Vancouver, ALCAN created a huge water-power reserve by damming the Nechako River. From this water reservoir, a 10-mile (16.1-km) tunnel was bored through the mountains to bring water down 2,600 ft (792.5 m) to the floor of the neighbouring Kemano valley, where the generators were located. The electric power from these generators was then transmitted 48 miles (77.23 km) to ALCAN's smelters at Kitimat.

ALCAN's generating station, with a capacity of 1.6 million horsepower, would "generate more electricity than any other plant in operation, except that at Grand Coulee."[23] In 1955, Ferranti UK provided the four 71,000-kVA power transformers needed to boost the transmission voltage up to 301,000 volts from the generators located on the main floor of the powerhouse at Kemano, BC. At the ALCAN smelters in Kitimat, three 37,000-kVA, forced-oil, forced-air Ferranti power transformers stepped incoming transmission down to 13,200 volts.

Ferranti UK's involvement with the ALCAN project is indicative of the inroads that foreign manufacturers had made into the Canadian market. In the ALCAN project, Ferranti UK was not in direct competition with its Canadian subsidiary; the design and manufacturing sophistication of the Kitimat transformers went far beyond Ferranti Canada's capabilities.

Anti-Combines Investigations

While Ferranti Canada and Packard Electric grappled with foreign competition, their business practices came under intense government scrutiny. Post-war Canada had become increasingly sensitive to combines. In 1889, Canada had become one of the first countries to legislate against combines. But the action proved completely ineffectual. In the years that followed, Canada's many efforts in this area met with minimal success. The meagre sums allocated for anti-combines investigation and enforcement reflect the low priority given to anti-combines law.

Restoring free competition after wartime price controls had become the cornerstone of the government's orderly transition to a peacetime economy. Any restraint of trade was painted as injurious to the public good. As a result, Canada's anti-combines machinery geared up. The Combines Investigation Act, however, had several weaknesses, and, by 1950, with inflation becoming a serious problem, the government's inability to control price-fixing became a hot political issue.

Criticism of combine legislation started to mount. Sparked by the

Liberal government's mishandling of a report on combines in the flour-milling industry, the Conservatives and the CCF demanded changes to the act. Continued opposition attacks led to a committee of inquiry, headed by Mr. Justice J.H. MacQuarrie of the Supreme Court of Nova Scotia. In response to the committee's report, Parliament in 1952 amended the existing act. The new legislation continued the traditional "cops and robbers" approach: "the major function of the anti-combines machinery is to prepare the prosecution and punishment of a small minority among businessmen who abuse positions of economic power or engage in unfair economic practices. These men are criminals, and the criminal law is the basic tool for dealing with them."[24]

In 1954, the director of the Combines Investigation and Research Division of the Department of Justice received a formal complaint from "the City Solicitor of the City of Ottawa in which the statement was made that when the Ottawa Hydro Electric Commission asked for tenders in early 1954 for watthour meters the prices quoted by the six suppliers were exactly the same."[25] In light of the government's sensitivity to mounting opposition criticism over combines, an investigation was launched immediately. The five firms involved were Canadian General Electric (CGE), Canadian Westinghouse, Ferranti Canada, Packard Electric, and Sangamo. It was quickly extended to cover the transformer business as well. Within two weeks of Ottawa Hydro's complaint, combines officals, empowered to seize without notice whatever documents they thought pertinent, entered the premises of every manufacturer of heavy electrical equipment.[26] All of Canada's manufacturers of transformers and watt-hour meters were being investigated for possible price-fixing violations.[27]

Meanwhile, the minister of justice launched criminal proceedings, on 10 September 1954, against ten Canadian wire and cable companies for price-fixing; these cases came to trial 10 January 1955. After nearly ten weeks of testimony, Chief Justice James C. McRuer, of the High Court of Ontario, found all the defendants guilty of operating a combine: "The irresistible conclusion from the evidence is that whenever there was a suggestion of competition raising its head, the combined action of all the accused was brought to bear, not only for the purpose of lessening it, but to extinguish it."[28] The bad publicity and guilty verdict no doubt fuelled further suspicions concerning the transformer and watt-hour-meter manufacturers.

The manufacturers set up a Law Committee to ensure timely exchange of information. In October 1954, fourteen solicitors representing all the companies met at the Royal York Hotel in Toronto to plan a co-ordinated response. Because of the large volume of documents seized, and later returned after copies had been made, the group agreed to establish a common pool of information. Packard Electric's solicitor, Murton Seymour, wrote to Tom Edmondson,

Several of the Solicitors present who have been through the Dental, Paper, and Wire & Cable combines investigations, were very strongly of the opinion that we should immediately have all the documents which have been ex-tracted from the various companies by the investigators, examined and cross-indexed by some person competent to do the work so that every company would have an idea of what the other company's documents are and it could be determined whether there is any pattern of investigation disclosed by the types and dates of documents extracted by the investigators.[29]

What conclusions could the government draw from the thousands of documents seized? What kind of case could T.D. MacDonald, director of investigations and research, prepare from the available evidence? How effective would it be? Good answers to these questions had to be found before the companies' solicitors could plot their strategy. To provide these answers, the companies organized an impartial investi-gation and chose R.H. Hogge to conduct it for them. The thousands of pages of seized documents were carefully analysed, and officials in all the companies were interviewed.

Some of the documents seized were no doubt very sensitive and never intended to be seen by competitors. Tom Edmondson was thus very reluctant to let Hogge have access to the most confidential items. Hogge wrote to Murton Seymour:

In regards to the confidential documents, I appreciate that these may place you in an awkward position with your client. However, if I may, I would like to make a few general observations on this point.

First of all, my position is that of an impartial analyst. In this regard, these documents, in my hands, should fare no worse than being in the hands of the government investigators.

In any event, every effort should be made to place my investigations on an equal footing with those being conducted by the Government. Such equality can only be obtained by placing all the documents seized by the investigators at my disposal.

Last of all, it is extremely difficult to assess the value of a document as it stands alone. In the investigations I have conducted thus far on the Watthour Meter problem, I find that there are a large number of documents, which, taken by themselves, appear meaningless in a combines inquiry. However, when taken and placed with a series of documents taken from other compa-nies, they form segments of a complete picture.[30]

By 1955, a member of the Restrictive Trades Practices Commission and government officers were taking sworn testimony. Selected offi-cers from each company were asked to respond to specific questions put forward by the investigators. J. Thomson, A. Brace, and J. Pratt testified for Ferranti Canada, while T. Edmondson and D. Martin represented Packard Electric. The officials were free to add any evi-dence that they felt necessary to support their side of the story.

According to government documents, "the evidence secured [by the government] indicated that collusive agreements were entered into by the industry in 1927 relating to the establishment of common prices, terms and conditions of sale [of transformers], and that they fell into disuse during the war."[31] One had only to look at the steady decline in the transformer price index since 1949 and the intense domestic competition in transformers to realize that formal price-fixing arrangements had long ceased to exist. But in certain circumstances, price-fixing had given way to a very informal, "follow-the-leader" kind of arrangement. Many of the old-timers at Ferranti Canada and Packard Electric remember that it had been common practice for smaller companies, such as their own, to follow the pricing lead of the bigger companies. As we shall see, Tom Edmondson argued quite convincingly that it was absurd to think that small companies, such as Packard Electric and Ferranti Canada, could ever set prices. This system of price leadership was by no means an organized conspiracy.

As the investigations dragged on for over eighteen months, the Law Committee met many times in an effort to reach a consensus on strategy. Uncertain as to how far the government was willing to go with the evidence at hand, "One or two counsels expressed the view that the companies might just as well throw up their hands, plead guilty, save the costs of the examination and the trial and endeavour to keep the fines to a minimum."[32] Others felt that the government was still a long way from making a final decision on whether to proceed. By the end of 1955, T.D. MacDonald still had not sent the case to the Restrictive Trade Practices Commission, which would advise the government whether to prosecute.

Most on the Law Committee believed that even if the case got to the minister, he would have a hard time convincing cabinet to go along with laying charges. Seymour wrote to Tom Edmondson: "Some of us believe that ... the Cabinet may find it very difficult to justify the laying of charges against an industry which is so obviously in a loss position and not one making substantial profits as was the case in previous prosecutions. Then, too, this is an industry which does not deal directly with the public, of which the public is really little aware and, therefore, there is not likely to be any public clamour for prosecutions as could be the case with an industry whose products are sold directly to the public."[33]

For Edmondson the matter was clear. The idea of price conspiracy was ridiculous, and Packard Electric had not violated the Combines Investigation Act. Edmondson had instructed Seymour to raise the subject of price leadership with the lawyers of the other companies. In Edmondson's view, if the industry were guilty of anything, it was price leadership, and that this did not represent a conspiracy to fix prices.

When Seymour raised price leadership with the other lawyers, it met with little response. After discussions with Edmondson, Seymour persisted in pressing this view: "After two or three meetings ... some of the counsels began to agree that it presented if not a complete answer, at least the only possible way out and that the information they had obtained from their own clients tended to support that view."[34] Seymour then pointed out to Edmondson: "in the discussion they [i.e.

the various lawyers] had with their clients they found that their clients had been approaching the matter from a somewhat wrong viewpoint and making assumptions as to the price fixing activities of the group that were not really justified after examining and re-examining the situation. Finally Westinghouse came around to that view and Mr. Bruce [its lawyer] and I felt the time had arrived to discuss it with counsel for Ferranti ... and with counsel for C.G.E."[35]

Lawyers for Ferranti, CGE, and Westinghouse were still unconvinced about the price leadership approach. But Tom Edmondson demonstrated quite convincingly that price leadership, not collusion, was the only way to explain the evidence gathered by the government. For price-fixing to work, some sort of sales-quota system must be worked out within the combine. Edmondson argued that it would be absurd for smaller companies like his own to enter any such arrangement with the larger companies, such as CGE and Westinghouse, without some sort of quota system on the supply of grain-oriented steel to the various members of the combine. Edmondson, through his lawyer, presented data on the purchases of grain-oriented steel that showed the absence of any quota system. This argument won over the lawyers of CGE, Canadian Westinghouse, and Ferranti Canada.

Seymour felt that a consistent presentation of this argument would make it difficult for the combines machinery to continue the investigation. Getting all the lawyers to agree to this approach was the turning point in the companies' case. "It has not been easy," wrote Seymour to Edmondson, "to swing counsel to our viewpoint, but I think it has been successful, therefore I think that we have made a very real and substantial contribution."[36]

Ferranti Canada, Packard Electric, and the other companies anxiously awaited the government's decision. On 9 April 1956, T.D. MacDonald wrote Edmondson: "In the matter of the Combines Investigation Act and in the matter of an inquiry relating to the manufacture, distribution and sale of transformers – I wish to advise you that, due to lack of detailed evidence, and the recent dissolution of arrangements among certain of the companies, I have decided to discontinue this inquiry."[37] He also dropped the investigation of watt-hour meters. But in that case, he wrote in a separate letter, "Some of the documentary evidence indicated the likely existence, some years ago, of arrangements contrary to the Combines Investigation Act, among certain companies. There is no substantial evidence, however, that such arrangements have continued into recent years and, in these circumstances, I felt that no useful purpose would be served by continuing the inquiry."[38]

Four years later, in 1960, the electical industry came under government scrutiny again. In both cases, in 1956 and 1960, the government used the Combines Investigation Act during a period when the industry was facing serious foreign competition and losing money. Timing of these actions raises serious questions. Does ensuring the lowest possible prices in the marketplace always serve the national good? Is unbridled competition always desirable if it threatens the survival of a vital industry?

New International Trading Relations

The debate over the role of protective tariffs for the electrical industry raged on throughout the 1950s. Some in the industry believed that Canada had given too much away too soon in the General Agreement on Tariffs and Trade (GATT). The Knox Report concluded that the new tariff reductions were not responsible for the industry's plight. From its earliest days, the industry had been nurtured under a cover of protective tariffs. The National Policy had sought to encourage the growth of an indigenous manufacturing capacity.

However, after 1945, Canada entered a new era of international trade relations. As a signatory to the first GATT treaty, in 1947, it hoped to stimulate economic development by a general lowering of tariffs. It wanted to secure foreign markets for its traditional resource-based exports: agricultural, fishery, forest-derived, and mining products. In return for lowering tarrifs on imported manufactured goods, Canada obtained lower tariffs for its resource-based exports.

By 1955, tariffs on imported electrical goods reached their lowest level in 75 years.[39] Some felt that the reduction of tariffs had taken place too hastily and had precipitated a crisis in the industry. The president of the CEMA, Kenneth Farmer, protested in 1955 that Canada had become a "sitting duck" for world manufacturers.[40] Pointing to the disastrous effect of tariff reduction on the textile industry, he argued that a similar fate could befall electrical manufacturers. For the CEMA, "every indication pointed to a similar trend in the electrical manufacturing industry."[41]

Industry spokesmen warned government that the industry was too vital too suffer that fate. At the height of Cold War tensions, the president of Canadian Westinghouse pointed out: "the Canadian electrical manufacturing industry is a repository of a wide variety of skills, all vital to defense ... Certainly in the interests both of the defense of our country, and of a healthy economy, Canada needs a thriving electrical manufacturing industry. And any menace to the health of that industry threatens to weaken not only the Canadian economy, but, in the long run, the very capacity of the nation to meet whatever challenge the future may bring."[42]

While manufacturers were protesting the growing penetration of foreign imports, some economists were arguing that the increase in foreign competition represented a return to a more balanced partition of the market. In a submission to the Royal Commission on Canada's Economic Prospects in 1956, C. Barber, a Queen's University professor of economics and an author of the Knox Report, explained:

During the war and again during the period of defence buildup after the outbreak of the Korean War in 1950, imports were restricted by priorities and the unavailability of supplies. Again during much of the post-war period foreign suppliers were too busy producing for their domestic market to pay much attention to the Canadian market. For a short period from 1948 to 1950, the availability of imported electrical equipment was further restricted by the dollar saving import restrictions that the government imposed near the end of 1947. These special limitations have gradually disappeared during the past few years and as result there has been a rapid increase in the import share of the market.[43]

Tariff reductions were not at the heart of the problem. Neither were superior technology and productivity. Canadian know-how and labour productivity were comparable to those in competing nations. Rather, the Knox Report pointed to major post-war currency devaluations as the reason for the startling success of imported European power transformers. British currency had been devalued relative to the Canadian dollar during the war. But an even bigger devaluation occurred in the fall of 1949. From September 1949 to the end on 1953, the British pound sterling fell by 32 per cent relative to the Canadian dollar,[44] giving British power transformer manufacturers an important competitive advantage.

Since labour is such a major component in the making of power transformers, Canadian producers stressed the high cost of Canadian labour. The post-war boom in the mining- and forest-products industries drove wage levels up, as manufacturers had to compete with these industries for workers. This fact, coupled with the ability of organized labour to win higher wages in prosperous times, increased Canadian wages to 327 per cent of their pre-war levels.[45]

A condensation of the Knox Report, prepared by the CEMA, singled out labour costs as a major reason for Canada's inability to compete: "The rapidity of the recent rises in wages paid to Canadian electrical workers, which has been faster than the rise in wage rates in any competing country, and faster than the rise in productivity per worker in the Canadian electrical manufacturing industry."[46] But the Knox Report had pointed out that, after devaluation was factored out, British wage rates had grown just as fast as Canadian ones.[47]

Heated debate ensured as to whether excessive wage demands by organized labour had crippled the industry's competitiveness. Every company in the industry was touched directly by this debate, as labour and management struggled to impose their views. This battle raged on within Ferranti Canada, and later Ferranti-Packard, for years and resulted in bitter labour conflicts and strikes. At the Toronto plant, a touchy situation was worsened by a union whose leadership was clearly out of step with most of the labour union movement in Canada.

Ferranti Canada's New Plant

Changing market requirements had created demand for ever-larger power transformers. The increased demand for electrical energy in

Canada's urban areas greatly increased the load, as measured by kVA, which power transformers had to carry. As load requirements for transformers rose, so did the physical size of transformers. In addition, higher transmission voltages which require bigger transformers were being used to send power further.

By the early 1950s, Ferranti Canada realized that its existing facilities could not build larger and larger power transformers. From realization to implementation took five years. Finally, in early 1955, the board of directors agreed to a $2.6-million program of modernization and expansion. Capitalization for this project had started in 1949, when Ferranti UK had pumped more money into its Canadian subsidiary, increasing authorized stock from $500,000 to $3 million, while the value of shares held by Ferranti Ltd jumped from $500,000 to $2 million. By 1956, stock purchases poured in more capital: the value of authorized stock for Ferranti Canada had risen to $6 million, and Ferranti UK owned $3 million in shares.

On 8 February 1956, Vincent Ziani de Ferranti officially opened Ferranti Canada's impressive new transformer manufacturing facility. This spacious new plant was built to handle very big power transformers – as large as 100,000 kVA, it was claimed.

With the new plant, Ferranti Canada tried to make one giant step from 7,500 kVA to 100,000 kVA. The company's transformer sales and profits had peaked in 1952 and continually declined thereafter. Nonetheless Dr. John Thomson, president and general manager, had pushed for the new plant on the grounds that it was essential. Ferranti UK's board had approved the plan. Unfortunately, Canadian output of transformers had reached its peak. Within one year of the plant's opening, the total value of Canadian production plunged. As the reader will recall, the Depression had hit just when the first factory was built in 1929.

Labour Relations at Ferranti Canada

No sooner had Ferranti Canada started operations in its new plant than, on 14 May 1956, workers' frustration over contract negotiations erupted into a strike. At the centre of this strike was one of Canada's most controversial unions, the United Electrical Workers (UE), which today is known as the United Electrical, Radio and Machine Workers Union. Events leading up to, and during, the strike reveal the destructive role that suspicion and lack of communication can have on management-labour relations. These problems were spawned by union militancy and the company's reluctance to accept the union's new post-war bargaining power. To appreciate the militancy and Ferranti Canada's perception of it, one must examine the turbulent history of this union.

The UE was created in 1937 as part of a growing form of worker organization called industrial unionism. By the 1930s, many in the factory-based segment of the labour movement had become disgruntled with the concept of craft unions. Membership in a particular

Access to new markets often requires new facilities. In 1956, Ferranti Electric built a major addition to its Industry Street plant in Toronto in order to accommodate the construction of large power transformers. (Ferranti-Packard Transformers Ltd.)

union comprised all workers from a given craft, or trade, regardless of their place of work. Futhermore, in any one plant, there would be as many unions as there were definable crafts. This type of horizontal organization greatly limited unions' bargaining strength and excluded the mass of semi-skilled and unskilled workers.

In contrast, an industrial union would represent all workers in a given plant – "one union, one boss." Such a method seemed utopian to craft union leaders, such as Samuel Gompers, president of the American Federation of Labour (AFL). But in the United States, the Wagner Act of 1935, passed under President Franklin Roosevelt's New Deal, offered industrial unions new opportunities for organizing: "At one blow, the Wagner Act created a legal procedure which forced the employer to accept an orderly, legal process by which workers could choose their own bargaining agent."[48] In the wake of the Wagner Act was born the American Congress of Industrial Organizations (CIO) in 1935. The CIO's success in organizing industrial unions was astonishing.

The Canadian equivalent of the CIO, the Canadian Congress of Labour (CCL), was formed in 1940 out of an uncomfortable alliance between the Co-operative Commonwealth Federation (CCF) and the communist-run Workers Unity League in Canada. For the communists, who wanted to turn the CCL into a radical political force, the grass-roots western socialist party became an obstacle that had to be destroyed.

The UE was one of the first affiliates of the CCL, and, under C.S. Jackson's leadership, its communist sympathies were evident from its inception. Jackson's attachment to Soviet communism was nowhere more apparent than in contradictory positions that he, and other Canadian communists, advocated as the war in Europe continued. In a balanced view of the Canadian labour movement's struggle for economic and social justice, Desmond Morton observes: "Until only weeks before the outbreak of the war, the communists had been almost frenzied in their efforts to build a popular front against Hitler and fascism. No issue mattered more. Suddenly, with announcement of the Nazi-Soviet pact, no issue mattered less. Never had the contradictory orders from Moscow demanded a more humiliating change of line. In hours the popular-front slogans were forgotten. Loyal Communists, open and secret, accepted a fresh directive: the war with Hitler was the last gasp of a decaying bourgeoisie and should be sabotaged in any useful way."[49]

Prime Minister William Lyon Mackenzie King's tolerance of the communists and their anti-war, pro-Moscow stance ended in 1941 with the internment of 98 prominent communists. Among them was C.S. Jackson. The UE, however, has a different version of events. Preferring to gloss over the communists' opposition to the "phoney war," the UE casts Jackson as a martyr in the labour struggle against Canadian General Electric (CGE):

Thus the first concrete steps toward a collective agreement with the giant CGE were taken. However, it was not without great cost. Fifteen stewards and local leaders were hauled into court and fined $120 each for participation in an unlawful strike, and UE President C.S. Jackson, active in the CGE organization and strike, was whisked off to an internment camp and held there for six months.

CGE's complicity in this internment was clearly indicated in the ensuing months which they utilized to win over some of the union leadership to a company union status, and to pressure that group into signing off on a weak and company union-type contract, on the threat of Jackson's impending release from internment.[50]

When Hitler broke his non-aggression pact with the Soviet Union in the summer of 1941, the war took a new turn for Canada's communists. The Soviet Union had now become a member of the Allied

Forces. Once again, communists flipped back to their earlier position that the war was a crusade against the evil forces of fascism. Suddenly, the communist-led unions became an unexpected ally of the King government. By condemning strikes and other labour disruptions as unpatriotic, the communist labour leaders helped maintain labour peace during the war. With this new patriotic stance, the communists were able to mount sufficient public pressure to get Jackson and others released.

Dissatisfied with the International Brotherhood of Electrical Workers (IBEW) and attracted by the militant promises of the UE to win better conditions, workers at Ferranti Canada voted in the UE in the fall of 1943. The first wage agreement between the new union and management was signed on 4 February 1944, and it included "one weeks vacation after one year's service – 'till that time you had to work three years to get one week vacation'."[51] The UE's success in organizing the Ferranti Canada plant was indicative of its rising fortunes. As one Canadian historian noted, "patriotism brought rewards. Jackson's union reached a peak of thirty thousand members by 1944."[52]

Part of the price that management and government paid to ensure wartime labour stability was to give labour the right to organize and bargain collectively. As a result, union membership doubled by 1945. The new rights accorded to labour were implemented as orders in council, under the government's wartime powers. Labour and employers both realized that with war's end the federal government's jurisdiction in these matters would expire. The years from 1945 were marked by many bitter, sometimes violent, labour-employer conflicts. Labour was determined to entrench its newly acquired rights, while employers refused to accept any extension of those rights into the peacetime economy. As far as employers were concerned, the rights to organize and bargain collectively were temporary measures required by the war effort.

Labour unrest was also fuelled by inflation. During the war, prices and wages had been tightly controlled. In 1945, the government faced the difficult task of removing controls in an orderly fashion. Labour found government's "orderly decontrol" of the economy unfair. By 1946, the prices of many items were rising to new levels, but wages were still pegged at 1926–29 levels. "The number of man-working hours lost as a result of strikes and lock-outs rose from a low of 490,139 in 1944 to 1,457,420 in 1945 and 4,516,393 in 1946."[53]

The Jackson-led UE quickly erased all traces of its non-strike pact and embarked on a campaign to prove its militancy to members and break the vestiges of wartime wage restraints. Many strikes were called in an attempt to win wage increases and benefits. These strikes were also tests of strength, as the union and employers tried to assert their strength. During this period, basic fringe benefits were the key items of negotiation for the UE local at Ferranti Canada. Paid statutory holidays were introduced. In fact, Ferranti Canada became the first local in the UE to win a full eight statutory holidays per year. In

1947–48, the union negotiated a hospital insurance plan, and vacations were increased from 2 weeks after 15 years to 2 weeks after 3 years. But the employees still lacked a pension plan, and considerable strife would arise over this issue.

In the late 1940s, the UE came under increasing attack from the labour movement itself. In 1947 Pat Sullivan, a prominent communist union leader, revealed the dirty side of communist unionism to the press. This news intensified the struggle to win back control of the CCL from the communist unions. One communist union after another was expelled from the CCL.

The last communist bastion in the CCL was Jackson's UE. In 1949, the CIO expelled the American United Electrical Workers from its ranks. It gave a break-away group from the UE, the International Union of Electrical Workers (IUEW), official jurisdiction in the United States. The IUEW campaigned to get UE locals to switch over to it. This inter-union warfare spilled into Canada. Canadian companies such as CGE saw this as an opportunity to rid themselves of the UE, and they encouraged IUEW certification. Though supportive of the anti-communist IUEW, CCL's leadership could not be seen encouraging the raiding of CCL member unions. The UE had to be expelled. But how? Jackson was shrewd enough not to give the CCL any justifiable cause. In 1949, the executive of the CCL discovered that the international office of the UE had forgotten to send in the Canadian UE's dues. This oversight gave the CCL executive, according to a strict reading of the by-laws, the right to expel the union.

Contract negotiations at Ferranti Canada had, from the outset, been carried on with the usual confrontational posturing by labour and management. The union wanted more benefits for its members, while management sought to keep input costs down. The union always accused management of lying and concealing profits; management vehemently complained that the "pinko" union was destroying the company's competitiveness. Nonetheless, contract differences seemed to get resolved with a minimum of disruption. In 1956, however, a series of circumstances turned mutual mistrust into bitter confrontation.

The union complained that it had not received a wage increase since 1953, while inflation had continued to erode the value of its members' pay cheques. The company pointed to the crisis gripping the entire industry and argued that it could not compete with offshore producers if its direct labour and overhead costs kept increasing. The workers' militancy was further fuelled by the company's inability to resolve the long-standing issue of pensions. From about 1950 on, the union had been asking for a company pension plan. Management had agreed to look into the matter but kept putting off a decision. With a number of workers nearing retirement, the question had become very sensitive. By 1956, the union claimed that it had waited long enough and wanted action. The dispute stemmed from a fundamental distinction between two views of labour: wage as a living and wage as a cost.

These two views could have been reconciled and a compromise

found, but the union's militancy and management's stubbornness had built a wall. The union refused to believe the company's pleas that it was in serious financial trouble. In 1955, Ferranti Canada suffered one of its biggest losses since the Depression, and, with the industry under siege from foreign imports, the future did not look any brighter. Everyone in the union, from the rank and file to the negotiators, refused to believe the financial losses. The union pointed to the brand new, multi-million-dollar facility as proof that the company had money.

The union did not appear to understand that modernization and expansion were essential to competitiveness; that the money for the plant came from Ferranti Ltd, in England; and that the new plant, poorly timed and overly ambitious, had too much excess capacity to be profitable in the market circumstances of the day. The union did not realize that it was possible for a company to live beyond its means. As far as the union was concerned, a new factory meant profits to be shared. And to this day, former shop employees still insist that the firm must have been making substantial profits if it could afford to build a new factory. Even access to the books might not have convinced the union of the company's claims, because unions at that time often claimed that the books were rigged. Moreover, the executives of Ferranti Canada, already upset over the growing infringement of labour on management's former prerogatives, were not about to let the union peer into its books.

Ferranti Canada's resolve to resist UE's demands was reinforced by stiffening industry opposition to unions. In 1955, during hard negotiations with Canada Wire and Cable, UE officials miscalculated the resolve of the firm and consequently found themselves in a strike that they never intended to call. At the same time, the UE started threatening strike action against Canadian Westinghouse. The UE suffered a costly defeat at the hands of Canada Wire and Cable. The 107-day strike cost the union the support of workers at Canada Wire and Cable and allowed the IUEW to be voted in as the new representative. With a greatly depleted strike fund, the UE started to tread softly in its negotiations with Canadian Westinghouse and CGE.

The UE looked more vulnerable than ever. The *Financial Post* advised that it was time to take a stand against the UE.[54] The crisis in the transformer industry forced Ferranti Canada to lay off 60 per cent of its plant employees. The company reasoned that such reductions would temper the militancy of those remaining. So when the UE put its demands to Ferranti Canada, the firm felt confident that it could get tough with the union and win. It countered by demanding a 10-per-cent cut in wages. Management misread the union. The rank and file were convinced that their pension demands were fair and were within the company's budget. They believed that Ferranti Canada merely wanted to break the union. After a year of setbacks, the UE could not afford to show any weakness. A confrontation was inevitable.

On 14 May 1956, 97 per cent of those voting called for strike

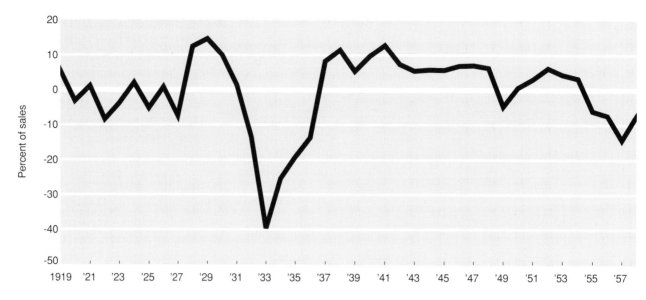

Ferranti Electric Ltd. profits as a percentage of sales, 1919-1958

action. As the strike dragged on, it became apparent that each side had misjudged the other's determination. Weeks turned into months. Finally, the union got management to agree to a mediated solution. Once the mediator was accepted, a settlement was reached in three days. After 135 days, the workers went back to the shop floor on 26 September 1956, ending the longest UE strike in Canada. Although the union got its pension plan an a small wage increase, both sides made concessions. The strike had taken its financial toll on both company and workers. But even more important, it had reinforced mistrust and lack of communication. In the years to come, confrontation became the reality between labour and management.

Merging in Order to Survive

In the midst of the electrical industry's competitive predicament, a smaller corporate drama was being played out in which Tom Edmondson and Vincent Ziani de Ferranti were the principal actors. By the mid-1930s, stock in Packard Electric was being concentrated in the hands of a smaller and smaller group of shareholders. It had become a tradition for management and professional staff to own some shares. Edmondson had always encouraged his staff to buy into the company. Whenever any stock was up for sale, he would first offer it to his staff. By promoting stock ownership among employees, he had given everyone a vested interest in the firm. With partial ownership came commitment and enthusiasm.

By the 1950s, most of the voting stock, except for Ferranti UK's one-third, rested with the firm's management and professional staff. Over the years, the shareholders had developed an agreement that if

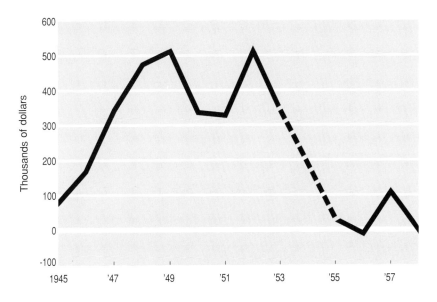

Packard Electric net income, 1945-1958

anyone wanted to sell his other shares they would offer them to other employee-shareholders. But many of these people were not in a financial position to buy up the shares when available, and they were not willing to mortgage their houses to finance such purchases. As a result, Edmondson would buy the shares himself to keep control within the company. By the time that Edmondson assumed the presidency, he had acquired the single largest block of shares.

In 1952, Packard Electric's future looked brighter than it had in its entire history. The company was building modern manufacturing facilities, and the market for electrical equipment was still very healthy. Despite all this good news, troubling thoughts started to fill Edmondson's cautious mind. With most of his wealth tied up in Packard shares, he was worried that if forced to sell under unfavourable conditions he could lose a lot of money. Then there was the problem of inheritance taxes. The real value of his stock holdings far exceeded their face value. At the time, inheritance taxes were based on real value, not face value. In the event of his death, his wife would be left nearly destitute if she had to pay the high inheritance taxes and still sell the stock at face value to other employee shareholders.

In 1952–53, Tom Edmondson decided that it would be best to sell his shares and convinced the other shareholders to sell with him in a block, in order to get the best price. All the shareholders had implicit faith in Edmondson and left it to him to get the best price. But sell to whom? According to Bert Wigley, the company's chief finance officer, there were some inquiries from other electrical manufacturers outside Canada, but nothing ever came of them. In Edmondson's mind, Ferranti UK offered the best hope. First, it already owned one-third of the common stock. Second, he knew Vincent Ziani de

Ferranti, and they both respected each other. And third, Ferranti UK was doing very well and had capital to invest.

The idea of selling out to Ferranti UK was a complete turn-about in attitude for Edmondson. Just a few year earlier, Edmondson, like Wyman before him, had been determined to buy back V.Z. de Ferranti's block of shares. In March 1950, he explained to A.B. Cooper that for "sentimental reasons he was willing to pay a fair price," and he offered Vincent $200,000.[55] The latter, however, did not accept. He interpreted "fair price" differently from Edmondson and reasoned that because Packard Electric had shown such remarkable earning power in the period 1945–50, his shares could be worth as much as $3 million! He had no intention of selling back his shares. His goal, as he confided to Cooper, was to merge Ferranti Canada with Packard Electric when the opportunity arose. Further, he hoped to recruit Edmondson to the Ferranti team. Edmondson's managerial tal-

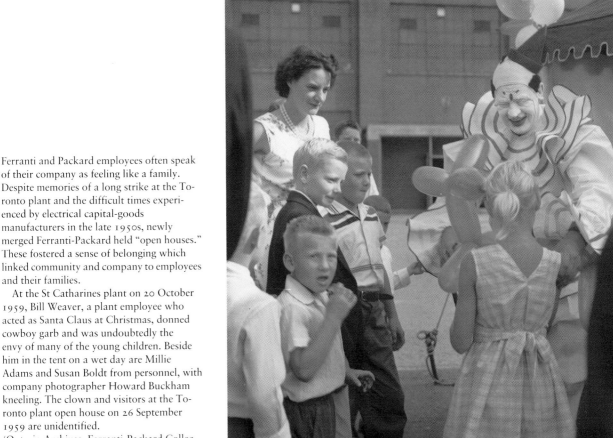

Ferranti and Packard employees often speak of their company as feeling like a family. Despite memories of a long strike at the Toronto plant and the difficult times experienced by electrical capital-goods manufacturers in the late 1950s, newly merged Ferranti-Packard held "open houses." These fostered a sense of belonging which linked community and company to employees and their families.

At the St Catharines plant on 20 October 1959, Bill Weaver, a plant employee who acted as Santa Claus at Christmas, donned cowboy garb and was undoubtedly the envy of many of the young children. Beside him in the tent on a wet day are Millie Adams and Susan Boldt from personnel, with company photographer Howard Buckham kneeling. The clown and visitors at the Toronto plant open house on 26 September 1959 are unidentified.
(Ontario Archives, Ferranti-Packard Collection, AO 1534, AO 1533)

ents had been recognized by Ferranti UK as early as 1943, when Cooper recommended him as his successor. Thus Edmondson's hostility to Ferranti UK's gestures of co-operation was of great concern to Vincent. "My main complaint," wrote Vincent, "as far as Tom is concerned is his unfriendly attitude toward us. If only he would treat us as partners, it would be much better for both parties."[56]

Edmondson's eventual negotiations were kept very secret. After a year of bargaining, he got his price, and V.Z. de Ferranti finally got Packard Electric and Edmondson. In 1954, Ferranti UK bought 13,275 preferred shares at $50 a share, and 18,625 common shares at $117 a share, for a total of just over $2.8 million. The purchase was done through Ferranti Canada. Not all of Packard Electric's shareholders were happy with selling out to Ferranti. Some of the younger ones were confident that the company could make it on its own. But Edmondson was more cautious. Did he already see signs

of the impending crisis in the industry? If he had waited a few more years, the crisis would have substantially reduced the value of Packard Electric stock.

Though not foremost in Edmondson's mind, an engineering dimension to the acquisition interested him. The technology for producing larger, higher-voltage–rated transformers was getting very sophisticated and costly. Ferranti UK, as a world leader in the design of large power transformers, offered technology for the smaller Packard Electric.

The Neelon Mill in St Catharines, where the Packard brothers set up the operations of Packard Electric in 1894, was built in 1882. The bee hive and wheat sheaves symbolized industry and bountiful prosperity. This decision in 1951 to relocate and build a new larger plant marked the end of one era and the beginning of another. The Neelon Mill was torn down in 1965 but as a symbol of its links to the past Ferranti-Packard saved the stonework of the bee hives and wheat sheaves. (Ontario Archives, Ferranti-Packard Collection, AO 1272, AO 1271)

After the purchase in 1954, though both Ferranti Canada and Packard Electric had financial difficulties because of intense offshore competition, Ferranti UK was content to let the two companies compete with each other. During this difficult period, Packard Electric stayed in the black, though barely. Its meter operations were always profitable – with net profits averaging 11 per cent of sales – and its transformer profits hovered between 1 and − 1 per cent of sales.

Ferranti Canada, however, was in serious financial difficulties. By 1954, its meter business had run into difficulties, and losses ensued for the next four years. But it was the crisis in the industry that really took its toll. The company's financial difficulties were further compounded by the fact that Ferranti Canada had just finished investing $3.7 million in a new plant and machinery in 1956. With two 120-ton cranes, and new impulse-testing equipment, the firm hoped to produce very big power transformers, as large as 100,000 kVA. Since Packard Electric was acquired through Ferranti Canada, the latter had to pay off the bank loan used to finance the acquisition. The resulting high overhead and heavy debt load accentuated the "cost squeeze" from foreign competition.

In 1958, as a result of the continued downward plunge of the Canadian transformer industry, Ferranti UK decided to merge the two companies, as Ferranti-Packard Electric Ltd, and rationalize its Canadian operations. Years later, the name was changed to Ferranti-Packard. The Toronto plant was to specialize in power transformers, and St Catharines in distribution transformers and meters. Each company had had about 15–20 per cent of the meter market. Everyone thought that the new company's meter business would be the sum of the two shares. Instead, the public utilities continued to give a total of 15–20 per cent of their business to the new company.

The president of Ferranti Canada, Dr. John Thomson, had been kept in the dark about the merger. V.Z. de Ferranti immediately appointed Tom Edmondson as president and CEO of Ferranti-Packard; Thomson because chairman of the board and was politely pushed aside. Vincent left the corporate details of the merger to Edmondson. The result was practically a wholesale replacement of the Ferranti management by Packard people. The new managers tried to bring some corporate focus to the Ferranti organization. The X-Ray Division was sold, and the activities of the Research Department, Electronics Department, and Ordnance Division were amalgamated into the Electronics Division, with John Fogarty as general manager.

From the very beginning, in 1935, V.Z. de Ferranti saw his purchase of Packard's shares as a long-term investment in the future of his Canadian operations. The idea of merging Packard Electric and Ferranti Canada was never far from his mind, but at the time Packard Electric's president, F.T. Wyman, would never have accepted it. Vincent Ziani de Ferranti was a patient man, and twenty-three years later he got his way.

7   *From Canadian to North American*

From 1955 to 1957, the value of manufactured-in-Canada power transformer shipments dropped from $92.5 million to $26.3 million, as a result of offshore competition and dumping.[1] In the midst of such a crisis, the merger of Ferranti Electric and Packard Electric was the only way of ensuring the survival of two of Canada's oldest electrical manufacturing companies and corporate cultures. Life after merger, however, did not turn out to be a bed of roses.

Ferranti-Packard's management wondered, as did the entire industry, if better times were not just around the corner. The early 1960s, however, did not offer any respite. Only two years after the merger, Ferranti-Packard found itself forced to lay off nearly 33 per cent of its labour force. By 1960, a slowdown in the growth of the Canadian economy and an excess electrical generating capacity had compounded the effects of foreign competition.[2] In 1961, the value of shipments registered a further drop of 23 per cent, and profit rates for the industry fell to their lowest since the Depression.[3] For Ferranti-Packard, these conditions translated into substantial losses in power and distribution transformer operations – 34 per cent and 15 per cent of sales respectively in 1963. The company's ability to survive weighed heavily on its leadership.[4]

The plight of Ferranti-Packard raised important issues. At stake was Canada's ability to sustain long-term industrialization and economic growth. The Canadian Electrical Manufacturing Association (CEMA) argued with the federal government that a healthy domestic industry was a strategic requirement. It warned that to leave the industry to foreign producers would return Canadians to being hewers of wood and drawers of water and create serious social and labour repercussions. The direct and indirect loss of 35,000 jobs between 1956 and 1960 was a chilling omen.[5]

People in the electrical industry called for swift government action. Some demanded greater protective measures, re-examination of tariffs, and better enforcement of anti-dumping laws.[6] Others outside industry, such as C. Barber, who had helped with the Knox Report on the state of the electrical industry, argued that the industry's problems were structural. The Canadian market was only a fraction of the size of the American market, but Canada still had as many domestic manufacturers as the United States. With so many competitors sharing a very small pie, the smaller companies found it difficult to generate sufficient profits to invest in future growth.

At times the calls for more protection became interwoven with economic patriotism. C.A. Pollock, president of Dominion Electrohome Industries Ltd, captured the mood of the industry in 1961:

What will our government do about curtailing the great Canadian fallacy of wanting to have our cake and eat it too? As long as it lasts, it will be great fun for our citizens earning good wages and salaries to buy products from low wage countries brought into Canada by enterprisers with little interest in building our industry. It will always be a truism that the buyer gets what he pays for – the long-term end-result of persistence in this folly will be that the public will buy for themselves a lower standard of living. When more Canadian lose their jobs, a bright clear light may dawn on enough people and a demand for quotas on importers' practices will be strong enough to force the government to recognize that the future development of Canada lies in the expansion of our secondary industry.

It's up to all of us to build Canada for Canadians – no one else will do it for us![7]

To buy or not to buy Canadian, that has always been a fundamental dilemma in Canada's economic and technological development. To buy from cheaper foreign suppliers was, in the CEMA's view, detrimental to the country's, long-term interests. The CEMA asked utilities to think about the nation's future and "Buy Canadian." Paying a little more for Canadian products was a small price to pay to bolster national industrial development and ensure greater socio-economic benefits for all. Throughout Europe, nationally owned utilities used their purchasing power to ensure the vitality of domestic industry. In the United States, a deeply rooted "Buy American" attitude had boosted the industry.

Basil Ziani de Ferranti was a member of the Ferranti UK board and was asked to monitor the company's overseas operations. Given that the firm had so much invested in Canada, he added his voice to the calls for buying domestic products. In a well-publicized speech before the Empire Club in Toronto, in January 1960, he warned: "You can't make a song and dance about the attractions of Canada to the industrialist wanting to set up business here and then go and buy subway cars overseas." He added: "You can't solve an unemployment problem by creating jobs in other countries. Canada's balance of payments has been largely supported by the inflow of foreign capital. But this will soon dry up if Canadian industry is not supported."[8]

If Canada wanted to play a prominent role in world affairs, it had to support indigenous industry. Canada "must give orders to Cana-

Ferranti-Packard transformers are a hidden but essential component of the CN Tower, a major communications facility and Toronto landmark. Here a small 2,000-kVA Ferranti-Packard power transformer is being installed in May 1975.
(Ontario Archives, Ferranti-Packard Collection, AO 672)

dian firms and people must stop pretending that it's always the other firm's duty to buy Canadian."[9]

Any calls for economic nationalism were bound to have provincial parallels, particularly in Quebec. Ontario and Quebec had been Canada's greatest producers of electrical power and greatest consumers of heavy electrical equipment. Since Ontario had always been the centre of the nation's electrical industry, calls to "Buy Canadian" were in effect calls to "Buy Ontario." This state of affairs did not sit well with the nationalist forces that had started to simmer in post-war Quebec. The production and sale of electricity became the focus of nationalist ambitions there. This situation affected the way in which Ontario-based electrical industry carried out business in Quebec. In Quebec's electrical market "Buy Canadian" was translated into "Buy Quebec."

Expanding into Quebec

Hydro-Québec emerged in 1944 from debate over public good versus private interests and developed into a powerful symbol of the province's new economic nationalism. Since its creation, every premier of Quebec, from Maurice Duplessis to Robert Bourassa, has used its economic clout as a central political tool in fostering his province's economic, social, and political aspirations. Deeply rooted in a rural economy, post-war Quebec faced the challenge of diversifying its economy through greater industrialization. The need to break away from a resource-based economy was nowhere more compelling than in the electrical industry. Throughout the 1950s and 1960s, Hydro-Québec used its enormous purchasing power, through a "Buy Quebec" policy, to encourage Canadian and foreign electrical manufacturers to invest and locate in the province.

In 1948, John Thomson, general manager of Ferranti Canada, decided that it had become imperative to begin manufacturing meters and small transformers in Quebec. On 23 December 1948, he made his plans known to the very surprised Canadian board of Ferranti Canada.[10] Thomson argued that he had discussed the matter in detail with V.Z. de Ferranti and had obtained his approval. Cooper, though disappointed that Thomson had purposely excluded him from the entire affair, arranged, as chairman of the Board, for formal approval of the project.

In truth, Vincent had received few, if any details. Furthermore, he believed that any expansion into Quebec, like all important capital projects, could be undertaken only if existing profits could justify new investments. While other transformer companies were making healthy profits in the late 1940s, Ferranti Canada's performance was mediocre. By 1949, the company was running into serious financial difficulties, and yet Thomson insisted on entering Quebec. Vincent saw Canadian operations as getting dangerously close to being out of control. On 22 March 1949 he wrote to Cooper and asked him and the board to reconsider seriously Thomson's plan: "I will say no more until I hear the result of your Board meeting and any advice you can

Not all the transformers were destined to stay in one place for the duration of their operational life. In mid-1964 Saskatchewan Power Corporation purchased this 5,000-kVA trailer-mounted transformer. It functioned as a miniature mobile transformer substation for use with construction or in a power outage. Saskatchewan Power also bought one of the five FP-6000 computers designed, manufactured, and sold by Ferranti-Packard. (Ontario Archives, Ferranti-Packard Collection, AO 699)

give me with regard to reorganization, so that the $2,000,000 invested in Canada will not evaporate."[11]

Interpreting the letter as a call for stronger leadership by the board, Cooper replied: "In the face of circumstances as they have developed, I now feel sure that you will want me temporarily now to give general guidance and direction, which will require enabling authority in proper course."[12] Cooper was unable to get from Thomson any detailed financial analysis of the Quebec project other than "a few paragraphs of generalities." After his own analysis, he wrote V.Z. de Ferranti that he would "give instructions to cancel the plans for the Quebec factory" at the upcoming meeting.[13]

Proud and strong-willed, Thomson refused to accept the arguments put forth by Cooper at the board meeting on 25 March 1949. The ensuing debate became quite heated, and, in the end, Thomson opposed the majority and voted against cancellation. In the minutes of the meeting, a single entry on the matter was made: "in view of the changed financial position of the Company as shown by the latest reports, the arrangements to proceed with the Quebec factory be cancelled."[14] Vincent totally supported Cooper's position and was stunned at Thomson's unorthodox behaviour: "I cannot for a moment understand John's reasoning or action at the Board meeting," he wrote to Cooper; "it is quite unheard of in our experience to have a vote on any subject as we find ourselves always able to come to an agreement with the facts in front of us."[15]

Packard Electric's plans to build in Quebec took more time to evolve. It needed to assure a market presence in Quebec. In response to intense competition, it asked itself whether it had truly developed all Canada's regional markets to their fullest. Outside Ontario, the large Quebec market offered the most fertile ground for increasing sales. In an effort to obtain more orders from Quebec, Tom Edmondson met in January 1956 with the new president of Hydro-Québec, J.-Arthur Savoie, and its other officers.

Savoie had climbed to the top of Hydro-Québec in the wake of Maurice Duplessis's rise to power. Upon assuming office in 1936, Duplessis made the usual patronage appointments, making his old friend Savoie director of Quebec's Liquor Control Board.[16] In 1939, when Union nationale went down to defeat, Duplessis found himself attacked from within the party for his handling of the election. Savoie and others, however, continued to rally around him.[17] In 1944, Duplessis once again led Union nationale to power. As a reward for his loyalty and assistance, Duplessis appointed Savoie one of the five commissioners on the board of Hydro-Québec.[18] On 1 June 1955, Duplessis named him president.[19]

While Edmondson wanted more business from Hydro-Québec, Savoie wanted more investments from Ontario-based electrical manufacturers. At their meeting, Savoie had made it "clear to [Tom Edmondson] that [Packard Electric] would get very little business from them until [the company] had a plant in the province of Quebec."[20] After lengthy discussion, Packard Electric's board concluded that a new plant in Quebec would give the company three to four hundred thousand dollars annually in additional orders, including ten to fifteen thousand meters.[21] The board therefore decided unanimously "to investigate the establishment of an operation in the province of Quebec for the assembly of standard distribution transformers, and at a later date, for meters."[22] On 13 May 1956, the sod was turned for a new factory in Trois-Rivières.

Meanwhile, Ferranti Canada had once again decided to build in Quebec. In 1949, John Thomson's insistence on building there, even in the face of serious financial difficulties, had nearly precipitated a direct confrontation with V.Z. de Ferranti. Six years later, in 1955, Thomson once again set his mind on Quebec. Given a piece of land for $1 by Quebec Power, Ferranti Canada had plans to build in Quebec City. But Duplessis did not share these dreams. Through Savoie, Duplessis told Ferranti Canada that Louiseville, a small town near Trois-Rivières, was the place to locate.[23] With Savoie's help, Ferranti

Canada found and bought a piece of land on which to build the new plant.

Locating in Quebec made very good business sense. One has to wonder why Ferranti UK allowed both of its Canadian holdings to pursue independent expansion programs in the province. Wasn't such a move a wasteful duplication of resources? After the acquisition of Packard Electric in 1954, the Ferranti family was content to let its two Canadian interests operate as competitors, in the belief that two companies could collectively secure more business than one. It thus made perfect sense for both Packard Electric and Ferranti Canada to pursue their own individual interests, one being to secure a bigger market share in Quebec. At a time when more rationalization was needed, the decision to allow the two firms to operate independently was baffling. Furthermore, by 1956, it had become common knowledge among Canadian utilities that Ferranti owned both companies. The independent policies taken by Ferranti Canada and Packard Electric in regard to locating in Quebec reflected the Ferranti family's inability to establish an unambiguous, co-ordinated, and unified strategy for its expanded Canadian holdings.

By late 1956, the advisability of building two plants in Quebec had become a moot point. A prolonged strike by the UE had brought Ferranti Canada to a grinding halt, and the ensuing losses forced the company once again to postpone any such plans. Then, with merger in 1958, a second plant in Quebec became redundant.

Why did Packard Electric locate in Trois-Rivières? Montreal, long the hub of Quebec's financial and manufacturing activities, would have seemed a more logical choice. The city was also the headquarters of Packard Electric's sales effort in the province. Little got done in Quebec without Maurice Duplessis's knowledge and consent. With an election about to be called, the premier let it be known that if Packard Electric wanted to do business in his province, then it would have to locate in his home riding of Trois-Rivières. In return, Savoie gave the company assurances that its share of the province's transformer and watt-hour-meter business would increase accordingly.

Through Savoie, a deal was struck to buy a piece of land from the St. Lawrence Paper Corp. on which to build the new plant. At the last minute, the corporation practically doubled its asking price for the land. Tom Edmondson became so furious that he threatened to call the deal off. At a meeting between Edmondson and the representative from St. Lawrence Paper, Savoie tried to get the latter to go back to its original offer, but with no success. Not about to let his own riding lose such an important venture, Duplessis personally intervened to save the project. In a speech at the ground-breaking ceremony for the new plant, the premier made light of how he got St. Lawrence to reconsider: "I got in touch with my friend Percy Fox, at the St Lawrence Corporation, and said: "Percy, what are thinking of? Do you want your assessment increased? [laughter] If your property is worth that much we should increase your assessment.' He said: "Not at all, not at all, it was a mistake.'"[24] In the same breath, Duplessis turned his

By the early 1950s Packard Electric had realized that sales to Hydro-Québec required a manufacturing presence in Quebec. In 1956 they decided to build a meter and transformer plant in Premier Maurice Duplessis's riding of Trois-Rivières. The 13 May 1956 sod-turning ceremony took place in the midst of a provincial election and Maurice Duplessis took advantage of the opportunity to make the ceremony a newsworthy event at which he extolled the virtues of his government's pro-business and anti-labour policies.
(Ed Love)

arm-twisting into an act of "understanding and generosity" on the part of the St. Lawrence Paper Corp.

Only after construction had started did Packard Electric discover that it had obtained several acres of quicksand. Poor soil conditions fostered some very innovative civil engineering; the plant stands on an extraordinary foundation that actually floats on the quicksand.

The sod-turning ceremony, in the midst of an election campaign, turned into quite an affair. Duplessis's campaign advisers made sure that the ceremony was carried out in style, while Packard Electric paid the bill. There was a marching band, plenty of media coverage, and a host of distinguished guests, including Savoie, president of Hydro-Québec; the mayors of Trois-Rivières, Nicolet, and St-Justin, as well as St Catharines, Ontario; and the curé of St-Philippe, who was there to give his benediction.

Brimming with confidence, Duplessis proclaimed, to the amusement of the partisan audience, that the sod-turning ceremony "was a good exercise for the grave we are going to dig for the opposition."[25] The arrival of companies such as Packard Electric represented an important step in the diversification of Quebec's resource-based economy. Duplessis used the investment as a symbol of the new economic relationship that Quebec was demanding from its highly industrialized neighbour, Ontario. Calling for more equitable regional development within Canada, Duplessis told his audience:

the province of Quebec receives the sunlight before Toronto and Ontario, because we are east and the sun rises in the east. We are always glad to share sunlight with Ontario. We supply timber to run the mill at Thorold and supply Ontario with 900,000 hp of electric power. We realize that you need light and power and we, as good brothers are always happy to co-operate. But co-operation cannot be a one-way street.

And you are starting to co-operate by establishing in Quebec, an industry with a good reputation, an important industry which will benefit Trois-Rivières, Quebec, and Canada.

The province of Quebec is a very fertile field for this kind of industry because we have here in Quebec more horsepower – I was inclined to say horse sense but I won't – than any place in Canada.[26]

Duplessis had already declared the United Electrical Workers union illegal in Quebec. "You may be sure," he proclaimed to his pro-business audience, "that here you will have stability. Not stability that means immobility, but stability that means real security. There is no room for communism in the province of Quebec."[27] He compared Westinghouse's strife with the UEW in Hamilton to the labour calm of that firm's lamp factory in Trois-Rivières: "The Canadian Westinghouse Company, which has also established a large plant in Trois-Rivières, has a union in their Hamilton plant that is led by communists. We don't stand for that in Quebec. The union here in

The sod-turning ceremony for the new Packard Electric plant at Trois-Rivières. Front row, left to right: George Murray, vice president and works manager, St Catharines; Tom Edmondson, president and CEO; Mayor Paradis, Trois-Rivières; Mayor Smith, St Catharines; Premier Maurice Duplessis; the Curé of St. Philippe; Marcel Ouellette, industrial commissioner of Trois-Rivières.
(Ed Love)

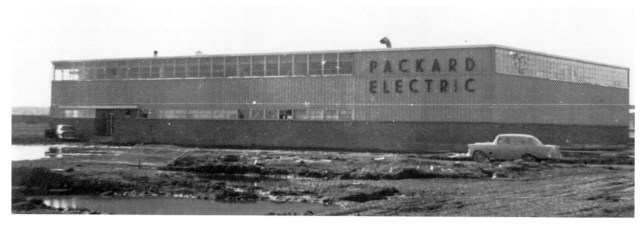

View of the Packard Electric plant in Trois-Rivières as it emerges from the construction site in 1957.
(Ferranti-Packard Transformers Ltd., Trois Rivières, Quebec)

Westinghouse's new Trois-Rivières plant is free of communism."[28]

Holding up his government's tough anti-labour stance as a model for other provinces, the premier proclaimed to the Quebec electorate: "We are giving an example. We don't want to meddle into the affairs of others, but we are glad of our policy, and we are glad of our stand."[29]

Business during the first four or five years of the Trois-Rivières operation was uncertain. Although Hydro-Québec had given Packard Electric a reasonable amount of meter business, it could not give the company any distribution transformer business until 1958, because of prior commitments to Brown-Boveri (Canada) Ltd. In 1951, Brown-Boveri started construction of a $2.5-million plant, in St-Jean, Quebec, for the manufacture of power and distribution transformers.[30] Brown-Boveri also built, at a cost of $500,000, an entire "integrated dwelling settlement adjacent to the factory site to accommodate a number of its employees. Thirty modern brick dwellings, completely equipped, have been built."[31]

For such an impressive investment, Brown-Boveri extracted important promises from the provincial government and Hydro-Québec. The province awarded the company the contract, in 1955, to supply Hydro-Québec's distribution transformer requirements. According to a confidential memo to Tom Edmondson from Bob Short, the man running Packard Electric's sales operations in Quebec, the "contract was extended to June 15, 1958, by political arguments put forward by Brown-Boveri."[32]

In the mean time, Packard Electric's only option was to sell distribution transformers to the province's private utilities. But the transformer price war of the mid-1950s had considerably eroded Packard Electric's share of the private utility market. According to one internal analysis prepared for Tom Edmondson, "we have latterly been deprived of a large part of this business due to pricing policy on the part of C.G.E. who are not content to obtain a reasonable share of

Shawinigan business but seem to want it all. In order to attain this end and, incidentally, embarrass those manufacturers actually making transformers in Quebec, they have resorted to deliberate price-cutting tactics."[33]

Sizeable orders for power transformers for the St Catharines plant, from Hydro-Québec in 1957, helped carry the cost of operating at Trois-Rivières. This cushion vanished in 1958 when Canadian General Electric extended price-cutting to power transformers. As a result, CGE "obtained an inordinate proportion of the power transformer business for 1958, leaving a relatively small share to be divided between other transformer manufacturers."[34]

Bob Short feared once again that Brown-Boveri would, on purely political grounds, obtain the entire order for Hydro-Québec's distribution transformers. His fears became very real when it was announced that Jean Barrette, a member of Quebec's legislative council (the upper house), and close friend of Duplessis, was elected director of Brown-Boveri (Canada) Ltd. For Short, "there was absolutely no question that this appointment was made to increase the influence of Brown-Boveri on Provincial politics and that it was timed to fit with their plan to persuade Hydro-Quebec to renew the distribution transformer contract without competitive bids."[35] Short urged Tom Edmondson to write J.-Arthur Savoie to plead Packard Electric's case for more business.

On 22 April 1958, Edmondson wrote to Savoie "to seek assurance that [Packard Electric] shall have an opportunity to participate in the 1958 distribution transformer business of Hydro-Quebec"[36]: "with the price levels of the past three years, Packard has been able to barely break even, although we consider we have an efficient organization. The current price levels throw us definitely into a loss position. Consequently, if we do not obtain some portion of the Commission's distribution transformer business, we must ask ourselves if we are economically justified in continuing our transformer operation in Quebec."[37]

Short arranged to meet Savoie on 25 April. On arriving at Savoie's office, Short discovered, to his chagrin, that Mr. Bernhardt, the president of Brown-Boveri, had just met with Savoie. In his talk with Savoie, Short presented Packard Electric as "anxious to help Quebec grow industrially; anxious to support the Province of Quebec and the Government of Mr. Duplessis, which has been very good to [Packard Electric]."[38] However, it became evident to Short that Savoie had already decided to renew Brown-Boveri's distribution transformer contract. Nevertheless, Savoie was sensitive to Packard Electric's predicament and, as a consequence, told Short that Hydro-Québec would renew Brown-Boveri's contract at the previous year's level. Any additional orders would go to Packard Electric. Furthermore, Savoie promised to give Packard Electric the contract, formerly held by CGE, for all of Hydro-Québec's subway-type transformer orders for 1958.

Because of space limitations in dense urban areas, or the importance of appearances in new developments, some distribution systems are installed underground. These "subway" transformers are placed in underground vaults; they are subject to complete submergence in water and therefore must be completely watertight.

After the merger, the combined sales efforts of Ferranti Canada and Packard Electric in Quebec were channelled through the Trois-Rivières plant. By the early 1960s, these operations had succumbed to the same market forces that had been plaguing the entire electrical industry. More favourable market conditions and the arrival of Charles Begin, a dynamic French-Canadian plant manager, allowed the plant to reach its true potential in the Quebec market.

Another Combines Investigation

In the midst of a deepening crisis, Canada's electrical industry called for government assistance; instead, it became the object of another combines investigation. On 8 April 1960, on orders from T.D. Mac-Donald, director of investigation and research, Combines Act, the government initiated an investigation of pricing policies in Canada's watt-hour meter and transformer industries. But such an investigation had been completed less than five years earlier. Like so many Canadian actions, this second inquiry appears to have been a knee-jerk reaction to events in the United States.

From the late 1950s, twenty-nine manufacturers of heavy electrical equipment, including the transformer manufacturers Allis-Chalmers, General Electric, Moloney, Pennsylvania Transformer, Wagner, and Westinghouse, were the object of a massive anti-trust investigation by the US Department of Justice. Evidence came to light that representatives from these companies met almost monthly throughout the 1930s, 1940s, and 1950s in order to control the prices quoted on transformers and other heavy electrical equipment. Based on the government's inquiries, the US Department of Justice launched legal proceedings against most of the American manufacturers. Labelled the "Electrical Conspiracy" by the press, the entire affair won considerable notoriety. After five years of court battles, the companies were found guilty of price-fixing, and some of the executives were even given prison sentences. In addition, various American utilities launched a $9-billion lawsuit against the manufacturers.

The great irony was that the price-fixing efforts had little, if any, effect on prices. According to Ralph Sultan, a former professor of business administration at Harvard University, who studied the effect of the meetings on actual selling prices:

the behaviour of prices in switchgear, transformers, and turbine generators lends poor support to the argument that the meetings stabilized, elevated, or standardized prices in the marketplace. Over the years reviewed prices seem to have been unusually unstable, cyclical, and nonstandardized. The meetings failed to influence prices because only some of the transactions were covered by the agreements, because there was widespread violation of the spirit

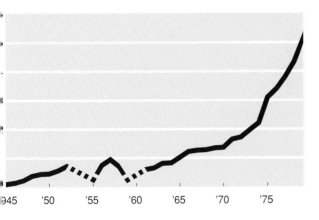

Value of Canadian transformer production, 1945-1979, Base Year 1945=100

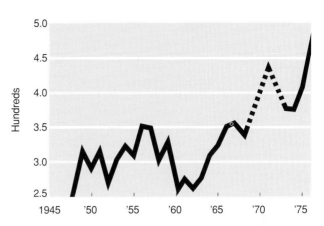

Value of Canadian meter production, 1945-1976, Base Year 1945=100

of the agreements, and because many other factors than the initial bid price influenced the utilities. Because these undermined the effectiveness of the conspiracy, forces of supply and demand ultimately established the market price level – even at the height of the conspiracy.[39]

Conditions in the Canadian electrical market in 1960 offered no grounds for suspecting price fixing. Intense competition often forced manufacturers to sell below cost. As a result, manufacturers were in very troubled financial waters. Ferranti-Packard was sustaining considerable losses. Not since the Depression had the industry's profits been so low. The US market, in contrast, had been insulated against low-priced European equipment by a deeply rooted "Buy American" tradition among electrical utilities. From 1949 to 1960, the US price index for transformers had climbed steadily, while the Canadian index had fallen to below its 1949 level. While unstable prices threatened electrical manufacturers such as Ferranti-Packard, the government was investigating these same manufacturers for price-fixing.

Sensing an opportunity to score political points, Canada's opposition parties pointed to the American convictions and accused John Diefenbaker's Conservative government of being "soft" on monopolies. On 6 February 1960, the Liberal MP for Burin-Burgeo, C.W. Carter, stood up in the House of Commons and asked: "In view of the fines levied on eight electrical companies in the U.S. for bid rigging and price fixing, will the minister tell the house whether any investigation is being made or contemplated by the combines investigation branch into similar practices by the Canadian counterparts of these electrical companies."[40]

In the weeks that followed, the opposition continued to ask if the electrical industry were being investigated. The Department of Justice ordered into action its Investigation and Research group which quickly discovered that the suspicions were totally unfounded. Two months after T.D. MacDonald issued the order to investigate

Ferranti-Packard, he wrote the company to announce that the investigation had been abandoned.

But this did not silence the opposition. With the US "Electrical Conspiracy" still in the news, the opposition continued to use any pretext to create a similar issue in Canada. On 22 March 1961, the MP from Assiniboia, Hazen Argue, announced to the House that he had evidence, from Kingston's public utilities commission, showing that the city "had received identical bids from various companies for the supply of electrical cables, transformers, meters, and street lighting."[41] The opposition wanted to know if the minister of justice would now launch a full investigation of the industry.

The government's anti-combine machinery perplexed and angered the Canadian electrical industry. The manufacturers felt that not only had they been unjustly singled out but the Combines Act accentuated the cost-price squeeze threatening the industry. Combines legislation is most effective in periods of high demand, when companies are in a position to extract excessive profits from the market. But during stagnant periods, combines legislation must be applied with sensitivity. On many occasions during his term of office as president of the Canadian Electrical Manufacturers Association, Tom Edmondson voiced concern over the harmful effect that the Combines Act was having on the troubled industry. In March 1961, he wrote in the *Monetary Times* that "the devastating price war that has raged in the electrical manufacturing industry for some years has been stimulated by the limitations placed on businessmen in the manufacturing sector by the combines act."[42] Edmondson also "deplored the fact that the necessity to make a reasonable profit was not a consideration in the administration of the Act."[43] The act was premised on the belief that the lowest price, through competition, was a good in itself. But the lowest price was not always in the public's long-term interest if it threatened a strategic Canadian industry.

One person's misfortune can sometimes be another's good fortune. The US "Electrical Conspiracy" had been a particularly traumatic and costly experience for American manufacturers. The aftermath of the scandal opened new market opportunities for Ferranti-Packard.

The Market from within and the Market from without

As with all manufacturers of heavy electrical equipment around the world, Ferranti-Packard's ability to carve out a sizeable and secure portion of the domestic market was a cornerstone of success. But its total reliance on the Canadian market had limitations. The market tends to be cyclical, and in Canada, the large number of suppliers fighting over a small pie merely exacerbated the harmful effects of any downturn in the market. Severe price competition and losses would often ensue as manufacturers scrambled to find enough orders to cover high overheads associated with large electrical works.

Soon after the merger, in 1958, Tom Edmondson realized that if

Ferranti-Packard were going to exploit its full productive capacity efficiently and profitably, then Canadian sales would have to be complemented by exports. An export market provided new avenues of profit and the cushion needed to absorb the fluctuations of the Canadian market. Three issues had to be adressed: where to export, what to export, and how to sell in the export market. Turning this goal into action would be a major test of marketing, manufacturing, and engineering skills.

Throughout the late 1950s and early 1960s, the federal government had helped Canadian manufacturers export heavy electrical equipment to Third World nations. Like many industrialized nations, Canada used its foreign aid to provide an outlet for domestic excess capacity while also helping underdeveloped nations build their own electric power infrastructure. Export credit policies, for example, provided long-term financing for purchase of costly equipment. This helped Ferranti-Packard supply power transformers to major electrification projects in India and Pakistan financed under the Colombo Plan.

Although the underdeveloped nations offered markets for Canadian power equipment, Tom Edmondson realized that there was a more stable market right on Canada's doorstep – the United States. The United States was the world's largest market for heavy electrical equipment. And for Ferranti-Pckard, even a small share in this market would contribute significantly to the company's order books. Many at Ferranti-Packard, however, were initially sceptical about the company's chances of penetrating the US market. Not only would the firm have to take on the far larger American electrical companies on their own home ground, it also would have to overcome the close relations between American investor-owned utilities and electrical manufacturers. This relationship had been both the product and the cause of the powerful "Buy American" ethos among US investor-owned utilities, which dominated the market. Public utilities such as the Tennessee Valley Authority also strongly favoured domestic purchases.

Ferranti-Packard did, however, have some factors in its favour. First, geographical proximity, a common language, and practically identical electrical standards all made the United States a more natural market than any other place in the world. Second, lower wages gave Canadian manufacturers an important cost advantage – a reverse of what had existed between Canada and Europe. The declining value of the Canadian dollar relative to the American dollar further accentuated this advantage. Third, in the early 1960s, the US market was able to absorb imports easily, as a result of a temporary undercapacity in the American electrical industry. Fourth, and perhaps most important, the US market was effectively closed to most of Ferranti-Packard's Canadian competitors. Being the subsidiaries of American firms, companies such as Canadian Westinghouse and Canadian General Electric could not export into the US market. Ultimately any success in that market would depend on how quickly and effectively Ferranti-Packard could demonstrate the technical excellence and reliability of its products, the quality of its service, the speed of its deliveries, and the competitiveness of its prices.

Tom Edmondson appointed Ray Taylor to lead a one-man assault on the US market. A graduate in electrical engineering from the University of Toronto, Taylor had started his career with Ferranti Canada in 1949. Almost immediately, he had found himself at odds with the company's abrasive manager of sales, Arnold Brace. He was not alone in this regard; Brace had alienated many in the firm. Realizing that only confrontation lay ahead, Taylor left Ferranti Canada and went to work for Packard Electric as a sales engineer.

There was nothing fancy or unusual about the way in which Ray Taylor tackled the US market. His methods entailed hard work and dogged determination. Thinking back on those tough days, Taylor recalled how he simply got a utility directory and started knocking on doors. "I spent 80% of my time in the US and called upon some 340 utilities all over the US."[44] All his perseverance would have been for nought had he not also had a well-thought-out sales strategy.

The investor-owned utilities' staunch support of American electrical manufacturers had long made it quite difficult for any foreign firm to get on these utilities' list of approved bidders. How could Ferranti-Packard compete on the basis of the quality and price of its products if it were not even given a chance to bid? Taylor's first and biggest hurdle was to get the private utilities to place Ferranti-Packard on their official bidding lists. The negative publicity raised by the "Electrical Conspiracy" made the utilities more receptive to Ferranti-Packard's sales overtures. Taylor exploited the timely anti-trust predicament. "Here was an opportunity," he later recalled, "to break the solidarity that had been established between the private utilities and the electrical manufacturers."[45]

In all his visits to American utilities, Taylor underscored Ferranti-Packard's complete corporate independence from all the US "conspirators." He stressed that this independence allowed his firm to give its American customers the benefit of lower Canadian transformer prices. The American market had escaped the intense price competition that characterized the Canadian transformer business throughout the late 1950s and early 1960s. As a result, Canadian subsidiaries of American transformer manufacturers were selling at lower prices in Canada than their parent firms could sell in the United States. Taylor would tell all prospective American customers that he wanted to give "them the same opportunity to benefit from the low prices GE and Westinghouse were selling at in Canada."[46]

Ferranti-Packard had to reshape its corporate image, balancing the advantages of two seemingly conflicting concepts: being associated with a well-known, innovative British firm and being seen as a very American company. Though the Ferranti name still conjured up a long and eminent tradition in electric power engineering, Ferranti-Packard had to create an unequivocal North American vision of itself in the minds of its American customers. In an effort to shed any ap-

Packard Electric's Sales Department, seen here in 1956, led the way into the United States market in the 1960s, despite the reluctance of American utilities to buy from a foreign company. Seated, left to right, Tom Good, Calgary; Ted White, Toronto; Ray Taylor, Toronto; Merv Conlin, Vancouver; Rolly Plamondon, Montreal. Standing, left to right, Tom Glover, Toronto; Larry Attwood, Toronto; Ian Mason, Toronto; Ken Beard, Toronto; Norm Acheson, Toronto; Ed Love, Toronto; Dave Durgy, Toronto. (Ed Love)

pearances of being "foreign," Taylor pointed to the company's historical ties with the United States. The American Packard brothers, founders of the company, later played a significant role in the American automobile industry. For many years, American investors had financed Packard Electric. Frank Wyman, who led Packard Electric for nearly three decades, had strong American roots and connections with the University of Pittsburgh and the Pennsylvania Transformer Co. Clayton Snyder, the talented engineer who for many years had guided transformer design at Packard Electric, had come from Pennsylvania Transformer.

Taylor also underscored the realities of the North American economy. Canada was not only the United States' closest ally, but also its biggest trading partner. With Canadians importing so many American manufactured goods, Americans should buy more manufactured products from Canada. Playing on the close ties between the two nations produced some awkward moments for Taylor. At the height of the Vietnam War, Canada's policy of harbouring American draft-dodgers and deserters often brought the wrath of the fiercely patriotic investor utilities down on his head. At the time, many Americans did not accept Canada's position on the war. Taylor's sales force did all it could to separate this highly charged political issue from the business of selling transformers.

Ferranti-Packard concentrated on the sale of specialty items. Its first exports to the United States were instrument transformers. "It was not a high volume item," Taylor later recalled, "but we had a complete line."[47] The break-through came in custom-engineered items such as furnace and power transformers. Relatively lower wage rates, currency devaluations, and many years of tough price competition in Canada gave the firm an important competitive price advantage in these highly labour-intensive products. But quality, reliability, and delivery time were equally, if not more, important.

Success in the US market did not come overnight. Time would be needed to win the trust and confidence of American customers. Each new order acted as a stepping stone to others. With each sale, Ferranti-Packard's reputation for quality, reliability, and service grew steadily. Commonwealth Edison, in Chicago, pleased with the performance and price of its first transformer, went on to place "millions and millions of dollars of orders for all kinds of transformers."[48] Once such a big investor-owned utility had placed major orders with Ferranti-Packard, others soon followed.

Technological Change and Matching Corporate Resources to Market Requirements

Ferranti-Packard's success in the American market depended on how effectively and quickly it could move up the so-called engineering learning curve for the design and manufacture of power transformer technology. Before the merger, neither Ferranti Canada nor Packard Electric had established a solid engineering tradition in the realm of larger power transformers. Despite any dreams that the two companies may have harboured, they never had the opportunity to build power transformers much above 15 MVA or for voltages above 138 kV. Design and construction of larger transformers were not, however, a simple matter of extrapolating from the company's existing range of small designs. With every major increase in capacity and voltage rating came challenges — most crucially, the competitive imperative for cost-effectiveness. It is extraordinarily difficult to get power transformers to operate efficiently at higher voltages and greater loads, and yet keep them as small and light as possible, without sacrificing reliability.

After the merger and rationalization of the two companies' power operations, Ferranti-Packard set about catching up. The first few years provided a learning period during which the Power Division slowly increased its design, testing, and manufacturing know-how. Mindful of the company's limitations, the Power Division moved very cautiously. In its initial marketing efforts in the United States,

Large power transformers must be able to withstand abnormally high voltage surges or spikes. In the Test Department of the Power Transformer Division in Toronto the impulse generator, and potential divider seen on the upper right, subjected larger transformers to a 2,000,000 volt surge. The stack of condensers which the workman is touching stored a charge which, when triggered, discharged with a wave shape similar to a lightning strike. The lower photo shows the spark flashover during the discharge. (Ontario Archives, Ferranti-Packard Collection, AO 657, photo 790)

Large power transformers designed to operate at very high voltages also had to be tested for ionization leakages within the interior of the transformer. This was done through Corona testing, as shown in this photo, taken in the Toronto plant. (Ontario Archives, Ferranti-Packard Collection, AO 660)

Ferranti-Packard was careful not to bid on too large a transformer. Wordie Hetherington, general manager of the Power Transformer Division, realized that going too far too fast could easily get the division into serious difficulties, which would damage the credibility of the new company. The division accordingly confined its design and manufacturing efforts to power transformers with power capacity up to 200 MVA or voltages up to 230 kV.

Just as the Power Division started to move along the learning curve, dramatic changes in market requirements greatly altered the limits of the relevant technology, the tempo of technological change, and the costs associated with research and development. Increased demand for electrical power and a shortage of new hydro-electric sites necessitated greater economies of scale in the generation of electricity. In the more remote regions of Canada, such as northern Quebec, where water-power remained untapped, massive hydro-electric developments were started.

For the rest of North America, steam-turbine–generator technology pointed the way to the future. Once considered inefficient, the steam turbine had, by the 1960s, become an extremely efficient piece of machinery capable of producing prodigious amounts of mechanical power. In 1958, the maximum output from a single steam-

Smaller distribution transformers, which required less elaborate set-ups and equipment, could be tested on an assembly line basis. Andy Barrowman is shown performing such tests during the 1960s in the Test Department of the St Catharines plant. (Ontario Archives, Ferranti-Packard Collection, AO 1229)

turbine–generator unit was 335 MW. By the start of the 1970s, the figure had climbed to 1,300 MW. With greater economies of scale came greater efficiency, and there seemed to be no limit to the size of steam-turbine–generator units that could be built.

Based primarily on fossil fuels, the technology was neither clean nor renewable. Nevertheless, its output capacity was not restricted by the hydrographic and topographic constraints of water-power. Furthermore, the rise of nuclear power technology produced an almost unlimited supply of energy to drive the steam-turbine generators and achieve even greater economies of scale. When several steam-turbine–generating units were combined under one roof, output rivalled the largest hydro-electric stations.

The rapidly escalating economies of scale carried the logic of the alternating-current central station, first advocated by Sebastian Ziani de Ferranti some eighty years earlier, to new heights. While fewer new stations were being built to meet increasing demand, stations were much bigger. With much higher capacities concentrated in fewer stations, transmission voltages expanded, nearly doubling in Ontario to 500 kV. In the mid-1960s, Hydro-Québec became the first utility in the world to transmit power at 735 kV. US voltages leapt from 345 kV to 765 kV, with research projects aiming at 1,000 kV.

These developments revolutionized power transformer technology. Never before had the voltage and load requirements of the largest power transformers risen at such a rate. Building a 600-MVA, 735-kV power transformer, such as those installed in Quebec's largest hydro-electric projects, required enormous budgets for research and development (R&D) that only the largest manufacturers could afford. This widened the gulf between the giants such as Westinghouse and the smaller companies such as Ferranti-Packard. Although the latter never held any illusions of competing with the giants at the top end of the market, its competitiveness in the intermediate range was influenced by the advances made in the largest sizes. As the frontiers of a technology are pushed to new limits, all the technology is pulled along. With the development of 735-kV transformers came further design advances for transformers in the 138–400-kV range.

In an industry dominated by large multinationals, Ferranti-Packard's success with power transformers would require effective incorporation of the "state of the art" into its own product mix. To accomplish this end, particularly in a period marked by rapid technological change, it had to maintain an appropriate level of R&D. Such efforts could be very expensive, and with limited capital resources, the firm had to concentrate on areas most responsive to its own particular competitive needs. In order to target the company's efforts wisely, Hetherington made it a point of knowing where the industry was going, particularly in the United States.

During the 1960s, as a member of the Transformer Committee of the Institute of Electrical and Electronics Engineers (IEEE), Hetherington was able to keep abreast of technological change. In 1969, he became the first Canadian to chair the committee. Besides discussing technical issues of immediate concern to the American industry, this committee examined long-term technological needs. Through the committee, a small Canadian company could easily tap into the mainstream of American developments and be better prepared to assess and plan R&D for the American market.

From a global perspective, Ferranti-Packard was also well positioned to keep abreast of the rapidly advancing transformer technology. Hetherington was also Canadian representative to the Transformer Committee of the Conférence internationale de grand réseau électrique à haute tension (CIGRE) during the 1960s and 1970s and, along with Charles Kiel, chief engineer for R&D, Power Division, participated in its numerous seminars and conferences. The committee would meet every two years; Hetherington later recalled, "we would have remarkably open discussions on technical matters regarding transformers. Discussions you couldn't have had if you visited your competitor's plant."[49]

Discussions at meetings during the 1960s made Hetherington realize that if Ferranti-Packard were to compete in the higher voltages and carry itself as a technically reliable firm among the big manufacturers in North America, then R&D into better insulation and testing techniques would have to be a priority. Impulse testing had long been

There is also concern over the noise level generated by transformers, particularly in urban areas or in the workplace. Consequently transformer manufacturers must also have audio equipment to measure the noise level in decibels.
(Ontario Archives, Ferranti-Packard Collection, AO 649)

essential in selling transformers to utilities. While it measured a transformer's ability to withstand lightning and switching surges, it could not detect any subtle weaknesses in insulation that might develop in the long term. After many years, these weaknesses could grow and result in serious failure, which was costly in terms of repairs and of disruption in the utilities' electrical service.

Utilities and industry therefore mounted a concerted effort to develop a more sophisticated testing technique to assess the long-term integrity of a transformer's insulation. They evolved methods to detect partial discharges during insulation tests commonly called Corona testing. First developed by the large heavy electrical equipment manufacturers, it was a costly technique that Ferranti-Packard had to have if it hoped to compete in the United States. Not only were utilities increasingly demanding more Corona testing, but this technique had become vital in designing and testing new insulation structures for the higher voltages. To Ferranti-Packard, improvements in insulation technology appeared essential for survival; they offered major cost reductions while also improving reliability in an intensely competitive environment.

R&D in Corona testing and insulation technology were too costly for Ferranti-Packard acting on its own. Other manufacturers had the same problem, and Hetherington helped set up an international consortium – Ferranti-Packard, Ferranti UK, Pennsylvania Transformer, and Industrie Elettriche di Legnano, in Italy. The purpose of this joint research was better to understand the complexities of insulation at different voltages, so as to reduce the amount of space taken up by insulation. Engineers sought to balance cost and reliability. Too much insulation produced transformers that might be more reliable, but far too expensive to be competitive. Too little insulation, and the transformer could fail if overstressed by a lightning stroke or switching

surge. Though complex, this research was propelled by market considerations. The goal was to reduce size and costs, but still maintain reliability.

With the help of the Canadian government, Ferranti-Packard spearheaded this research consortium. Through the Industrial Research Assistance Program (IRAP), Ottawa covered about 50 per cent of Ferranti-Packard's costs. IRAP's goal was to improve the export potential of Canadian manufacturers by helping them carry out the kind of R&D that would make them more competitive. Ferranti-Packard did some highly advanced work in insulation phenomena, which "enabled [Ferranti-Packard] here in Canada to compete in the U.S. market with giants like G.E. and Westinghouse which [the company] otherwise couldn't have done."[50]

While the Power Division was catching up in the area of high-voltage power transformers, it continued to lead in furnace transformer technology. From the earliest days of Packard Electric, success with furnace transformers had derived from the company's ability to extend its expertise beyond design and into application engineering. After decades of close collaboration with North America's top furnace manufacturers, Packard Electric had developed an unsurpassed knowledge of the operation of the various types of electric furnaces and how to design a transformer that would best suit the needs of any particular furnace. As a result of years of specialization, Ferranti-Packard had a vast fund of knowledge and experience in every facet

Short-circuit testing of large transformers (opposite) could not be done within the plant as the very large amounts of power needed to subject the power transformer to currents far higher than those found in normal operation could only be obtained at substations. Until provincial utilities built special facilities, Canadian transformer manufacturers could not perform short-circuit testing on large transformers. Hydro-Quebec provided the first such facility at IREQ in Varennes. Here Ferranti-Packard is testing a 10-MVA power transformer at Ontario Hydro's research centre on Kipling Avenue, Toronto, in April of 1971.
(Ontario Archives, Ferranti-Packard Collection, AO 659)

The Electronics Division of Ferranti-Packard became an early pioneer in computer technology during the 1950s and 60s. In the late 1950s the Transformer Division became an early user of computers for design and research purposes with a computer designed and built by the parent firm in the UK. The computer shown here with Geoffrey Langfield at the console is the Pegasus. This reliable vacuum-tube computer was taken out of operation in 1963.
(Ferranti-Packard Transformers Ltd.)

of furnace transformer design, manufacture, service, and operation that was second to none. Furnace transformers are so specialized that there are no textbooks on the subject. At Packard Electric, and later at Ferranti-Packard, knowledge and experience were passed from mentor to student. Each succeeding generation also innovated and added its own contributions. First there was Frank Wyman and Clayton Snyder. Then came Wordie Hetherington, who, in turn, passed on his expertise to W.G. "Bill" Cook.

Furnace transformers must supply an extraordinary amount of current, at a low voltage, to the electrodes of the furnace. High currents raise a special set of problems in the design of the transformer windings and cooling system. In order to accommodate very high currents flowing in low-voltage winding, the standard practice from 1920 to the 1950s was to replace the single continuous wire normally found in a transformer winding with a bundle of square wires.

By the early 1960s, Ferranti-Packard had pioneered the use of "strip winding." A 30-inch (0.76-m) strip of copper now replaced the bundle of square copper wires. Strip winding changed the furnace transformer's operation, mechanical integrity, and cost. The use of one wide strip eliminated the cumbersome, time-consuming, and costly process of trying to wind many wires in parallel. The wide surface area of the strip winding greatly increased the mechanical strength of the windings and provided superior cooling. This innovation also considerably lowered manufacturing costs. In furnace transformers, the transformer price war had little effect on the Power Division.

Throughout the 1960s, Ferranti-Packard kept setting new limits in the size of its furnace transformers. In 1963, with the delivery of a 18.7-MVA unit to the Atlas Steel Co. in Tracey, Quebec, it had built the largest arc furnace transformer ever put into service in Canada. In 1966, it built one of the largest and most complex furnace transformers in North America. Destined for the Interlake Steel Corp. plant at Beverly, Ohio, this 36-MVA unit could deliver an astounding 80,000 amperes to the furnace's electrodes. Though great engineering achievements, these large furnace transformers were few in number. The bulk of the company's orders came in lower-capacity units.

Ferranti-Packard's reputation as the leading innovator in furnace transformers continued when it introduced a more efficient voltage switching device. Operation of an open arc melting furnace requires a range of voltage and current levels at the electrodes. Tap changers are electrical-mechanical devices that allow a transformer's output to be switched between a fixed set of voltage values. The standard practice in North America was to use either off-load or on-load reactor tap changers. Off-load meant that the transformer had to be shut down while the switch was operated manually. Though off-load tap changers were very simple devices, they greatly increased the unproductive "downtime" of the furnaces. Changing the taps while the transformer is energized, or on-load, presents a whole new set of problems. Since it is imperative to keep the load current flowing in the

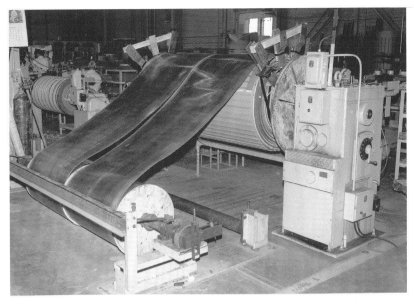

Ferranti-Packard pioneered the transition from copper cables to copper strips to carry the very high currents, sometimes as high as 60,000 amperes, in the windings of furnace transformers. In this photograph, taken 10 October 1963, wide copper winding strips are being wound onto the core of a furnace transformer being custom-built for Lake Ontario Steel.
(Ontario Archives, Ferrati-Packard Collection, AO 654)

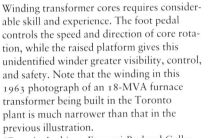

Winding transformer cores requires considerable skill and experience. The foot pedal controls the speed and direction of core rotation, while the raised platform gives this unidentified winder greater visibility, control, and safety. Note that the winding in this 1963 photograph of an 18-MVA furnace transformer being built in the Toronto plant is much narrower than that in the previous illustration.
(Ontario Archives, Ferranti-Packard Collection, AO 683)

transformer winding and to avoid any short-circuiting during tap changes, on-load tap changers are far more complex and hence more costly than off-load devices. They must be designed to limit voltage fluctuations during switching, keep the currents between taps during switching to a minimum, and minimize the duration of the arcing at the moment of switching.

The savings resulting from the furnace's higher operating efficiencies more than justified the added expense of the on-load tap changer. Standard North American on-load tap changers, however, had unacceptably long periods of arcing with each tap change. Tap changers are used extensively in furnace transformers. Long arcing periods led to considerable erosion of contact surfaces and excessive carbonization of the oil, which resulted in substantial maintenance costs. The Ferranti-Packard load-resistor transition tap changer reduced the problems of arcing, thereby increasing the lifetime of tap changer contacts by a factor of ten. The same changer also substantially decreased the maintenance devoted to the oil in the switch compartment.[51]

One of the hallmarks of a technologically astute company is the ability to acquire and put to good use technology developed by others. During the early 1960s, Ferranti-Packard pioneered the use of resistor transition tap changers in North America. Their use had become widespread in Europe, where Ferranti UK had been a leading innovator. Why didn't other North American manufacturers pick up on this development? Was it simply resistance to foreign ideas? Was it smug belief in the superiority of North American technology? Being a subsidiary of a British firm, Ferranti-Packard was more receptive to

Accidents are rare but they happen, as with this transformer being built for Commonwealth Edison in June 1972. In order to prevent heat losses due to eddy currents it has been standard practice since the 1890s to make transformer cores out of stacked sheets of steel. The heavy stacked cores are made horizontally, wrapped with bands to secure them, and then lifted vertically. Once in this position some of the bands are released and the coil lowered to enclose the core. In this case too many bands were released and the heavy steel core collapsed. The workman in the light coloured shirt is Bill Cook. (Ontario Archives, Ferranti-Packard Collection, AO 662)

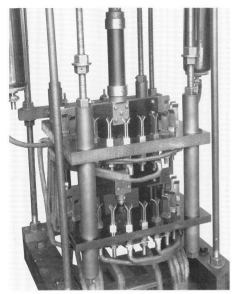

Tap changers allow transformers to switch operating voltages while still energized. In the UK Ferranti Ltd. had been a leading innovator in reactor transition-load tap changers. Ferranti Canada started with the parent firm's technology and then designed and built its own version during the 1930s. Three decades later, in an effort to reduce manufacturing costs and eliminate some operating problems, Ferranti-Packard engineers introduced resistor transition tap changers (shown on the right) to North America. (Ontario Archives, Ferranti-Packard Collection, AO 776, Ferranti-Packard Transformers Ltd.)

any promising European technology. Convinced of the superiority of the European practice, Ferranti-Packard hired Andy Elder, from Canadian General Electric, to develop an on-load resistor-type tap changer for the North American market.

The new tap changer had an unexpected benefit for the company's business in the United States. Any electrical utility seeks to provide uninterrupted service at a voltage that remains constant within well-defined limits. On early power-supply systems it was possible to control the voltage drop of transmission lines by varying the output of the generator. With the rapid growth of long-distance transmission networks and closely interconnected urban systems, automatic voltage control became essential. On-load tap changing had long been an essential feature of power distribution systems.

North American transformer manufacturers were still rooted in the *reactor* transition type of tap changer. As the more reliable *resistor* transition type slowly gained acceptance, Ferranti-Packard was well positioned to compete. Its experience in furnace transformers gave it a great advantage when it came to improving the long-term mechanical reliability of tap changers. Power transformers experience some 5,000 tap changes per year. A tap changer in a furnace transformer, however, may have some 1,000–1,500 tap changes in a day. As a result, data on the ability of a power transformer's tap changer to withstand the mechanical stresses of thirty years of operation may be gathered in less than six months of operation in a furnace transformer.

Ironically, Ferranti Canada had, during the 1930s and 1940s, developed a market niche in voltage regulation. By a combination of home-grown and parent-firm technology, it marketed a variety of successful automatic step-voltage regulators and on-load tap-changing devices. This tradition disappeared after 1945 but resurfaced in the 1960s as part of furnace transformer development, another Packard tradition.

Although Wordie Hetherington had cut the Power Division's losses during the 1960s, his efforts failed to put the division on a sound, profitable basis. External and internal obstacles foiled his efforts. In 1958, he rose to be general manager of the new Power Transformer Division, just as overcapacity was wreaking havoc with the entire electrical industry. Short of an imposed rationalization of the entire industry, the future did not hold out any relief from the intense competition. None of the players displayed any willingness to budge. With so much already invested, few could afford to leave. Closing a plant was costly and traumatic. For Ferranti-Packard, its power transformer operation in Toronto had become a "Catch-22" affair: too costly to stay in and too costly to get out of.

When Hetherington took over the Power Transformer Division, he sought to expand its engineering know-how in order to keep up with rapid technological changes sweeping the industry. By the end of the 1960s, the division was on a sound technological footing. With the addition of Bob Veitch, from Allis-Chalmers in the United States and formerly with Westinghouse Canada, as head of engineering, Ferranti-Packard had the expertise to produce the larger power transformers. Productivity, however, constantly eluded Hetherington's control. The quality of work was never the problem, but the pace was. Schemes to increase productivity ran into considerable resistance from the United Electrical Workers. For example, any effort to introduce a more flexible division of labour, by assigning work tasks as a function of the dynamic needs of the production schedule, was immediately rebuffed. An ingrained unco-operative spirit in labour-management relations threatened the future of the company.

Upon becoming general manager, Hetherington immediately set better labour relations as a priority. Despite the innovative management practices that he introduced with his professional staff, he found himself unable to elicit from the union the kind of co-operation for which he hoped. After a time he came to believe that low productivity and labour hostility had become an organic part of the Toronto plant's existence long before the merger. To this day, he sees his inability to improve labour relations as his greatest failure as general manager.

Ferranti-Packard gambled that it could carve out a profitable niche in this overpopulated industry, but by the early 1970s this outcome did not seem likely. Life for the Distribution Division, however, was much rosier.

The Distribution Division

Though not subject to the same offshore competition as the Power Division, Distribution faced equally stiff domestic competition throughout the early 1960s. After nearly five years of losses, it

Survival and successful entry into the American transformer market involved more than dispatching a capable sales force. In the 1960s the Power Division launched a major productivity and waste-prevention campaign. Wordie Hetherington's favourite equation was "productivity equals output divided by input," where output was measured by selling price and input by total costs. With selling prices falling, costs rising, and no real prospects for increasing the former, the key to survival lay in reducing costs. During the 1960s the word productivity made unions very nervous, so the emphasis was placed on reducing waste, an important part of productivity. It had also been a long tradition at the plant. Tom Edmondson, for example, toured the plant daily for years and never failed to examine scrap barrels, for what was thrown out often offered clues to better methods and areas which needed improvement. Wordie Hetherington's campaign placed great emphasis on reducing the amount of copper scrapped, recycled, or just plain lost from view. The waste-prevention campaign fit in with a major effort in the same area by the Canadian Manufacturers Association.

At the same time, Hetherington launched a major study to reduce the size and amount of insulation needed. The size, and consequently the cost, of a transformer is directly proportional to the thickness of insulation between layers in the winding. The Ferranti-Packard insulation research project, which was assisted by an IRAP grant from the National Research Council of Canada, reduced insulation thickness.
(Ontario Archives, Ferranti-Packard Collection, AO 1262)

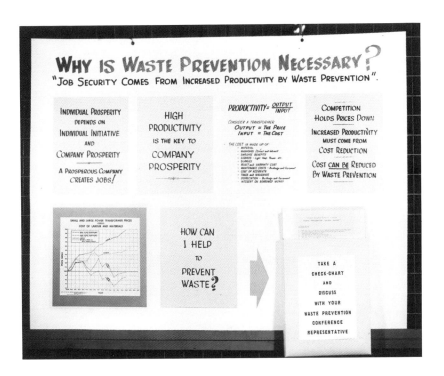

started, in 1965, a long period of stable growth and profits. The electronics and power operations, fraught with uncertainties, continued to struggle on. Unlike the dazzle of high-tech electronics or the awe-inspiring sight of power transformers delivering enormous amounts of power at previously unheard-of voltages, there was nothing glamorous about Distribution's products. Yet the division became the foundation of Ferranti-Packard's commercial survival throughout most of the 1960s and 1970s. The story of its success is one of singular market opportunities and the ability of management and labour to capitalize on them.

Located in the former Packard Electric facilities in St Catharines, the Distribution Division was created after the merger in 1958 to handle the watt-hour-meter, instrument, distribution, and small power transformer businesses. Trois-Rivières fell under the division's mandate. In its first few years, Distribution's bread-and-butter products were pole-top transformers and meters. After Packard Electric's invention of the Lock Wound core in the 1950s, the new division switched to the straight wound core in the 1960s. Sold primarily to Canadian utilities, pole-top transformers gave the division its greatest volume of business for most of the 1960s, with the bulk of the devices produced at St Catharines.

Producing some 4–5 power transformers per month, the division's business in small power transformers remained quite modest. Starting in 1967, a fortuitous chain of events brought the American firm Allis-Chalmers and Ferranti-Packard into a close and profitable collaboration which profoundly influenced the future of the Distribution Divi-

Reduced production costs helped keep Ferranti-Packard transformers competitively priced. In 1960 Jack Webb, a mechanical engineer at Ferranti-Packard, designed equipment to change taping from a manual to a mechanical process. The operator is unidentified.
(Ferranti-Packard Transformers Ltd.)

sion. Allis-Chalmers had developed a very good business in the United States selling both switch-gear and small power transformers for substations. In 1967, a prolonged strike in its Pittsburgh transformer plant threatened the profitable substation business. Tipped off by a friend about the predicament and the firm's search for an alternative supply of small power transformers, Jack Coopman, marketing manager for Ferranti-Packard's Distribution Division, flew down to Milwaukee to win some business. Having put off finding an alternative supplier and facing increasing presure from disgruntled customers waiting impatiently for delivery, Allis-Chalmers was anxious to find a supplier. A series of preliminary meetings culminated in an all-night negotiating session at the Holiday Inn, in St Catharines, which produced a one-year contract.[52]

In addition to convincing Allis-Chalmers that Ferranti-Packard could produce a high-quality product, Coopman also had to promise a now-frantic Allis-Chalmers that his firm could deliver a large number of transformers in a very short time. Although St Catharines had never before built so many transformers in such a short time, Coopman never questioned the plant's ability to meet the extremely ambitious production schedule that he had promised Allis-Chalmers. Everyone in St Catharines, from management to shop floor, threw themselves into the challenge with great dedication and fervour. The plant produced a lot of transformers very quickly. So pleased was Allis-Chalmers that it kept extending the contract year after year for fifteen years; it closed down its own transformer operations and made Ferranti-Packard its major supplier.

The consequences of the Allis-Chalmers deal were profound. The St Catharines plant started to build 8–10 transformers a week. This contract alone brought in between $1.5 million and $4 million annually.[53] More important, the contracts generated a great deal of good publicity and many new costumers in the United States. Although Allis-Chalmers put its own name plate on the Ferranti-Packard–produced transformer, it made no secret of the source. As a result, many of its prospective customers went to St Catharines to satisfy themselves that the plant there could produce the kind of quality that they required in the substation that they were buying from Allis-Chalmers.

Up to this point, Ferranti-Packard's transformer business was known to the American utilities primarily through the efforts of the Power Division. The Distribution Division at St Catharines had now opened up an entirely different market in the American industrial sector. Coopman recalls how companies such as Ford, General Motors, International Paper, Scott Paper, and Weyerhauser, and contractors such as Bechtel and Braun, came to inspect the plant. This boosted the plant's American reputation and attracted a great deal more business. The American automobile industry was booming, and it was not unusual for the plant to receive a single order for 30–40 small power transformers, in a business where orders usually came in threes and fours.[54]

Ferranti-Packard manufactured small power transformers, such as these made for Allis-Chalmers. This particular transformer was Askarel-filled, others were oil-filled. Askarel is the generic name for a synthetic cooling oil containing polychlorinated biphenyls or PCBs.

Transformers generate heat that must be removed to avoid damage to the insulation. The early insulator coolant oils had one major drawback: they were flammable. Askarel was far more fire-resistant. However, because it was more viscous and therefore flowed less readily, it conducted heat away more slowly. Consequently, when Wordie Hetherington designed Packard's first Askarel-filled transformers in the 1950s, he had to make the core and coils 15 per cent larger to compensate for Askarel's less-efficient cooling. At that time there were no suspicions that Askarel might be carcinogenic. In the mid-1970s Ferranti-Packard started working with Dow-Corning Chemicals to find a PCB replacement. By the early 1980s Ferranti-Packard had completely discontinued use of PCBs.
(Ontario Archives, Ferranti-Packard Collection, AO 658)

This success in the American market had given the St Catharines plant far greater economies of scale. It was a critical turning point for the Distribution Division. Coopman later recalled: "Instead of building one small power transformer at a time, as they had been built, we now had a semi-production line going. As a result we were able to standardize this class of transformer. That increased our productivity and reduced our costs. It also enabled us to be more competitive in purchasing. Our purchasing department was able to arrange larger contracts, on a forecasted annual basis, with quantities to be released as required, at better prices. This further increased our competitive position."[55]

The new economies of scale also positioned the division to become active in the sizeable network transformer market. The practice of using network transformers developed in urbanized areas, where the high density of customers made good voltage regulation and uninterrupted service a priority. Customers were linked to a number of transformers in a network instead of to one transformer. If one transformer failed, another would automatically take over the load without any loss of service. To make the system even more fail-safe, the network was fed by several different power lines so that the entire system did not depend exclusively on one source of power.

Network transformers must withstand far more rugged service. Because they may undergo many short circuits, they are built more solidly in order to cope with the large mechanical forces produced in the

The success of the Trois-Rivières plant as an efficient, cost-effective manufacturer of pole-top distribution transformers led to the need for more space. On 15 November 1984 Charles Begin (left), general manager of Ferranti-Packard transformers in Trois-Rivières, Gilles Beaudoin, Mayor of Trois-Rivières, and Barry Hercus, CEO and president of NEI Canada, officially opened the $2 million plant expansion shown on the far upper right.
(Opening photo courtesy Barry Hercus, plant courtesy Ferranti-Packard Transformers Ltd., Trois-Rivières, Quebec)

The staff of the Trois-Rivières plant in 1992. The abilities and enthusiastic dedication of the Trois-Rivières employees have made this plant one of the jewels in Ferranti-Packard's operations.
(Ferranti-Packard Transformers Ltd., Trois-Rivières, Quebec)

windings by short circuits. Network systems are usually placed underground. Because the cables are carried in ducts and the transformers are located in vaults below street level, flooding is common. As a result, network transformers for such applications must, in common with subway transformers, be watertight.

Ferranti-Packard had long specialized in building network transformers, but the Canadian market was relatively small. Now economies of scale at St Catharines gave the company a competitive edge. Development of its own disconnect switch increased this edge. Designed by engineer Eric Bergenstein, this high-voltage switch forms a critical part of the transformer's protective system. If the transformer develops any electrical problems, a "network protector" automatically disconnects the transformer's secondary winding from the network, and the switch disconnects the primary winding from the incoming power line. Ferranti-Packard was thus able to add much more value to its manufacturing process. With these manufacturing advantages, the Distribution Division reassessed its marketing strategy and decided to go after all the US utilities that used network transformers. By the early 1970s, Coopman remembers, St Catharines "started to sell a hell of a lot of small network transformers across the u.s."[56]

By the early 1970s, Ferranti-Packard's strategy to penetrate the US market had touched all but one of the company's operations. The meter business remained purely Canadian. The ability of the Distribution Division to capitalize on the Allis-Chalmers business and exploit the US market for small power transformers helped keep the company's head above water. So, too, did the Trois-Rivières plant's successful take-over of the pole-top transformer business formerly at St Catharines. From the moment that Charles Begin had been appointed manager at Trois-Rivières, he fought impatiently to give his plant a fully autonomous base. Increasing specialization in small power transformers at St Catharines allowed him to carve out a mandate for his own plant.

From Dependence to Independence with Charles Begin

Initially, Packard Electric envisaged the plant in Trois-Rivières as a gateway into the Quebec market for products from St Catharines. All components for distribution transformers and watt-hour meters would be produced in St Catharines and then shipped to Trois-

The Trois-Rivières plant excels in producing pole-top transformers. These photographs demonstrate some of the important steps in manufacturing pole top distribution transformers.

(a) Benoit Rouleau winding the low-voltage coil

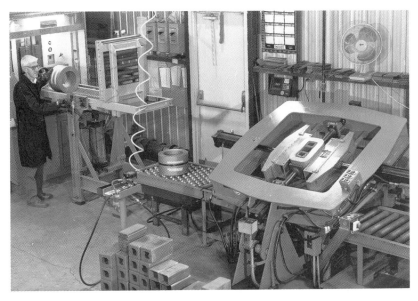

(b) Gilles Cossette shaping the wound core

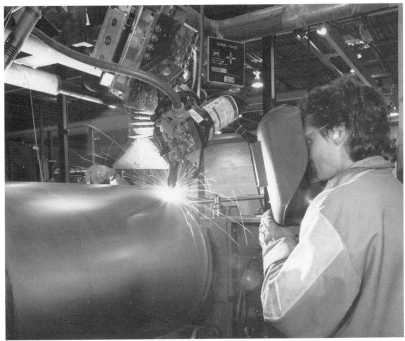

(c) Jacques Poirier and equipment for robotic
welding of transformer tank

Rivières for assembly. The same approach continued after the merger
in 1958. The assembly operation in Quebec added little, if any, value.
As a result, for several years Ferranti-Packard ran the Quebec plant as
a straight overhead cost.

In late 1960, Charles Begin replaced Walter Seline as manager at
Trois-Rivières. Born in the small town of Mont Joli, not far down the
St Lawrence from Trois-Rivières, Begin joined Ferranti Canada in the

summer of 1947, while studying electrical engineering at Laval University. After taking a year's leave of absence to complete his bachelor of engineering degree, he returned to Ferranti Canada in 1949 as a sales engineer in the Montreal office. By 1958, he had risen to be sales manager for Quebec. After the merger, there was room for only one Quebec sales manager, and Begin moved back down to sales engineer. Packard Electric's Quebec sales manager, Bob Short, assumed the same title for Ferranti-Packard.

When Begin took over at Trois-Rivières in late 1960, the volume of business had reached desperate lows. Intense price competition and a reduction in Hydro-Québec's orders as a result of a recession took their toll. Begin recalled the grim situation that he faced: "I was left in the plant with only three direct labour employees ... Only one person at a time was working on a transformer ... The volume was very low, very bad ... Two transformers was a big order."[57]

Begin wanted the plant to become a successful manufacturing operation. The more value the plant added, the more self-supporting it could become. Begin was convinced that the operation could, if given the equipment and opportunity, generate substantial profits. He had to convince his superiors to invest in equipment. He argued that production should be transferred from St Catharines because wage rates were lower in Quebec than in Ontario, sending parts to Trois-Rivières for assembly involved significant transportation costs, and Hydro-Québec was exerting more and more pressure for manufacturing facilities in the province.

The company's transformer operations were losing money. Begin later recalled, "everything was very hard to get. You not only had to present good figures, but you also had to be very persistent."[58] Not being part of Ferranti-Packard's inner circle compounded Begin's difficulties. He did not sit on the management committee. He reported to the general manager of the St Catharines operation, who had to approve any plans for Trois-Rivières before they went to the company's executive.

Begin set about patiently to increase his plant's manufacturing role in a well-calculated, incremental manner: "start with one manufacturing operation, perfect it, make it profitable and then go on to the next step."[59] The struggle to convince management in Toronto fostered a close-knit team spirit at Trois-Rivières. Every accomplishment was a source of pride, clear proof that Trois-Rivières could handle any challenge, and a declaration that "Made in Quebec" was a sound business decision.

After an uncertain beginning, the plant grew slowly and methodically from an assembly operation to a manufacturing facility with its own design capabilities. It exceeded all of management's initial expectations. Maurice Duplessis was right after all when he said: "Mr. Edmondson, you must realize the opportunities you will have by coming to Three Rivers and Quebec. We have an unsurpassed labour class and our workers are amongst the best in the world."[60]

(d) Aimé Gagné, left, and Gaétan Lemay painting pole-top transformer tanks

(e) Claude Poitras, left, and François Grenier lowering the core and windings into the tank
(The five preceding photographs courtesy Ferranti-Packard Transformers Ltd., Trois-Rivières, Quebec)

8 *Birth of the Electronics Division*

From the horrors and human suffering of the Second World War emerged a new economic, technological, and political order in Canada. At the outbreak of war, Canada was still in the grip of the Depression. By war's end most traces of the Depression had vanished. War production accelerated Canada's transformation from a mere producer of raw materials to a modern industrial state. In 1943, C.D. Howe, who as minister of munitions and supply oversaw wartime production, boasted that "never again will there be any doubt that Canada can manufacture anything that can be manufactured elsewhere."[1]

The war fostered a new relationship among science, technology, and national development, which became the cornerstone of post-war military and economic development. Never before had science and technology been so systematically exploited in the waging of war. Rockets, automatic fire control, guidance systems, radar, atomic energy, and the electronic digital computer were all consequences of wartime imperatives. Unfortunately, global tensions did not end in 1945. Former allies, the Americans and Soviets, polarized the world into two armed ideological camps, each accusing the other of seeking world domination. In this emerging Cold War, a nation's ability to apply science-based technologies to the defence of its borders became an urgent priority. Finding itself behind technologically, the Soviet military raced to catch up with the United States. Fearing that the Soviet Union would achieve technological parity, the American military greatly expanded its support of science and technology. In 1949, the Soviet Union tested it first atomic bomb. The importance of science and technology in any future world conflict was now frighteningly clear.

The Cold War and the difficulties of defending Canada's vast, sparsely populated territory shaped the Canadian military's approach to science and technology. Despite the nation's efforts to play the role of the "middle power" in the growing Cold War tensions, Canada could not escape taking sides. The Canadian military was too well integrated with the American forces not to take sides. With Canada caught geographically between the Soviet Union and the United States, its northern borders became a pivotal element of American defence strategy. Canadians realized that in order to reinforce their traditional claim of sovereignty over the Arctic they would have to take an active role in continental defence. "Otherwise, the U.S. might defend Canada out of her vast geographic future."[2]

Unlike the United States, where a mushrooming military-industrial complex could lavishly support research and development, Canada's military establishment had little money to spend on R&D. With limited funds, it tried to encourage the private sector to take a more active role in R&D. Canadian industry, however, lacked the capacity to carry on serious R&D in many of the newly emerging technologies. In the face of such deficiencies, government assistance would be needed to induce Canadian industry to take up pure and applied research. Even Howe, an ardent laissez-faire advocate, realized "that only government would have the strength to guarantee Canadians a future in science and technology."[3] The Canadian military had some money to prime the R&D pump, but industry would have to keep the pump operating. Could Canadian industry easily convert military-inspired innovation into commercially viable products?

Ferranti-Packard's entry into electronics emerged from this new relationship between industry and the military. With the birth of the Electronics Division in 1949, Ferranti Canada became a founder of Canada's computer industry. The history of the division displays the managerial, corporate, market, and engineering challenges faced by small, innovative companies trying to build an indigenous computer industry in Canada. Its history is a microcosm of the early history of Canada's computer industry; great innovation of itself cannot guarantee commercial success.

Rise of the Electronic Digital Computer

From the concerns of war and destruction grew one of the most profound technological achievements of the human mind in recent history, the computer. For thousands of years technology had sought to extend, multiply, and enhance the physical capabilities of humankind. The examples are endless: mechanical and electrical machines to increase the power and speed of the human body; optical systems, such as telescopes and microscopes, to increase the power of the eye; communications technology to extend the range of speech and hearing; transportation systems to increase mobility. There had been precursors, but the electronic digital computer marked the first significant technological extension of the human mind's ability to calculate.

In the United States, the electronic digital computer grew out of the necessity of producing accurate ballistic firing and bombing tables during the Second World War. To calculate these tables, one had to solve a complex set of equations that took into account the amount of charge used, the weight of the shell, the inclination of the cannon, the distance of the target, atmospheric conditions at various heights, air friction, the laws of gravity, and even the rotation of the Earth. Firing cannons and dropping bombs had grown into a complex science. The computational tools of the day – namely, mechanical desk calculators and mechanical analog computers – were too slow to meet wartime demand for ballistics firing tables. As the war continued, "the situation became hopeless. [The Allies] were incapable of producing more than 15 tables a week, yet the number of tabular requests had reached 40 a week."[4] A new kind of calculator, working on radically different principles, would be needed.

In England, efforts to break a highly sophisticated German code resulted in the application of electronic digital techniques to code breaking. Messages are coded in terms of rules that substitute different letters for those in the original message. If one knows these rules one can decipher the code. The Germans had developed an ingenious electro-mechanical teletype machine, called the Geheimfernschreiber, and could easily alter the coding rules from day to day by simply changing the settings on four drums. British intelligence labelled the teletype machine Enigma. Since the number of possible ways in which Enigma could code a message were in the trillions, the Nazis were firmly convinced of their system's indecipherability.

Both the Americans and the British needed a new kind of machine that could solve difficult problems by doing thousands upon thousands of simple arithmetical and/or logical operations in a very short time. In 1937, the eccentric and brilliant mathematician Alan Turing proved that a thinking machine could, in theory, be built to resolve any mathematical problem. In 1938, Claude Shannon, from MIT and the father of information theory, proved that the problems of mathematical logic could be handled by electronic switching circuits.

The theoretical work of Turing and Shannon found concrete expression in two projects of far-reaching importance. The Americans started work on a top secret project to build a radically new computational device based entirely on digital electronic principles. The result was an Electronic Numerical Integrator and Calculator (ENIAC). As Herman Goldstine, a mathematician and liaison officer between the US Army and the ENIAC group, later said, "the automation of [ballistic table computations] ... was the raison d'être for the first electronic digital computer."[5] By the time the University of Pittsburgh group had built ENIAC, the war had ended.

On the other side of the Atlantic, British scientists and mathematicians started work on an electronic digital computer called Colossus. After the Polish underground captured an Enigma machine, the British group set about studying its operation. British intelligence then used Colossus to emulate the mechanical operation of the Enigma machine, but at very high speeds using electronic switching circuits. Colossus would decode an Enigma-generated code by going through all the possible drum settings of the Enigma machine until a meaningful message emerged. From 1943 to the end of the war, and unbe-known to the Nazis, the British were regularly decoding the German High Command's radio transmissions. Breaking the Enigma code was instrumental in winning the war, and without Colossus it would have been impossible to decipher Enigma.

Colossus was neither a calculating machine nor a programmable computer. The 2,400–vacuum tube machine was a special-purpose digital electronic device capable of making logical comparisons at high speeds. ENIAC was more complex. It was not, in appearance or operation, like any computer we think of today. It consisted of 18,000 vacuum tubes, weighed 30 tons, covered a floor space of about 1,800 square feet (about 200 m^2), and consumed a staggering 174 kW of power – enough power to heat an apartment building. For all its monolithic presence, it could not compete with the smallest of today's microcomputers. Nevertheless, ENIAC opened people's eyes to the immense computational power of the electronic digital computer.

Military interest in the computer did not end with the war; it only intensified. Wartime and immediate post-war developments such as radar, ENIAC, the atomic bomb, the German V-2 rockets, and the transistor reflected a new relationship between pure scientific research and technological development. Technological development now required much greater scientific and mathematical sophistication. The electronic digital computer offered the computational power and speed needed to squeeze out practical answers from highly abstract and complex mathematical models.

The computer represented more than just a fast, automatic calculating machine. By means of its high-speed Boolean logic, it could "intelligently" operate other machines. The implications of a computer's ability to control other machines was not lost on the post-war military mind. During the war, there was intense interest in automated weapons systems such as radar-directed anti-aircraft gunfire control and guidance systems for aircraft. From these efforts arose a new discipline called cybernetics. Cybernetics, derived from the Greek word "kubernetes," meaning to steer a ship, deals with the study of self-correcting systems. Using "feedback," a machine can readjust itself automatically and continuously by analysing past performance. As post-war weapons systems grew in complexity, the computer provided the "hardware" needed to implement cybernetics and create intelligent weapons systems.

The post-war rise of Operations Research (OR) also heightened interest in the computer. OR had its start in Professor P.M.S. Blackett's efforts "to introduce scientific methods and attitude of mind" into British Army operations. In 1940, Blackett set up the first Army Operations Research. Blackett's OR group, nicknamed Blackett's Circus, made some crucial contributions to the British war effort. Soon other OR groups sprouted up throughout the British and American armed forces. One of the six original members of Blackett's team was a young physicist named Arthur Porter. Nineteen years later,

Porter would come to Canada to lead Ferranti Electric's first digital electronics research group.

By using rather sophisticated mathematical models, the proponents of OR claimed to provide an impartial, scientific, and quantitative basis for making complex decisions. The growth of OR, like other applied mathematical models, required considerable computational power. The parallel development of electronic digital computers greatly increased the power and scope of OR. OR was infectious and soon found a wide range of applications, from military logistics to scientific management.

The Computer and Canada's Post-War Technological Needs

With little money at its disposal, Canada's Defence Research Board (DRB) sought to stimulate and co-ordinate industrial R&D in areas of military interest. According to D.J. Goodspeed, author of *A History of the Defence Research Board of Canada*, "there was a belief that, as more and more research was done in this country, Canadian industries would realize that scientific projects of their own were not only feasible but also profitable."[6] This research, however, could not be done in a vacuum. Canada needed foreign knowledge and capital. DRB's biggest challenge was to induce the parent firms of Canadian companies to establish R&D in Canada.

The development of a broad spectrum of electronics technologies was a prime DRB concern in the post-war years. As a report to the Royal Commission on Canada's Economic Prospects (1956) pointed out: "Prior to World War II, government contracts played little or no part in the development of the electronics industry in Canada. However, the rapid growth of the electronics industry after the outbreak of the war was largely the result of government contracts. Factories were built and equipped with funds obtained through capital assistance contracts. As a result of the large-scale cancellations of government contracts upon the termination of hostilities, the output of the electronics industry shrunk considerably in 1945 and 1946."[7]

The Canadian electronics industry's poor record of applied R&D further hampered DRB's initiatives to stimulate military-oriented R&D. A good deal of electronics R&D came to Canada, in the form of technology transfer from US multinationals to their subsidiaries. As a result, the Canadian electronics industry had a poorly developed infrastructure for carrying out its own innovative work.

In an attempt to foster more applied electronics research in Canada, DRB distributed a confidential list, in August 1948, of Canadian armed forces applied R&D requirements and called for proposals from industry. DRB specified four areas of electronics research: (1) precision servo-systems for computers, including automatic following devices for radar systems; (2) frequency control and crystals; (3) unattended power supplies; and (4) radar systems.

In a letter to Vincent Ziani de Ferranti, Capt. E.G. Cullwick, director of the DRB's Electrical Research Division, wrote: "The Defence

Research Board intends to initiate a program of applied research in Canadian industry in fields related to the use of electronic equipment in the Armed Forces. Such a program would balance the Board's program of basic research in the Canadian Universities, and would, it is felt, prove a valuable foundation for the Canadian production of Service equipment. *The value of such work to the problems of defence will of course depend on the degree to which the program can be carried out with Canadian facilities and personnel* [emphasis added]."[8]

This letter produced a flurry of memos between V.Z. de Ferranti and his senior managers and engineers on both sides of the Atlantic. How should Ferranti UK best respond to DRB's requirement that all the work be carried out in Canada? Ferranti UK had the engineering and scientific manpower, facilities, and proven experience; Ferranti Canada in Toronto had neither the experience nor the manpower to undertake any applied research in electronics. More important, Ferranti Canada did not have the appropriate financial and management resources. Ferranti UK had the resources but was unwilling to set up an electronics research group in Canada at its own expense.

By October 1948, V.Z. de Ferranti had decided that an independent electronics research group could be developed in Canada. It would be formed around a small nucleus of Ferranti UK experts, with the bulk of the engineers and technicians being Canadian. Though Ferranti UK was willing to supply management support and technology transfer, it was unwilling to underwrite the cost. De Ferranti wanted assurances that the Canadian government would provide sufficient defence contracts to make the new group self-supporting.

On 18 October 1948, V.Z. de Ferranti met in Ottawa with Dr. Ormond Solandt, chairman of the DRB, and other members of the board, and put forward his company's proposal to set up an electronics research group in Canada. Also present were Dr. John Thomson, from Ferranti Canada in Toronto; Richard Davies, from Ferranti Electric Inc. in New York; and Eric Grundy, John Toothill, and John Stewart from Ferranti UK. On Grundy's recommendation, V.Z. de Ferranti pushed electronic servo-control, digital electronics, and computers during his meeting with DRB.[9]

Vincent was looking for financial inducements to justify applied research in Canada, but DRB had none. The meeting disillusioned and upset the Ferranti delegation. It had come so far for so little. In his official reply, Solandt rejected the proposal because it could not be sufficiently supported by current or projected commercial activity: "It was felt that, since we are just beginning a policy of subsidizing research and development for defence purposes in industry, we should for the present confine our efforts to the beginnings of a research and development organization in Canada for purely commercial purposes. It was felt that we had not yet reached the stage where we could undertake to support a research venture such as the one which you propose which has no direct commercial value but is entirely dependent on government support."[10]

Was it still worthwhile for Ferranti Canada and Ferranti UK to pursue development contracts with DRB? V.Z. de Ferranti sent a copy of Solandt's letter to several of the people who had been at the meeting. The reactions were not encouraging. John Thomson wanted nothing to do with DRB. A.B. Cooper, president of Ferranti Canada, re-marked sarcastically that "Solandt leaves a small loophole open for us to be associated with the Board, provided we will work for nothing."[11] Richard Davies replied: "It seems to confirm our impression that the Defence Research Board have few resources at their command, and probably are acting only on a broad directive to support industrial research and development. It is not necessary to point out that if research and development facilities exist and are supported on a purely commercial basis, there is no need for any government subsidy to make them available for defence purposes."[12]

Despite their disagreement with the DRB's position, many supported Cooper's advice to de Ferranti that "it might be in our general interest nor to ignore Solandt's suggestion of unpaid co-operation."[13]

Birth of the Electronics Division

After the disappointing meeting with Solandt, the prospects of Ferranti doing military electronics work in Canada were quite dismal. But a young naval lieutenant, named Jim Belyea, and Digital Automated Tracking and Resolving (DATAR) saved the day. DATAR represented a comprehensive inter-ship electronic information processing and communication system that Belyea had been formulating since 1946. Belyea envisaged DATAR as a system that would allow a fleet of ships to gather, share, and display radar and sonar data regarding enemy aircraft, ships, and submarines. From his experience with naval training simulators, Belyea knew that conventional electrical analog computation and display of data would not work. As a research officer of a Canadian naval electronics laboratory, Belyea had access to American and British scientific intelligence. After reading about the work already done on computers, Belyea's intuition told him that DATAR had to be based on digital electronics. However, he had no idea how to make it work.

Belyea was searching for companies to convert his dream to reality. Belyea knew of the 18 October meeting and had "heard that the DRB and Ferranti groups didn't hit it off."[14] He seized the moment and approached the Ferranti group with the idea of DATAR and R&D money. Unlike DRB, Belyea's Navy lab could provide Ferranti with the money to set up an electronics research group in Canada. Furthermore, to a technology-driven company such as Ferranti UK, the challenge and potential of DATAR were too tempting to turn down. Recalling the initial discussions of Belyea's ideas, Kenyon Taylor, who later came from England to head the research group, wrote: "it seemed to our group that what he had in mind was very much the proper thing to be doing. It was a system for the acquisition, digital processing, transmission and display of naval information, a first step in push-button warfare. Lt. Belyea was thinking 15 years ahead of his time and Sir

Vincent de Ferranti and the rest of our party were well in tune with him."[15]

Belyea proposed a rather odd form of funding, which, to his surprise, V.Z. de Ferranti accepted. Because Belyea had authority to approve contracts only for $5,000 and under, he broke up the DATAR proposal into a series of small, $5,000 contracts: "I discovered a scheme, from a junior person in the Deputy Minister's Office, of getting large contracts out. If you needed $15,000, the trick was to put out three contracts at $5,000, all under different names, to the same outfit."[16] Through this method, Belyea was able to provide a considerable amount of money for the first year of the DATAR project.

Before Solandt had a chance even to reject officially de Ferranti's proposal, Ferranti UK had already decided to embark on DATAR. On 19 January 1949 Ferranti UK sent a team of four to start up an Electronics Research group at Ferranti Canada. Kenyon Taylor left on the maiden voyage of the *Caronia*, while John Harben, Donald Walker, and G. Ross set sail for Canada on the *Empress of France*.

On arriving in Toronto, Taylor set up the Research Department, the forerunner of the Electronics Division, in a 1,500-sq-ft (139.4 m²) area at the far end of the X-ray assembly shop.[17] He then set about recruiting a core of bright young electronics engineers, many of whom had just graduated from university: Gordon Lang and J. Williams, from Western; Tom Cranston and Les Wood, from Toronto; H. Ristow, from Queen's; Dave Nuttall, from UBC; and P. Levers.

Solandt's letter of 7 January 1949 to V.Z. de Ferranti reveals that Solandt was unaware of Belyea's initiative. Solandt was trying to consolidate DRB's authority to co-ordinate all R&D in the Canadian military. Belyea's independent negotiations with Ferranti Canada were a flagrant encroachment on DRB territory. Ironically, it was Capt. Cullwick, a fellow naval officer and director of DRB's Electrical Research Division, who not only told Belyea of the unsuccessful meeting but also recommended that Belyea meet with the Ferranti delegation.

V.Z. de Ferranti did not want his company caught in the middle of an intragovernmental squabble. Fearing that Solandt would react badly to the DATAR project, thus jeopardizing future contracts, de Ferranti wrote to Solandt informing him of the Navy work and reassured him that the newly formed Canadian electronics group was ready to assist DRB if needed. Although some frictions arose between DRB and Belyea's Navy research laboratory, Solandt supported the Navy's initiative on DATAR as an "engineering development" project, not "research."

DATAR: Canada's First Steps in Computer Technology

To build a realistic prototype of DATAR required far more money than Belyea's financing scheme could provide – it would require selling the project to the Navy's highest echelon. A preliminary demonstration was needed to convince skeptical senior Navy officials of the merits of digital transmission. Funded by Belyea, the new Research

The original equipment used by Ferranti Electric in February 1950 in establishing a radio link between Toronto and a Navy laboratory in Ottawa to demonstrate the merits of digital-data transmission. (John Vardalas)

Department at Ferranti Canada set about proving that radar tracking data could be reliably represented and communicated in a digital format via a radio link.

By February 1950, the Ferranti Canada group had successfully demonstrated the merits of digital data transmission. In a radio link between Ottawa and Toronto, it transmitted the x, y coordinates of light fictitious targets from Toronto and then graphically displayed the targets in Belyea's Navy laboratory in Ottawa. The special display monitor, a cathode ray tube, was developed by Computing Devices of Canada Ltd. Impressed by what they saw, the Navy admirals authorized $900,000 to develop a full scale demonstration with two ships and a land station to simulate a third ship.[18]

Half-way through phase 1 of DATAR, V.Z. de Ferranti sent Dr. Arthur Porter from England to Canada to take charge of Ferranti's Research Department and DATAR. A distinguished British physicist who had done pioneering work in differential analysers, Porter was also a noted authority in control theory, servo-control mechanisms, and operations research. Many years later, Porter established the Department of Industrial Engineering at the University of Toronto, which he chaired for many years. Sir Vincent felt that a man of Porter's international stature would add considerable credibility to the Research Department's operations and enhance its ability to obtain further defence contracts.

Preferring the academic title of "Head of Research" to that of "Manager of the Research Department," Porter added a professorial dimension to the fledgling Research Department. Together, Porter and Taylor moulded the department into a research institute where business planning took a back seat to the excitement of invention. As with Taylor before him, Porter lost no time in recruiting some of the finest young engineers that Canadian universities had to offer.

In contrast to Porter's theoretical approach to research, Taylor was a "hands-on" engineer. Impatient with the constraints of formal education, Taylor had spent two years at the University of Manchester before leaving out of boredom. In 1931, he joined Ferranti as a "lab boy." From 1931 to 1972, his exceptional inventive talents produced seventy-two patents, in fields as diverse as textile machinery, TV and radio, radar, grain-drying machinery, air-bearing magnetic drums, the track-ball, xerography, and automobile detectors used in traffic signal systems.

It was often difficult for management to subordinate Taylor's inventive drives to corporate constraints. Basil Ziani de Ferranti, Vincent's son, once remarked to Barry Hercus, general manager of Electronics: "every organization can only afford one Kenyon Taylor." He paused and added: "and you've got him."[19] Taylor was difficult to manage, but his inventions had put enough money in the coffers that he was allowed to continue his innovative escapades.

The DATAR system developed by Ferranti Canada clearly demonstrated the power of electronic digital technology for naval operations. Perhaps the earliest such system in the world, DATAR was

Canada's first successful effort in electronic computer warfare systems. In 1953, Ferranti Canada demonstrated the DATAR system on Lake Ontario using two minesweepers, HMCS *Digby* and *Granby*, and a shore station on Scarborough Bluffs which simulated the third ship in a convoy. The demonstration showed that an electronic digital computer and communication systems could track the movements of enemy aircraft, ships, and submarines relative to the motion of ships in a convoy, process the tracking information, store it, and then display it for analysis.

In the operations room of each ship there were large rear-projection displays of the movement of friendly and hostile ships, aircraft, and submarines. Don Ritchie developed DATAR's impressive display system. By means of a track-ball, developed by Longstaff, Cranston, and Taylor, one could move a cursor over any object on the screen and obtain data on its heading, speed, altitude, or depth. Herb Ratz, one of the young engineers on the project and later associate dean of engineering at the University of Waterloo, remembers the incredulity with which a group of American military observers greeted the sophisticated display system of DATAR. Some even looked suspiciously under the displays, as if hoping to find the trick behind the operation.

Jammed within the tight confines of each minesweeper was a rudimentary hard-wired computer consisting of some 30,000 vacuum tubes. This computer processed the radar and sonar data, controlled access to the magnetic drum memory, and ran the various display options of the system. Getting the system to work on cue was like playing Russian roulette; one never knew which of the 30,000 tubes would burn out. Dealing with such large electronic systems presented a whole new set of problems. In fact, one of the early objectives of the DATAR project was to gather statistical data on the performance and reliability of vacuum tubes in such large and complex electronics systems.

Quickly finding and replacing defective tubes became an art in itself. Every engineer associated with DATAR remembers with great amusement the elaborate system that Ferranti Electric's engineers had devised to ensure that DATAR always worked on cue when being shown to distinguished visitors. Visitors were always first ushered into a room where they would be given a lecture on DATAR's operation. Unbeknown to the visitors, Ferranti's engineers had installed a green light at the back of the room. If the light was off, the lecturer was to keep speaking because the system was down. Meanwhile, Fred Longstaff and Herb Ratz, stripped to the waist and armed with cartridge belts of vacuum tubes, roamed the hot confines of the computer, deftly locating any of the 30,000 tubes that had failed. As soon as the system was "up," the green light would come on and the unsuspecting visitors would be immediately taken to see the system in its "normal" operation.

What was unique and bold about DATAR was the way in which Ferranti Canada had used digital electronics to marry communication, computation, and display into one information system. Gordon

Great modern inventions are rarely the work of one individual. While travelling to Ottawa for a meeting on DATAR (Digital Automated Tracking and Resolving) sometime in early 1952, Tom Cranston and Fred Longstaff conceived the idea for a trackball. On their return they described the idea to the members of the Research Department. Kenyon Taylor contributed the air-bearing concept and undertook to construct a model. The Canadian game of five-pin bowling provided the inspiration for the ball used in the prototype. The bowling ball used in American ten-pin would have been unworkable. However Ferranti Electric could not patent the idea because DATAR was a secret military project. Today the trackball is used widely, but is best known in its inverted form as the "mouse."
(John Vardalas)

Lang developed DATAR's communications equipment. At the outset in 1949, the group had decided to base DATAR's communications technology on a new and rarely used technique, discovered just before the war, called pulse-coded modulation (PCM). Today, PCM is used throughout the communications industry.

In Arthur Porter's view, Ferranti Canada's engineers had produced "the most advanced system of its kind in the world." Yet DATAR never went beyond the demonstration stage. Why? First, there was the American military's NIH (not invented here) syndrome. In the sensitive area of defence, the Americans were afraid that buying foreign technology would leave them very vulnerable. The powerful American defence industry, which sought to protect its own commercial interests, further nurtured this attitude. Second, in Canada, DATAR technology promised to be far too expensive for the Navy's budget in 1952. It was estimated that the costs of implementing DATAR throughout the Navy's fleet would have run as high as $80 million.

Third, the vacuum tube limited the use of DATAR as a practical naval counter-measure warfare system. It made digital electronic circuitry very cumbersome. With all the communications and computer equipment installed on the two minesweepers, some though it a small miracle that the ships did not sink under the weight. DATAR needed transistors, but reliable solid-state electronics were five years in the future.

Although DATAR never produced any commercial results, it allowed Ferranti Canada to get in on the ground floor of a new and revolutionary technology. Before the creation of the electronics group, electronic digital techniques were non-existent in Canada and few people had ever heard of an electronic digital computer. Everything about DATAR was new and unexplored territory for Canadian technology. With DATAR, the engineers at Ferranti Canada broke new ground as they learned. For a group of young engineers fresh out of university, it was a dream come true.

The technical success of DATAR instilled new confidence within the Research Department. With new confidence came great ambitions. Having gotten a taste of computer design, the engineers now yearned to be Canada's first producer of commercial computers.

Canada's First Electronic Digital Computer

From the moment in 1949 when Ferranti UK committed its resources to commercializing the electronic digital computer, speculation turned to whether Ferranti Canada, with its newly established digital electronics group, could follow the same route in Canada. In 1948, the British government gave Ferranti UK nearly £175,000 to turn Manchester University's pioneering computer into a commercial venture. The first sale of this new computer was to go to England's Atomic Energy Authority. Progress in nuclear technology depended on extracting practical solutions from very esoteric scientific theories. The computer offered the only means to grind out answers quickly from complex mathematical formulae.

In 1949, a group at the University of Toronto, under Dr. Calvin Carl "Kelly" Gotlieb, received funding to start research on a computer called UTEC (University of Toronto Electronic Computer). UTEC's principal supporter was Dr. W.B. Lewis, head of the research section of Canada's Atomic Energy Project in Chalk River. The project needed computational power, and Lewis hoped that UTEC could eventually fill the need. In October 1949, Solandt suggested to Porter that Ferranti Canada was the obvious organization to commercialize the computer being developed at the University of Toronto. On another occasion, Dr. Bowden, a key man in the Computer Group at Ferranti UK, while on a visit to Chalk River asked Lewis "if there was any possibility that Ferranti, Toronto, might be given a contract to build a computer on the same sort of terms as Ferranti Ltd. had."[20]

The idea that Ferranti Canada could commercialize UTEC was very

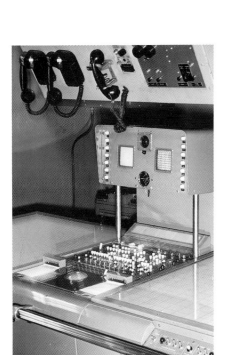

The idea for the DATAR (Digital Automated Tracking And Resolving) system originated within the Canadian Navy in 1948, but Ferranti Electric designed and built the hardware. DATAR clearly demonstrated the potential for applying electronic digital technology to military operations. This "double plot" displayed all the tracking information stored in the computer. Note the trackball at the front centre of the control console.
(Ferranti-Packard Transformers Ltd.)

appealing. However, Ferranti UK had a fully operating and proven computer to start with. Despite the progress made by the University of Toronto group, UTEC had still not gone beyond the highly experimental stage. By 1951, there was nothing in UTEC that Ferranti Canada could commercialize. The UTEC team needed time to turn its experiment into a reliable computer. Time, however, was something it didn't have. Chalk River needed a computer desperately, and Lewis lost patience with UTEC.

In a controversial move that still elicits debate, Lewis pulled the plug on UTEC. He arranged for the University of Toronto to purchase in its place the Ferranti Mark I computer from Ferranti UK. The demise of UTEC proved of little consequence to Ferranti Canada's heady ambitions to design, build, and sell computers. As a result of DATAR, the firm had assembled an engineering group that was second to none in Canada. There was little that the UTEC group could teach Ferranti Canada.

The DATAR experience convinced Porter that Ferranti Canada had acquired the technical expertise to go into the computer business. What it lacked, however, was a customer. On one occasion, over lunch, Porter boasted to E.L. Davies, vice chairman of the DRB, that Ferranti Canada "could produce a computing machine as efficient if not better than the present Ferranti equipment [the Ferranti Mark I], in approximately twelve months for roughly $150,000."[21] On 30 June 1952, Davies offered Porter an opportunity to make good on his claims and launch Canada's computer industry:

I am suggesting a method by which Ferranti Canada could effectively and cleanly cut the throat of Ferranti England, and this depends on whether or not your statement at the very pleasant lunch last Thursday was affected by the liquid refreshments! ... We do not have in Canada, at present, any need

Below the decks of seemingly conventional minesweepers, room had to be found to cram in the racks holding the 30,000 vacuum tubes for DATAR's computer needs. (Ferranti-Packard Transformers Ltd.)

During DATAR tests in 1953, two minesweepers with onboard computers traversed Lake Ontario while the third major component, the DATAR shore station shown in this photograph, lower right, remained on Scarborough Bluffs. The acquisition display is on the right, tracker display on the left, with ASDIC simulator which provided sonar data to DATAR in the rear. (Ferranti-Packard Transformers Ltd.)

The University of Toronto Electronic
Computer (UTEC), shown here with (left to
right) R.F. Johnson, Dr. J. Kates, and
L. Casciato, was built in 1951. It was
Canada's first attempt to design and build a
general-purpose electronic digital
computer.
(John Vardalas)

for a further computer but we have heard that Dr. Ellis Johnson, Director of
the Operations Research Office [in Washington, DC] ... is considering purchasing one of the Ferranti machines for roughly $300,000. This is your
chance to go to it, and earn some U.S. dollars for Canada, our contribution
being the know-how we have paid for in your development of DATAR.[22]

Ferranti Canada did not get the contract, but Porter promoted the
company as a serious manufacturer of computers. Was he unrealistic
in his belief that Ferranti Canada could leap directly from DATAR to
commercial production of computers? With UNIVAC the only North
American commercial producer of computers, entry into the embry-
onic business must have seemed deceptively simple to Porter. Thanks
to DATAR, Ferranti Canada had become one of the few companies on
the continent with engineering experience in the key facets of computer hardware: digital logic circuit design, magnetic memory drum,
and display technology.

At a time when computers were reserved for a handful of elite research institutes and secretive defence installations, few understood that commercial success would depend on identifying, understanding, and fulfilling customers' needs. In 1953, an established office machine company became another late entry into the computer business. But International Business Machines put marketing first and foremost and became famous as IBM: "While the technological leaders in the early computer days ... were product-focused and technology-focused, the punch card salesman who ran IBM asked: 'Who is the customer? What is value for him? How does he buy? And what does he need?' As a result, IBM took over the market."[23]

The same military funding that created and nurtured the electronics group at Ferranti Canada also moulded a "product-focused" and "technology-focused" management, with little appreciation of marketing. Like so many others, Porter did not realize that selling computers would involve a lot more than good engineering. This oversight would haunt the business operations of the electronics group for over two decades after DATAR. How would Ferranti Canada, and later Ferranti-Packard, convert a centre of great innovative potential into a profit-maker? Managing the electronics group would not be easy for a company that had its roots in the electric power business. Power technology dealt in thousands of amperes (kiloamps) of electrical current; digital electronics dealt in thousandths of an ampere (milliamps). These quantitative differences symbolized markedly different perspectives on R&D, innovation and product cycles, marketing and selling, and manufacturing practices – in short, very different corporate mind sets. Turning the electronics group into a profitable operation would require bridging the chasm separating the company's traditional kiloamp mentality from the new milliamp mentality of electronics.

On the completion of DATAR, military R&D funding ceased and the Research Department had to find commercial outlets for its talents. Arthur Porter left in 1955 to become dean of engineering at the University of Saskatchewan. His replacement, Kenyon Taylor, had to find work for all the engineers recruited during the days of heady research on DATAR. He found it particularly stressful trying to make the department profitable. Many years later, he observed: "I was feeling very keenly my responsibility to keep our good engineers employed usefully, and had become depressed by our everlasting red Profit and Loss account."

As with Porter before him, Taylor's management style was driven by technology. The brilliant inventor thought that superior technical merit would always win the day in the marketplace. But it did not. Taylor would often lament that his group was "always too far ahead of the market technically and people seemed to want simple things rather than efficient things."[24] Frustrated with his inability to turn elegant engineering into profit, he yearned to return to inventing and so left the management to someone else.

The years from 1953 to 1956 were difficult. The Research Department's engineers got some very interesting contracts with Atomic Energy of Canada Ltd (AECL). ZEEP and NRX were the first Canadian nuclear reactors. Both were built at Chalk River, where the NRU reactor was to open in 1957, a gateway to CANDU research and development for electric power generation. Under the direction of Les Wood, Ferranti Canada developed an analog computer simulator of the proposed new NRU reactor. The simulator was used to derive the design parameters of the power control system. This in turn led to the contract for the control rod sequencing unit and subsequently to the manufacture of the pile face amplifiers and control desk by the new Electronics Department. Work also started on a remarkable idea, code-named JANET, to improve military data communications in the Arctic by bouncing digital communications off the ionized trails of meteorites.

The Transistor and Canada Post

Between 1949 and 1956, the perception of computers' utility changed significantly. Computers had slowly moved out of elite university research centres and secretive military installations and found their way into business and industry. These "engines of the mind" were now being seen as invaluable tools for data processing and automation.

In mail sorting, data processing and automation promised great gains in efficiency. In the early 1950s, mail in Canada was still sorted manually. The complexity and number of Canada's geographical subdivisions made manual sorting bewildering. There were 2,600 mail agglomerations in Ontario, and the city of Toronto alone was divided

Ferranti and Packard participated in many leading-edge projects in Canada. From 1953 to 1956 Ferranti Electric worked with Atomic Energy of Canada Ltd. This control system was designed and built to handle the automatic start-up, operation, and shutdown of the 200-megawatt NRU reactor at Chalk River.
(Ferranti-Packard Transformers Ltd.)

To Catch a Falling Star

Because of the vast expanse of Canada's sparsely populated terrain, the quest for more effective long-distance communication has always been a primary concern. The advent of radio marked the dawn of a new era in Canadian communication. By means of radio waves, remote areas, beyond the reach of telegraph or telephone, could be linked up in instantaneous communication.

A key aspect of this break-through was the ionosphere – a layer of ionized particles that surrounds the Earth. By bouncing radio waves off the ionosphere, a transmitter could reach distant receivers located far beyond the horizon. Much of the radio spectrum could not be used, however, because the ionosphere was transparent to radio frequencies beyond the HF band – namely, above 30 MHz. Consequently, the HF band could easily become over-congested as the use of radio increased. Frequencies greater than 30 MHz were useful only for short-range, line-of-sight communication. As well, solar storms can affect the ionosphere over Canada's north. Highly energized charged particles produced by the Sun can make the ionosphere highly unreliable as a reflective medium for radio waves.

The unreliability of the ionosphere in northern latitudes was of particular concern to Canada's military. With the tensions of the Cold War, defence of the north became a paramount concern. Effective and reliable communication in the north was crucial. The JANET system allowed relatively low-power, point-to-point communication over ranges of 500–1,000 km (310.5–621 mi) that avoided the ionospheric disturbances that plagues HF radio.

JANET, a code name derived from Janus, the Roman god of the doorway who looked both ways at once, used the ionization trails produced by meteors to bounce radio signals between two points in Canada. It required frequencies beyond 30 MHz. Meteor trails are random events but happen frequently enough to serve as a basis for reliable communication. Most meteor trails are produced by pin-head-sized meteors that burn up in the atmosphere.

The idea of JANET was first proposed by a research group at Canada's Radio Propagation Laboratory (RPL), in Ottawa. In 1956, RPL asked Ferranti-Packard to turn JANET into a workable communication technology. Ferranti-Packard assigned the task to its talented digital communication engineer, Gordon Lang. The technical challenges were formidable. The system had to be able to adapt its operation to the conditions of the transmission medium – the meteor trails. Quick detection of meteor trails and rapid selection of those suitable for communication were essential. Because of the nature of meteor trails, digital information had to be communicated in bursts of varying lengths at irregularly occurring times. In the intervals between suitable trails, JANET would accept messages and store them until the next burst.

By 1956, Ferranti-Packard had developed much of the expertise needed to make JANET work. It had already pioneered in digital transmission technology, with DATAR, and led the industry in high-speed computer input and magnetic storage technology. Ferranti-Packard implemented JANET with remarkable success. It showed that random meteor bursts could sustain constant communication between teletype machines going at 60 words per minute.

A substantial portion of funding for JANET came from the US Army. The Americans, too, wanted secure and reliable communication systems to help defend the north against possible Soviet aggression. With the launching of its first satellites, the American military lost interest in JANET. Communication satellites eased northern communication. Nevertheless, satellites are vulnerable, and the concept of JANET offers an alternative.

Early in the project, Kenyon Taylor realized the broader commercial potential of the technology and lobbied Canada's Defence Research Board to loosen the security restrictions surrounding JANET. In time, these restrictions were lifted, but Ferranti-Packard never succeeded in developing a commercial market for JANET. Several decades later, and under more favourable market conditions, the JANET technology was resurrected and turned into a viable commercial undertaking by another Canadian company.

into 10,000 sections. In 1951, Dr. Maurice Levy, a French engineer who had immigrated to Canada to work briefly for the DRB, started toying with the notion of automatic sorting while an engineering consultant for the Post Office.

Levy's system consisted of five key elements: a postal code; an encoding terminal, where the postal code could be put on the envelope as a fluorescent bar code; an optical scanner to read the code on the envelope; conveyors and mechanical gates that would channel letters to collection bins for different destinations; and a computer to interpret the data from the scanner and control the gates.

Levy found complete support from W.J. Turnbull, deputy postmaster general. Turnbull, who had been W.L. Mackenzie King's principal secretary from 1940 to 1945, took a very pragmatic approach: "I don't care much about gadgets," he told Levy; but he added, "I'll support your work on two conditions; it will make the mail move faster and save us money."[25] Once convinced that Levy's system would greatly benefit the Post Office, Turnbull, in the face of considerable opposition, courageously supported the project.

The first step was to show that it was feasible to route mail electronically. Levy searched for a Canadian company knowledgeable in electronic digital computer technology that could design and build a small working model of the concept. Already familiar with Ferranti Canada's reputation in the area, Levy approached the company in 1953 and asked Porter's group to build a small prototype of the computer needed to sort mail. Porter gave the task to Gordon Helwig, a young engineer of Jamaican extraction. Helwig, like so many of his colleagues in the department, had been part of that first wave of highly motivated and bright ex-servicemen who went to university after returning from war. Helwig, who had already been involved in DATAR, lost little time in applying this experience to Levy's problem. Levy was immediately struck by Helwig's talents and the technical excellence displayed by the department.

Radio waves travel long distances in straight lines. But, because of the curvature of the earth's surface, the signals are lost or greatly reduced in intensity unless bounced back to the earth as is now done by satellite. JANET, a code name derived from Janus, the Roman god who could look both ways at once, was a secret project aimed at using trails from meteors as a reflective surface to bounce long-distance radio waves towards the earth. In 1956 Canada's Radio Propagation Laboratory asked Ferranti Canada to turn the concept into workable communication technology for long-distance data transmission. The resulting system was assembled at the Ferranti Research Division Mt Dennis plant in Toronto. High-speed optical punched-tape readers developed by Ferranti were a key component of the JANET system, which was secretly tested by American Army mobile units which were shipped to Arizona for secret field tests. (Ferranti-Packard Transformers Ltd.)

DATAR technology provided the basis for
using a computer to automatically control
mail sorting. The computer in this photograph, taken in Toronto in 1955, was the
experimental vacuum-tube version that led to
the world's first computerized mail-sorting
system.
(Ferranti-Packard Transformers Ltd.)

After the success of the prototype, a few more years would pass before Levy could win the necessary funding to embark on a full-scale
system. During this time, a profound change in electronic technology
opened a new era for computers. DATAR's technology, like all computer technology of the period, was based on the vacuum tube. Lee
De Forest's 1906 invention of the triode gave birth to electronics, but
a half-century later he remarked: "there is nothing wrong with electronics that the elimination of vacuum tubes would not fix."[26] The
vacuum tube's heavy consumption of power, relatively short lifespan, and large size blocked the computer's technical and commercial
progress.

The transistor offered a perfect solution to the impracticality of
building larger and more complex computers with vacuum tubes. It
consumed very little power and was a fraction of the size of a vacuum

This transistorized computer was developed and built by Ferranti in 1956 as part of a pilot project to develop automatic mail sorting for the Canadian Post Office. The open door reveals the few rows of transistor cards which replaced many racks of vacuum tubes, such as those shown in the background on the right. The memory drum above the cabinet used a patented air-suspension system, a key element in Ferranti Electric's computer for the Canadian Post Office mail sorter. This same technology was used in 1956 to build the TASC computer for the University of Illinois.
(Ferranti-Packard Transformers Ltd.)

tube. Transistor technology, however, met with considerable opposition in the electronics industry. In the early 1950s the transistor was not universally acclaimed as the basis of an electronic revolution. For example, "as late as 1953, there was still suspicion among some leading British physicists that the transistor was no more than a piece of good publicity for Bell."[27] In North America, "the transistor was still not recognized as any sort of trailblazing commercial triumph."[28]

While others in Canada, and elsewhere, may have been laggards, Kenyon Taylor and his electronics research group immediately grasped the significance of the transistor. As historians of technology today acknowledge: "The transistor was not just a new sort of amplifier, but a harbinger of an entirely new sort of electronics with the capacity not just to influence an industry or a scientific discipline, but change a culture."[29] As soon as the transistor became commercially

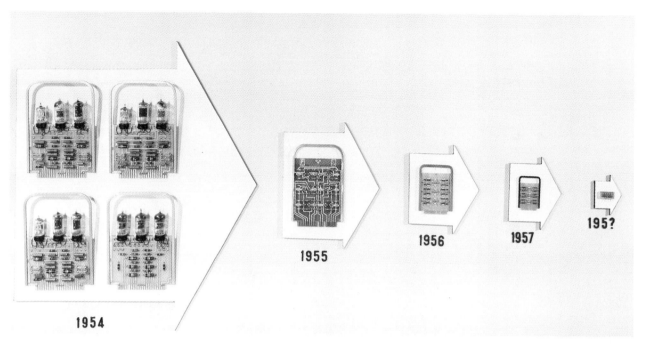

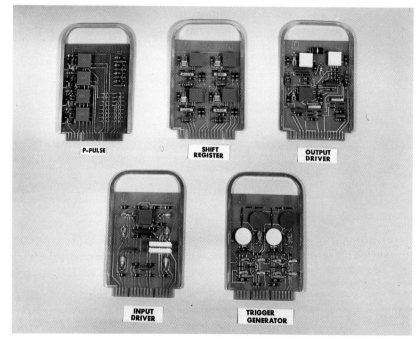

These three photographs clearly depict three elements in Ferranti Electric's vision of the future in 1957: continuing miniaturization, small circuit cards and boards designed for specialized functions, and modular assembly of working equipment.

In its efforts to commercialize the digital computer, Ferranti Electric had lived through several generations of miniaturization. By 1957 one small transistorized card, which consumed far less energy, would replace four larger vacuum tube cards used in 1954.

Ferranti Electric also foresaw ever-increasing use of standardized electronic digital circuit cards. By the late 1950s Ferranti-Packard had embarked on a program to manufacture and market several of their applications, such as flip-flops, logic gates, and shift registers for computer and communication applications.

The standardized cards became part of a system of plug-in modular components (far right) which replaced racks of individually wired tubes.
(Ferranti-Packard Transformers Ltd.)

available, the electronics engineers at Ferranti Canada studied and experimented with the new device. The Research Department reformulated its knowledge of digital circuit design to use the potential of the transistor.

Hundreds of pages of published technical notes attest to the thoroughness and fervour with which the Research Department studied

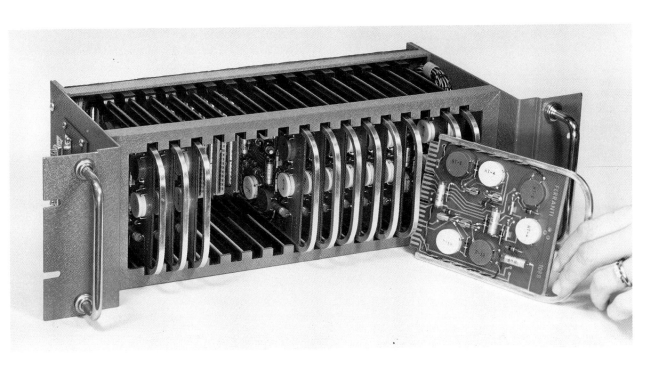

the transistor's implications for digital circuits. Everyone realized that they were getting in on the ground floor of a major technological revolution. Gordon Helwig remembers this period as "an extremely exciting time. Everyone was learning about transistors ... It was a fabulous place to work at. Moody would come down from Ottawa and there would be a lot of exchange between the Ferranti group and Moody's group."[30] Norman Moody spearheaded transistor research at the Defence Research and Telecommunications Establishment (DRTE) in Ottawa in the early 1950s.

The appearance of the first high-speed transistor, the Philco SB-100, started an important chapter in the Research Department's computer design efforts. Don Ritchie, who was a design engineer for Ferranti Canada and now works for Control Data Canada, still recalls with pride that he "personally brought back the first batch of SB-100's to Toronto." Throughout 1955, the electronics group studied digital switching circuits based on the Philco transistor; it obtained some 3,000 SB-100s and compiled an extensive and pioneering set of statistics on the transistor's operation in digital circuitry. This research put Ferranti Canada in the forefront of transistorized digital switching techniques in North America. The Lincoln Laboratories at MIT were also developing switching circuits based on the Philco SB-100 transistor, and Ferranti Canada offered to share its research with them.[31]

In 1956, Levy received funding approval for $1 million to build an experimental sorter in the Ottawa post office. He immediately gave Ferranti Canada the contract to build the optical scanning system and computer for the mail sorter. Armed with SB-100 transistors, Ferranti

Canada started work on the world's first computerized mail-sorting system. Once again Gordon Helwig designed the computer. The Route Reference Computer became the earliest solid-state computer designed and built in Canada, but it was still a hard-wired, special-purpose device. The only other solid-state computer in Canada was a general-purpose one being developed at the DRTE under the direction of David Florida. "Dirty Gertie," as the DRTE computer was affectionately called, did not go into complete operation until 1960.

Based on diode-transistor logic, rather than the older resistor-transistor logic, the brain of this mail-sorting system contained some 1,100 transistors and 500 diodes. Its memory consisted of an air-bearing magnetic drum, another specialty item developed at Ferranti Canada, with a capacity of about 500,000 bits.

The "eyes" of the system, also designed by Ferranti Canada, were an optical system that could read fluorescent bar code markings imprinted on the back of envelopes. The information was sent to the computer for processing. The computer checked for coding errors, consulted a giant look-up table in drum memory, and decided which series of gates to activate along the conveyor belt for each letter.

The experimental mail sorter could process over 36,000 letters an hour. Levy claimed that a bigger installation could easily be built that would be ten times faster.[32] Canada was several years ahead of other nations in this type of installation. Observers from many countries came to Ottawa: "The U.S. sent a group of congressmen to check on the Canadian system before congress voted five million dollars to a research laboratory in Washington D.C. for a similar study."[33] The first automated US post office went into service in 1960, in Rhode Island. Great Britain followed in 1966.[34]

The future looked bright for Ferranti Canada. The initial contract with Canada Post was quite substantial, and any large-scale production would have been a most profitable venture. The defeat of the Liberal government in 1957 by John Diefenbaker's Conservatives shattered these dreams. Levy and Turnbull received little sympathy from a technologically unsophisticated governing party which, when in opposition, had called the mail sorter "the million dollar monster."[35] The new government ended Levy's involvement with the mail sorter. Turnbull, who had enough of what he called Diefenbaker's "stupidity and vindictiveness," resigned in disgust from his position as deputy postmaster general.[36] He saw that the new government was determined to stamp out all vestiges of the previous government, and Levy's project was a thorn in the Conservatives' side. Levy was soon engaged by the US Post Office to advise it on development of its automatic mail sorter.[37] While the Diefenbaker government was killing the only Canadian-built computer, a royal commission looking into the electronics industry estimated Canadian demand for computers to be at $175 million![38]

Despite cancellation, the Post Office computer proved an invaluable experience. The optical scanning system made Ferranti Canada a pioneer in bar code–scanning technology. More important, however, was the experience gained in the design, manufacture, and assembly of solid-state computers. With an eye to the future, Ferranti Canada built the computer around standardized circuit cards. In the assembly of even the most complex computers, a small number of fundamental digital circuits, such as flip-flops, shift registers, inverters, and pulse generators, are used repeatedly in great numbers. By standardizing these circuits onto mass-produced cards, the electronics group hoped to standardize the manufacture of future computers and at the same time develop a secondary business selling components to other designers of digital processing systems. This standard-card approach formed the basis for much of the group's future computer development. Unfortunately, the idea of a components business based on standardized circuit cards was too premature for a technology that seemed to be changing almost overnight. Semi-conductor electronics, and their use in digital circuits, were moving too fast to be standardized on cards.[39]

Merger and Reorganization

The merger of Packard Electric and Ferranti Canada, in 1958, brought about important organizational changes. In order to streamline management and rationalize cost-accounting procedures, the Research, Ordnance, and Electronics departments were amalgamated into the Electronics Division, with its own general manager. As we saw in chapter 4, the Ordnance Department had been created in 1941 to manufacture Magslips for anti-aircraft guns. In 1952, it received a substantial contract to manufacture a large number of "artificial horizons," of Ferranti UK design, for the Royal Canadian Air Force.

The Electronics Department had been created in 1955 to take on work for Atomic Energy of Canada Ltd. The Electronics Department built the nuclear reactor control and simulator equipment for the NRU reactor at Chalk River. It also produced meters for measuring radiation levels and exposure. In an age of expanding nuclear energy research, Ferranti Canada saw a good business opportunity in contamination meters. It reasoned that increased handling of radioactive materials would lead to concern over radiation exposure and safety, and significant market demand for contamination or radiation meters. This market never materialized for Ferranti Canada. Nevertheless, the idea behind the formation of the Electronics Department made sense. It was to be the "product"-selling and -manufacturing arm of the electronics business. It would try to capitalize on the Research Department's development contracts to generate a few "volume" stable products.

After the merger, Packard people filled most of the top management positions of Ferranti-Packard. The electronics business perplexed the new corporate leaders who, like their predecessors, were seasoned electric power veterans. They felt it wiser to let the Electronics group run its own house. Their business sixth sense, however, told them that the division's history of depending on a series of single cus-

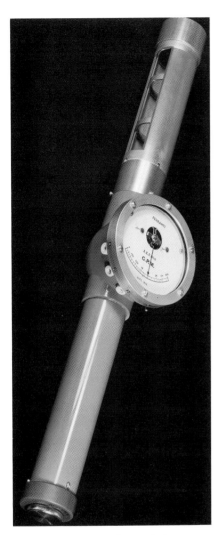

New technologies usually raise high expectations about the extent and rate of change they will bring. During the early 1950s both expert and public opinion predicted widespread use of atomic energy and radioactive devices. Ferranti Electric reasoned that there would be an important, safety-driven, commercial market for devices to measure radioactivity. The "Contamination Meter" produced in 1956 with interchangeable probes to measure alpha, beta, and gamma radiation was a technically important early application of transistorized circuits for miniaturization. It had three transistors, two no. 2N78 and one 2N34, and was designed with pin jacks for head phones or recorder. However, atomic energy moved much more slowly than predicted and the Contamination Meter was not a commercial success. (Ferranti-Packard Transformers Ltd.)

tomers or unique solutions could not be the basis for a profitable business. Profits would depend on repeat sales and standardization. This concern found expression in the appointment of John Fogarty as general manager of the Electronics Division.

Fogarty had been with Ferranti for twenty-three years and had "graduated through all phases of production planning and estimating." He was a member of the planning committee which, in 1943, started the Edinburgh research and production facility of Ferranti UK. Having joined Ferranti Canada in 1950, he became works manager of the Ordnance Division in 1951. He had little experience in electronics or computers, but since he had managed the Ordnance Department very well, it was thought that his experience in large-volume manufacturing would add new discipline and direction to the commercial efforts of the Electronics Division.

Fogarty's influence was felt most in terms of organizational structure and product development. Under his leadership a conventional organizational structure emerged, consisting of a sales force, an engineering group, an R&D group, a production planning group, a manufacturing group, and an accounting section. The division also began thinking in terms of actual products as well as systems, but change would take time. In terms of engineering and product specialization, little changed under Fogarty's management. The work in high-speed tape readers, magnetic drum storage, and computer systems started under Ferranti Canada was continued. In three years a fourth product base would emerge: displays systems.

Despite the buildup of tape reader and drum business, manufacturing of computer systems promised money and prestige. As an ambitious man, Fogarty gambled on computers. However, he also knew that a well-co-ordinated global effort within the entire Ferranti organization would be needed if Canada were to achieve any long-term commercial success in the computer business. Unfortunately, Ferranti UK was unwilling to develop one co-ordinated transatlantic computer business strategy.

Unexpected Spin-Off

Post-war economic expansion greatly increased the volume of financial transactions. The daily number of cheques cleared through North America's large banks rose to staggering proportions. By the late 1950s it was clear that the banks needed high-speed automated cheque-sorting technology. The problems of sorting cheques resembled those of sorting mail. Officials at New York City's Federal Reserve Bank had heard about Ferranti-Packard's work on the automated mail sorter in Ottawa. They sent a consultant, from Stanford University, to meet with Kenyon Taylor and see the system in operation. Helwig remembers how "the consultant liked the work that [they] had done and recommended that the Bank start a pilot project in its four branches."[40]

Ferranti-Packard received the contract to develop the computer,

An artist's conception of the modular cheque-sorting system that Ferranti-Packard pioneered in the late 1950s. The system, which read MICR- (magnetic ink character recognition) encoded cheques, was first installed in the Federal Reserve Bank in New York in 1959. The system reflects Ferranti-Packard's modular or building block design philosophy, which combined various plug-in units, each with specific capabilities. It consisted of a central dictionary look-up reference module, drum-load and print-out facilities, simulators, controls, and power supplies. When fully expanded to include three cheque sorters, it could sort up to 290,000 cheques per hour. It did all of this on conventional 115-volt 60-cycle office current and operated under normal office environmental conditions.
(Ferranti-Packard Transformers Ltd.)

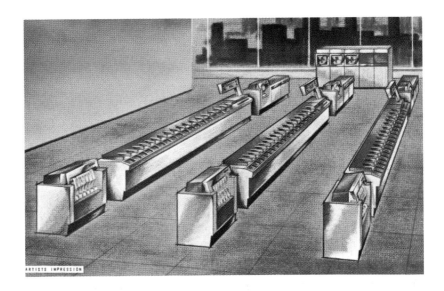

while Pitney Bowes built the mechanical sorting system and General Electric built the scanners. The computer for the cheque sorter was a direct transfer of the technology used for the mail sorter. It, too, was hard-wired rather than programmed. Instead of optically scanning a postal code, the cheque sorter scanned MICR (magnetic ink character recognition) encoded cheques. It was customary to sort by each individual digit on the cheque, but Ferranti-Packard used the computer to scan all eight coding digits at once and then sort the cheque by reference to a look-up dictionary stored in memory. In this way, the system could process 135,000 cheques an hour.

The cheque sorter represented the first truly commercial sale for the Electronics Division. The success of the Federal Reserve Bank cheque sorter convinced the division that a profitable business could be built around cheque-sorting equipment. By 1961, Ferranti-Packard was ready to market an enhanced version. In a clear attempt to standardize components, the Electronics Division developed a modular approach. The plug-in-module concept gave prospective customers a system that would grow with their needs. All the elements of success were there: a vast market of banking institutions across North America, market presence and credibility as a result of the Federal Reserve Bank experience, and an excellent product based on customer requirements.

The heart of the system was a hard-wired computer, designed to perform specialized functions; it can be reprogrammed to do other tasks only by physically rewiring the computer. Because of the high costs of programmable computers, hard-wired, or special-purpose computers were often cost-effective for certain data-processing needs. But rapid improvements in price, flexibility, and performance soon made general-purpose computers very attractive, even for special applications.

Ferranti-Packard's ambitions to sell automated cheque-sorting equipment were threatened by the growing availability of general-purpose computers as manufacturers, such as Honeywell, explored more flexible solutions to cheque sorting. The general-purpose computer could not only process cheques but could also be programmed to handle a multitude of other data-processing tasks. To stay competitive, Ferranti-Packard would have to develop comparable technology – a general-purpose computer.

Moving People

The first opportunity to build a general-purpose computer evolved from the operational needs of Canada's national airline. Canadian air transportation underwent dramatic changes during the 1950s. From 1951 to 1956, the number of passengers increased by 104 per cent. The increased passenger and flight loads put tremendous strain on the flight-booking system at Trans-Canada Airlines (TCA), because of the enormous volume of scheduling and reservation data. Some fifty ticket offices across Canada were connected to one control centre by 29,000 miles of teletype and telephone lines. Every day the TCA communications system handled over 35,000 message units, most of that in an eight hour period. All TCA's booking requests and scheduling changes were forwarded to the control centre, where they would be manually processed. The inventory of booked and available seats was then written on a big wall display called VSIB (visual seat indicator board). One can easily imagine how messy that board must have looked. The system was barely coping, and the spectre of even greater passenger volume worried TCA managment.

Hired by TCA in 1949, Lyman Richardson remembers that as it got closer to departure date the board got filled with so many erasures and rewrites that "it looked like a dog's breakfast." As early as 1953, Richardson realized that automated high-speed information processing would be needed. A radio operator and radar instructor during the war, Richardson had returned to Canada to pursue a technical career at the Radio College of Canada. Soon after starting work for TCA, he began studying communications engineering by correspondence. He quickly rose to communications engineer and then took on the task of improving TCA's reservation system.

Richardson had heard of computers but knew nothing about them. Nevertheless, he has convinced that a computer was the only solution to problems confronting the airline's reservation system. The idea of an electronic computer handling the entire seat inventory was completely alien to the TCA hierarchy. In 1953, Richardson demonstrated to it how a computer for airline reservation would work by using the University of Toronto's Ferranti Mark 1 computer, better known as FERUT, with J. Kates, L. Casciato, and R. Johnston as consultants.[41]

A more realistic field test took place three years after a suitable input/output device, called the "transactor," was designed and built by Ferranti Electric to meet Richardson's general requirements. Six

The Development of RESERVEC, a computerized national airline reservation system, for Trans-Canada Airlines was a pivotal point in Ferranti-Packard's efforts to design and market a commercially viable "Made-in-Canada" general-purpose computer system. The name RESERVEC, sometimes spelled RESER-VEC, came about as a result of a contest among TCA employees. Trans-Canada Airlines changed its name to Air Canada on 1 January 1965. Harry J. Simper, passenger office manager at Lethbridge Alberta, won $100 for the name RESER-VEC, derived from Reservations Electronically Controlled. In this 1959 photograph the vice-president of Trans-Canada Airlines signs the contract with Ferranti-Packard to start work on the project. Seated beside him is John Fogarty. Standing left to right are unidentified, Earl Mann, Don Ritchie, Bill Davis, Les Wood. (Ontario Archives, Ferranti-Packard Collection, AO 1527)

transactors were remotely linked to the FERUT computer in a demonstration for the president and board of directors of TCA. This demonstration exhibited all the key aspects of a reservation system: input/output by agents, data communications over telephone lines, and computer processing power.

The rapidity of the system's response so impressed the president and the board that "within 5 minutes, they accepted the entire concept."[42] In 1959, TCA authorized $3.25 million for construction of a system that would embrace the entire TCA operations in thirty-nine cities. Ferranti-Packard received the contract to design and build the entire system – the hundreds of transactors in all the TCA ticket offices, the digital data communications interfaces that covered the TCA network, and the computer.[43] In 1959, $3.25 million was an enormous amount of money. Not only was TCA's move a bold one for an airline, it was even more courageous to go with a Canadian company, when large corporations, such as IBM, were twisting a lot of arms.[44]

D.K. Ritchie, a Ferranti-Packard engineer, and an unidentified TCA agent give the press a public demonstration of RESERVEC. The agent marked the information or flight requested on the transactor card and then inserted it into the desk-top Business Transactor which was linked to the central data-handling system computer. Within two seconds the system would respond to the request by punching notches on one end of the card. Previously one might have had to wait from hours to a day or more. (Ontario Archives, Ferranti-Packard Collection, AO 1269)

TCA's decision shows the critical role that government purchasing can have in the development of Canadian technology and business.

IBM and UNIVAC had also vigorously pursued the contract. IBM was working on a computerized airline reservation system, called SABRE, for American Airlines. Because of the IBM mystique and Canadians' general reticence about trusting their own technology, it took courage for TCA to work with a Canadian company. Once again, as with the computer for the mail sorter, the desire to give the contract to a capable Canadian firm had helped Ferranti-Packard win the job. Richardson recommended Ferranti-Packard because he was pleased with the work that the company had done on the Transactor and was impressed by its growing reputation as an innovator.

RESERVEC I, designed and built by Ferranti-Packard, was a remarkable engineering achievement. It was a total information system that married communications technology to computers in a commercial environment. It was also a first in Canada, perhaps the first of its kind in the world. While RESERVEC I was being developed by Ferranti-Packard, IBM was developing SABRE. However, with the success of RESERVEC I, Ferranti-Packard had proven that Canadian companies could compete with the world's best. It had exhibited bold and imaginative engineering and then built reliable systems. RESER-

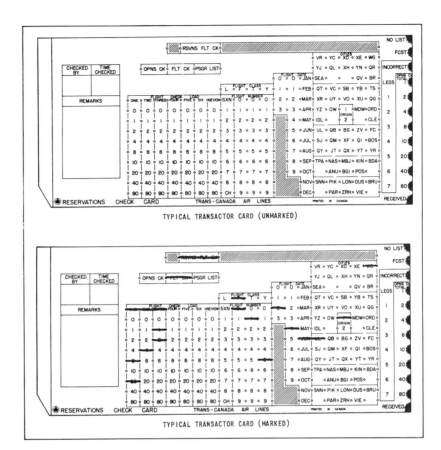

TYPICAL TRANSACTOR CARD (UNMARKED)

TYPICAL TRANSACTOR CARD (MARKED)

Typical transactor cards, marked and unmarked, as used by Trans-Canada Airlines.
Similar cards could be used for many other
information applications.
(Ferranti-Packard Transformers Ltd.)

RESERVEC I operated almost flawlessly for over ten years before it was replaced by the newer technology of RESERVEC II.

RESERVEC I combined two major engineering achievements: the
Gemini computer and the data communications system. Gemini was
a programmable computer, which actually consisted of two computers, Castor and Pollux. Not only did these two function as each
other's backup, but they also worked together, sharing the processing
load. The overall design was Fred Longstaff's brain-child. Harvey
Gellman's group did the programming.

Like many of the electronics engineers at Ferranti-Packard, Fred
Longstaff graduated from the University of Toronto in engineering
physics, in 1950. In 1951, he obtained his master's degree in engineering physics. His career spans the history of computer technology in
Canada. He started with DATAR, and today he works as a senior engineer and trouble-shooter for Motorola Information Systems in Toronto. His achievements are matched only by his great modesty, and
every engineer who worked with him has nothing but admiration for
his brilliance. His grasp of both the hardware and software of computer design is extraordinary. During the 1950s and early 1960s he
was, in the words of Ian Sharp, a founder of I.P. Sharp Associates and
a former Electronics Division colleague, "the consummate hardware

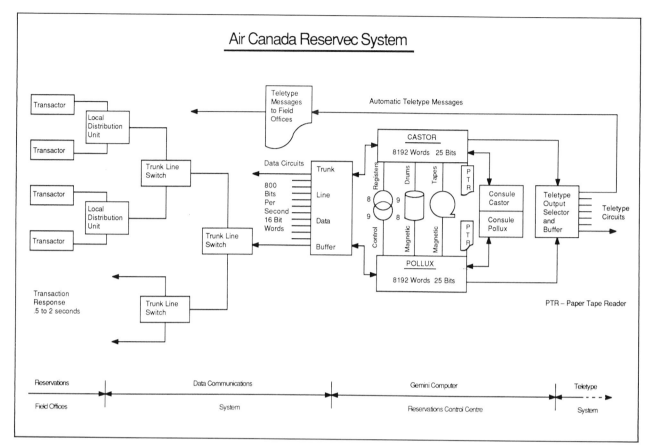

Air Canada Reservec System

Transactor

Transactor

Local Distribution Unit

Trunk Line Switch

Transactor

Transactor

Local Distribution Unit

Transaction Response .5 to 2 seconds

Trunk Line Switch

Trunk Line Switch

Teletype Messages to Field Offices

Automatic Teletype Messages

Data Circuits

800 Bits Per Second 16 Bit Words

Trunk

Line

Data

Buffer

CASTOR
8192 Words   25 Bits

Registers

Control

8   9

9   8

Drums

Magnetic

Tapes

Magnetic

P T R

P T R

Consule Castor

Consule Pollux

Teletype Output Selector and Buffer

Teletype Circuits

POLLUX
8192 Words   25 Bits

PTR – Paper Tape Reader

| Reservations | Data Communications | Gemini Computer | Teletype |
| Field Offices | System | Reservations Control Centre | System |

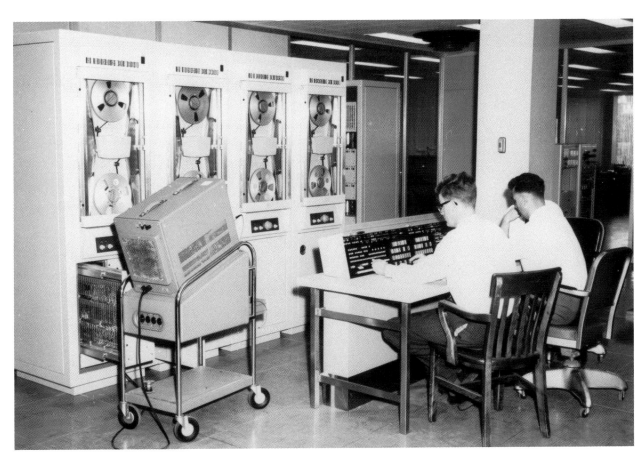

A schematic view of RESERVEC (opposite, top), now known as the Gemini system. Two transistorized Ferranti-Packard computers labelled Castor and Pollux constituted the heart of the system. RESERVEC was Canada's first commercially built transistorized computer system. The system linked reservation offices across Canada to the centralized computer system on Bloor Street in Toronto.

A delegation from Trans-Canada Airlines visiting the Transactor Manufacturing facilities (opposite, bottom). Although Ferranti-Packard saw the Business Transactor as having a wide range of business applications, such as reservations, stock control, mail order handling, and freight services, they were unsuccessful in attempts to market it widely as a basic input/output device.

The RESERVEC I/Gemini computer system (above) was installed in TCA offices on Bloor street in Toronto in 1961. Ferranti-Packard engineers are shown doing final on-site testing.

(Ontario Archives, Ferranti-Packard Collection, AO 1528, AO 1529; Ferranti-Packard Transformers Ltd.)

and software designer."[45] Longstaff stands out as the technical wizard behind many of the computer designs of Ferranti Canada and Ferranti-Packard.

The communications system, which was Gordon Lang's responsibility, could transmit data at 800 bits per second over standard voice-channel circuits to the computer. Lang's earlier work on DATAR and JANET had established him as the division's expert in information theory and digital communications technology. RESERVEC I's real-time response time was an astounding two seconds. The two seconds started when an agent in any TCA office in Canada used the transactor to make an inquiry. The digital message then travelled to Toronto, where the computer compared the reservation request with the existing seat inventory and flight schedule. Updates to seat inventory were made, and a message was sent back to the agent about the status of the inquiry. All this took only two seconds.

No profit figures are available for the RESERVEC contract, but with $3.25 million allocated by TCA, Ferranti-Packard must have found it profitable. After the first sale to TCA came the real question: who would buy the next one? Canada had only one national airline, so the sales would have to be international. Ferranti-Packard ran into real difficulty in trying to market the RESERVEC system. Don Ritchie, who headed the sales effort, recalls: "we tried to sell it to Lufthansa, we tried selling a similar system to the Swedish State Railways, and we even tried to sell it to Australia, but none of these efforts were successful."[46] Systems for national transportation carriers would invariably be bought domestically. Years later, Ritchie reflected on his experience with international sales and concluded that there was no saleable product called RESERVEC. Each prospective sale needed a new system designed to meet particular requirements: "What you really have to sell is experience and not a product. In this regard we suffered quite a bit from a credibility point of view. Here we were a small, few hundred man, operation in the colonies beating [the bushes of] the world trying to sell large computer systems. It didn't work."[47]

In the United Kingdom, Ferranti UK wanted to develop and sell its own system to British Airways rather than market its subsidiary's proven RESERVEC I system. Ferranti-Packard's failure to get participation by Ferranti UK reflected the parent firm's inability to formulate one company-wide development and marketing strategy for computer systems. As a result, the Canadian computer group often worked at cross-purposes with its English counterparts.

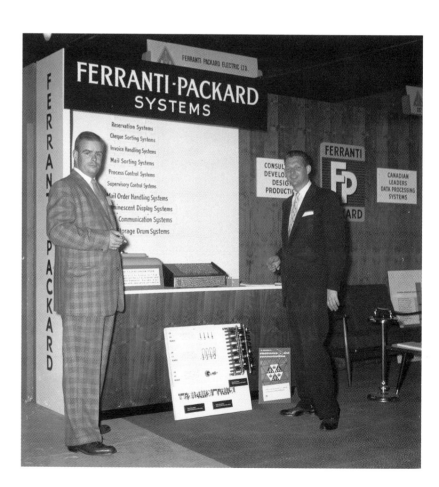

By 1961 Ferranti-Packard had become one of Canada's industrial leaders in designing and manufacturing information-processing systems. This is a typical trade show exhibit with Frank Squires, left, and Ray Taylor manning the booth.
(Ferranti-Packard Transformers Ltd.)

9 *The Rise and Fall of Canada's First Commercial Computer*

The Electronics Division was born, in 1949, out of the Canadian military's interest in the use of thinking machines for automated warfare. In the years that followed, it nurtured the dream of designing and manufacturing a commercial general-purpose computer. Starting with DATAR, the division moved inexorably in that direction. By the early 1960s, the company was poised to leap into the commercial computer business. As Ferranti-Packard would soon discover, technical excellence did not guarantee commercial success. In addition to the technical questions to be answered, another fundamental question remained: was the domestic market ready for a made-in-Canada computer?

Ferranti-Packard's destiny as a manufacturer of computers was to a great extent, as we shall see in this chapter, moulded by corporate decisions made in England. A crisis in the parent firm engendered a deep crisis within the Electronics Division, which threatened Ferranti-Packard's entire computer development effort. This crisis, however, only served to provoke crises and plunge the division into a long period of disarray. Underlying all the division's problems were the difficulties of converting innovative engineering into profitable product lines.

Canada's First Commercial General-Purpose Computer

By 1961, many of the Electronics Division's engineers were becoming increasingly frustrated with what they perceived to be a lack of direction and interest on the part of their corporation's top executives. Ferranti-Packard was reluctant to commit its resources to creating a general-purpose computer business. The Electronics Division's general manager, John Fogarty, reassured his staff that he was working on a deal to manufacture a computer in Canada – the ATLAS. The ATLAS was no ordinary mainframe. It was the largest, most powerful, and most expensive computer in Ferranti UK's product line. For a time, it was the world's leader in computing power.

In 1961, no general-purpose computers were being produced in Canada. Fogarty's plan to manufacture a computer, even under licence from the foreign parent firm, would have been a major step forward. The Canadian government saw the obvious technological and economic advantages in building computers in Canada and expressed great interest in Ferranti-Packard's proposals.[1] It gave "assurances that the Government would be interested in supplying funds to assist in development required for the manufacture of large computers."[2] In anticipation of the new undertaking, Ferranti-Packard was ready to spend $200,000 to provide more space for future manufacturing capacity, but first an agreement with the parent firm would have to be struck.

It was symptomatic of the government's confused policy on technological development that it offered industrial development grants to manufacture computers in Canada, but its very tax laws discouraged this development. Ian Sharp recalls that "there was a positive disincentive to manufacture systems in Canada ... The duty rate on components was almost three times the duty rate on a complete system. Federal sales tax was charged on the end price paid by the end user if the equipment was manufactured here. It was only payable on the cross-border company to company price if it was manufactured by a company such as IBM in the States."[3]

In the summer of 1961, John Fogarty and Les Wood travelled to England to discuss the project in depth and got no support. According to Les Wood, both Basil and Sebastian de Ferranti thought that the English company was already exposed to enough technical risk from the then far-from-complete ATLAS computer. Moreover, the English team was too absorbed in its own work even to think about bringing Canadians into the fold.[4]

In retrospect, failure was a blessing in disguise. Not only would ATLAS have put Ferranti-Packard in direct competition with IBM, but the design of the ATLAS computer would have been a marketing disaster in North America. ATLAS was a technology-driven product aimed at the scientist and engineer, but the real market for computers lay in business applications. Fogarty's efforts, however, had raised expectations, and the subsequent letdown proved frustrating. Feeling that management was unresponsive to their aspirations, several engineers in the Electronics Division tendered their resignation to Fogarty in 1961, in protest. Les Wood says: "We had some difficulties after the merger when we felt we were being ignored even more. A whole bunch of us had enough of this and we were going to resign ... [The corporation] wouldn't invest anything in us." Helwig also remembers how the division "wanted to make a computer and the company refused to put any money into making one. To make a lot of money we knew we had to have a computer."[5] Tom Edmondson, the president, met privately with many of the parties concerned at Les Wood's house and convinced them to stay on.

The discontent was soon forgotten when the news of Paul Dixon's sales coup spread. Dixon, a systems engineer, realized that the

By the early 1960s institutions that handled great volumes of data, such as the Toronto Stock Exchange, realized that computerization was essential.
(Ferranti-Packard Transformers Ltd.)

cheque-sorting business was threatened by the efforts of companies such as Honeywell to introduce general-purpose computers. Dixon convinced New York's Federal Reserve Bank that the next step in data processing was a general-purpose computer. The success of Ferranti-Packard's computerized cheque-sorting system had given the bank a great deal of respect for and trust in the division's abilities. Dixon was able to convince the bank to buy a general-purpose computer from Ferranti-Packard. This contract gave birth to the FP-6000. Amid all the celebrations, no one seemed to worry that the division had not even designed and tested a prototype of this computer.

Ferranti-Packard's approach to the design of the new FP-6000 was greatly influenced by the troubles that its parent firm was having with its own computer business. Although Ferranti UK had produced remarkably high-powered computers for scientific and engineering applications, the company could not address the needs of the business customer interested in electronic data processing and office automation. This large, untapped market held the key to the commercial success of computers. Ferranti UK built engineering marvels that experts could appreciate, but it chose not to design or market computers as solutions to business problems. As a result, its strategy led to inefficiency and inflexibility in the systems supplied. In 1961, the error of

The Toronto Stock Exchange invested in innovative Canadian technology to solve its enormous data-processing needs. Ferranti-Packard's FP-6000 computer was delivered to the Toronto Stock Exchange on 23 December 1963. Santus Claus was Orville Lesarge, a main-gate security guard at the Industry Street plant who played this role every year. The woman adorning the gift is believed to be a Toronto Stock Exchange employee.
(Ferranti-Packard Transformers Ltd.)

this strategy became painfully evident; Ferranti UK lost nearly $450,000 that year in its computer operations, and the future did not look any brighter.

Determined to reach a wider market, Ferranti UK embarked on a new computer, ORION. But once again, the penchant for innovation led the firm to develop a new kind of circuitry called the Neuron. The advantages of Neuron circuitry never materialized, and, as a result, the design of the ORION was fraught with technical problems, cost overruns, and substantial delays. Fearing that the technical and financial problems might be insurmountable in the time allotted, Ferranti UK decided to start work on a backup computer, ORION II. Its design would be based on a more conventional type of circuitry used successfully in the design of RESERVEC I. In a reverse transfer of technology, from subsidiary to parent firm, engineers Gordon Helwig, Ted Strain, and Peter Stevens went to England in the fall of 1961 to help build ORION II. Helwig remembers: "the logic work had already been done for ORION II. We were just applying the circuit techniques that we had developed for RESERVEC I to their logic design."[6] The two groups worked in parallel: one in Manchester building ORION, and the other in Bracknell building ORION II. The Canadian group spent three months at Bracknell.

ORION was finally completed, but huge cost overruns made it too expensive for the middle–lower-price segment of the market for which it was intended. The ensuing losses were straggering. From 1962 to 1964, the Computer Division lost nearly $7.5 million. The ORION project contributed significantly to Ferranti's withdrawal, several years later, from commercial general-purpose computers. It was a sad ending for a company that had pioneered the commercial production of general-purpose computers.

While ORION was being designed, Fred Longstaff and Don Ritchie went to England to get corporate approval for the new computer that they were proposing for the Federal Reserve Bank. They also needed permission to make a full entry into the general-purpose computer market. Their idea was to build on RESERVEC I technology and design a mid-sized computer that would appeal to a middle market. The computer group at Ferranti UK in Manchester did not agree with its Canadian counterparts design approach and did not want anything to do with it. Nevertheless, because there was a customer and the basic RESERVEC I circuitry had proven itself in ORION II, Ferranti-Packard got the green light to proceed with the FP-6000. "It was also agreed that if the development went well the Computer Department [of Ferranti UK] would offer it for sale in the UK and the rest of Europe and if it sold well manufacture would then be undertaken in the UK."[7]

Although the circuit logic for the FP-6000 was based on RESERVEC, the team at Ferranti-Packard came up with a very original and advanced concept for the FP-6000. Once again Fred Longstaff was the man behind new architecture and system design. There was no single creator or hero. Significant contributions to logic, hardware, and software design came from individuals such as George Collins, Gor-

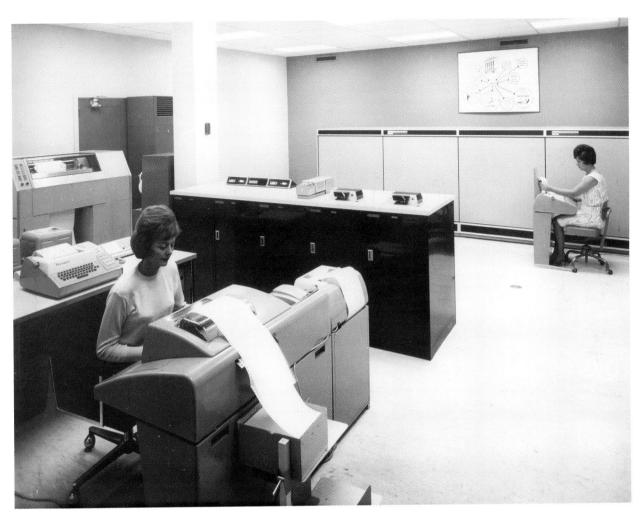

Behind the frenetic, seemingly chaotic trading-floor activity at the Toronto Stock Exchange, the FP-6000 quietly recorded the day's trading. In this 1964 photograph the office is presented as an oasis of tranquil, orderly productivity.
(Ferranti-Packard Transformers Ltd.)

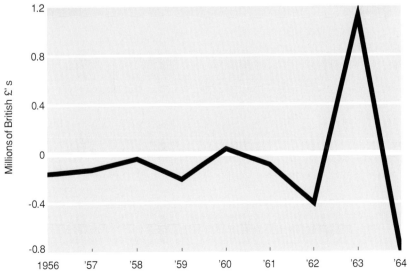

Ferranti - U.K. commercial computer business, profits and losses, 1956-1964

The FP-6000 at a Glance

The FP-6000 was marketed as a fast, medium-sized computer system with the multi-programming capabilities of very large systems. The computer's architecture, which was Fred Longstaff's brain-child, used a two-address instruction format. The computer operated with words of 24 binary digits; a 25th bit was used for parity checks. This small word length was an error in judgment, as Longstaff later recalled. The FP-6000 operated in a parallel mode, with a one-MHz clock rate. The Arithmetic Unit consisted of three full-length, 24-bit, flip-flop registers; a variety of smaller registers; and the Mill. The Mill contained a 24-bit parallel adder, carry circuitry, and a set of right- and left-shift gates. The adder circuitry consisted of a set of 8 NOR gates for each of the 24 binary digits in the addition. Multiplication and division were handled by repeated additions, or subtractions, and the appropriate right or left shifting. Addition and multiplication required 7 and 40 microseconds, respectively.

The FP-6000 was provided with a minimum ferrite-core working memory of 4,096 words. The core memory could be increased on modules of 4,096 words, to a maximum of 32,768 words; it was not divided into predefined blocks or sections. Rather, the EXECUTIVE assigned core memory to program in a dynamic fashion. The first eight core registers of an assigned block became the Accumulator registers for the program in question. This allocation of memory was a cornerstone of the FP-6000's multi-programming capabilities.

Written by Audrey Williams, the EXECUTIVE was the FP-6000's operating system. The EXECUTIVE organized all peripheral transfers and allocated the central processor's time to the various programs running simultaneously. The FP-6000 came with a business program assembly system called AUTOCODER, Fortran and Algol compilers, programming debugging software, and a library of standard sub-routines for business and scientific work.

The engineers at Ferranti-Packard designed as well a whole line of peripheral devices that could be added to the computer. Development of most of these peripherals was a natural extension of the firm's considerable know-how in high-speed tape and magnetic storage devices. Most peripheral devices had their own control unit. Once initiated by the EXECUTIVE, transfers between computer and peripheral proceeded autonomously. Thus the computer was free, during data transfers, to execute other programs. Unlike in other, larger computers, the peripherals of the FP-6000 were not equipped with logic circuitry to handle addressing and counting operations. Since the FP-6000 was to be a medium-sized computer, Ferranti-Packard had decided, for reasons of cost, that the computer's central processing unit would handle these functions. The engineers felt that the subsequent small loss in performance was more than compensated for by the FP-6000's more affordable price.

don Helwig, Mike Marcotty, Roger Moore, John Parsonage, Don Ritchie, Ian Sharp, Ted Strain, and Audrey Williams. The idea was to bring the most advanced technology, available only in the largest of computers, into an affordable, mid-sized computer – an ambitious undertaking for a group that had yet to build a full-scale general-purpose computer.

But the unqualified success of RESERVEC I gave the computer engineers confidence, which was vindicated by the speed with which they designed and assembled the first FP-6000. "We had one year, from the day somebody said 'go', to have a machine working on the customer's premises. Now that isn't a very long time to design and build a computer. Granted there was not much software and there weren't many peripherals running but we actually had the basic machine plus paper tape and some other stuff for the Federal Reserve Bank, running in a little over a year."[8]

Multi-programming stands out as the FP-6000's greatest technical achievement. It allowed many programs to run simultaneously and in such a way that each program ran as if it had exclusive use of all the computer's resources – namely, memory and input and output devices. Before multi-programming, even the largest computer could

The Electronics Division had its own well-equipped machine shop and staff of highly skilled machinists to build the many parts and prototypes needed for the Division's technology-driven research and development program.
(Ferranti-Packard Transformers Ltd.)

handle only one program at a time, an extremely inefficient use of a very expensive resource. Throughout the 1950s, computer engineers faced the highly complex technical problem of increasing the volume of work that a computer could handle in a given time. Multi-programming greatly improved the economics of computer use.

Multi-programming environments were first developed in the very big and expensive computers. The FP-6000 introduced highly efficient multi-programming features into an affordable, mid-sized computer. Much of the credit must go to Fred Longstaff for the way in which he integrated software and hardware to achieve a very efficient and innovative multi-programming environment. The software handling the complex task of managing the input, output, memory, and processing needs of many programs "simultaneously" was achieved through a resident program called the Executive and written by Audrey Williams. It was during the course of the FP-6000 project that Ian Sharp and Audrey Williams met and married. A special team headed by Ian Sharp developed the Executive, along with all the software for the FP-6000, which included ALGOL, FORTRAN, BUSINESS AUTOCODER, REPORT GENERATOR, and SORTS, along with a library of routines, general utility routines, and monitoring routines. As the first multi-programmable computer designed and built in Canada, the FP-6000 established Ferranti-Packard as the nation's leading designer and manufacturer of computers.

The Demise of the Computer Business

The FP-6000 was a milestone in the history of Canada's computer industry. For a machine that compared favourably to the highly successful IBM 360, its sales were a big disappointment. From 1962 to 1965, Ferranti-Packard managed to sell only five, to the Federal Reserve Bank, the Toronto Stock Exchange, the Saskatchewan Power Corp., the Defence Research Establishment in Dartmouth, Nova Scotia, and Ferranti UK in Britain. While Ferranti-Packard sought a bigger share of the computer market, a corporate drama was being played out in England that would forever change the Electronics Division in Canada.

Ferranti UK was finding it difficult to make a profit from its computer operations. Moreover, its limited equity base had become a competitive handicap. By the early 1960s, competitive realities for large commercial computers had altered significantly. For Harry Johnson, at the heart of computer development at Ferranti UK, "it was becoming clear that the business, particularly in the burgeoning commercial applications sector, was one in which only a small number of suppliers prepared to invest on an enormous scale could compete successfully."[9]

Nothing illustrates Johnson's view better than IBM's approach to the IBM 360. Put on the market in 1964, the IBM 360 represented an ambitious program, which "some compared with the massing of troops and equipment for the D-Day invasion of France during World War II."[10] With the 360, IBM was determined to ensure its dominance of the market. IBM had never previously reported annual capital expenditures of more than $340 million. By 1966, two years after the 360 entered the commercial market, the figures had risen to an unbelievable $1.6 billion! From 1961 to 1967, IBM's long-term liabilities rose by $1 billion.[11] The firm had significantly increased the stakes needed to stay in the commercial computer market. The world's computer manufacturers had two options: invest heavily in marketing and manufacturing capacity, or fold computer operations.

To compete successfully against the likes of IBM, Ferranti in Britain and Canada had to develop a more "market-driven" approach and greatly expand its equity base. For a privately owned company, such a massive infusion of capital could have come about only through merger or the issuance of public stocks. The Ferranti family, however, rejected any such options. From the time that Sebastian Ziani de Ferranti regained control in 1923, the family was determined to keep Ferranti UK a privately owned company, under family control. Ferranti UK was the living embodiment of the Ferrantis' vision of what an innovative, forward-looking company should be. Going public, or merging, meant losing control of its image.

At I.C.T it's all go

I told the wife I delivered
seven 'undred, thousand
quids worth of computers
for ICT this week
and she said pity you
don't 'ave time to weed
the garden.

I.C.T. now have over 500 orders for 1900 Series computers, announced only twenty one months ago. Of these 131 have been delivered, together with the necessary software. Delivery rate is building up to eight a week. What's more, these I.C.T. systems will be there for a long time. No matter how a business grows, the I.C.T. 1900 can grow with it. It was designed that way—to keep the buyer's original investment secure. That's why 500 systems — worth £61 million — have been ordered: a third of these for export.

Britain can be proud of **I.C.T.**

International Computers and Tabulators Limited

The ICT 1900 series was the British response to IBM's 360 series of mainframe computers. The 1900 series was based on the Canadian-made computer the FP-6000, whose rights ICT purchased directly from Ferranti UK, the parent company. This 1966 ICT advertisement took first prize in Milano at the Premio Europeo Rizzoli. The announcement that ICTs 1900 series computers were European-made and ready for delivery came a full year before the IBM 360 series, which did not reach Europe until 1967.
(Oxford University Press)

Ferranti UK's problems mirrored the state of the European computer industry. Mounting capital requirements called for new economies of scale. National governments regarded a viable domestic computer industry as crucial. The British government concluded that the future health of the nation's computer industry would require a national policy of rationalization. France came to the same conclusion in 1965, with the commercial failure of "Compagnie Bull," the country's key computer manufacturer. Finding IBM's dominance of the computer market "intolerable," the French government "caused the formation of a private company, the Compagnie Internationale de l'Informatique, CII, as a joint venture of three electrical companies and contributed a grant of $80 million ... CII was to develop a comprehensive (small to large) line of computers and software."[12] Unlike the British and French, the Canadian government did not seem to be interested in an indigenous computer industry.

In 1963, Ferranti transferred its entire commercial computer operations – which included manufacturing facilities, research laboratories, sales departments, along with the entire work-force – to the British company International Computers and Tabulators (ICT). Soon afterward, ICT changed its name to International Computers Limited (ICL). As with IBM, ICT had its roots in the office machine and equipment business. ICT had market presence and knew how to sell machines and computers to business but needed access to technology. Though a severe blow to the Ferranti corporate ego, the transfer was not a bad financial arrangement. Ferranti UK became a substantial shareholder in ICT and was able to rid itself of its financially draining commercial computer operations while still retaining its lucrative defence-oriented computer work.

This arrangement promoted the interests of the British computer industry but thwarted the ambitions of Ferranti-Packard. According to John Pickin, a former technical director and member of the board of Ferranti UK, the rights to the FP-6000 were a key element in the deal. Picken later recollected: "without the FP-6000 I don't think we would have succeeded in getting the deal we wanted from ICT. The FP-6000 was the golden brick in the sale of our operations."[13] In the words of another former member of the board, Donald MacCallum, the FP-6000 was "the jewel in the crown that ICT had bought."[14]

The real value of the FP-6000 for ICT became apparent when the company produced its 1900 series of computers. Faced with the market challenge of the IBM 360, ICT was anxious to develop a competitive line of products. After examining the various computer designs that it had acquired, ICT decided to base its new 1900 series on the FP-6000. The ICT 1900 was an exact copy of the FP-6000. Johnson, who was an important figure in computer development at Ferranti UK, writes that "the 1900 range proved very successful and with several updatings of design as technology advanced had a surprisingly long life."[15] ICT sold these computers all over the world. The success of the 1900 series firmly established ICT, and later ICL, as the dominant player in Britain's computer industry.

The sale was an enormous and unkind blow to Canada. There had been no consultation with the Canadian group, and the sale of rights to the FP-6000 effectively stripped Ferranti-Packard of its entire computer systems operations. Ferranti-Packard received $1 million in compensation. In a last-ditch attempt to save the computer systems work at Ferranti-Packard, the Electronics Division soon approached ICT with a proposal to design and manufacture the 1905 and 1906, two of the computers in the proposed 1900 series. The computer systems groups at Ferranti-Packard argued that they were well positioned to design and market such a computer, especially in North America, but ICT had plans that did not include Ferranti-Packard.

ICT's refusal to enter into a joint computer venture marked the end of Ferranti-Packard's twenty-five – year journey to establish a commercial computer business in Canada. In the summer of 1964, realizing than an era had come to an end, most of the hardware design team resigned, followed by the entire software development team. In all, fourteen engineers left and a key industrial centre for computer design disappeared.

It took many years, much money, and a good deal of effort to develop this centre of excellence; this centre, however, was very fragile, and its closure and the subsequent dispersal of highly trained personnel posed serious threats to Canadian technological development. This happened at Ferranti-Packard, and then again with cancellation of the AVRO Arrow and the ensuing "brain drain" of aeronautical engineers to the United States. Closure and cancellation are sometimes necessary, but Canada has collected a considerable number of examples of the wrong way to do this.

The resignations of almost all of the computer systems group at Ferranti-Packard, though an incalculable loss for the company, led to significant spin-offs for Ontario and Canada. Gord Lang, Fred Longstaff, Don Ritchie, and Ted Strain, the hardware engineers, left to create ESE, a new company which continued doing innovative work in digital electronics. ESE was later acquired by Motorola and became a key element of Motorola Information Systems. Today, Strain is president of Motorola Information Systems, Longstaff vice-president of systems, and Lang vice-president of R&D. The software development team, David Butler, Brian Daly, Bob Johnston, Ted McDorman, Jim McSherry, Roger Moore, Audrey Sharp, and Don Smith, which had been led by Ian Sharp, left to form I.P. Sharp Associates. I.P. Sharp maintains an extensive on-line global database service in a network and is one of the largest software houses in Canada. In 1987, I.P. Sharp Associates was acquired by Reuters. In the late 1960s, Cliff Bernard, Rod Coutts, Lawrie Craig, and Al Vandeberg left Ferranti-Packard to create Teklogix, another successful digital electronics company.

The sale of the FP-6000 to ICT has engendered considerable debate. The FP-6000 was more than just a good product; it was a symbol of a dream that Canadians could become serious manufacturers of computers. Was the FP-6000 a unique commercial opportunity that was snatched away from Canada by foreign interests? Does the success of the 1900 series prove the point? Before pointing an accusing finger at Ferranti UK, one should ask: had the rights to the FP-6000 not been sold, could Ferranti-Packard have developed it into a profitable business? It is difficult to find an answer without engaging in speculation.

Back in 1961, the brash young computer engineers at Ferranti-Packard were convinced that, with the right technology, they could carve out a profitable niche in the North American computer market. By 1963, the Digital Equipment Co. (DEC) was proving that, with the right product, a small company could find a chink in the IBM marketing armour. Formed in 1957 by Kenneth Olsen, an engineer who had previously worked on the Whirlwind computer for MIT, and two other engineers, DEC started in an old woollen mill in a suburb of Boston with only $70,000 of capital, put up by a local venture-capital firm.

Unlike companies such as IBM, Sperry Rand, and Ferranti UK, which were advocating large, complex, and expensive computer installations, Olsen felt that there was a real need for small computer systems. By the time that the competition realized what had happened, DEC had a pioneering product that virtually captured the minicomputer market. In 1966, when DEC went public, the initial $70,000 investment was worth $228.6 million. DEC's early computer lines represented a marketing break-through achieved with rather ordinary technology. The early PDP computer series produced by DEC consisted of simple, cheap computers for specific situations. The Ferranti-Packard group, however, had a different vision of the mid-sized computer. It wanted to use superior technology to build a small computer with the attributes of a large mainframe.

Today, with the wisdom of experience behind them, all those associated with the FP-6000 feel that it was naive to believe that Ferranti-Packard could create a viable general-purpose computer business. The FP-6000 was an attempt to build a standardized, off-the-shelf, general-purpose computer and market it to a diverse, non-specialist market. All five sales of the FP-6000 were made by engineers selling to technically sophisticated users. The Electronics Division was ill-equipped to reach the market for which the FP-6000 was designed. The chief designer, Fred Longstaff, put it more bluntly: "Our marketing was zip. We were poles from IBM."[16] In the quest for engineering excellence, the division lost track of the simple truism that a business is determined by its customers, not its products. In the words of Peter Drucker, one of the founders of the "modern management science":

What the business thinks it produces is not of first importance – especially not to the future of the business and to its success. The typical engineering definition of quality is something that is hard to do, is complicated, and costs a lot of money! But that isn't quality; it's incompetence. What the customer thinks he is buying, what he considers value, is decisive – it determines what a business is, what it produces, and whether it will prosper. And what the customer thinks he is buying is never a product. It is always utility, that is, what a product or service does for him.[17]

Marketing a Canadian computer, in a conservative domestic market dominated by IBM, proved far more difficult than its design and manufacture. Like so many other technology-driven companies, the Electronics Division failed to see the role that astute marketing played in growth. Engineers selling innovation to data-processing customers was not the most effective way to market the computer. Selling, no matter how aggressively done, does not constitute marketing. In a recent study of innovation and business growth, Funkhouser and Rothberg described marketing as

both a philosophy of business and a versatile set of tools and techniques. In addition to advertising and sales, the marketing umbrella covers pricing, packaging, distribution, product development, and research, and everything else that is involved in bringing the firm and its customers together ... 60% of high-tech product introductions that reached the commercialization stage failed because of marketing problems ... Many a new product idea owes its success to being catapulted out of the incubation phase by an effective marketing system. Many a good product has died a squalid death because it lacked one.[18]

The marketing of the FP-6000 was further hampered by the Canadian corporation's inability to raise the financial resources to promote, service, and support the computer over a large North American market. As we saw earlier, these were weaknesses shared by the entire Ferranti organization. With twenty-five years to reflect on the question, Harry Johnson concluded that "there was no possible way in which Ferranti, let alone its Canadian subsidiary, could, in the relevant time scale, have established or acquired the manifold skills and facilities necessary to undertake the transformation of the basic design into the comprehensive range of processors, associated peripheral equipment, operating systems and other supporting software that constituted the 1900 series. Nor could Ferranti have financed the necessary manufacturing, marketing and field support activities on an adequate scale."[19]

Another problem in selling the FP-6000 was the attitude of the Canadian market. Canadians tended to view home-grown solutions with suspicion. In 1962, looking at the armed force's support of industrial development, the Glassco Commission underscored the defence establishment's "marked lack of confidence in Canadian science and technology as a whole."[20] Many excellent and reliable Canadian innovations have been passed over for off-the-shelf foreign technology. While Americans are prone to believe that all great things were invented by the United States, Canadians' diffident psyches tend to view all great things as having been invented elsewhere.

Purchasing patterns of governments reflected this troubling lack of confidence in Canadian goods. Ian Sharp is still very caustic in his

In addition to designing and building computers, Ferranti-Packard developed an important market niche in perforated-paper tape readers during the 1950s and into the 1960s. Perforated-paper tape, along with punched cards, were the first principal means of storing information. Early punched-tape readers, however, were slow because they used mechanical pins to sense the holes during reading. Ferranti-Packard greatly improved the speed of perforated-tape readers through the innovation of optical scanning. Ferranti-Packard not only sold many of its tape readers to the military but also developed a good market in the business sector. This photograph shows a Bell Telephone Co. of Canada data-reading installation, installed at Ontario Hydro, based on Ferranti-Packard tape readers. (Ontario Archives, Ferranti-Packard Collection, AO 1525)

criticism of government unwillingness to use its purchasing power to foster Canadian goods and services: "the Government of Ontario had a campaign on to buy Ontario produts. They were buying a large computer at that time but they did not give the FP-6000 the time of day."[21] In 1963, Metropolitan Toronto rejected Ferranti-Packard's bid to use the FP-6000 for the world's first computerized traffic control system which it was about to build. The UNIVAC machine, which was Metro council's choice, had no technical superiority over the FP-6000. Though promising significant Canadian content in the manufacturing, the cheaper UNIVAC system was assembled in the United States, with no economic spin-offs for Toronto. The FP-6000, in contrast, would have been manufactured entirely in Toronto – a boost to the local computer industry.

The BUIC Incident

With the demise of computer systems business, the Electronics Division intensified efforts to expand activities in such traditional product lines as memory drums. On learning that the US military was develop-

Preparing the magnetic-memory drums required very precise machining. In this photograph the vertical drum is being rotated past a cutting tool which slowly moves vertically to turn the drum to the proper diameter and finish the surface.
(Ontario Archives, Ferranti-Packard Collection, neg. 490E)

ing a back-up system to SAGE, Ferranti-Packard prepared a bid to build the system's mass memory storage. In a subcontract to the American firm Burroughs, the division was to design and manufacture the high-capacity, fast-access memory drums for the Back Up Intercept Command (BUIC) system.

Ferranti-Packard was a respected manufacturer of large magnetic memory-drum systems. Magnetic-drum storage technology developed as an outgrowth of computer systems work. Fast and reliable memory drums were essential components of Ferranti-Packard's computers. Rapid-access memory – random-access memory, as it is called today – was so expensive that it had to be complemented by magnetic memory drums. The Ferranti-Packard drums rested on an elegant, but simple exploitation of aerodynamic principles. Jets of air stabilized and positioned the rather large drum very precisely as it turned at high speeds. The read/write heads could be accurately positioned very close to the floating drum's surface by air-servo control mechanisms. Later technology would introduce a floating head. Ferranti-Packard's memory drums were known for their speed, reliability, and storage capacity.

Starting with DATAR, the company's interest in magnetic drums grew out of its computer systems work. Ferranti-Packard's magnetic-drum memory systems were an integral feature of the mail-sorting computer for the Canadian Post Office, the cheque-sorting computer for the Federal Reserve Bank, RESERVEC I, and the FP-6000. The company used this expertise to develop a business selling memory systems. Its biggest single customer for drums was the US military. Sales, though profitable, remained relatively small and sporadic.

Bill Lower, the division's marketing manager, saw the BUIC project as an excellent opportunity to expand the company's drum business. Unlike previous drum designs, the BUIC drums were to be based on a new technology using "floating heads." Only a few companies in the world were working with floating head drums, as the technology was still experimental. Today, floating heads are standard practice for disk memories. This technology aims at improving the efficiency and economics of drum memory by placing the magnetic sensing heads as close to the drum's surface as possible. The closer they are placed, the more information can be packed onto the drum's tracks. As the drum rotates at high speeds, it drags a very thin layer of air around with it. In a "floating head" system, the read/write heads floated approximately 200 micro-inches above the surface of the drum, on this very thin cushion of air.

Before BUIC, Ferranti-Packard had experimented with floating heads but had never built or even tested a marketable product. Nevertheless, the company's engineers felt confident that they could tackle BUIC. They had an apparently successful model, and only the tight schedule seemed worrisome. Moreover, the division had an enviable record of achievement under tough circumstances. Little did Bill Lower, an electronics engineer by profession, realize that a small piece of Teflon would totally wipe out his vision of great profits.

Both electronic and magnetic-core memory were very expensive during the late 1950s and early 1960s. Magnetic-drum memory proved to be a slower, but more economical, way of storing and retrieving data for a variety of applications. With its patented and innovative air-bearing drum, Ferranti-Packard developed another market niche in the design and manufacture of magnetic-drum systems. Drums similar to the one shown here, which is about 24 centimetres high, were used in many Ferranti Canada computer systems in the late 1950s and early 1960s. These drums had 240 tracks, with as many read/write heads. Each track could store up to 4,000 digits. With air-suspension the drum could rotate at speeds up to 18,000 rpm. (Ontario Archives, Ferranti-Packard Collection, AO 693)

The read/write heads are very small pieces of metal embedded in a larger housing called a shoe. In the BUIC system, the shoe and the head floated as one unit over the drum. Ferranti-Packard's engineers reasoned that a very soft material, such as Teflon, would protect the surface of the drum in the event of any contact between the two. To the engineers' surprise and dismay, when the system was tested, the 200 Teflon heads crashed onto the surface and stripped the information-carrying nickel-cobalt surface from the drum.

What started out to be a straightforward project turned into a nightmare. After considerable experimentation and many drum failures, the cause of the problem became clear. Any speck of dust squeezing through the minute gap between the shoe and the drum would embed itself in the soft Teflon. This speck would then rub against the drum and lift off the drum particles of the nickel-cobalt surface, which, in turn, would also embed themselves in the soft Teflon shoe. In a short time, the soft Teflon shoe took on the appearance and texture of a piece of sandpaper and scraped the drum clean.

With time running out, an alternate material had to be found. Ferranti-Packard engineers concluded that a highly polished stainless-steel shoe was the answer, but more time was needed to perfect these new shoes. Burroughs insisted that Ferranti-Packard meet its deadlines according to the original specifications of the contract. Ferranti-Packard had to make a design work that it knew was basically flawed.

Many at Ferranti-Packard involved in the project saw Burroughs's director of procurement as behind the intransigence and nicknamed him "gunslinger," apparently a fitting phonetic parody of his name. "He was doing everything to make us default," recalled Bill Lower. "He put everything in our way to try to stop us from finding a technical solution."[22] Bad feelings developed after Burroughs threatened a lawsuit. Ferranti-Packard negotiated a termination of convenience which included a stiff penalty. The division lost $1–2 million on the BUIC contract.

Immediately after Ferranti-Packard defaulted, Burroughs awarded the drum contract to a rival US company which had just hired Burroughs's intransigent director of procurement. Was Ferranti-Packard sabotaged? It is a difficult, perhaps unanswerable question. One might fault the Electronics Division for drawing up a contract in which, as a result of over-confidence, an R&D problem was treated as a manufacturing problem. But this happens frequently in rapidly changing fields; those not willing to move boldly into new areas soon recede into the background. Burroughs, inexplicably, was unwilling to allow design modification or extension, even though these are common with emerging technologies. Burroughs seemed more intent on getting away from the contract than on having its needs met. Even before termination of the contract, supposedly for non-performance, Ferranti-Packard had delivered the new drum design with stainless-steel heads to the Saskatchewan Power FP-6000 system, where it worked very well.

Clearly something had gone wrong. Was it a severe case of person-

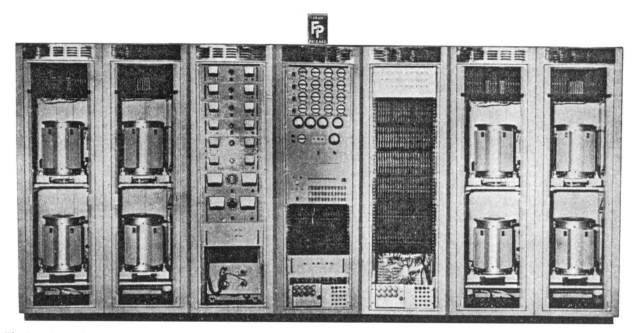

The American military were Ferranti-Packard's biggest customers for memory-drum systems. This eight-drum memory system was used by the Strategic Air Command during the 1960s. (Ferranti-Packard Transformers Ltd.)

ality conflict? Was it an early sign of the exodus of imagination, technical wizardry, and confidence which would be so apparent as Burroughs slipped from once mighty manufacturer to supplier and maintainer of technology from other manufacturers? Whatever the cause, Ferranti-Packard was able to produce enough parts for the willing Saskatchewan Power Corp. only by misleading the watchful Burroughs monitoring team, which was there under a contract clause giving it unlimited access to the Ferranti-Packard plant. According to Les Wood's recollection, production records were doctored and a secret third shift was put to work, hidden from the Burroughs team. But even when a solution was produced, manufactured, and proven, Burroughs would have none of it. The redesigned floating drum head would benefit others. The redesigned drums installed for the FP-6000 system at Saskatchewan Power ran for 40,000 hours without a problem.

After the BUIC disaster, Tom Edmondson and the board followed the operations of the Electronics Division with greater care. Unhappy with the general manager's handling of the project and the general financial picture of the division, Edmondson in 1965 replaced John Fogarty with Bill Lower.

The Electronics Division Struggles

Bill Lower faced the unenviable challenge of instilling a new sense of purpose in the division's engineering and business operations. He inherited a technology-driven division which was breaking up into a number of engineering islands with little business direction from the top. In the absence of any coherent, long-term business plan, engineering vision, rather than sound market analysis, governed business planning. Like Stephen Leacock's now immortal rider, the division appeared to be jumping on its engineering horse and riding madly off in all directions.

The diversity of this small division's activities in the 1960s leaves one breathless: superconductivity, fuel cells, thin film research for integrated circuit technology, electro-magnetic disk information display systems, numerical readout systems for machine tools, magnetic disk memories, magnetic memory drums, high-speed photo-electric tape readers, bar code scanning technology for automated shipping and inventory, electronic control systems for large mail-order businesses, and various top secret communications projects for the Canadian military.

The many activities were spreading already limited resources dangerously thin. Cut from the same cloth as the other engineers in the division, Lower found it difficult to resist an exciting engineering

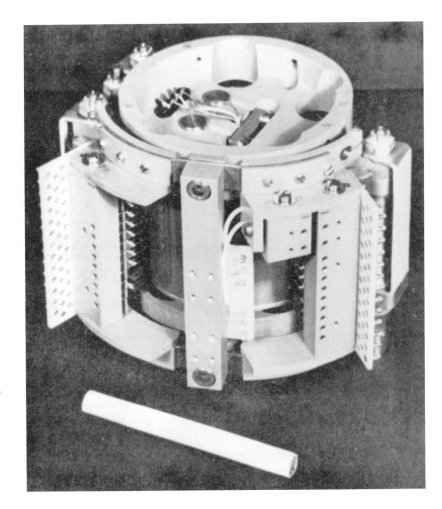

Miniaturization was an important trend in the design and manufacture of memories to military specifications. This small magnetic-memory drum unit, shown with a cigarette to give a sense of scale, was designed around 1959–60 to be used in military aircraft. The drum is surrounded by two detachable columns on which the many read/write heads rested. One of Ferranti-Packards smallest drum units, type 217, was 2 inches (5.1 cm.) in diameter, stored 20,000 bits of information on 20 tracks, and had access times of 2.5 milliseconds when the drum rotated at 25,000 rpm. (Ferranti-Packard Transformers Ltd.)

challenge and, try as he might, was unable to impose business discipline on the division's innovative drives. The company's top management did little to help.

The executive and board had long maintained an arm's-length approach to the division. At times, this attitude bordered on indifference, at least as perceived by those within the division. As Wordie Hetherington, at the time general manager of the Power Transformer Division, later recalled, the executive group of division managers "never took the time to understand how they were really trying to run the Division as a business."[23] This indifference was in part a consequence of serious financial troubles resulting from a very tight transformer and meter market.

In terms of revenue, capital investment, and corporate tradition, Ferranti-Packard was first and foremost a manufacturer of transformers and watt-hour meters. Getting the company's transformer and meter business out of the red weighed heavily on the executive, to the neglect of the Electronics Division. There was a communications obstacle arising from two different engineering mind-sets. "At management meetings," recalls Hetherington, "the other managers, from the electrical side, really couldn't assess the technical significance of the Electronics Division's operations, and as a consequence really couldn't assess the business side ... One dealt in milliamps. The other dealt in kiloamps ... and never the twain shall meet."[24]

It was also not easy for the company's executive to impose a "bottom line" on the division's R&D. Mesmerized by new technologies whose commercial merits they could not assess, the corporation's top managers harboured the hope that one day the Electronics Division would hit the jackpot. Hetherington can still "remember listening to the wonderful tales of the things they were going to do. I remember thinking that was great. I don't ever remember, in those days, ever questioning how they were going about ensuring that they would eventually make a profit ... I remember saying: 'Gee, this might be good business.' That's the truth!"[25]

Research on fuel cells and superconductivity illustrates the hold that visionary engineering had on the firm's management. A fuel cell is a device which, like a battery, produces electricity from a chemical reaction. Unlike a battery, however, the reactants are continuously fed into the cell and the products of the chemical reaction are continuously removed. As long as the cell is supplied with fuel, it will continue to generate electricity. Thus a fuel cell resembles an engine rather than a battery in that it does not run down and can be refuelled rapidly. Fuel cells were first developed as a reliable and compact means to supply electric power for spacecraft. These cells used esoteric fuels and were very expensive.

Superconductivity refers to the fact that as the temperature of a conductor decreases, so does its resistance. If the temperature of a conductor is lowered toward "absolute zero" (-273 Celsius), electrical resistance drops dramatically and almost disappears. Temperatures close to absolute zero are obtained by liquefying nitrogen,

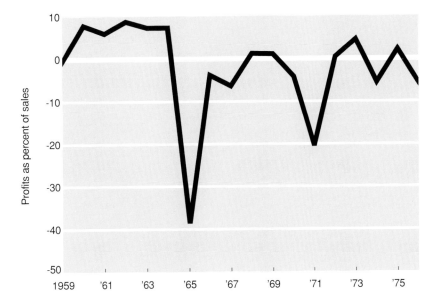

Electronics Division financial performance,1959-1976

helium, and other gases. As one gets closer to absolute zero, the economic benefits of superconductivity rise dramatically.

Fuel cells and superconductivity have enormous implications for the electrical power industry. Suppose that every home was equipped with a fuel cell that could operate with a cheap fuel such as natural gas. While natural gas could directly meet the bulk of the home's heating and cooking needs, the fuel cell would supply all the electricity needed for lighting and other electrical appliances. Such decentralized electrical power generation would drastically reduce the need for long-distance AC transmission and considerably reduce the need for transformers and generators. The potential economic, social, and technological ramifications are deep and far-reaching.

Superconductivity first interested Kenyon Taylor, the Electronics Division's head of research, as a means of developing faster and larger memory systems for computers. Taylor, however, also realized that superconductivity had important implications for the power business. He later wrote: "I felt that as our company business is in electricity handling, transmission and use, know-how on something without electrical resistance was vitally important."[26] Superconductivity could radically improve the efficiency of electrical power transmission by reducing the losses caused by resistance in the conducting wire or cable. With such power losses virtually eliminated, much finer wire could be used to construct miniature superconducting power transformers and generators. Unlike fuel cell technology, which offered decentralized electrical power systems, superconductivity promised more efficient and economical centralized power production.

These are the kinds of arguments that Taylor used to convince

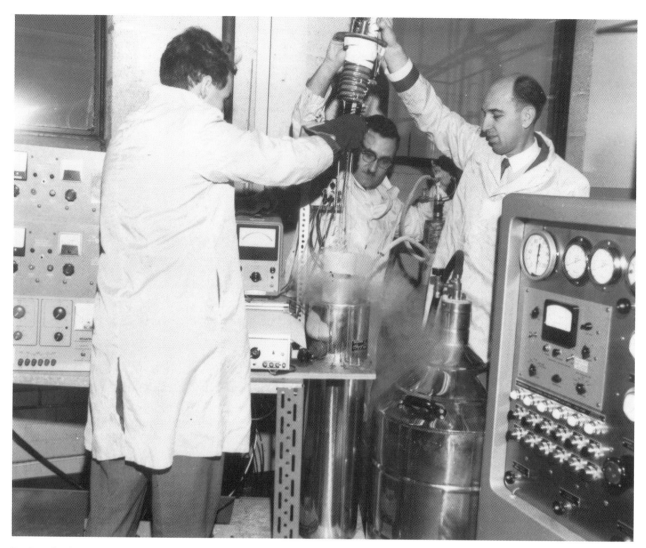

Dr. David Atherton, shown with his colleagues working in the Electronics Division "clean room," was hired in 1962 to head a small cryogenics and superconductivity team. Ferranti-Packard researchers were very talented individuals, some of whom ended up at Canadian universities. Dr. Atherton went on to teach physics at Queen's University in Kingston, Dr. Herb Ratz went to the University of Waterloo via the University of Saskatchewan.
(Ontario Archives, Ferranti-Packard Collection, neg. 1480–3)

Ferranti UK, Ferranti-Packard, and the Canadian government to fund the initial R&D in these areas. Taylor's letter to Sebastian Ziani de Ferranti in 1964 convinced Ferranti UK to pay 25 per cent of the initial R&D costs – a small price for research with so much potential. In 1962, Taylor hired Dr. David Atherton, a physicist who later taught at Queen's University, to head up a small research team in superconductivity In 1964 he brought on Dr. H.J. Davis from Energy Conversion Ltd, in England, to start up the fuel cell research. Both projects were, in their initial stages, relatively modest and supported jointly by the company and government.

The transition from small-scale laboratory experiments to practical commercial application required considerable R&D. The risks were high, and millions of dollars would have to be invested before there was even the possibility that anything commercial might emerge. With fuel cells, the challenge was to develop a cell that could produce electrical power reliably and at a price that was competitive with the standard methods of generating and transmitting power. Ferranti-Packard estimated that it would take $3 million to develop a 50-kW commercial model. This was a conservative figure, as R&D costs somehow invariably seemed to exceed initial estimates, and modest in comparison to the efforts of big American companies. Pratt and Whitney, for example, spent over $50 million on fuel-cell R&D between 1967 and 1972.[27]

Once again, as with the FP-6000, the division was moving into financial waters beyond the company's depth. How could Ferranti-Packard possibly finance such costly undertakings? The FP-6000 had been tried alone. For fuel cells, Ferranti-Packard tried to go beyond its capital limitations by proposing that a consortium carry out the R&D, manufacture, and marketing. It would contribute its R&D experience in the area, while the other partners would provide the capital. In the fall of 1969, a presentation was made to senior officials of the Department of Industry in an effort to enlist government assistance to form a consortium. Government officials rejected the idea and suggested instead that the project be given over to Atomic Energy of Canada Ltd.

Unwilling to give up its potential commercial stake in fuel cells, Ferranti-Packard approached a candidate that had much to gain from exploitation of fuel cells. Consumers Gas expressed a keen interest in the venture, and after some discussion it was agreed in May 1970 that the two companies would commission a study on the state of fuel cell R&D and its potential market. A.D. Little Inc. would do the survey and study. If the results were favourable, Consumers Gas would enter into a two-year fuel cell development program. It and Ferranti-Packard were no strangers to each other. Financial links had already been established in a previous venture. The two companies had invested $800,000, with Consumers Gas putting up $700,000, to create a new firm, T-Scan, with Lyman Richardson, who had championed the RESERVEC concept at TCA, as its president. The purpose of the enterprise was to manufacture and sell a much-improved version of the Transactor used in RESERVEC I.

The A.D. Little Report came out in November 1970, and its conclusions were not as positive as Consumers Gas wanted. The company changed its mind on the joint venture and proposed instead a consortium of itself, American Gas Development, and Ferranti-Packard. When American Gas decided against the venture, Consumers Gas pulled out of the whole affair. Ferranti-Packard was left to cover the overhead costs associated with the fuel research group. It notified the government that it could no longer maintain the program and planned to wind it down in January 1971.

In a last-ditch effort to give the program an additional one-year lease on life, a financial package was suggested for Shell Oil, the Canadian government, and Ferranti UK in Edinburgh. On 27 January 1971, Lower reported to top management that "the Shell Oil Co. has indicated an interest in investing $30,000 in this program to keep it

This advertising photograph was prepared by Ferranti-Packard to help market the products of its superconductivity research. Ferranti-Packard managed to sell a variety of very powerful superconducting magnets to various research centres, such as McGill University in Canada and others in the United States. Nonetheless, Ferranti-Packard's efforts to commercialize cryogenics ultimately failed.
(Ontario Archives, Ferranti-Packard Collection, neg. 1525–1)

going until March 31, 1972, at which time the program would be reviewed with a view to establishing a joint venture arrangement for the second phase of development. The total cost to run the program for the year would be $100,000. Continuation for the year would be contingent on $60,000 from the Defence Research Establishment, $30,000 from Shell Oil, and $15,000 from Ferranti Edinburgh."[28]

For unstated reasons, Shell Oil changed its mind. In March 1971, Ferranti-Packard was forced to wind up its fuel cell project. In this undertaking, as in the computer business, the Electronics Division had once again managed to push the corporation into an area that required capital resources beyond the capacities of a subsidiary of a privately owned corporation. But this time, upper management was seeking ways to get around this limitation through joint ventures and consortiums. Unfortunately, Ferranti-Packard's commercial ambitions were too far ahead of existing technology and Canadian venture capital.

Upper Management Looks at the Division's Operations

By the late 1960s, Ferranti-Packard was pulling out of a difficult financial period for its meter and transformer business. The company was also formulating a North American market strategy for transformer sales. In an aggressive decision, it stated that survival depended on moving beyond the limited Canadian market to the larger American one. With the return of profits in the company's power business, it would pay greater attention to the problems in Electronics.

In August 1968, Wordie Hetherington presented the Canadian position to the top executives of all the Ferranti UK trading groups, at a meeting at Gleneagles in Scotland. He declared North America the prime market for the Canadian transformer business and proposed a new direction for the Electronics Division: "It is hoped that through further introduction of U.K. technology to North America we can build a strong and growing business. Without this technology the Electronics activity in North America will be difficult to develop. This report will outline the reasons why Canada can be an effective base for U.K. electronics operations in North America, participating in the tremendous market potential available in North America."[29]

The proposal that the Electronics Division become a gateway for British electronics assumed that the infusion of British technology and products would increase the division's competitiveness in the United States: "Since 70% of our Electronics business is in the United States and thus is expected to increase, our plans must take into account the need to compete with U.S. technology and to follow the changes in the U.S. market which generally lead to Canadian demand."[30] Further, "if U.K. technology is not available, then we have David battling the U.S. giants on rather unequal terms, but if our role of a subsidiary is recognized, we can expect business growth up to 25% per year."[31]

The Canadian presentation made it clear that Ferranti-Packard's

CANADA'S FIRST COMMERCIAL COMPUTER 273

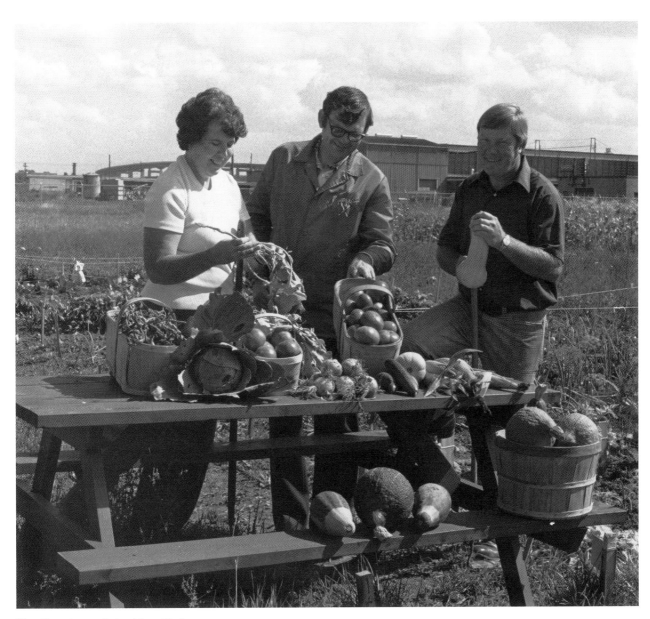

Not all employee relationships with the company centred around machines, factory work, and technology. In St Catharines, Ferranti-Packard provided about seven acres (2.8 ha) of fertile land for garden plots. Ron Pay, shown on the right in September 1976, organized the garden-plot activities. With him are Louise Sumbler and Bob Babyk.
(Ontario Archives, Ferranti-Packard Collection, AO 676)

management wanted the Electronics Division to leave military-oriented business and pursue a civilian commercial market. Ferranti-Packard mistakenly believed that technology-driven Ferranti UK could help it establish commercially oriented product lines. Ferranti UK's biggest strength was military electronic systems. It was a frustrating meeting. On the surface, gentlemanly cordiality reigned, but nothing changed. The Electronics Division continued its quest for commercial purpose.

The inability of the division's management to chart a clear business direction and produce long-term growth was creating serious morale problems. Tom Edmondson asked Wordie Hetherington in 1970 to run the division as acting general manager and do an unobtrusive study of the division's business operations and assess the performance of the division's managers. An astute businessman with a meticulous mind and a good engineer who could also be a generalist, Hetherington was an excellent choice for this delicate task.

After several months of study, Hetherington confirmed what everyone suspected. The division was a highly innovative, technology-driven group with little business and manufacturing discipline. New design changes were being instituted before the previous ones could be studied. Preoccupation with improving everything led to production delays and high production costs. It also made standardization very difficult. The division's financial problems arose from management's inability to control the rate at which the designs of products were being modified, plus an overly complex but inaccurate costing system which consistently underpriced jobs. Hetherington was raising an important issue: at what point does technical improvement for its own sake become counterproductive?

Hetherington also recommended key changes in personnel, overhauling the division's management structure, and rationalizing the division's activities. In a private memo to Edmondson, he wrote: "The three product groups and four profit centers may have been right if growth had materialized but, for the present and immediate future, it involves too much overhead; cost accounting and reporting have become too complicated."[32] The division had spread itself too thin and had developed small pockets of research. As a result, it could not maintain an adequate level of R&D in all areas. Cost-cutting measures had reduced the R&D effectiveness of many departments: "Except for Fuel Cells and Superconductivity, R&D is almost negligible. This has been done to cut overhead but it is very shortsighted and if allowed to continue much longer, the Division will not be able to recover."[33] The solution was to focus resources and energies into the most promising short- and long-term commercial avenues.

Hetherington recommended that a five-year business plan be implemented to move the division's operations into respectable profitability. He also urged Edmondson "to move fairly quickly, otherwise the situation will worsen due to the loss of key personnel and that technical troubles would develop due to very low morale."[34]

10   *End of an Era*

If crisis was the crucible in which Ferranti-Packard was created, then Tom Edmondson was the craftsman who forged the union between two of Canada's oldest electrical manufacturing firms. His decision in 1954 to join forces with the Ferranti organization remains the most significant event in the company's history. Faced with the ever-deepening financial crisis in the Canadian electrical industry, Vincent Ziani de Ferranti in 1958 asked Edmondson to oversee the consolidation and rationalization of the Ferranti holdings in Canada. Only with Edmondson in charge did Vincent feel confident that the best of both companies would be brought together to produce a competitive, self-reliant, and profitable operation in Canada.

From 1958 to 1971, Edmondson adroitly steered Ferranti-Packard through very troubled waters as it sought to find its proper role in Canada's industrial development. Realizing that the Canadian market had become too small to absorb the Canadian industry's production capacity, Edmondson set his company's marketing sights on larger horizons. He realized that long-term survival was contingent on breaking away from the restrictive confines of the Canadian market and integrating more into the North American economy. Although the idea of market expansion into the United States seems commonplace today, in 1960 it represented a bold move for a Canadian electrical manufacturer.

Within a decade, the Ferranti-Packard marketing and sales team turned the US market into a cornerstone of the company's manufacturing activities. By the late 1960s, Ferranti-Packard's exports to the United States had grown so much that 50 per cent of its workers owed their jobs directly to these exports, which helped create a six-fold increase in overall sales from 1960 to 1971.[1] As the reader will discover in this chapter, Ferranti-Packard's commitment to the US market continued to grow throughout the 1970s, culminating in 1977 with construction of a transformer-manufacturing facility in Dunkirk, New York.

In 1971, Tom Edmondson, at the age of 65, fell victim to the same mandatory retirement policy that he had instituted many years earlier. After twenty years at the helm, first at Packard Electric and then at Ferranti-Packard, he passed the reins of leadership to Wordie Hetherington. He stayed on as chairman of the board until the age of 70. To mark his departure in 1976, after 55 years of service, Sebastian Ziani de Ferranti arranged for Edmondson to visit Buckingham Palace for an audience with the Queen. On 28 February 1988, after several years of declining health, Edmondson passed away in St Catharines at the age of 82.

In 1921, at the age of 15, Edmondson went to work as an office boy at Packard Electric. He took home study courses, studied at night school, and eventually became a certified general accountant. Packard Electric executives noticed his diligence and abilities, particularly in financial matters, and he rose steadily in the firm. Despite all the financial and administrative experience that he obtained, he never had the opportunity, nor did he feel the need, to acquire the in-depth scientific and engineering knowledge on which his company's products were based. On several occasions while president, however, Edmondson had taken Hetherington aside to ask for tutoring on the principles of electrical theory. Edmondson's limited knowledge of electrical engineering was more than compensated for by his astuteness and his business vision. A strong believer in consensus building, communication, and the importance of people, Edmondson's greatest talent lay in his ability to manage people by allowing them to do what they did best. He had a keen eye for character and talent and surrounded himself with people whose understanding of electrical manufacturing he could trust.

Ferranti-Packard had come a long way from merger under Edmondson's leadership. Many serious questions remained unresolved, though, when he stepped down as president in 1971. Survival of the Power Division still hung in the balance. The Electronics Division, as driven by technology as ever, lacked focus and seemed to drift from one poor year to another, despite the great hopes everyone had for it. For the company's oldest product line, the watt-hour meter, the handwriting was on the wall: too many suppliers chasing a rather small and static market. Then there were the problems associated with just getting bigger. As the complexity and scale of the company grew, so did the need for more unified and systematic management practices. A well-structured framework was needed to co-ordinate the diverse, and sometimes opposing, needs of various divisions. This was particularly true in capital investment, where limited financial resources required difficult choices between immediate and long-term needs.

Wordie Hetherington now had the task of accomplishing what Edmondson had been unable to do: ensuring consistent profits throughout the entire organization. Little did he realize that his efforts would be greatly complicated by profound global economic changes. By the early 1970s, it became evident to most economists that the long-sustained post-war growth was slowing. The Western economies were falling into deep recession, and rising unemployment was eating away at the social fabric. All efforts to fight the recession and unemployment merely fuelled inflation. By 1975, a new economic phenomenon, "stagflation," had gripped the industrialized world. Not only was the world's economy stagnating, but there was galloping inflation.

In Canada, the slowing of economic growth was accompanied by a pronounced drop in productivity. The latter caught economists completely off guard. Many reasons were given, but none seemed adequate. Baffled, Canadian economists made the unusual admission that they did not have the answers.[2] In this regard Canada was not alone. Its largest single trading partner, the United States, was undergoing similar slow-downs in productivity.

In 1973, political turmoil in the Middle East fanned the flames of inflation and shook the economic order of the Western nations. After the October 1973 Arab-Israeli War, the Organization of Petroleum Exporting Countries (OPEC), under pressure from its Arab members, imposed an oil boycott on the United States and other nations which they felt had supported Israel. Imposed scarcity drove up the price of oil, and in turn, the price of oil and inflation fed off each other. The four-fold increase in the price of oil created severe balance-of-payments problems as large amounts of wealth shifted to the oil-producing Arab nations. The crisis revealed plainly how dependent the West had become on the Middle East for its basic energy supplies.

Seeing inflation as a far greater social and economic evil than unemployment, governments around the world switched their focus from unemployment to bringing inflation under control. However, this decision created considerable dissent as left-of-centre politicians pointed to the injustices of such an approach. In Canada, Pierre Trudeau's Liberal government instituted extraordinary measures to combat inflation. In 1975, the Anti-Inflation Board was established by an act of Parliament to administer a wage-and-price control program. The government's authority to impose such a measure was challenged in the courts. Viewing the threat of inflation as a national emergency, the Supreme Court of Canada ruled that the government was empowered to enact such drastic measures for the national good.

World-wide recession, oil crisis, declining Canadian productivity, and inflation all had a profound effect on Canada's electrical industry. Throughout the twentieth century, the growth of the heavy electrical industry had been based on a doubling of electric generating capacity every ten years. For transformer manufacturers, this growth pattern had led to an average annual increase of 7.5 per cent in demand. Then in the mid 1970s, growth collapsed to about 3 per cent. The general economic slowdown, a pronounced energy conservation program brought on by the oil crisis, and growing environmental opposition to the construction of nuclear power stations had slowed construction of new generating stations. These events further amplified the existing over-capacity in the heavy electrical industry, and competition became even more intense.

Over-capacity had become a way of life in the heavy electrical industry around the world. Throughout the 1960s, the substantial engineering and capital needed to compete in the industry produced a wave of mergers and acquisitions. The slowdown in economic growth only reinforced ongoing global rationalization of the industry; the 1970s offered little respite from growing corporate concentration. These changes hurt both Ferranti-Packard's competitiveness in North America and the parent firm's long-established position in the transformer business. Ferranti-Packard's new relationship to Ferranti UK dramatically altered its corporate destiny.

These new global realities help explain the course of events at Ferranti-Packard under Hetherington's leadership.

New Management Policy

With Hetherington's rise to the presidency of Ferranti-Packard came a new style of management. Unlike Edmondson, who preferred a more intuitive and informal approach, the methodical and analytical Hetherington liked well-defined and rigorous management systems, which suited the growing scale, complexity, and diversity of the firm's operations.

During the 1960s, Hetherington, along with R.J. "Jim" Martin, general manager of the Distribution Division, had attended a short management course at Queen's University. There they had learned about "management by objectives."[3] Peter Drucker had coined the phrase in his classic study, *The Practice of Management*, which argued that organizations contain forces that misdirect and diffuse the manager's energies away from established goals. While Martin dismissed the approach as too formal and unnecessary, Hetherington immediately embraced it as a powerful tool to promote excellence, foster self-motivation, and channel talents toward a common set of objectives.

In management by objectives, each manager must formulate a set of concrete objectives which he, or she, feels best respond to the overall goals of the corporation. To be effective, the objectives must be simple; focused on what is important; genuinely created from the bottom up, as the objectives are drafted by the person who must live up to them, with no constraining guides; and a "living" contract, not a form-driven exercise. These targets then become the standard by which superiors measure and judge each manager's performance. If done properly, management by objectives encourages self-discipline and self-motivation and leads to better performance. It also encourages managers to see themselves within the broader context of the company's overall goals. These were the kinds of attitudes that Hetherington felt essential if Ferranti-Packard were to succeed in the rapidly changing and highly competitive global marketplace.

Hetherington's introduction of management by objectives was the first attempt in the company's history to provide a well-structured method for setting management's objectives and measuring performance. His efforts forced managers to re-examine their understanding of what the company was all about. This engendered considerable corporate soul-searching. Minutes from management meetings were filled with discussions of fundamental questions. Who are we? What is our business? Where do we want to be in 10 or 20 years? There emerged an explicit reaffirmation of the company's traditional values: the importance of remaining a fiercely self-reliant and autonomous company capable of financing its own development; pride in being a progressive Canadian electrical and electronics company, eager to prove itself in the marketplace; uncompromising commitment to high quality and good service; and belief that people are the company's greatest assets. These corporate reflections crystallized the company's mission and gave managers a renewed sense of purpose.

In setting overall objectives, Hetherington placed particular emphasis, as had Tom Edmondson, on the relation of profits to the capital that the company needed to generate them. Increasing sales, though important, did not reveal how efficient or productive the company actually was. For a small firm with relatively limited access to capital, being self-reliant and financing growth through profits demanded wise capital investments. Every investment had to be justified by the return that it would generate. Along the same principle, Hetherington also introduced the turnover of capital employed as a measure of effective use of capital.

Low-range objectives were set from these two measures, return on and turnover of capital employed. This approach represented a tough challenge to management. Each year an annually updated three-year plan was developed, with the first year of the plan being the profit plan for the coming year. Hetherington tried to set the two key ratios in the profit plan as high as possible, without being unrealistic. Whether his application of management by objectives succeeded is difficult to say, because no one will ever know what performance would have been like without it. Hetherington had to be flexible. His managers were not all equally enthusiastic about the system, and it was not easy convincing many of them of its merits.

While Ferranti-Packard's transformer operations had their difficulties and problems, the Transformer Division of Ferranti UK fell into disarray and instability.

Victim of Its Own Traditions

For decades, the Ferranti fortunes were made on transformers. Then, in 1970, staggering losses in transformer operations shook the already debt-ridden organization to its foundations. Major technical problems with power transformers supplied to the Tennessee Valley Authority in the United States exacerbated the situation. The difficulties, however, stemmed from deeper and older forces, long at work undermining the company's ability to compete.

Throughout the 1960s, the world's heavy electrical equipment industry was concentrating in response to growing competition and the search for economies of scale. From 1965 to 1970, there came a wave of mergers and acquisitions. Four new major corporate groupings had emerged in continental Europe: Kraftwerk and Transformatoren in West Germany; C.G.E.-Alsthom in France; Brown-Boveri in Switzerland; and ASEA in Sweden. They joined the Japanese and American multinationals as dominant players. In Britain, once populated with many electrical manufacturers, G.E.C. and Reyrolle-Parsons became the leaders. In all these cases, national governments, through their control of utilities, pushed for rationalization in order to ensure a healthy domestic industry.

Vertical integration was central to this process. Generator manufacturers teamed up with producers of steam turbines. Power transformer companies teamed up with switchgear manufacturers. The mergers and acquisitions produced large corporations able to manufacture all parts of power-generating stations – prime mover technology, turbine-generators, power transformers, and switch-gear – and offer an array of project management and engineering consulting services to the public utilities.

With the growing scale and complexity of new generating-station projects, utilities sought companies that could handle the entire project. Despite Ferranti UK's acknowledged expertise in the very large, high-voltage power transformers for power stations, it could not offer a "turn-key" solution to the utilities' generating needs, and, to make matters worse fewer new stations were being built each year. During the early 1960s, Britain's government-owned utility had predicted that the nation's electrical power system would continue to expand; as a result, Ferranti UK expanded its Hollinwood facilities to produce more power transformers. When the predicted growth did not materialize Ferranti UK was left with substantial over-capacity.

Ferranti UK received overtures from other companies interested in merging. The last occurred in the late 1960s, when Reyrolle-Parsons sought amalgamation. Ferranti UK also needed to raise far more capital to support its electronics operations. In both cases, corporate restructuring would have been essential. Fearful of losing control, the Ferranti family stubbornly refused any attempts to merge or go public.

Sebastian Ziani de Ferranti, eldest son of Sir Vincent, knighted in 1960, was running the company at this time. His rejection of amalgamation stemmed from the powerful hold of his father and family tradition and from personal characteristics that made him unable to share power. In 1904, the company had gone into voluntary bankruptcy. After it was restructured, the family had lost its controlling interest. By the end of the First World War, it had regained control. From that time, running Ferranti UK as a wholly owned private company had become a tradition. The founder and his son and successor, Sir Vincent, had seen themselves as patrons of technological innovation who also happened to be entrepreneurs. To them, profits ensured innovation, not the other way around. The family felt that any corporate arrangement, other than its total control, would comprise its vision of the firm and how it should be run. Sebastian Ziani de Ferranti did not want to be the one who lost the company.

The board of Ferranti UK in the 1960s.
Sir Vincent Ziani de Ferranti is third from
the left in the front row. His sons Basil and
Sebastian are on his left and right
respectively.
(Ferranti Family Archives, Macclesfield,
Cheshire, England)

By 1970, the demise of Ferranti UK's transformer operations was
apparent to all within the company, except the family. From 1970 to
1975, the staggering losses pushed the debt-ridden firm toward collapse. Tradition, however, prevented Sebastian from closing down the
Hollinwood transformer operations. His brother Basil, deputy managing director of ICT – the company that bought out Ferranti UK's
general-purpose computer business – had suggested that the Transformer Division at Hollinwood be closed down. Trained as an engineer, he had a deeper understanding of the dynamics of technological
development. But primogeniture held sway, and when their father
had retired as managing director of Ferranti UK in 1958, he passed on
the running of the company to Sebastian.

On one occasion, however, Basil spoke to his father about closing
Hollinwood. Although Sir Vincent had long retired from active management, he still exercised considerable authority. Word that Basil
wanted to dismantle the "House That Sir Vincent Built" preceded his
visit, and his father was not pleased. As father and son walked silently
around the peaceful lake on the family's magnificent estate, Henbury
Hall, Sir Vincent stopped, looked his son straight in the eye, and said,

"I hear you want to close down *my* transformer factory." That ended the conversation.

 Caught between Hollinwood's past glories and harsh competitive realities, Sebastian kept postponing any decision, hoping for a miracle. In the end, the decision to leave the electric power business would be taken entirely out of his hands. In 1975, he wrote in the company's publication *Ferranti News*:

A more ruthless financially oriented policy might have decided that in face of the total collapse of the CEGB's forward forecasts of transformer demand, and with a world surplus of manufacturing capacity, we should have closed down the Division five or six years ago, or let it go out of our control and be merged with some giant organization.

I didn't do this because ... well, because I didn't believe it was the right thing to do. I have trust in our engineering ability. The people concerned I have known all my life, and I would not wish to betray that trust by taking a short-term commercial view. Ferranti has, from the very start, been a name in power transformers. The list of Ferranti technological firsts in transformer design is almost tediously long. Highest voltages, largest sizes, most efficient thermal designs – we pioneered them all, and the Ferranti name – my grandfather's and my father's name – means something whenever transformer design is discussed.

With that sort of background you don't lightly give up just because times become difficult.[4]

For many years, Ferranti UK had been walking on a financial tightrope. The losses suffered by its transformer business pushed the company off the high wire. As its activities grew and diversified, access to investment capital became a central concern. Avionics, computers, semiconductors, and other high-tech adventures demanded considerable working capital. The family's refusal to go public left the company always scrambling for capital. For nearly four decades, the firm had depended on loans from the banks. When interest rates were low, borrowing to finance new levels of production seemed rational. But by the 1960s, the company lost control of its borrowing at a time when interest rates started to climb.

In 1968, all the top executives of all the trading divisions, led by John Pickin and Donald MacCallum, organized a conference in Gleneagles, Scotland, called "Operation Cashflow." As we have seen, Wordie Hetherington tried there to convince Ferranti UK that Ferranti-Packard offered a gateway into the North American market. The main purpose of the conference, however, was to convince Sebastian de Ferranti of the need for fiscal reform and going public in order to raise more money. Ferranti UK's overall expanding trade, coupled with high inflation, had extended it beyond its resources. But Sebastian kept telling everyone, "The banks will see us through."[5] With nearly $24 million in debt, he argued that the banks could not afford to let the firm go under.[6]

Then in 1973, after a series of major loan defaults resulting from failure in the tourist industry, National Westminster Bank, which held the company's loans, got nervous and "pulled the plug." Because Ferranti UK was a major supplier of advanced electronic equipment for the military, the British government could not let it go bankrupt. On 14 May 1975, eight months after Ferranti UK first approached Harold Wilson's Labour government for help, the secretary of state for industry announced to the House of Commons that the government would increase the company's existing asset base of £24 million by £15 million. In exchange, the government, through its National Enterprise Board, obtained a 50-per-cent voting share in Ferranti UK.[7] The board insisted that a man of its choice replace Sebastian at the helm.

Sebastian Ziani de Ferranti, however, still hoped to continue in charge. Lord Goodman, the firm's adviser throughout the negotiations with the government, was given the task of explaining the reality to him. John Pickin recalls: "We had lunch at the Savoy. When you are bankrupt you go to the Savoy. At the end of the lunch, Sebastian raised the question that he couldn't see the necessity to change the management structure of the company. Then Lord Goodman said, 'Sebastian, you just have to face it that you can no longer run this company. And furthermore, you have to look pleased about it, even if we have to send you to the Royal Academy of Dramatic Arts for three months!'"[8]

After the National Enterprise board's takeover, Derek Alun Jones, as chief executive officer, had to bring Ferranti UK back to financial health. He first wound down the Transformer Division, ending ninety distinguished years of history in the British electric power industry. With Ferranti UK no longer in the transformer business, Ferranti-Packard now found itself an orphan in an industry filled with giants. Furthermore, very little synergy remained between Ferranti-Packard and the parent company. Could Ferranti-Packard survive as an independent producer of transformers, or would it now succumb to rationalization and corporate buy-outs? The British government's takeover, with its promise of selling shares to the public, further fuelled talk of making Ferranti-Packard as self-reliant as possible, possibly by going public.

Diversification

The cyclical nature of the heavy electrical equipment business had long inhibited Ferranti-Packard's efforts to develop a consistent pattern of profits, especially in its power transformer operations in Toronto. Relatively short periods of frenzied production were being followed by longer downturns. As the cost of doing business continued to mount and market swings became more intense, it became harder for small companies to weather the downturns. If Ferranti-Packard were to survive, it would have to dampen the disruptive effects of these severe fluctuations.

As other manufacturers had already discovered, diversification was

The flip-disc display, one of Kenyon Taylor's deceptively simple inventions, brought considerable profit to Ferranti-Packard and fundamentally changed the business direction of the Electronics Division. These drawings are taken from Taylor's 1961 patent application.

The upper figure (opposite), gives the overall view of a number of discs, each mounted on a single axle, while the middle figure shows the mounting in more detail. The lower figure shows the all-important flip mechanism. On the back of disc number 54 is a permanent bar magnet, number 60. There is also an electromagnet, the ends of which are marked as 58. While the poles of a permanent magnet do not change, the poles of an electromagnet can be reversed by reversing the connections or polarity of an electromagnet circuit. When the electromagnet is energized, the fixed north pole of the permanent magnet will be attracted to the south pole of the electromagnet. When the electromagnet circuit and polarity are reversed, the formerly south pole of the electromagnet becomes a north pole, which now repels the north pole of the bar magnet and attracts the south pole. As a result the flip disc flips over or rotates on its axis, and the opposite side of the disc is displayed. One side of the disc is black, the other a light colour such as white or fluorescent green. The pattern of light and dark creates the numbers, letters, or figures in the display. Every disc must have its own electromagnet, switch, and control; the principle is simple but designing and building an entire system requires great attention to detail.

(Canada Patent Office, Patent 641,350)

the answer. And for Ferranti-Packard, the Electronics Division held the key. From its birth in 1949, as the Research Department, it explored the frontiers of electronic digital technology. But managing its commercial activities proved difficult for a company rooted in the older technology of electric power. Data processing technology was new and unfolding rapidly. Its innovation cycles, R&D requirements, market dynamics, and general capital needs differed from those of heavy electrical equipment. Its engineers were constantly pushing the firm into areas for which the management and financial resources were not ready. Ferranti UK's sale of the FP-6000 technology to ICT abruptly ended any dreams that the division may have harboured of becoming a successful computer manufacturer. For several years afterward, the division floated aimlessly in search of purpose. Many, on the electric power side of the business, wondered if the division would ever earn significant profits.

On becoming president in 1971, Wordie Hetherington set diversification as a priority and began trying to make the Electronics Division profitable. After a disastrous loss, −27-per-cent return on capital employed, in 1971, action was needed.[9] Hetherington believed that only a new general manager could accomplish this, and in the same year he brought in Barry Hercus. A mechanical engineer by training, Hercus came from a highly disciplined, high-volume manufacturer. He had been general manager of Standard Coil, a Toronto manufacturer of tuners for the Canadian television industry. Standard made electronics components but was not involved in research and development. Hercus concluded that the Electronics Division had "no structured selling or marketing program and no knowledge, or skills, to speak of, of basic manufacturing assembly."[10] He gave himself three years to change the division's engineering, marketing, and manufacturing philosophy and practices.

It was no easy task to alter long-established traditions and patterns of thinking. To stimulate thought, and provoke change, Hercus introduced an element of management by conflict. Management meetings were, in the beginning, confrontational, as opposing views of the division's future collided. Hercus recalled that whenever Hetherington, a calm man, would sit in on the division's meetings, he would leave shaking his head in disbelief. In 1988, Hercus reflected: "I felt we were getting the best out of it. Not everyone was completely comfortable. So when it came time to make management changes, it wasn't too difficult to convince those in question to leave. They were tired of being shouted at and of shouting back. I was tired of shouting, so we thought there was an easy solution for both of us. We would give the individual a chance to look for another job while we looked for a successor. It sounds a little brutal, but I felt that we had to keep the pressure on to get people to change their thinking."[11]

Engineers had traditionally dominated all aspects of the division's operations, and in Hercus's view it "couldn't afford to have that many engineers." De-emphasizing engineering was bound to meet with resistance. Some of the division's senior engineers, such as Bill

Lower and Les Wood, soon crossed swords with Hercus. Some in the division felt that Hercus neither appreciated nor undertood the role of creative engineering in an electronics company. In their view, Hercus would not last long with his "autocratic management style." To the board, however, Hercus represented the kind of direction that the division so desperately needed. Although the board and the company's executives were supportive, they continued their arm's-length approach. Only now they believed that a sound business plan was being pursued.

Hercus, like his predecessors, had to select and develop one major commercial product base, from the division's many engineering pursuits, around which to rebuild the division. By 1973, the choice was becoming obvious. Superconductivity and fuel cells had been eliminated because of the excessively high investment costs of R&D. High-speed tape proved unprofitable as other technologies appeared. The drum business, which had floundered since the BUIC affair, would soon fall victim to new technologies. Numerical read-out for machine tools, which at first seemed promising, faltered because of Ferranti Edinburgh's inability to meet supply requirements. The division would have to build a business based on display technology.

Display Technology Saves the Day

At the time when RESERVEC was being installed, TCA challenged the Electronics Division to come up with a practical way to display arrival and departure information at airports. Kenyon Taylor's Research Department took up the challenge with its usual unbounded enthusiasm. Everyone ran around working on inventions of their own. In the end, Taylor solved the problem.

Taylor came up with the idea of displaying any character – letter or number – in a line of information by means of a fixed array of dots. The size of each dot and the number of dots in the array would depend on the size of the character being displayed. Each dot was made of a thin metal disc which was black on one side and white on the other. Initially, the discs were attached to nylon threads at the top and bottom. The thread acted as an axis around which the disc could rotate. A small permanent magnet was affixed to the back of each disc and an electromagnet installed behind each disc. A small pulse of current to the electromagnet then rotated any disc from its white side, or "on state," to its black side, or "off state." Each disc thus became a mechanical pixel in a computer-driven display. This type of system consumed very little power, and, unlike light sources of the time, the white dots were legible even in brightly lit surroundings. Each disc was controlled by special data-processing circuitry.

In the early experimental prototypes, nylon threads from women's stockings had the best operational characteristics. On one occasion, Taylor sent Dr. Sidney V. Soanes to the women's section of a local department store to buy an enormous quantity of stockings. A very reserved, shy, and proper gentleman, Soanes still remembers the

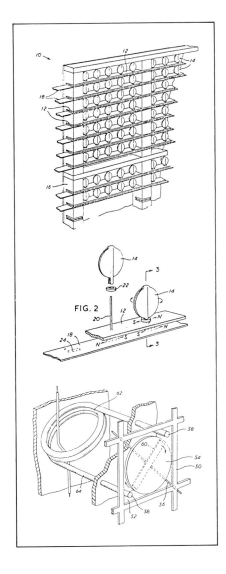

FIG. 2

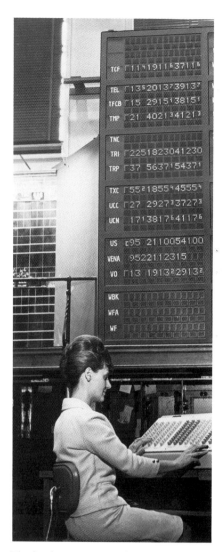

The first big opportunity for the Ferranti-Packard's flip-disc display system came in 1961 when the Montreal Stock Exchange decided to modernize its method of displaying trading information. Here a limited display, using the new technology, is being tested on the trading floor. One end of the huge chalk board on which trading data was written by hand is visible on the left.
(Ontario Archives, Ferranti-Packard Collection, AO 1264)

embarrassment of having to explain to a sceptical saleswomen that all these stockings were for an important engineering experiment.

The brilliance of the invention lies in its engineering simplicity and economic attractiveness. It was an ideal way to display information that must be continuously and quickly updated in large, well-lit public areas. This display technology also complemented the division's experience in computer and electronic data processing. When Taylor patented the flip-disc technology in 1961, management was less than enthusiastic. Taylor could not get the general manager, John Fogarty, interested. Ferranti UK could not envision such a "toy" as the basis of a business. To make matters worse, TCA, which had instigated the development, lost interest.

Just when the future looked bleakest for Taylor's invention, good news arrived. In 1960, the Montreal Stock Exchange decided to move to new quarters in Place Victoria. George Cruikshank, the executive vice-president, was committed to modernizing operations and facilities. Up to that time, all data arriving from trading on the floor was written by hand on huge chalkboards. Cruikshank wanted a modern electronic information system that could display stock quotations minute by minute to the traders on the floor. Hearing of the exchange's interest, the Electronics Division assigned Henry Peprnick to pursue the prospect. Hired in 1960 to write the manuals and documentation for RESERVEC, Peprnick quickly moved into sales. It took him nearly two years, and "well over 35 visits to Montreal," to sell the firm's display technology to the stock exchange.[11]

In 1961, fifteen prototype modules represented the sum total of Ferranti-Packard's experience in the display business. Peprnick, today a successful realtor in Brampton, Ontario, still shakes his head at the sale: "When I look back at one of those early modules, I still wonder how the hell we ever managed to sell a seven hundred thousand dollar system to Montreal."[12] Without an actual system to demonstrate, Ferranti-Packard had devised an imaginative graphic demonstration that caught the eye of the exchange's board. In an old warehouse, across from the old exchange, Ferranti-Packard replicated the entire proposed 60-ft (18.3-m) wall display using silk-screened panels 4 ft by 8 ft (1.2 m by 2.4 m). The panels were an exact graphic representation of how the stock-quotation data would appear. Here and there, pieces were cut away from the panels and replaced by actual modules that operated. Members of the board still wondered if this relatively small company could deliver the goods.

Westinghouse, the other main bidder for the job, was pushing its electro-luminescent display. Although the proposal was technically and economically inferior to Ferranti-Packard's, Westinghouse had the prestige and corporate resources that often instill confidence in prospective customers. Technical merit won. Ferranti-Packard obtained the contract on grounds of superior reliability and extremely low power consumption, both of which translated into much lower maintenance costs.

Ferranti-Packard had twelve months to install a partial system in the

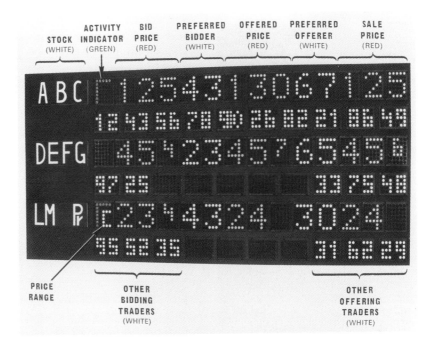

An explanation to show how to read Montreal Stock Exchange trading data as displayed in Ferranti-Packard flip-disc technology. Note that in addition to the black backs, discs came in white, green, and red. Using three colours for display information made the system easier to use. It was user-friendly before that term had been invented.
(Ontario Archives, Ferranti-Packard Collection, AO 1257)

The Ferranti-Packard trading-display system was actually installed for the first time in 1962, when the Montreal Stock Exchange moved its operations to Place Victoria. This photograph was taken in 1967.
(Ontario Archives, Ferranti-Packard Collection, AO 1270)

During the 1970s Ferranti-Packard invested in mass-production technology by buying injection-moulding equipment to make the flip-disc modules to insure its competitive advantages in the display business when its patents on the flip-disc ran out. Embarking on mass production during the 1970s was a new direction for Ferranti-Packard. (Ontario Archives, Ferranti-Packard Collection, AO 678)

old stock exchange, with the complete system to be installed six months later in the new quarters. Manufacturing problems soon threatened substantial delays. Nine months into the contract, the Electronics Division had still not produced a reliable and properly functioning module. Peprnick complained that without working modules further sales would be difficult. As a reward for his complaints, he was taken off sales and made project engineer for the Montreal system.

The division had sold the system to Montreal on the basis of an improved module developed by Dave Winrow, an engineer in Taylor's group. The module used small metal pins instead of nylon thread. Winrow's contributions produced several patents for Ferranti-Packard. But the division had promised a new module without any serious study of its manufacturing implications. Plastic injection moulding companies claimed that moulds with precise, small holes could not be produced to accommodate the pins to the required tolerances. Peprnick got Winrow to look into the problem; Winrow simply bought a small injection moulding machine and proved that it could be done. A a consequence, Ferranti-Packard produced all the plastic mouldings for the entire display, and on time.

Surprise and chance are important elements in engineering and manufacturing. Digital electronics drives the Ferranti-Packard display and allows it to interface with various input terminals. The logic-circuit designer for the Montreal system was a Hungarian-born engineer named Imry Fekete. Unable to finish the design before he was scheduled to go on vacation, Fekete promised to finish the job in Hungary. When border officials in Hungary saw the sheets of logic-circuit designs, they immediately thought that the material was of some strategic importance. Detained and afraid of arrest, Fekete had to do some quick talking to convince officials that all that complicated circuitry was to make harmless little discs flip back and forth.[13]

The Montreal Stock Exchange display became a showpiece for Ferranti-Packard's technology and reliability. The system's durability was dramatically demonstrated when it survived the FLQ bombing of the exchange. Much of the original system is still operating. With the firm's credibility well established, other orders started to come, from the Chicago Board of Trade and the Chicago Mercantile Exchange.

When Barry Hercus joined Ferranti-Packard as general manager of the Electronics Division in 1971, the display business was already poised for pursuit of international markets. The stock exchanges in São Paulo and Tokyo were expressing serious interest. The prospect of "going international," however, raised concerns within the board. Did Ferranti-Packard have the human and capital resources to support systems around the world? Experience in North America had shown that it took considerable engineering manpower to supervise installation of display systems. In 1972, the Electronics Division was losing $12,000 monthly in service contracts. Could the company afford to service installations in far-flung parts of the world?[14]

The same engineers who were designing the product were also run-

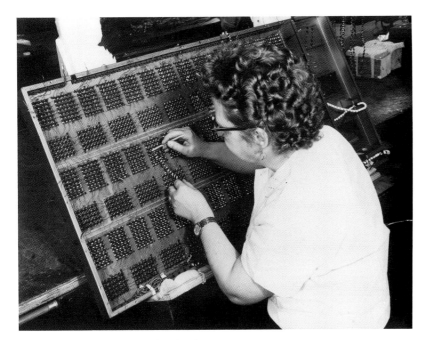 

Women usually did the meticulous hand assembly for the display system. In the photograph upper left, an unidentified woman is installing the tiny electromagnets required to flip each disc. The other woman is installing the actual dots, or discs.
(Ontario Archives, Ferranti-Packard Collection, AO 1258, AO 1259)

ning the servicing. As a result, when delivery schedules were tight, there was a tendency to shift basic design problems to the servicing contract. Hercus therefore took servicing away from the design engineers and set up a Service Department as a separate "profit centre" managed by Doug Greenwood. Greenwood had come in the late 1950s from Ferranti UK in Scotland as a technical adviser to assist in the sale of numerical read-outs for machine tools. To minimize costs, the new Service Department selected and trained support staff in the countries where displays were being installed.

Hercus felt that the division "would have to rationalize the product and exercise some discipline in what was sold and in the designs."[15] Only a shift from custom engineering to more standardized display systems could reduce development and manufacturing costs. Hercus's determination to shift the division toward standardized manufacturing intensified his differences of opinion with his marketing manager, Bill Lower. Hercus saw Lower as "a great developer, but when things got standardized he lost interest."[16] The clash was a consequence of differing views on the role of innovation in the division. Lower was not alone in his disagreements with Hercus. He found employment elsewhere, and Hercus brought in Bud Tucker as the new marketing manager. Tucker had sold radio equipment systems internationally for RCA.

The company sold display systems to commodity and stock exchanges all over the world: Winnipeg, Toronto, New York, Minneapolis, Kansas City, New Orleans, Buenos Aires, London, Turin, Tokyo, and Seoul. By 1977, it had won 50 per cent of the world market for display systems in commodity and stock exchanges, as well as

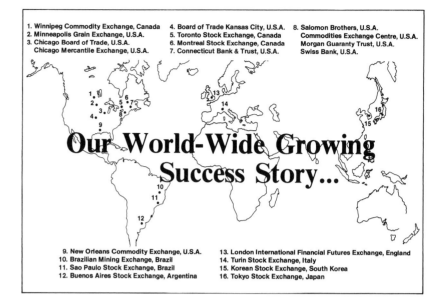

1. Winnipeg Commodity Exchange, Canada
2. Minneapolis Grain Exchange, U.S.A.
3. Chicago Board of Trade, U.S.A.
   Chicago Mercantile Exchange, U.S.A.

4. Board of Trade Kansas City, U.S.A.
5. Toronto Stock Exchange, Canada
6. Montreal Stock Exchange, Canada
7. Connecticut Bank & Trust, U.S.A.

8. Salomon Brothers, U.S.A.
   Commodities Exchange Centre, U.S.A.
   Morgan Guaranty Trust, U.S.A.
   Swiss Bank, U.S.A.

Our World-Wide Growing Success Story...

9. New Orleans Commodity Exchange, U.S.A.
10. Brazilian Mining Exchange, Brazil
11. Sao Paulo Stock Exchange, Brazil
12. Buenos Aires Stock Exchange, Argentina

13. London International Financial Futures Exchange, England
14. Turin Stock Exchange, Italy
15. Korean Stock Exchange, South Korea
16. Tokyo Stock Exchange, Japan

As this promotional map indicates, Ferranti-Packard sold large-scale display technology to some of the largest financial trading floors in the world.
(Ferranti-Packard Transformers Ltd.)

half of the world's market for highway traffic signs using display systems.[17] Selling only turn-key display systems, however, made it difficult to maintain a sufficient flow of new business to cover overheads and make some profit.

Introducing Stability

Display systems generated a financial roller-coaster. Business was never constant; a big project with much activity would be followed by an indeterminate wait for the next order, while production capacity lay idle. Long-term planning was impossible. Similarly, the firm could not plan long-term capital investments in modernizing production equipment and enlarging capacity. Morale dropped as hourly paid shop personnel were laid off and then rehired. They grew to feel that they were being used. Unstable labour conditions also meant that better workers would look for more secure positions; when they left, they took skills and experience perfected over time. Ferranti-Packard constantly had to retrain new workers.

The display business clearly needed a constant flow of orders. Ferranti-Packard concluded that it should complement display systems with components; the two operations would act as separate profit centres.

Looking for a man to launch a components business, Hercus, on the advice of Bud Tucker, hired Don Smart in 1973. After Tucker left RCA, and prior to coming to the Electronics Division, he had worked at Westinghouse's Electronics Division in Hamilton, where he got to know Smart. After twenty years with Westinghouse, Smart had no interest in changing jobs. In 1973, however, news that Westinghouse was going to restructure its Electronics Division and phase out his section changed his thinking.[18]

The strategy for developing the components business was simple and classic: encourage others to develop uses for the product and then sell them the components to build products. Smart realized from the outset that the Electronics Division would have to change its approach to product development and find second parties who could run with the flip-disc technology.

The absence of standardized display components blocked profitable manufacturing of components. Smart faced a "hodge-podge" of products at Ferranti-Packard. As a rule, each display system was custom designed to customers' specifications. The basic components for these different systems formed a relatively disconnected set of products. There seemed little continuity in size, functionality, interchangeability, design, and operation. A good deal of the problem stemmed from the "engineering-driven" environment of the Electronics Division.

Smart observed, as had other senior executives at Ferranti-Packard, that display development was inspired more by technical interest than by the market. "Some components," according to Smart, "were technically very interesting, but virtually unmanufacturable in quantity, at any economic cost."[19] As the man responsible for marketing the display components, Smart had to work closely with engineering staff to "convert an odd collection of products into a continuous and flexible range of products."[20] The conversion took many years and was characterized by many small decisions, constant reassessment of how old and new products fitted into the company's product line, and continual monitoring of the product line's relation to market requirements.

In the beginning, interaction between the engineering people and Smart was far from enthusiastic. The systems people saw the components group as competition and felt threatened by the basic premise of the components business: high-volume, standardized manufacturing, with engineering development work left to second parties. Some of the sales people were also upset because Hercus had set up a parallel sales force to market components. Hercus's confrontational style did little to calm the fears of those in engineering. Today, Smart can still remember when he first experienced the hostility that some of the systems people had for the idea of splitting display into systems and components: "One month after I joined the company, a senior member of the systems staff came to me and said I should look for another job because I would never make a go of this. This person then added, 'Why are you wasting your time here? The Division doesn't want this to happen.'"[21]

Smart realized that Ferranti-Packard's flip-disc display technology "didn't lend itself to widespread applications."[22] How to find second parties that the Ferranti-Packard system could help? Smart compared the challenge to "looking for a needle in a haystack." He saw it as a question of numbers: "If you look at enough applications, you are bound to find a few that match up with Ferranti-Packard technology."[23] He first set up a good sales network, using manufacturer representatives, throughout the United States.

Ironically, the earliest break-through came from a Dutch manufacturer of gasoline pumps. In the late 1960s, Ferranti-Packard had developed a seven-segment bar-type display component for the display system that it installed at the American Stock Exchange in New York City. Looking for another application of this component, the firm approached a number of people whom it felt might have use for it, including makers of gasoline pumps, which were just starting to use electronic technology. The Europeans, far ahead of the Americans, were looking for a display technology for the new generation of electronic pumps. None of the available electronic displays could be read easily in brightly lit surroundings.

In 1973, Leo Koppens, president of Koppens Automatic in Holland, had seen Ferranti-Packard's seven-segment display component and became convinced that it would work well in the gasoline pumps that he was designing. Koppens Automatic did a lot of development work for Royal Dutch Shell, in all areas of gasoline station design. When Koppens first spoke to Ferranti-Packard, many of the engineers in the Electronics Division expressed considerable doubt. They did not think that the display module, as designed, could function reliably. Koppens disagreed and "dragged Ferranti-Packard kicking and screaming into the gasoline pump display business."[24]

Together, Koppens's company and Ferranti-Packard worked several years to redesign the module to function properly in the Dutch firm's pumps. By 1976, the first gas pumps with Ferranti-Packard's new seven-segment display modules appeared on the European market. Many other European gasoline-pump manufacturers bought Ferranti-Packard display modules. Today, Europe is a key market for the company's components.

Koppens Automatic was a small, aggressive company competing against much larger manufacturers. Leo Koppens believed that Ferranti-Packard's display technology offered him a clear edge over his competitors, and, as a result, he pressed the company for exclusive rights before he would develop and introduce the module in his pumps.

For years, Ferranti-Packard had sought an application for one of its modules, and here was Leo Koppens with a solution. But Smart vigorously objected to giving Koppens Automatic exclusive rights. He recommended that Ferranti-Packard call Koppens's bluff; if the product were indeed good, then other, far bigger companies would buy it. But if the product were bad, it would die whether it were in Leo Koppens's hands or not. Smart and Hercus argued over this point, and Koppens tried to play one level of management off against the other. In the end, Ferranti-Packard refused Koppens exclusive rights — a wise decision in light of the great growth of this market in Europe. Koppens, though displeased, had no choice but to go along.

Another major application for Ferranti-Packard's display modules

Ferranti-Packard had to cultivate new market applications for its display technology. The Funabashi Race Track in Japan bought the system in 1977.
(Barry Hercus)

soon presented itself quite accidentally. After a long, frustrating day of seeking business around Dallas, Texas, Don Smart and his sales agent for the area, Bill Pearson, were deciding whether to go for dinner. Out of the blue, Pearson suggested calling on a friend who worked for Luminator, which made electrical fixtures for buses, and with whom he had already had some dealings in connection with other electrical products. Pearson had heard a rumour that Luminator was developing a variable-destination display sign for the front of buses. He phoned and arranged for an immediate meeting. When he and Smart arrived, Smart produced a small sample display system which he carried around for demonstration purposes; Luminator's representative was impressed. He took Smart and Pearson into a laboratory and showed them a display system already developed by Luminator. The electronics worked well, but the liquid crystal units were totally inadequate for his company's needs. The manufacturing engineer and a Luminator vice-president were called in, and for several hours the fivesome explored the possibility of interfacing the Ferranti-Packard display modules with the electronics that Luminator had developed.

On the day that he returned to his office, Smart received a telephone call from George Lively, president of Luminator, asking to meet Smart and Hercus in Chicago. After a late-night meeting in their hotel in Chicago, a deal was hammered out. In 1974, after several months of development work, Ferranti-Packard display modules were installed on several buses, on a trial basis. By 1977, the bus display business was so well established and growing so quickly that its sales soon surpassed those for gasoline pump displays.

Bus and gasoline pump displays became the basis of a display components business. The critical sales to Koppens Automatic and Luminator gave Ferranti-Packard entry into these very important markets. By the end of the 1970s it appeared that the future of the Electronics Division display technology lay in components. With its patents about to run out, however, the company faced the spectre of intense competition. Management had foreseen this eventuality when it set up the components business. While Ferranti-Packard still had its exclusive patent rights covering the flip-disc display technology, the Electronics Division used the opportunity to finance a major modern-

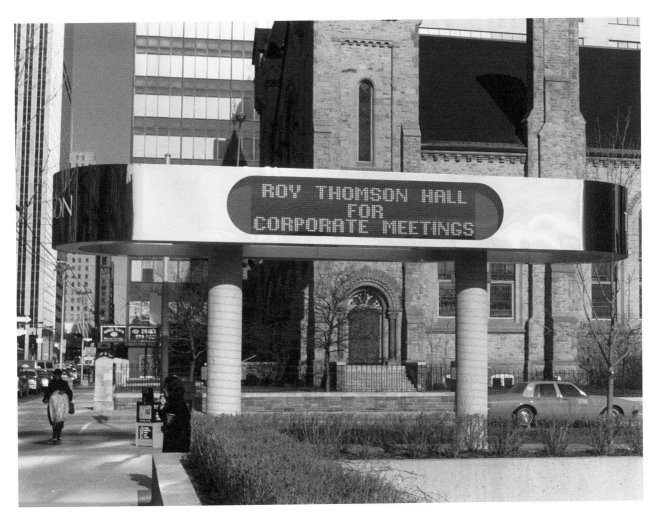

ROY THOMSON HALL
FOR
CORPORATE MEETINGS

Gas pumps also provided a large market for the display technology in Europe. Flip-disc technology has been used on buses across North America and Europe. It has also been used extensively on public information displays, as shown here at Roy Thomson Hall in Toronto
(Barry Hercus)

ization of its manufacturing facilities and improve its mass production techniques.

A great deal of manufacturing engineering is required to mass produce the display modules. Management felt that heavy investment in automation could reduce unit costs so much that when Ferranti-Packard's patents expired, prospective competitors would find entry costs prohibitive. In 1979, the Electronics Division moved from the building that it had occupied since 1950 into new facilities in Mississauga, just outside Toronto. This strategy – of compensating for loss of patent protection by dramatically reducing production costs – worked. Nonetheless, it is unclear how long the company will be able to maintain this manufacturing advantage. At the time, competing display technologies posed questions about the size and direction of the firm's future R&D investments.

Developing a Second Product Line. Management felt that it needed a secondary product line to achieve balanced long-term growth. While

PR	CAT.#	SF	REFER	COLOR	SIZE	LOT	PRICE			PB #
					6					
					8					
	5734					5	L/24	.65	SINKERS	346
R	5817					16	EA	3.49	LAND NET	346
R	5820					16	EA	2.88	LAND NET	346
R	5851					16	EA	3.29	CREEL	346
	7001					16	EA	4.88	GLOVE RHT	351
	7002					16	EA	4.88	GLOVE LHT	351
	7003					16	EA	3.88	GLOVE RHT	351
	7004					16	EA	3.88	GLOVE LHT	351
	7021					16	EA	6.88	GLOVE RHT	351
	7022					16	EA	5.88	GLOVE LHT	351
	7023					16	EA	5.88	GLOVE LHT	351
	7030					16	EA	6.88	GLOVE LHT	351
	7035					16	EA	9.94	GLOVE RHT	351
	7036					16	EA	9.94	GLOVE LHT	351
	7065					16	EA	19.94	GLOVE RHT	351
	7066					16	EA	19.94	GLOVE LHT	351
	7067					16	EA	15.94	GLOVE RHT	351
	7068					16	EA	15.94	GLOVE LHT	351
	7115				5	21	PR	5.94	SHOE	351
					5½	22				
					6	23				
					6½	24			MED WIDTH FITS C/D	
					7	25				
					7½	26				
					8	27				
					8½	28				
					9	29				
					9½	30				
					10	31				
					10½	32				
					11	33				
					11½	34				
					12	35				
					12½	36				
					13	37				
	7150					38	EA	.79	BASEBALL	351
	7155					39	EA	1.09	SOFTBALL	351
	7157					40	EA	1.09	BASEBALL	351
	7159					41	EA	1.49	BASEBALL	351
	7160					42	6/MR	1.32		6 - 7.92	
	7163					43	EA	1.79	SOFTBALL	351
	7164					44	EA	.75	BASEBALL	351
	7171					45	EA	1.47	BASEBALL	351
R	7172		29			46	6/MR	1.32	BASEBALL	351
			30			47	EA	1.95	BAT	351
			31			48			NS - BILL 30	
R	7173					49	EA	2.39	BAT	351
						50				
						51				
						52				

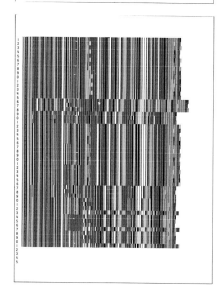

Between 1959 and 1962 Ferranti-Packard worked with one of the world's largest mail-order houses, Spiegel Inc. of Chicago, to develop a network of optical bar-code scanning terminals, called "Document Transcribers," all of which were tied to a central computer. "Director Cards" were a key feature of the system. These 8.5 × 11 inch (22 × 28 cm. cards) displayed information in English on one side. The other side contained bar-coded information produced automatically from plain-language input. The machine language was based on modified teletype code using ordinary ink and could be optically scanned into the computer. Note that the Transcriber operators at Spiegel (opposite) have specially constructed office furniture. Ferranti-Packard advertised the

the Electronics Division historically had been overdiversified in product R&D, total dependence on display technology left it vulnerable. Within his first year as general manager, Hercus decided that scanning technology offered the best route to diversification.[25] He knew that he was tapping into R&D roots that went back to the mid-1950s, when Ferranti Canada pioneered the technology for electronically sorting letters by optically scanning bar-coded routing information. Ferranti-Packard then developed its innovative computerized cheque-sorting system for the Federal Reserve Bank.

At that time, Simpson Sears in Canada wanted to improve the speed and accuracy of its mail order business, as well as reduce losses from pilferage. It wanted a system to read bar-coded labels on parcels as they went by on conveyor systems and then, by means of a computerized sorting system determine where the parcel could be automatically tipped off its tray and into the shipping box. It offered to help pay for the R&D. After in-depth R&D, partially funded by IRAP, into laser and video scanning, Ferranti-Packard adapted the latter technology for the problem at hand.

In 1959, the company entered a three-year R&D collaboration with Spiegel Inc., of Chicago, the third largest mail-order house in the world. Kenyon Taylor had convinced the Spiegel brothers that his firm's experience with optical bar-code scanning would help Spiegel Inc. cope with the mountain of data processing needed to handle the ordering and shipping of 40–50 million items of merchandise per year.[26] The resulting Document Transcriber could efficiently process orders, control inventory, expedite shipping, and monitor sales by means of a network of optical bar-code scanning systems tied electronically to a central computer system. So successful was the project that Spiegel ordered 200 document transcribers, at a total installation cost of $1.5 million.[27] As a result, other large mail-order catalogue companies in North America looked to Ferranti-Packard.

When Hercus joined Ferranti-Packard, the firm was developing an "on-the-fly" scanner and had patents for this technology. Tony Tyler, a physicist who wanted to work as an applications engineer for a change, championed development of scanning products within the Electronics Division. His claims that Ferranti-Packard could build a $16–20-million business over five years, with the right system, elicited excitement within the company.

Several years later, Ferranti-Packard perfected a scanning and sorting technology that could read the labels on parcels moving on a conveyor belt at speeds up to 400 ft/min (122 m/min) and then sort the parcels for shipping. J.C. Penney and Montgomery Ward bought these units.[28] Ferranti-Packard's efforts to develop a viable scanning/sorting business received a further boost when Canada Post decided to incorporate this type of technology in the modernization of its Toronto and Montreal operations.[29] Unfortunately, its requirements differed from the scanners developed for mail-order catalogues. Scanners based on different optical principles had to be designed and built.

As a result of the $2-million contract from Canada Post, the Elec-

Document Transcriber as "a new concept in machine reading providing printed copy and computer input" with "many diverse, time saving economical applications". It was "most useful where documents are being prepared containing fixed information from a large file together with certain valuable data." Many types of work fit this description including "sales order entering, invoicing, preparation of purchase orders and automatic letter writing."
(Ferranti-Packard Transformers Ltd.)

tronics Division had a particularly good year in 1977; scanning products provided 21 per cent of sales. There were, however, only four large mail-order houses in North America, and a few in Europe. After modernization of Toronto and Montreal's postal operations, there was little opportunity for repeat sales to Canada Post. In a confidential analysis of display systems commissioned by the parent firm in 1978, Price Waterhouse & Co., of London, England, observed: "The market for this type of product is limited and sales are restricted by the high price."[30] Ferranti UK felt the same way about scanning.

After five years and considerable restructuring, Electronics was still not consistently profitable. Under pressure to show results, Hercus was committed to developing the scanning business. But he concluded that label-scanning technology would have to be taken in new directions if markets were to be found. This outlook led to acquisition of an American firm whose technology complemented Ferranti-Packard's label-scanning technology.

In 1977, after having scouted out several US companies, Hercus came across Identicon in Franklin, Massachusetts. It had run into financial troubles and had filed for protection from creditors under "Chapter 11 Bankruptcy" while it tried to find new capital or a buyer. Identicon's more flexible light pen and beam scanners system offered a compact alternative to Ferranti-Packard's scanner. Hercus convinced both the Canadian and British Boards that Ferranti-Packard should invest $350,000 to buy what little remained of Identicon.

After the acquisition, Hercus thought of using charge coupled diode

(CCD) video technology as the basic for future scanners, but he was hesitant about pursuing the costly R&D needed to adapt this technology. In the meantime, a competitor came out with a scanning tube based on CCD technology. Hercus decided to drop video and just pursue the product mix that Identicon already had: light pen and beam scanners that could read bar codes of automobiles at toll booths and cartons in warehouses and had other, similar applications.[32]

Hercus could devote only part of his time to managing Identicon. Every two weeks he spent a few days at its plant and offices in Boston, where he tried to co-ordinate accounting, engineering, manufacturing, and sales. Trying to run a financially troubled and technologically sophisticated operation part time was a mistake, which was reflected in slow growth. In 1979, a full-time general manager was hired to run the operation. Unfortunately, he failed to turn the company around. Worse, he saddled Ferranti-Packard with a financially disastrous contract.

In 1979, Hughes Aircraft was planning to build the factory of the future, which was to include a network of 1,000 terminals scanning bar codes, identifying where each product was in the manufacturing process and, in addition, monitoring many aspects of the labour process. All these terminals would, in turn, be linked to a constellation of four or five mainframe computers. In addition to developing the terminal, Ferranti-Packard, through Identicon, also agreed to design the hard-disc–equipped interface units.

According to Hercus's recollection, "anyone who listened found the concept convincing."[33] But there were substantial hardware and software challenges. Moreover, the budget was too small, and there were too few engineers. Software people at Hughes Aircraft thought themselves better suited to do the systems work. In the end, it cost Ferranti-Packard nearly $2 million to extract itself from the contract.[34]

The costly experience with Identicon reflected errors in judgment at many levels within Ferranti-Packard, but it taught the company an important lesson. Do not get involved with a financially troubled outfit unless you are prepared to supply a great deal of money and management talent. The incident was one more setback in an eight-year effort to obtain profits from the Electronics Division capable of compensating for downturns in the electric power business.

Diversification had been frustrating and unprofitable. Work on components increased sales, yet the division's profit column was usually written in red. Ferranti UK wanted results. It had become oriented entirely toward electronics and so hoped that the Electronics Division would in time become more profitable. "If Ferranti [UK] Limited had one wish for Ferranti-Packard, it would be that the proportion of electronics should increase," John Pickin, technical director of Ferranti UK, wrote to Wordie Hetherington in the fall of 1977.[35] But Pickin, like others on the British board, was starting to doubt the division's ability to turn a profit: "We are beginning to build up a history now of lack of success in this field."[36]

This photograph from 1929 was taken in the final assembly and test area for meters on the fourth floor of Packard Electric's Neelon Mill building in St Catharines. Manufacturing meters, such as the Type S meters being made here, was highly skilled work which was usually reserved for men in the early decades of the twentieth century. Of the eleven people in the photograph, ten are men. Making light bulbs was largely the work of women.
(Ontario Archives, Ferranti-Packard Collection, AO 797)

Pickin had little quarrel with the abilities of the Canadian managers, whom he saw as capable, hard-nosed businessmen. But he expressed concern as to the wisdom of pursuing the flip-disc technology. But 1977, he felt justified in wondering whether "the growth pattern of flip discs has indicated it is a new technology which is catching on." "In some ways it is a worry that we cannot see a competitor with basically the same product doing better than we are, because at least this is a sort of existence theorem."[37] By "existence theorem," Pickin meant proof that someone was making money from flip-disc display technology.

All doubts vanished when the division's sales and profits started to grow consistently in the early 1980s. The success of the display business in the 1980s justifies, in retrospect, the decision to emphasize components and high-volume manufacturing.

Canadian Watt-hour Meters

The watt-hour meter played a central role in the birth, growth, and development of Ferranti-Packard's history in Canada. At the turn of the century, Packard Electric became, after Canadian General Electric, the second Canadian company to manufacture watt-hour meters. In England, these meters had long been the bread and butter of Ferranti UK, and creation of Ferranti Canada was a clear extension of this meter business into North America. By the end of the First World War, the proliferation of companies selling watt-hour meters in Canada had dropped to five: Canadian General Electric, Canadian Westinghouse, Ferranti Canada, Packard Electric, and Sangamo.

By the end of the 1920s, relative market shares had reached rough equilibrium, with Packard Electric and Ferranti Canada each at about 15 per cent. This partition of the market continued more or less unchanged until 1958, when Packard and Ferranti merged. Ferranti-Packard hope thereby to combine market shares, but provincial and municipal utilities did not wish to become overly dependent on any one source and readjusted their orders downward. Ferranti-Packard wound up with only about 20 per cent of the market.[38]

Until 1971, Ferranti-Packard's profits from the meter business were reliable but never large enough to offset the wild downward swings of the transformer business. After 1971, Ferranti-Packard's meter business saw one poor year after another. According to Bob MacKimmie, the engineer who ran the meter operations at the time, there were several reasons for this poor performance. (1) The union tried to com-

Men still did the skilled machining operations in making watt-hour meters after the Second World War. Women, however, did much of the "nimble" assembly work once done by men. Photos taken during the 1960s. The woman seated and testing a toroidal winding is the late Rita Winkworth (far left). The machine operator is Fred Cullen. The women seated and working in the Assembly Department (right) are (clockwise from left) Dorothy Berger, Martha Voth[?], Mary Rempel, Ann Caperchione.
(Ontario Archives, Ferranti-Packard Collection, AO 710, AO 712, AO 714)

promise the effectiveness of the Meter Department's incentives program. (2) The highest price that Canadian manufacturers could charge and still remain competitive was determined by the US price, duty, and exchange. The General Agreement on Tariff and Trade (GATT), signed by Canada, the United States, and many other countries, gradually reduced tariffs and, as a consequence, the Canadian price advantage. (3) Meter manufacturing depended heavily on traditionally cheaper female labour, but the union brought women's pay up to male rates. (4) Higher wages necessitated increased dependence on labour-saving equipment, but Ferranti-Packard's small scale of manufacture made it difficult to justify expensive capital equipment.[39]

Too many manufacturers were competing for a relatively small domestic market. Canada had one-tenth the population of the United States but supported the same number of meter suppliers. As a result, Ferranti-Packard had barely enough volume to justify the kind of capital investment in machinery and R&D needed to stay profitable. The watt-hour meter is composed of hundreds of small parts that have to function perfectly, and precisely, for over twenty-five years. The technology is sophisticated, and developing more innovative designs can be costly. Because watt-hour meter standards were the same in both countries, Ferranti-Packard's competitors – Canadian General Electric, Canadian Westinghouse, and Sangamo – had access to their US parent firms' vast R&D resources.

Meter standards in Britain and North America were so different that Ferranti UK could transfer little technology to Ferranti-Packard.

Meter testing, shown here in a photo from Packard Electric in 1930, was also once a male preserve. Women had taken on the job of testing before the 1960s when the second photograph was taken. While the man in the earlier photograph is unidentified, the woman in the later photograph (opposite) is Faye Dolynsky, who is still an active employee in the St Catharines plant. She is a lift truck operator and her husband is a foreman in the Winding Department. (Ontario Archives, Ferranti-Packard Collection, AO 789, AO 707)

Developing competitive new designs drained Ferranti-Packard's resources. Furthermore, new designs introduced in Canada by competitors had already been tested extensively by their parent firms, over several years, in the large US market. Every time that Ferranti-Packard introduced a new meter, it would invariably have to spend considerable time and money working out the various "bugs," or problems, that could develop after installation.

Meter technology was changing rapidly around the world. Ferranti-Packard realized that it had neither the market base nor the capital resources to keep up with R&D. Also, substantial investment in new automation technology would be required to remain competitive. The company's fears were further fuelled by talk in the industry of a radical change in technology, such as electronic meters and remote reading. Such developments threatened to make its entire meter-manufacturing facility obsolete.

With five successive years of losses, these fears finally pushed Ferranti-Packard out of the watt-hour meter business. Unable to find a buyer for its meter operations, it sold its manufacturing equipment, in 1977, to Canadian General Electric. It negotiated a long-term contract with that firm to service Ferranti-Packard meters in the field. Although this was a sad event for the company, everyone, except those in the Meter Department, felt relieved. Management, financial resources, and a good deal of manufacturing space were now available for more profitable activities. Pole-top transformers in Trois-Rivières and small power transformers in St Catharines could now receive more attention.

Some within the Meter Department argued that the operations could have been saved. Years later, Bob MacKimmie, its chief engineer, pointed out that the radical changes in meter technology never materialized and that, had the entire operation moved to Trois-Rivières, it could have been made cost-effective: "The loss of the meter operation [was] a very real loss to other areas where repetitive manufacturing is important. Expertise which we had in industrial engineering [was] being lost. The fully-staffed tool room required for meters was a wealth of mechanical know-how. Inspection made use of sophisticated statistical techniques. The meter production systems provided a frame-work that other sections could make use of when required."[40]

Management at Ferranti-Packard made the right decision. In England, Ferranti UK's meter business underwent the same fate some ten years later, when it was bought out by Siemens. As predicted by Ferranti-Packard's management in the 1970s, the Western world's entire watt-hour meter business ended up in the hands of five multinationals.

In 1977 Ferranti-Packard bought out financially troubled British Columbia Transformer Co. in order to gain a stronger market presence on the west coast.
(Ontario Archives, Ferranti-Packard Collection, AO 682)

Consolidation and Expansion

Initially conceived of as an assembly operation, the plant at Trois-Rivières was built to respond to Hydro-Québec's policy of buying within the province. All the cores, windings, tanks, and so on were built in St Catharines and shipped to Trois-Rivières for assembly. As manager, Charles Begin lobbied senior management for a greater manufacturing role for his plant. By the 1970s, Begin had transformed the plant into a highly productive and profitable manufacturing operation. As the US market for small power transformers grew, Ferranti-Packard decided to divide its production along geographical lines; St Catharines specialized in small power transformers, and Trois-Rivières, in pole-top transformers.

From the two plants, Ferranti-Packard could cover all of the Canadian market. But a major market for distribution transformers in British Columbia remained difficult to penetrate because a local supplier enjoyed preferential pricing from B.C. Hydro. By late 1976, high costs and low sales placed the British Columbia Transformer Co., in North Burnaby, in serious financial difficulty. When the board at Ferranti-Packard heard that the company was about to close, it decided to acquire all of the firm's assets and continue to operate it. But, to compete profitably, Ferranti-Packard planned to reduce production costs by introducing its own well-established, cost-effective designs and manufacturing methods. Design and manufacturing engineering services, however, were to come from St Catharines. Management hoped that in British Columbia it could replicate the productivity and efficiency of its two existing plants.

It was a question of establishing a local manufacturing presence in order to obtain a larger slice of B.C. Hydro's orders. With the acquisition, Ferranti-Packard effectively covered the Canadian market. A manufacturing plant in British Columbia was a strategic point from which to penetrate the US west coast. Although success would depend on substantial orders from B.C. Hydro, the company recognized that business from other customers in British Columbia and exports to the United States would have to be developed to reduce the plant's dependence on one customer.

After one year of operating the BC plant, the company received the largest single order that B.C. Hydro had ever placed. The $4.2-million portion of the order covering 8,000 pole-top transformers turned the nearly idle BC plant into a beehive of activity. New equipment had to be installed and manufacturing facilities reshaped quickly. The remainder of the order, for $2.7 million worth of 300- and 500-kVA pad-mounted transformers, went to St Catharines. As happened when Ferranti-Packard opened its Trois-Rivières plant in Quebec, a manufacturing presence in British Columbia also created opportunities for the St Catharines plant that otherwise would have been unavailable.

With such a good start, management had little cause to doubt the long-term viability of its BC investment, and talk started of building new manufacturing facilities in Vancouver. In 1982, Ferranti-Packard moved its BC operations into a new plant in Surrey. This move, initiated by Barry Hercus, by then president and chief executive officer, proved premature; a sluggish BC market for distribution transformers resulted in substantial over-capacity. Without sufficient sales, the plant's overhead became a financial burden.

Extending and consolidating its market presence throughout North America had been a major theme at Ferranti-Packard. By the mid-1970s, it was apparent that any further penetration into the US market would be difficult without a US identity. Despite success in that country, significant segments of its market were still closed to Ferranti-Packard because of a strong "Buy American" attitude. After lengthy discussions and analysis, the board decided in 1977 to build a US facility for the manufacture of small power transformers. Throughout the 100-year history of electrification in North America, foreign makers of heavy electrical equipment, particularly American ones, had set up branch plants in Canada. Ferranti-Packard's decision represented the first time that a Canadian electrical manufacturer had reversed the process.

Dunkirk, New York, was chosen as site of the new plant. Why Dunkirk? It was close to St Catharines and offered easy access to regional American markets. Moreover, the municipal government was willing to provide fully serviced land adjacent to the airport, along with other incentives to help build the new facility. But there was more to the site than people realized. Nearly fifty years earlier, when the Canadian electrical industry was riding high on the prosperity of the 1920s, Packard Electric had decided to build a new plant in Dunkirk. It had also decided to send the up-and-coming young Tom Edmondson there as general manager. The crash of the stock market in 1929 and ensuing depression halted those dreams of US expansion.

In order to proceed with the new project, Wordie Hetherington needed the blessing of Ferranti UK and the British government, which held controlling interest. In his presentation to Britain's National Enterprise Board, he explained that Ferranti-Packard had given a great deal of thought to the question of locating in Dunkirk – fifty years' worth, to be precise. He recalls with a smile that this seemed to impress these earnest and conservative gentlemen "no end."

On 10 May 1977, a ground-breaking ceremony took place at Dunkirk, and R.J. "Jim" Martin's widow, Wilma, turned the first sod. Prior to his untimely death in 1976, Martin, as vice-president and general manager of the Distribution Division, had been a driving force behind the project. Municipal officials named the road in front of the new plant after him.

No sooner had the plant opened than it received its first major order, from the US government, for twenty-two small power transformers to be installed at Social Security Headquarters of the General Service Administration. By 1979, the plant had already surpassed target profits and accounted for nearly 9 per cent of the company's output. The American identity created by the plant also made it easier to get additional business for St Catharines. With new and modern manufacturing facilities, Dunkirk promised to be a cornerstone of Ferranti-Packard's US marketing strategy.

For Ferranti-Packard, 1977 proved a year of ambitious expansion. The firm leased new facilities for the Electronics Division in Mississauga, acquired Identicon and the British Columbia Transformer Co., and started construction in Dunkirk. It also quit the watt-hour meter business. Even the trouble-ridden Power Division staged a remarkable comeback. But world-wide over-capacity left Ferranti-Packard as vulnerable as ever. The company had long ceased to be an integral part of Ferranti UK's long-term strategy. With Ferranti UK out of the transformer business, the Canadian firm had become effectively orphaned in an industry populated by large multinationals.

Northern Engineering Industries

It is often said that some of the most important business decisions take place on golf courses or at parties. Ferranti-Packard's destiny was rewritten at just such a chance encounter. Donald MacCallum was general manager of Ferranti UK's Edinburgh operations and a member of Ferranti UK's board. His old friend Duncan McDonald was first managing director of newly created Northern Engineering Industries (NEI).[41] When the two met at a party, MacCallum broached the subject of selling Ferranti UK's transformer operations in Hollinwood.

NEI was a product of the rationalization sweeping the world's heavy electrical equipment industry. Based at Newcastle, in north-

To further strengthen its presence in and share of the American capital goods market, Ferranti-Packard built a factory in Dunkirk, New York, to produce small power transformers. R.J. "Jim" Martin played a crucial role in the growth of Ferranti-Packard and was a driving force behind the project to build a plant in Dunkirk. Unfortunately he died tragically in a plane crash before work on the Dunkirk plant started. To honour his contribution his widow, Wilma Martin, turned the first sod in the ground-breaking ceremony, attended by company executives and elected city officials. The plant at Dunkirk was a relatively short drive from the site of the Packard Brothers old summer estate on Lake Chautauqua.
(Ontario Archives, Ferranti-Packard Collection, AO 679)

eastern England, NEI had been created in 1977 by the merger of Bruce Peebles, Clarke Chapman, and Reyrolle-Parsons. NEI was a full-line manufacturer of heavy electrical equipment and had diversified extensively. With over $1 billion in annual sales, NEI was active in many areas, including boilers, cranes, electronic equipment, marine equipment, motors, nuclear components, process plants, switch-gear, transformers, and turbine generators.

Duncan McDonald replied that NEI really had no use for the remnants of Ferranti UK's transformer operations, but if it were willing to sell Ferranti-Packard, then a deal could indeed be struck. Ferranti-Packard had become a square peg in a round hole for Ferranti UK, and the sale would generate much-needed money. Ferranti-Packard's then-promising business outlook would certainly command a better selling price at this time than in leaner or less optimistic times. For NEI, Ferranti-Packard offered two important assets – an established and successful market presence in North America and the Electronics Division to complement NEI's electric power equipment business. NEI had manufacturing facilities in the major markets of the world except for Canada and the United States. For NEI, Ferranti-Packard offered a natural gateway to the world's largest single open market, North America. For Ferranti-Packard, NEI offered a far more synergistic relationship than did Ferranti UK. Because of the confluence of needs, a

As with the modern plant in St Catharines, the spacious interior view of Ferranti-Packard's successful transformer plant in Dunkirk, New York, is much different than the cramped quarters and the infamous, but fondly remembered, "Pit" in the old Neelon Mill building. Modern transformer plants are very clean workplaces. The overhead travelling crane in the background and the powered roller conveyers on the floor make handling heavy materials safer and more convenient. Although much has changed, a successful transformer manufacturer still relies on the coordinated efforts of many dedicated people: no job is unimportant. (Ontario Archives, Ferranti-Packard Collection, AO 681)

deal was struck fairly quickly, and NEI agreed to buy Ferranti-Packard.

John Pickin and Wordie Hetherington, however, disagreed on what to do with the Electronics Division. Pickin wanted it to stay with Ferranti UK, and he was ready to fight for it at the board.[42] Only two years earlier, Pickin had seriously questioned the viability of the flip disc as a display technology! The division's promising position in 1979 undoubtedly influenced him. Hetherington and the board knew that all his ambitions for diversification and balanced business growth hinged on keeping the division. Realizing the threat that Pickin posed, Hetherington flew to England to argue personally for retaining the division. Derek Alun Jones's only concern was to get the full price that NEI had agreed on, and he feared that if the division were removed from the deal, the value of the sale would drop considerably. Pickin doubted that the division held any importance for a large manufacturer of electric power equipment. However, he had not counted on the fact that NEI also wanted to buy diversity. As Hetherington subsequently found out, NEI would probably have withdrawn its offer if the Electronics Division had not been included.[43]

All parties were in agreement. One final hurdle remained. Any corporate takeover of a Canadian-based company, even if it involved a simple change of foreign owners, required the approval of Canada's Foreign Investment Review Agency (FIRA). In June 1979, a formal application was made to FIRA for approval of the sale of Ferranti-Packard to NEI by Ferranti UK. FIRA wanted assurances from NEI that the management would stay Canadian, R&D spending in Canada would reach a certain level, and capital expenditures would be undertaken. Other conditions included offering at least 20 per cent of the Canadian company's voting shares to the Canadian public, at an unspecified but appropriate time. After over three and a half months, FIRA had still not made a decision, and NEI was becoming impatient.

Behind FIRA's indecision lay a fundamental question over the future of the industry. Was it in the country's best interests to have Ferranti-Packard bought by another Canadian company, or by a foreign firm? Hetherington subsequently found out that an official in the Department of Regional and Industrial Expansion had asked FIRA to stall the application while the department tried to solicit prospective Canadian buyers. Incensed by FIRA's delay, Hetherington met on 17 October 1979 with his MP, Michael Wilson, then minister of state for international trade. He explained how the sale of Ferranti-Packard to another Canadian firm would be completely detrimental to his company's long-term interests. After all, selling Ferranti-Packard to a Canadian firm meant nothing more than selling to an American subsidiary. Once owned by an American company, Ferranti-Packard could say good-bye to its profitable sales effort in the United States.

In a letter to Wilson, Hetherington reiterated his company's position: "If the alternative to acceptance of the NEI application was rejection on the grounds that a wholly Canadian-owned company proposed to try and acquire Ferranti-Packard, this could be much less favourable from an operating point of view. Ferranti-Packard needs association with a major international company non-U.S. controlled and NEI satisfies this requirement. This is more important than Canadian ownership with no access to international marketing and transformer technology."[44]

Soon after Hetherington's presentations to Wilson, FIRA gave its blessing to NEI's takeover. Ferranti-Packard was split into Ferranti-Packard Transformers Ltd and Ferranti-Packard Electronics Ltd. Both companies answered to the newly created NEI-Canada, a wholly owned subsidiary of NEI-Overseas Ltd.

The sale was cause for both sadness and joy. A long, fruitful, and close relationship between the Canadian company and its British parent firm had ended while another was about to start. Ferranti-Packard had certainly changed since those early days when Packard Electric and Ferranti Canada set out to carve a place for themselves in the Canadian market. Throughout the company's nearly 100 year history, Ferranti-Packard made many contributions to Canadian engineering and industrial capability.

Epilogue: Ferranti-Packard's Journey to Rolls-Royce

When future business historians turn their attention to the long-term trends and developments of the 1980s, their studies will necessarily go beyond continuing technological innovation to encompass global corporate concentration and ownership changes, as well as often surprising shifts in product lines. These areas will certainly interest anyone writing about Ferranti-Packard in the years from 1979 to 1993, which saw two changes of ownership and a narrowing of areas of manufacturing activity.

The headline in the February 1979 issue of the *FP Newsletter* announced not that Ferranti-Packard had been acquired by someone but that "Ferranti-Packard Acquires a New Owner," and that is in fact what had happened. A year earlier, Ferranti UK had decided to sell its Canadian operations. Ferranti-Packard's management could see that the company simply was not large enough to survive on its own in the increasingly concentrated, highly technical business of manufacturing transformers. The question was: "would British or American owners be best for Ferranti-Packard and its employees?" Given its long history of excellence and innovation, management wanted to find new owners who would continue the tradition and encourage growth and increased exploitation of the American market. Northern Engineering Industries (NEI) seemed ideal. With approval in late 1979 by Canada's Foreign Investment Review Agency, Ferranti-Packard was folded into NEI Canada Ltd, with Wordie Hetherington as chairman, president, and chief executive officer (CEO).

At the same time, Ferranti-Packard Transformers Ltd and Ferranti-Packard Electronics, Ltd were created as subsidiary companies of NEI Canada. A number of NEI sales and service divisions continued as part of NEI Canada, with their managers reporting to their associated companies in Britain. Although NEI Canada reported to NEI in Britain, there were no restraints on the ability of the Ferranti-Packard companies to develop, design, manufacture, and market their products world-wide.

Wordie Hetherington, in addition to his responsibilities at NEI Canada, was also president of Ferranti-Packard Transformers. Barry Hercus, also a professional engineer, was president of Ferranti-Packard Electronics. In 1982, at NEI Canada, Hetherington, who would chair the board until 1984, retired as CEO, and Hercus became president and CEO.

The mid-1980s were difficult for Ferranti-Packard Transformers. Depressed markets forced prices so low that the few sales, which helped keep workers and plants active, were made at a loss. By 1987, the power transformer business was in desperate straits. The plant on Industry Street in Toronto was closed, and the property sold. NEI Canada moved its head office to leased quarters at 10 Carlson Court, near Pearson International Airport. Investments were made in the St Catharines plant, and equipment was moved from Toronto to build power transformers up to 30 MVA. In 1991, the plant was again upgraded so that transformers of more than 100 MVA could be built in St Catharines.

In an attempt to gain greater access to the BC market, Ferranti-Packard had purchased the assets of B.C. Transformer Ltd in Burnaby, and it opened a new manufacturing plant in Surrey in October 1982. Though promising, the plant was overly dependent on one customer, and loss of a major order forced its closing in 1985.

In the 1980s, Ferranti-Packard Electronics had good and bad years. Orders for display systems were sporadic, but the display component business continued to grow, particularly in the European market, and in 1989 a small manufacturing plant was opened in Cobourg, Ontario. In the same year, Hercus left the company, and Paul Cassar, who had joined NEI Canada in 1985 as vice-president, finance, became president.

Ed Lamoureux, who had from 1974 to 1985 been a division manager of Westinghouse Canada in St-Jean-sur-Richelieu, Quebec, and later was president of Renold Canada Ltd, served as president of Ferranti-Packard Transformers from 1990 to mid 1993.

In 1989 Rolls-Royce purchased the shares of NEI in the United Kingdom. Despite the change of ownership, NEI remained intact in Britain, where D. Terry Harrison continued as chairman. In Canada, where Rolls-Royce had substantial operations, the change in ownership had significant repercussions. Effective 1 January 1990, Canadian operations of both Rolls-Royce and NEI were reorganized into Rolls-Royce Industries Canada Inc., with Tom Parker, formerly head of Rolls-Royce in Canada, as president and CEO. Paul Cassar became vice-president, finance. Terry Harrison was appointed in September 1992 as chief executive officer of Rolls-Royce, PLC (public limited company).

On 1 March 1991, Tom Parker retired as president and CEO of Rolls-Royce Industries Canada, He was replaced by John Cheffins, formerly president of Rolls-Royce (Canada). Ferranti-Packard Transformers, headquartered in St Catharines, with additional plants in Trois-Rivières, Dunkirk, and Guanjuato, Mexico, continued to prosper and looked forward to celebrating its centennial in 1994. With acquisition of the entire share capital of Transformadores Parsons Peebles de Mexico, S.A. de C.V., the operation's name was changed to Ferranti-Packard de Mexico, S.A. de C.V. With this change, all operations within Ferranti-Packard Transformers represented themselves under a common banner.

The newly created Rolls-Royce Industries Canada Inc. employed some 3,500 personnel across Canada and had sales in excess of $500 million from five operating companies.

In 1990, the display business that had been such an important part of Ferranti-Packard Electronics was sold to Luminator through Dayco Products Canada Inc. Luminator was a major customer for display components used for variable-message bus signs. It wanted to secure the supply of components, and Rolls-Royce Industries found electronic signs to be outside its core business. With the change of ownership, the display business continued under the name of F-P Electronics, and no alterations were made to management personnel and other employees.

It is fitting that the names Rolls, Royce, Ferranti, and Packard should be united. Charles S. Rolls, a Cambridge graduate in mechanical sciences, was captivated by the advanced technology of his day, both as manufacturer and as successful racing-car driver and world land-speed record-holder. Henry Royce, later Sir Henry, was born into grinding poverty, had only two years of formal schooling, and left an apprenticeship for lack of funds. By age 21 he was founding co-partner in a pioneering electrical engineering and manufacturing company known for innovative design and uncompromising quality. His Canadian cousins, James, Allan, and George Royce, were trailblazers in Canadian electrical history, and George helped carry the Ferranti name to Canada.

Sebastian Ziani de Ferranti, founder of Ferranti UK, is recognized as one of the world's pioneers in electrical technology. He had many inventions of electrical equipment to his credit and helped launch the development of alternating current power systems.

The Packard brothers, too, had been pioneers in the electrical industry before attaching their family name to the automobile industry, also as a byword for quality and leadership. It would be hard to find two brothers whose interests, strengths, talents, and training more complemented each other's. William Doud Packard was the consummate salesman and disciplined businessman. James Ward Packard was the adventurous mechanical engineering graduate of Lehigh University who was drawn to the emerging electrical industry.

But as different as these men might be, they were all entrepreneurs pursuing personal visions of the potential created by new technology. Today these names are united in Ferranti-Packard Transformers Ltd., A Rolls-Royce Company.

Chronology

1894   Packard Electric Co. Ltd incorporated 30 August, with light-bulb manufacturing in Montreal and head office in Toronto. Four equal shareholders: J.W. Packard, W.D. Packard, J.H. Howry, and H.K. Howry.

1895   Manufacturing and the head office of Packard Electric relocated to St Catharines, Ontario, on the Neelon Grist Mill property.

1896   Transformer manufacturing begins at the Packard plant in St Catharines.

1902   Manufacture of watt-hour meters begins at the Packard plant, St Catharines.

1905–7 Oldsmobile automobiles made by Packard in St Catharines.

1912   Ferranti Electric Co. of Canada Ltd formed in Toronto, Ontario, by Ferranti Ltd. in England, from an agency created by the Royce family to sell Ferranti meters.

1915   Design and manufacture of transformers starts at Ferranti Electric.

1919   Assembly of watt-hour meters starts at Ferranti Canada in the Noble Street plant, Toronto.

1920   Frank T. Wyman becomes president of Packard Electric in St Catharines.

1922   Ashton Bert Cooper appointed general manager of Ferranti Canada in Toronto.

1924   Ferranti Canada plant on Noble Street, Toronto, extended to increase transformer manufacturing capability.

1930   Ferranti Canada opens new factory on Industry Street, Toronto.

1936   Ferranti UK, in England, acquires a 33-per-cent interest in Packard Electric.

Ferranti Canada starts an X-ray business by purchasing Solus X-Ray Co.

1949   The Electronics Research Department, under Kenyon Taylor, set up at Ferranti Canada's site on Industry Street, Toronto.

1950   Dr. Arthur Porter comes from England to be head of the Research Department at Ferranti Canada.

1951   Packard Electric opens a new plant, in St Catharines, on the Queen Elizabeth Way near the Welland Canal. Tom Edmondson becomes president.

1954   Ferranti UK buys the remaining shares of Packard Electric to become its sole owner.

1955   The Electronics Department created at Ferranti Canada in Toronto; computer manufacturing begins.

1956   Ferranti Canada, Toronto, opens new facilities at its Industry Street plant for the manufacture of very large power transformers.

Dr. John Thomson appointed president of Ferranti Canada.

1957   Packard Electric opens a plant in Trois-Rivières, Quebec, to manufacture pole-top distribution transformers and, later, watt-hour meters.

1958   Ferranti-Packard Ltd formed through the merger of Ferranti Canada and Packard Electric. Tom Edmondson becomes president and CEO, and John Thomson, chairman of the board.

1960   Ferranti-Packard begins marketing transformers in the United States.

1965   Ferranti-Packard ceases to design and produce general-purpose computers.

1971   Wordie Hetherington takes over as president and CEO of Ferranti-Packard. Tom Edmondson remains as chairman until 1976.

Barry Hercus brought in as general manager of the Electronics Division.

1977   Identicon Corp., in Franklin, Massachusetts, acquired to expand Ferranti-Packard's bar-code-scanning business. Discontinued in 1980.

Manufacture of watt-hour meters discontinued.

Assets of B.C. Transformer Co. purchased, and manufacture of Ferranti-Packard distribution transformers begins in Vancouver. New plant opened in 1982 in Surrey; closes in 1985.

Plant to make small power transformers opened in Dunkirk, New York.

The Electronics Division's display business moved from Industry Street in Toronto to leased premises in Mississauga.

1979 Northern Engineering Industries (NEI) Ltd. of Britain buys all the shares of Ferranti-Packard from Ferranti UK. NEI Canada Ltd formed to manage Ferranti-Packard Transformers Ltd. and Ferranti-Packard Electronics Ltd. Wordie Hetherington remains as president and CEO of NEI Canada.

1982 Barry Hercus becomes president and CEO of NEI Canada.

1987 Manufacture of large power transformers ceases at Toronto's Industry Street plant. Equipment moved to St Catharines, and range extended.

1989 Rolls-Royce, PLC of the United Kingdom buys NEI. Rolls-Royce and NEI in Canada reorganized into Rolls-Royce Industries Canada Inc., with the transformer business continuing under the name Ferranti-Packard Transformers Ltd., with headquarters in St Catharines.

1990 Ferranti-Packard's display business sold to Dayco Products Canada Inc., a division of Mark IV Industries (Luminator). Display-manufacturing plants in Mississauga and Cobourg continue under the Ferranti-Packard name.

Notes

Preface

1 V.Z. de Ferranti to A.B. Cooper, 14 July 1941, letter no. 614, Ferranti UK Archives.

2 For an introduction to confusion and unrealistic expectations as normal products of significant technological change see Norman R. Ball, "Essential Connections: Past and Future; Technology and Society" in Paul Beam, ed., *Beyond The Printed Page: Online Documentation, Proceedings, Second Conference on Quality in Documentation* (Waterloo: Centre for Professional Writing, University of Waterloo, 1992), pp. 11–28.

3 John Baglin as quoted in Ball, "Essential Connections," 27.

4 Reynor Banham, *The Architecture of the Well-Tempered Environment* (Chicago: University of Chicago Press, 1969), p. 64.

5 J.K. Thomas, "A Hundred Million Workers," *Electrical News and Engineering* 59 (15 June 1950): 82.

6 R. Schofield, Report to Board of Directors on Visit to Canada, 23 Feb. 1923, p. 2, Ferranti UK Archives.

Chapter One

1 Raynor Banham, *The Architecture of the Well-Tempered Environment* (Chicago: University of Chicago Press, 1969), p. 64.

2 The term "magneto-electric machines" applies to the early generators that used permanent horseshoe-type magnets to provide the magnetic field. When electro-magnets were used to provide the magnetic field, the generators became known as dynamos. Dynamos also provided a rectified AC current that very closely resembled DC. The term "alternators" later denoted electric generators that produced AC.

3 Ellen Glasgow, *Phases of an Inferior Planet* (New York, 1898); quoted in S. Kern, *The Culture of Time and Space* (Cambridge, Mass.: Harvard University Press, 1983), p. 29.

5 Lewis Mumford, *Technics and Civilization* (New York: Harcourt Brace Jovanovich, 1963), p. 225.

6 Editorial, "Electricity and Civilization," *Electrical Review* 37, no. 6, p. 122.

7 W.L. Randell, *S.Z. de Ferranti – His Influence upon Electrical Development* (London: Longmans, Green, 1946), p. 6.

8 Gertrude Ziani de Ferranti and Richard Ince, *The Life and Letters of Sebastian Ziani de Ferranti* (London: Williams & Norgate, 1934), p. 52.

9 Ibid.

10 R. Moise and M. Daumas, "L'Électricité industrielle," in M. Daumas, ed., *Les techniques de la civilisation industrielle, tome IV: Énergie et matériaux"* (Paris: Presses universitaires de France, 1977), p.369.

11 Jarvis Mackechnie, "The Generation of Electricity," in Charles Singer, E.J. Holmyard, A.R. Hall, and Trevor Williams, eds., *A History of Technology* (Oxford: Clarendon Press, 1979), vol. V, p. 200.

12 Address given by Nikola Tesla, at the Ellicot Club, in Buffalo, on 12 Jan. 1897, on the Occasion of the Commemoration of the Introduction of Niagara Falls Power, reprinted in full in *Electrical Review*, 27 Jan. 1897, p. 46.

13 Merill Denison, *The People's Power* (Toronto: McClelland & Stewart, 1960), p. 93.

14 Ibid., p. 46.

15 In 1889, Edward Adams, whom J.P. Morgan insisted oversee the American Niagara Falls syndicate, set out to discover if electrical technology was sufficiently advanced to make power transmission profitable. Adams reflected: "While I know that electrical development has proceeded with great rapidity, I am not yet sufficiently informed to decide upon the investment of a large sum of money based upon the theory that the electrical development in this direction has reached a commercial basis." Adams to Coleman Sellers, 30 Sept. 1889, Sellers-Peale Correspondence, American Philosophical Society, quoted in R.B. Belfield, "The Niagara Frontier: The Evolution Of

Electric Power Systems in New York and Ontario, 1880–1935," PhD thesis, University of Pennsylvania, 1981, p. 7.

In an attempt to choose the electrical technology appropriate for commercial exploitation of the American side of the Falls, Adams travelled throughout Europe assessing the state of the art. In Belfield's view, Adams was most swayed by his visit with Sebastian Ziani de Ferranti. Ferranti's plans for Deptford convinced him that the Niagara project should be based on a high-voltage, central-station approach.

16 James Wilson and John Fiske, eds., *Appletons' Cyclopaedia of American Biography* (New York: D. Appleton and Co., 1888), vol. v, p. 484.

17 A.D. Shaw to Casimir Gzowski, 16 Dec. 1889, RG 38, C-1, Box 7, File 381-390-1889, Niagara Parks Commission General Correspondence, Archives of Ontario, Toronto. Hereafter this collection will be referred to as Niagara.

18 The Canadian historian H.V. Nelles argues that Shaw "skilfully haggled the commissioners down to a $10,000 advance and then set about peddling his property among likely prospects. After initial overtures to some local New York State industrialists failed to produce a firm offer he tried to interest an English syndicate, organized around S.Z. Ferranti's technical abilities, in the hydro-electric possibilities of Niagara Falls." *Politics of Development* (Toronto: Macmillan, 1974), p. 33.

Several facts appear to contradict this interpretation. First, there is the letter from Shaw to Gzowski, 16 Dec. 1889, referred to in note 17. The letter indicates quite clearly that Shaw, in association with a "leading Electrician," i.e. Sebastian Ziani de Ferranti, is asking for an exclusive concession to the Falls. The proposal of 16 December was the first that the commissioners had entertained from Shaw and the sole basis for granting Shaw and Ferranti a concession. A prior request from Shaw, for an option "in the interest of an English company" to develop electric power at the Falls, was turned down because the commission was negotiating with the "Niagara Falls Electric Co.," a local company. Shaw to Gzowski, 30 Sept. 1889, File 321-330-1889, Niagara. Furthermore, Shaw made no payment of $10,000, nor was it mentioned in Gzowski's acceptance. The commissioners did, however, want $50,000 to be paid immediately, the equivalent of two years' rent.

19 Cited in Rowland Pocock, *The Early British Radio In-*

dustry (Manchester: Manchester University Press, 1987), p. 165. Comparing the pioneers of radio to the earlier pioneers of electric power, Pockock writes (pp. 165–6): "They were also linked by a common enthusiasm for social reform. In this respect, too, they differed from the established telegraph engineers, finding themselves in sympathy with the electrical power engineers – such as Sebastian de Ferranti. The application of electrical science to industry became a moral crusade for these applied scientists. Electric lighting, which created no fumes and did not consume oxygen, had already contributed to the reduction in respiratory illness among office workers. A more widespread utilisation of electricity would eliminate much of the pollution associated with earlier power sources. As Lodge said, it would '… restore our large towns to their old habitable beauty and healthfulness before the smoke-demon destroyed the vegetation and blackened the sky.'"

20 Ziani de Ferranti and Ince, *Life and Letters*, p. 124.

21 Ibid.

22 Ferranti to Shaw, 16 Jan. 1890, File 1-10-1890, Niagara.

23 Shaw to Gzowski, quoting the entire contents of Ferranti's telegram of 21 Jan. 1890, File 21-30-1890, Niagara.

24 Lord Wantage to A.D. Shaw, 28 Feb. 1890, File 41-50-1890, Niagara. It was Lord Wantage who made the offer of $10,000 in order to save the Ferranti-Shaw concession, contrary to Nelles's claim that Shaw had "skilfully haggled the commissioners down to a $10,000 advance."

25 Thomas Hughes, *Networks of Power* (Baltimore: Johns Hopkins University Press, 1983), p. 240.

26 Gzowski to Shaw, 17 March 1890, File 51-60-1890, Niagara.

27 S.Z. de Ferranti to Gzowski, 16 Sept. 1890, File 181-190-1890, Niagara.

28 The loss of business was caused as much by legislation as by mishap. In May 1889, bowing to extreme pressure from small DC electric lighting companies, politicians decided "to reduce the territory sought by LESC [London Electric Supply Co.] and to allow competition between AC and DC systems within the company's London districts"; Hughes, Networks, p. 242. The decision favoured decentralized DC utilities and seriously compromised the economic benefits of Ferranti's central-station approach. Had the company been given the monopoly over electric power distribution

for which it had lobbied, it would not have lost all its customers after the fire. Furthermore, the LESC would have had a larger market area to pay for the large start-up capital costs of its central-station approach.

29 Randell, *S.Z. de Ferranti*, p. 11.

30 Ibid.

31 Gzowski to James Wilson, 4 March 1891, File 51-60-1891, Niagara.

32 S.Z. de Ferranti to Gzowski, 20 Feb. 1892, File 21-30-1892, Niagara.

33 S. Lilley, *Man, Machine, and History* (London: Lawrence & Wishart, 1965), p. 122.

34 Hughes, in *Networks*, p. 87, points out that section 18 of the British Electric Lighting Act (1882) states that "the undertaker [supplier of electricity] shall not be entitled to prescribe any special forms of lamp or burner to be used by any company or person ..." As a result, Gaulard had to design a transformer that would allow the consumer to select any one of a number of voltages between 45 and 91 volts. In this way, the user became "independent of the producer" and could "apply the current he receives to any purpose he may please, such as arc lighting, incandescent lighting, the generation of power, or of heat." *Engineering*, 35, 2 March 1883, p. 205.

35 "The Frankfort Test," *Electrical Review* 19, no. 12, 14 Nov. 1891, p. 166.

36 Dolivio-Dobrowolsky, "The Transmission of Power by Alternating Currents Differing in Phase (Rotary Currents)," *Electrical Review* 19, no. 4, 19 Sept. 1891, p. 63.

37 Georg Siemens, *The History of the House of Siemens. Vol I: The Era of Free Enterprise* (Munich: Karl Alber, 1957), p. 123.

38 "Favors the Meter System," *Canadian Electrical News*, April 1904, p. 72.

39 Jas Milne, "Meters," *Canadian Electrical News*, July 1896, p. 152.

40 A. Dion, "Meter and Meter Rates," *Canadian Engineer* 6, no. 7, July 1899, p. 66.

41 In 1895, Canada had its first three-phase hydro-electric power plant, transmitting power from Rapid Plat to the St-Hyacinthe, Quebec, 4.5 miles (7.2 km) away. In 1897, an even longer transmission was achieved when the North Shore Power Co. transmitted electric power 17 miles (27.4 km) from the Batiscan River to Trois-Rivières, Quebec. In 1898, the Cataract Power Co. built a station to transmit electric power 32 miles (51.5 km), at 11,000 volts, from

DeCew Falls to Hamilton, Ontario.

42 Reinhard Filter, *The Barber Dynamo: A Perspective* (Cheltenham, Ont.: Boston Mills Press, 1977), p. 12.

43 J.K. Thomas, "A Hundred Million Workers," *Electrical News and Engineering* 59, 15 June 1950, p. 82.

44 Michael Bliss, *Northern Enterprise: Five Centuries of Canadian Business* (Toronto: McClelland and Stewart, 1987), p. 303.

45 R.T. Naylor, *The History of Canadian Business*, vol. 2 (Toronto: James Lorimer, 1975), p. 62.

Chapter Two

1 See, for example, Norman R. Ball, "The Technology of Settlement and Land Clearing in Canada Prior to 1840," PhD thesis, University of Toronto, 1979, and Norman R. Ball, "Technology Assessment and the Upper Canadian Bush Farmer," in T.A. Crowley, ed., *Proceedings of the 2nd Annual Agricultural History of Ontario Seminar* (Guelph: University of Guelph, 1977), pp. 90–106.

2 This process may be seen clearly in parts of the Canadian mining industry where, in order to counter rising costs of production and lower-cost foreign competition, committees have been established to bring together miners, mining engineers, and experts in microelectronics and microprocessors to identify problems that may be solved readily by the application of these fields. Companies such as INCO and Falconbridge have been very successful with this approach.

3 The steam-engine was working and had undergone various improvements before the birth of the field of thermodynamics, which grew out of the need to explain certain aspects of steam-engine operation. Once the science had advanced considerably, it served the technology that had given it birth.

4 Norman R. Ball, "Petroleum Technology in Ontario during the 1860s," MA thesis, University of Toronto, 1972.

5 Terry Martin, "The Packards of Warren: The Years before the Marque," in Beverly Ray Kimes, ed., *Packard: A History of the Motor Car and the Company* (Princeton, NJ: Automobile Quarterly Library Series, 1978), p. 16.

6 Ibid., p. 19.

7 For the most notable example of how these changes created opportunities for Canadian manufacturers and industrialists, see Merrill Denison, *Harvest Tri-*

umphant: *The Story of Massey-Harris* (Toronto: Mc-Clelland and Stewart, 1948).

8 Martin, "Packards," p. 20.

9 Ibid., p. 21.

10 Ibid., p. 21.

11 Ibid., p. 22.

12 William Doud Packard, Diary, 28 Nov. 1898, private collection, copy courtesy Terry Martin, Warren, Ohio.

13 Ibid., 29 Nov. 1898.

14 Ibid., 7 Dec. 1898.

15 Ibid., 23 Jan. 1899.

16 Canadian Association of Stationary Engineers, *Souvenir Number of the Fourth Annual Convention of the Canadian Association of Stationary Engineers* (Montreal: Association, 1893), p. 73.

17 See the major writings of Harold Adams Innis; see also Ball, "Technology of Settlement." For introductory overviews to various aspects of the history of Canadian technology, see Norman R. Ball, *Mind, Heart and Vision: Professional Engineering in Canada 1887 to 1987* (Ottawa: National Museum of Science and Technology in co-operation with the Engineering Centennial Board, 1987); Bruce Sinclair, Norman R. Ball, and James O. Petersen, eds., *Let Us Be Honest and Modest: Technology and Society in Canadian History* (Toronto: Oxford University Press, 1974); Norman R. Ball, ed., *Building Canada: A History of Public Works* (Toronto: University of Toronto Press, 1988).

18 For an introduction to the spread of electric power and its displacement of artificial gas, see Arnold Roos, "Electricity," in Ball, *Building Canada*, pp. 169–94.

19 Ball, *Mind, Heart and Vision*, pp. 38–42.

20 Ibid., pp. 28–30.

21 X.E. Bollinger, "Electrical Engineering," in *The Canadian Encyclopedia*, vol. 1 (Edmonton: Hurtig Publishers, 1985), p. 560.

22 Martin, "Packards," p. 23.

23 Stationary Engineers, *Souvenir*, p. 73.

24 Packard Electric Co., Minutes, 23 Jan. 1897.

25 Martin, "Packard," p. 23. The diaries of James Ward Packard have disappeared since they were last used by Martin. When last heard of, they were in the hands of an individual in California and are no longer available for research.

26 W.D. Packard, Diary, 22 Jan. 1898.

27 Martin, "Packards," p. 22.

28 "The New Packard Lamp Works," *Canadian Engineer* 3, Sept. 1895, p. 126.

29 *Electrical Review*, 26 May 1897, p. 244.

30 Robert E. Ankli and Fred Frederiksen, "The Packard Electric Company of St. Catharines, Ontario," *Automotive History Review* 14, fall 1981, pp. 5–8; David E. Nye, *Image Worlds: Corporate Identities at General Electric, 1890–1930* (Cambridge, Mass.: MIT Press, 1985), pp. 18–19.

31 *Canadian Engineer* 4, no. 2, June 1896, p. 1.

32 Ibid. 6, no. 11, March 1899, p. 1.

33 Ibid. 4, no. 2, June 1902, p. xxv.

34 Ibid. 4, Aug. 1902, p. xvii.

35 Ibid., June 1896, p. 57.

36 *Canadian Electrical News*, April 1893, p. 63.

37 See *Electrical Review*, 32 no. 3, 1898, pp. 45, 386.

38 Ibid., p. 45.

39 Packard Electric Co., *Jandus Series Alternating Arc Lighting System, Bulletin No. 21* (St Catharines: Packard Electric Co., Feb. 1905).

40 "The Packard Electric Company," *Canadian Electrical News* 17, no. 10, Oct. 1907, p. 326.

41 Ibid.

42 Ibid.

43 "The Packard Transformer," *Canadian Engineer* 3 no. 7, July 1896, p. 76.

44 Ibid. 9, no. 6, June, 1902, p. 161.

45 Ibid.

46 *Canadian Engineer*, Nov. 1902, p. 41.

47 Packard Electric Co., Proposal and Contract to Supply Transformers to the Ontario Power Company of Niagara Falls, 18 March 1907, Ontario Hydro Archives, Toronto.

48 Engineer in Charge to R.C. Board, Esq., Secretary Treasury, The Ontario Power Co. of Niagara Falls, Fidelity Building, Buffalo, N.Y., May 16th, 1912, Ontario Hydro Archives.

49 Ankli, "Packard Electric," p. 5.

50 Ibid., p. 6.

51 Ibid., p. 8.

52 Ibid, p. 6.

53 "Electrical Apparatus," *Industrial Canada* 6, June 1905, pp. 721–2.

Chapter Three

1 *Report of the Royal Commission on Dominion-Provincial Relations* (Rowell-Sirois Report) (Ottawa, 1940), p. 66.

2 Ibid., p. 67.

3 Ibid.

4 Oscar Skelton, *General History of the Dominion: 1867–1912* (Toronto: Publishers Association of Canada, 1913).

5 Canada, Dominion Bureau of Statistics, Census for 1891, 1901, and 1911.

6 Census, 1891, 1901, 1911.

7 J.F. Wilson, *Ferranti and the British Electrical Industry, 1864–1930* (Manchester: Manchester University Press, 1988), p. 55.

8 Ibid., p. 57.

9 Ibid., p. 73-4. Wilson writes: "Most steam alternator contracts included such penalty clauses, and in many cases they were enacted with dire consequences: in 1900 the Cardiff City Council was awarded compensation of 2,000 [pounds] and the Ferranti steam alternator free of charge by the courts after the one-per-cent-per-week penalty had exceeded the contract price of 5,000 [pounds]. In fact, on the first twenty contracts for steam alternators, worth 60,000 [pounds], the company lost 28,300 [pounds], and even with a healthy Meter department such a lame duck could not be sustained."

10 W.L. Randell, *S.Z. de Ferranti – His Influence upon Electrical Development* (London: Longmans, Green, 1946), p. 22.

11 James Salmon, *Rails from the Junction* (Toronto: Lyon Productions, 1958).

12 Ibid., p. 7.

13 Ibid., p. 10.

14 Fred Rowntree, History of the Ferranti Co. of Canada, 1951, p. 5, Ferranti UK Archives, Manchester, England.

15 Ibid.

16 Albert Schofield, History of Ferranti Canada, 1951, p. 14, Ferranti UK Archives.

17 Statutes of Canada, An Act Respecting Patents of Invention, CAP, XXVI, 14 June 1872; also quoted in R.T. Naylor, *The History of Canadian Business*, vol. 2 (Toronto: James Lorimer, 1975), p. 45.

18 Rowntree, History, p. 7.

19 W.A. Coates to A. Schofield, 27 Oct. 1950, Ferranti UK Archives.

20 *The Canada Year Book 1907*, Second Series, Ottawa, 1908.

21 *Canadian Electrical News*, Oct. 1907, p. 17.

22 Ibid.

23 H.J. Doughty, Early History of Ferranti in Canada, personal recollections, 1951, Ferranti UK Archives.

24 By-Law 25, Minutes of Ferranti Electrical Co. of Canada Shareholders' Meetings, 3 April 1914, Ferranti-Packard Archives, Toronto.

25 By-Law 26, Ferranti Minutes, 12 May 1914.

26 Rowntree, History, p. 13.

27 Ibid., p. 8.

28 Skelton, History, p. 203.

Chapter Four

1 The 48-per-cent drop was calculated from statistics in *Report of the Royal Commission on Dominion-Provincial Relations* (Rowell-Sirois Report) (Ottawa, 1940), p. 91.

2 F.H. Leacy, ed., *Historical Statistics of Canada*, (Ottawa: Statistics Canada, 1983), Series S59.

3 The editorial, in the 16 June 1917 issue of *Electrical World*, shows how Canada not only averted any serious wartime energy shortages but was able, thanks primarily to its hydroelectric potential, to expand the production of electricity for unprecedented wartime demand. Thermal electric power played a lesser role.

4 Albert Schofield, History of Ferranti Canada, 1951, p. 20, Ferranti UK Archives.

5 Ibid.

6 E. Parmelee, Recollections, 1951, Ferranti-Packard Archives (hereafter F-P), Toronto, Canada.

7 Fred Rowntree, History of the Ferranti Co. of Canada, 1951, p. 15, Ferranti UK Archives.

8 Ferranti Electrical Co. of Canada Annual Audited Report, 1918, Prepared by George Touche & Co.

9 Ibid.

10 F.C. Burnett and E.J. Brunning, "Electric Heating Device," Canadian Patent Number 170839, applied for 29 April 1916, granted 18 July 1916.

11 Rowntree recalled: "During the summer of 1918, I received a long distance call from Mr. James Royce, who was living in Syracuse, N.Y., looking after the Syracuse [Rolls-Royce] plant himself. He said he wanted to go to the Long Island plant and wanted me to come over to look after his interests in the Syracuse plant where he had seven floors in the Franklin Motor Car plant, which was devoted to making the crankshaft, camshaft and one of the gear cases for the eagle airplane. Ten Rolls-Royce inspectors from England were at that plant," Rowntree, History, p. 17. So important was the war production of Eagle airplanes that James Royce got the British minister in Washington, Sir Henry Japp, to call General Mewburn, in Ot-

tawa, and obtain Rowntree's release from the Artillery branch at Camp Petawawa.

12 "When the War made it impossible to borrow in London, Canadian industry, provinces and municipalities turned to New York. Between 1913 and 1921 the total United States investment in Canada rose from $780 million to $2,300 million while British investment fell slightly"; Rowell-Sirois Report, p. 109.

13 According to Albert Schofield, "The type C meter had apparently been designed to suit the service conditions in Canada, having special removable shunt coils because we lost so many due to lightning surges. However, the design was superior to the older model and fewer coils required replacement. The simple assembly proved a good selling feature and the demonstration by taking the meter apart and rebuilding it during an interview, always brought favourable comments and generally, an order. The spring seated jewel and the reversible pivot was a great asset and, above all, the carrying handle for the convenience of the installer, who generally had to walk to the customer's premises in those days. Also to our advantage was the fact that our polyphase meter could be supplier self contained for 500 volt and up to 100 amps. per phase, whilst other makers advocated step-down potential transformers for all above 200 volts"; History, p. 22.

14 Ibid., p. 23.

15 Surprisingly, Ferranti officials in Britain expressed concern that use of the Ferranti name would only hinder the company in its attempt to build a strong Canadian image. After considerable discussion, the name was kept. The Canadian board believed that it was in its long-term interests to use the name.

16 A.B. Cooper, General Manager of Ferranti Electric Ltd., to the Board of Directors of Ferranti Ltd., in the U.K., 3 July 1934, p. 6, Ferranti UK Archives, Manchester, England.

17 R. Schofield, Report to Board of Directors on Visit to Canada, 23 Feb. 1923, p. 2, Ferranti UK Archives.

18 Ibid.

19 Details of the deal are contained in a letter from R.H. Schofield to A.W. Tait, 16 Oct. 1922 F-P.

20 Cooper to R. Schofield, 27 Oct. 1922, Ferranti UK Archives.

21 Ibid.

22 According to one British historian: "Tait was initially very cautious about restoring Dr. Ferranti to such a powerful position but, with Whittaker as adviser on the Executive Committee, the Chairman [Tait] hoped that the new Technical Manager's well-known disposition for continual experimentation could be harnessed in a beneficial manner"; J.F. Wilson, *Ferranti and the British Electrical Industry, 1864–1930* (Manchester: Manchester University Press, 1988) p.119.

23 R. Schofield, Report, pp. 3–4.

24 Ibid., p. 4.

25 Ibid., p. 5.

26 Ibid., p. 6.

27 Vincent Ziani de Ferranti to Cooper, 25 Sept., 1925, Ferranti UK Archives.

28 A.B. Cooper to V.Z. de Ferranti, Sept. 1923, Ferranti UK Archives.

29 A. Schofield, History, p. 26.

30 Rowell-Sirois Report, p. 116.

31 J.T. Johnston "Water Power Resources of Canada and Their Development," paper presented at the Second World Power Conference, Berlin, Germany, 16–25 June 1930, reprinted in *Engineering Journal* 13, no. 6, July 1930, p. 409.

32 The figure for the increase in the generating output of the public utilities is derived from Tables Q75–80 of Leacy, *Historical Statistics*. The figure for the increase in new capital investment comes from Rowell-Sirois Report, p. 116.

33 In justifying his actions to the parent firm, Cooper wrote: "I have felt that, particularly with reference to the uphill fight which we may have to undertake on this side of the water to put the Surge Absorber across, the Doctor's title might prove a real asset to the company"; Cooper to Vincent Ziani de Ferranti, 21 July 1932, Ferranti UK Archives.

34 The Dominion Bureau of Statistics did not keep any statistics on radio production prior to 1925. The 1925 manufacturing figure is 48,531 radio sets and the 1931 figure is 291,711. Taken from Leacy, *Historical Statistics*, Series R738.

35 "Yesterday and Today" (London: Ferranti UK, Nov. 1957), p. 15.

36 Vincent Ziani de Ferranti to Cooper, 2 July 1929, Ferranti UK Archives.

37 Vincent Ziani de Ferranti to Cooper, 2 Feb. 1931, Ferranti UK Archives.

38 Rowntree, History, p. 23. According to A. Schofield, History, p. 27, "The audio frequency transformer which we imported from Ferranti Ltd., England, to sell to the radio trade in Canada, did more to establish the Ferranti name in the minds of the Canadian public than any form of advertising had hitherto done.

Everybody was deeply interested in Radio and by introducing Ferranti audio frequency transformers in the amplifying circuit of their receivers, many people could hear quality reproduction of broadcast music for the first time."

39 A. Schofield, History, p. 26.

40 Cooper to Vincent Ziani de Ferranti, 18 Sept. 1928, Ferranti UK Archives.

41 Ibid. Cooper argued that the purchase of 6–10 acres was also a wise real estate investment: "Land of this sort, properly chosen, will definitely appreciate in value, so that the acquisition of extra property may safely be looked upon as an investment rather than a risk." Nearly sixty years later, Cooper's words took on the aura of an uncanny prophecy. When Ferranti Canada closed its large power transformer operations on Industry Street in Toronto, the land that Cooper had bought for $35,000 had become a very valuable piece of real estate.

42 Ibid.

43 Ibid.

44 G. Gale, "Hydro-Electric Industry of Canada: Some Economic Aspects," paper presented at the Second World Power Conference, Berlin, Germany, 16–25 June 1930, reprinted in *Engineering Journal* 13, no. 6, July 1930, pp. 455–62.

45 J. Smith and C. Christie, "Generation, Transmission and Distribution of Electricity in Canada," paper presented at the Second World Power Conference, Berlin, Germany, 16–25 June 1930, reprinted in *Engineering Journal* 13, no. 6, July 1930, pp. 435–44.

46 Ferranti Minutes, 11 Jan. 1929.

47 V.Z. de Ferranti to Cooper, 2 July 1929, Ferranti UK Archives.

48 At a meeting of the board of Ferranti Canada, in Toronto, on 31 May 1931, V.Z. de Ferranti "informed the Directors that the Canadian Company would not be restricted in the sale of transformers to any export market"; Minutes of Board of Directors, Ferranti Canada, 31 May 1931, p. 2. His good news was a bit premature. As the Depression finally hit the electrical industry by the end of 1931, the international contraction in the electrical market made the announcement a mere pipe dream for Ferranti Canada.

49 D.C. Durland, "Canadian Electrical Industry Is Prosperous," *Canadian Engineer* 58, no. 2, 14 Jan. 1930, p. 131.

50 Ferranti Minutes, 25 Nov. 1932, p. 2.

51 1932 is the last year in which any mention of the Radio Department appears in the company's balance sheet;

52 In a confidential examination of Ferranti Canada's financial stability, Dunn & Bradstreet described the company's situation: "The erection of plant here has used up considerable working capital. It is pointed out that trade liabilities are chiefly to parent company which is reputed very wealthy, and general standing of both the English concern and its Canadian company is high. Subject concern does not borrow in local financial circles, and while the company has felt the effects of general conditions, have sufficient capital at their disposal." CD.18-7 34, 27 Nov. 1933, F-P.

53 Unidentified clipping, 1932.

54 Michael Bliss, *Northern Enterprise: Five Centuries of Canadian Business* (Toronto: McClelland and Stewart, 1987), Bliss, p. 412.

55 Albert Schofield, History of Ferranti Canada, 1951, p. 32, Ferranti UK Archives.

56 In a letter to John Stone, chief engineer of Britain's Central Electricity Board, dated 23 November 1933, Cooper observed: "In presenting the surge absorber, we found it difficult to change the habit of thinking of lightning protection purely in terms of amplitude reduction. Amplitude reduction would, in itself, be of prime importance except for the fact that transformer engineers have, over a period of years, developed insulation which is essentially proof against any stress of the major insulation which can reach the transformer without spilling over the line insulation. It is, however, economically impossible to provide throughout the transformer sufficient insulation between turns and sections to withstand the stresses resulting from the rapid change in the voltage associated with the steep wave front surges, ... [against] which the discharge type arrestor offers no protection. (Ferranti Ltd Archives).

57 Ian Drummond, *Progress without planning* (Toronto: University of Toronto Press, 1987), p. 61.

58 Advertisement appearing on page 67 of the *Ferranti Electric Bulletin* (Toronto: Ferranti Electric, 1937), 103-4.5M-3-37, F-P.

59 Ibid.

60 Ibid., 393 – 3.5M-7-37, p. 4, F-P.

61 Cooper to V.Z. de Ferranti, 4 Sept. 1935, Ferranti UK Archives.

62 "They do no advertising other than stereotyped electrical journal advertising; they have no direct-by-mail or catalogue advertising. They have a much smaller

engineering and draughting staff than we find advisable to maintain. They maintain no factory cost record system and no office check on factory stock or inventory." Ibid.

63 Ibid.

64 The impact on Ferranti Electric is clear from a letter written by Cooper in 1936: "The actual dollar value of business was materially lower in the period ending March 31, 1936, than in the previous year. This is due to two specific conditions arising from the same source. First: the price of the transformers sold was very materially reduced because of the competition from the Commonwealth Company. Second: the Commonwealth Company obtained during this period considerable business, and although no definite figures are available, I estimate that they equalled our volume of business. This competition as you know, became increasingly severe toward the end of the calendar year 1935, and reached its conclusion two months ago." A.B. Cooper to V.Z. de Ferranti, 25 April 1936, Ferranti Ltd Archives.

65 Frank Wyman to Filer-Smith Machinery Co., 9 Aug. 1934, FP.

66 Signed agreement between Andrew Tait and Ferranti Ltd, 3 Oct. 1936, FP. At the time of Tait's sale of shares to Ferranti Ltd. there were 20,000 class "A" and 30,000 class "B" Packard Electric shares in existence. Only class "B" shares, also known as ordinary shares, carried voting rights.

67 There are no known copies in existence of Packard Electric's annual financial statements before 1936. The earliest existing copies date to 1936, and these were found in Ferranti Electric files. Now they are in the Archives of Ontario, Toronto.

68 Interview with Tom Edmondson, St. Catharines, Aug. 1988, John Vardalas interviewer, FP.

69 Cooper to V.Z. de Ferranti, 27 April 1942, Ferranti Ltd Archives.

70 A.B. Cooper to V.Z. de Ferranti, 2 Oct. 1935, Ref no. 6126, Ferranti UK Archives.

71 A.B. Cooper to V.Z. de Ferranti, 2 Oct. 1935, Ref no. 6127, Ferranti UK Archives.

72 Ibid.

73 Albert Schofield, History of Ferranti Canada 1951, p. 31, Ferranti UK Archives.

74 "Electrical Apparatus and Supplies Industry," Canada, Dominion Bureau of Statistics, Census, 1939, 1941.

75 Ferranti Electric Ltd Annual Audited Reports, 1939, 1940, 1941, F-P.

76 Ibid.

77 Ibid.

78 On 17 April 1941, the board voted a stock dividend in the form of 1,500 shares in capital stock, at a nominal value of $100 each, to Ferranti Ltd, in England.

79 Ferranti Minutes, 24 Nov. 1944, p. 2.

80 Ibid.

81 Ordnance Division, Ferranti Electric Ltd, to the Deputy Minister, Department of Munitions and Supply, Canada, 3 Nov. 1943, F-P

82 Ibid.

83 Ibid.

Chapter Five

1 Minutes of the Packard Electric Co. Limited. Incorporated Under The Ontario Companys Act October 31, 1912, p. 20.

2 Ibid., p. 21.

3 Ibid., p. 27.

4 Ibid., p. 47.

5 Ibid., p. 32.

6 Ibid., p. 41.

7 Ibid., p. 37.

8 Ibid., pp. 39, 41.

9 Ibid., p. 40.

10 Ibid., p. 48.

11 Ibid., p. 48.

12 Ibid., p. 49.

13 Ibid., p. 51.

14 Ibid., p. 54.

15 Ibid., p. 60.

16 John Herd Thompson and Allen Seager, *Canada 1922–1929: Decade of Discord* (Toronto: McClelland and Stewart, 1986), p. 11.

17 Ibid., p. 81.

18 As quoted in ibid., p. 81.

19 Ibid., p. 81.

20 Ibid., p. 81.

21 Ibid., p. 83.

22 Ibid., p. 83.

23 J.A. Fleming, *Fifty Years of Electricity. The Memories of an Electrical Engineer* (London: 1921), p. 200.

24 "Westinghouse Large Electric Transformers," Oct. 1930, p. 22, unidentified clipping.

25 Minutes, p. 70.

26 Ibid., p. 74.

27 Ibid., p. 76.

28 Ibid., p. 78.
29 Ibid., p. 39.
30 Ibid., pp. 85, 86.
31 Ibid., pp. 54.
32 Ibid., p. 69.
33 Ibid., p. 71.
34 Ibid., p. 71.
35 Ibid., p. 80.
36 Ibid., p. 81.
37 Ibid., p. 88.
38 Ibid., p. 91.
39 Ibid., p. 114.
40 Ibid., pp. 117, 125.
41 Ibid., p. 130.
42 Ibid., pp. 153, 160–3.
43 V.Z. de Ferranti to A.B. Cooper, 14 July 1941, Letter no 614, Ferranti UK Archives.
44 Minutes, 16 April 1930,
45 Ibid., 1 June 1931, p. 163.
46 Ibid., ratification of decision of 2 Jan. 1934, p. 6.
47 Ibid., p. 8.
48 Ibid., 26 April 1935, pp. 16–17.
49 Ibid., 5 April 1937, p. 26.
50 Ibid., 2 Nov. 1937, p. 30.
51 Ibid., 12 Feb. 1938, p. 33; see also 5 April 1937, p. 26.
52 Ibid., 3 Oct. 1938, p. 37.
53 Ibid., 15 Nov. 1938, p. 39.
54 Ibid., 9 June 1939, p. 43.
55 Ibid., 26 Oct. 1939, p. 45.
56 "Manufacturers of Electrical Equipment," *Industrial Canada* 34, no. 9, Jan. 1934, p. 62.
57 Minutes, 25 Jan. 1940, p. 47.
58 H.L. Palmer, "Electrical Modernization in Industry," *Industrial Canada* 36, no. 9, Jan. 1936, p. 61.
59 Ibid., pp. 60–5.
60 "New Type Furnaces Replace Old Style Installations in Montreal Plant," *Industrial Canada* 36, no. 9, Jan. 1936, p. 68.
61 "Steel Sheets Now Made by Cold Reduction Process in Hamilton," ibid., p. 80.
62 "Extensive Improvements to Alloy Steel Plant," ibid. 35, no. 3, July 1934, p. 124.
63 "Important Additions to Automobile Factory," ibid. 35, no. 8, Dec. 1934, pp. 44–5.
64 "Formal Opening of New Electric Foundry," ibid. 36, no. 1, May 1935, p. 62.
65 "Doubling Size of Electric Furnace Foundry", ibid. 36, no. 7, Nov. 1935, p. 52.
66 "New Alloy Steel Plant Commences Operations," ibid. 36, no. 10, Feb. 1936, p. 66.
67 "Report On Canadian Limestones," ibid. 34 no. 2, June 1933, p. 56.
68 *Minutes*, 26 Oct. 1939, p. 45.
69 Ibid., 16 Aug. 1940, p. 54.
70 Ibid., 22 Nov. 1940, p. 56.
71 Ibid., 9 May 1941, p. 60.
72 Ibid., 25 July 1941, p. 64.
73 Ibid., 12 Oct. 1943, p. 77.
74 Ibid., 7 Oct. 1941, p. 67.
75 As reported in "Electrical Industries," *Industrial Canada*, 42, no. 1, May 1941, p. 78.
76 "Packard Electric Expanding Plant Capacity," ibid. 42, no. 5, Sept. 1941, p. 86.
77 John R. Read, "Electrical Industries," ibid. 42, no. 1, May 1941, pp. 78–9.
78 "Making Specialized Ordnance Steels," ibid. 43, no. 9, Jan. 1943, p. 105.
79 Ibid. 44, no. 4, Aug. 1943, caption to photo, p. 95.
80 "Ford Motor Company Again Expand Foundry," ibid. 44, no. 2, June 1943, p. 130.
81 "Electric Furnace Firm Erecting Plant Addition," ibid. 43, no. 2, June 1942, p. 121.
82 Minutes, 16 Dec. 1946, p. 98.

Chapter Six

1 J. Wilson, "Canada May Lead in Per Capita Consumption of Electricity," *Electrical News and Engineering* 55, no. 5, 1 March 1946, p. 15.
2 T.H. Hogg, "Ontario to Build up Power Reserves," ibid. 55, no. 6, 15 March 1946, pp. 65–7.
3 "Unprecedented Activity in Electrical Industry," ibid. 57, no. 12, 15 June 1948, p. 37. In 1945, Canada had 83,178 miles (133,862 km) of pole lines. By 1958 this figure had grown to 285,306 miles (459,154 km) F.H. Leacy, ed., *Historical Statistics of Canada* (Ottawa: Statistics Canada, 1983), Series Q126-130.
4 K.J. Rea, *The Prosperous Years: The Economic History of Ontario, 1939–75* (Toronto: University of Toronto Press, 1985).
5 Interview, Bob MacKimmie, St. Catharines, 17 July 1987; John Vardalas interviewer, F-P.
6 Bob MacKimmie, untitled article on post-war meter developments at Packard Electric and Ferranti-Packard, c. 1979, pp. 39–40, F-P.
7 Ibid., p. 2.
8 By 1945, Canada had produced some 26,000 distribu-

tion transformers. By 1949, this figure had jumped to approximately 72,000. "The Electrical Apparatus and Supplies Industry," Canada, Dominion Bureau of Statistics, Census, 1945, 1949.

9 "Equipment Review," *Electrical News and Engineering* 55, no. 4, 15 Feb. 1946, pp. 114–15; "New Products," ibid., 63, no. 21, 15 Oct. 1954.

10 J. Coltman, "The Transformer," *Scientific American* 258, no. 1, Jan. 1988, pp. 86–95.

11 D.A. Wiegand, "New Core Design for Distribution Transformers," *Electrical Digest* 24, April 1955, pp. 33–4.

12 "Electrical Apparatus and Supplies Industry," Census, 1948, 1955.

13 "The Story in Pictures of Our Electrical Development," *Electrical Digest* 22, June 1953, pp. 83, 84.

14 Yearly financial audits of Ferranti Ltd. world-wide operations, 1957. These audits include financial figures for Ferranti Electric and Packard Electric after 1954, F-P.

15 Kenneth Farmer, "Special Message from CEMA President: The Industrial Profits Slashed! ... Government a Contributing Factor," *Electrical Digest* 24, Sept. 1955, p. 35.

16 "The Canadian Electrical Industry ... A Report for 1956," *Monetary Times* 124, no. 3, March 1956, p. 39.

17 "Monetary Times 1955 Report on the Canadian Electrical Industry," ibid., 124, no. 3, March 1955, p. 41.

18 "Report Shows Electrical Manufacturing Industry Faces Serious Recession," *Electrical News and Engineering* 64, no. 4, 15 Feb. 1955, pp. 88–90.

19 F.A. Knox, in association with C.L. Barber and D.W. Slater, "The Canadian Electrical Manufacturing Industry: An Economic Analysis," report produced for and published by the Canadian Electrical Manufacturers Association, Toronto, 1954.

20 Edmondson to Packard Electric employees, 3 June 1954, F-P.

21 Ibid.

22 "The Kitimat Project," *Electrical Digest* 21, Jan. 1952, pp. 38–45.

23 Ibid., p. 38.

24 G. Rosenbluth and H. Thorburn, *Canadian Anti-Combines Administration, 1952–1960* (Toronto: University of Toronto Press, 1963) pp. 29–30.

25 In the matter of an inquiry under the Combines Investigation Act relating to the manufacture, distribution and sale of watthour meters, from T.D. MacDonald, Director of Investigation and Research, to the Restrictive Trade Practices Commission, Ottawa, 9 June 1954.

26 Under the new combines legislation, the director of investigation and research could launch an investigation (1) as a result of an official complaint lodged by six citizens, (2) on request from the minister of justice, or (3) on his own initiative.

The director's investigation proceeded in stages. The first was a preliminary investigation to assess if a formal investigation were required. This usually involved examining generally available data about the industry. In the majority of cases, the director would drop the case after the preliminary investigation.

If, however, the preliminary investigation suggested carrying the case further, the director could send his officers to search, without notice, the company's records and seize whatever was thought relevant. The business community found the new powers of search and seizure most distasteful, an invasion of its privacy, and a violation of its legal rights. At this point, the director could, at his discretion, drop the case for lack of evidence, without giving any written reasons.

If the evidence seized lent more credibility to the suspicion of combines activity, the investigation would then proceed to a more formal level. Company officials were asked to respond, under oath, to specific questions from the director. Company officials were also free to present whatever additional evidence they felt appropriate. Finally, after going over the testimony, the director would put written questions to the company to which it would have to give written returns, under oath.

27 The companies in question were Ferranti Electric, Packard Electric, Canadian Westinghouse, Canadian General Electric, Moloney Electric of Canada, Supreme Power Supplies Ltd., Cansfield Electric Works, Sangamo, English Electric, Reliance Electric, Pioneer Electric, and Brown-Boveri of Canada.

28 Unidentified newspaper clipping, 1955, F-P.

29 Packard Electric Solicitor to Tom Edmondson, 13 Oct. 1954, F-P.

30 R.H. Hogge to Packard Electric Solicitor, 28 Feb. 1955, F-P.

31 In the matter of the Combines Investigation Act and in the matter of an inquiry relating to the manufacture, distribution and sale of transformers, T.D. MacDonald, director of investigation and research to the Restrictive Trade Practices Commission, 8 April 1960,

obtained from the Canadian Ministry of Consumer and Corporate Affairs under the Access to Information Act.

32 Packard Electric Solicitor to Tom Edmondson, 2 Dec. 1955, p. 2, F-P.

33 Ibid.

34 Ibid.

35 Ibid.

36 Ibid.

37 Letter no. 1 from T.D. MacDonald, Ottawa, to Tom Edmondson, 9 April 1956, F-P.

38 Letter no. 2 from T.D. MacDonald, Ottawa, to Tom Edmondson, 9 April 1956, F-P.

39 Farmer, "Special Message," p. 35.

40 "Monetary Times 1955 Report on the Canadian Electrical Industry," Monetary Times, 124 no. 3, March 1955, p. 41.

41 Ibid., p. 42.

42 Ibid.

43 C. Barber, untitled brief to the Royal Commission on Canada's Economic Prospects, 1956, p. 12.

44 Knox, "The Canadian Electrical Manufacturing Industry," p. 60.

45 Ibid.

46 Canadian Electrical Manufacturers Association, "A Condensation and Digest of the Knox Report," Jan. 1955.

47 The CEMA chose to use a table from the Knox Report which gave the rise of foreign wage rates relative to Canada in Canadian dollars. To use devaluation as one cause of the industry's plight and then to use wage rates based on devalued figures is an erroneous argument. The Knox Report pointed out that British wages rose 320 per cent over the same period, as compared to the Canadian figure of 327 per cent. The discrepancy, however, was significant relative to American manufacturers, where wage rates rose 282 per cent. Knox Report, p. 60.

48 D. Morton, Working People (Toronto: Deneau, 1984), p. 154.

49 Ibid., p. 166.

50 United Electrical, Radio and Machine Workers of America (UE), Canadian Section, A Brief History of UE – 1937–1977: 40 Years of Militant, Progressive, Rank-and-File Trade Unionism, 1977, p. 13, Courtesy UE.

51 Untitled history of local 525 of the UE, 1968, p. 5, courtesy UE.

52 Morton, Working People, p. 203. According to Mor-
ton (p. 203), the communist labour movement's patriotism led to important gains throughout the CCL: "Communists came to dominate not only the Electrical Workers and the Canadian Seaman's Union but the British Columbia district of the International Woodworkers of America, the Shipyard and General Workers Union, and much of the United Auto Workers and the International Union of Mine, Mill and Smelters, heir of the old Western Federation of Miners. Within the CCL, at least a third of the members were organized in Communist-run unions, and their voice, carefully rehearsed and reinforced by communists in other unions, was even more dominant."

53 W. Easterbrook and H. Aitken, Canadian Economic History (Toronto: University of Toronto Press, 1956, reprint 1988), p. 570.

54 J. MacArthur, "A Red-Line Union Is Dying," Financial Post, 28 July 1956, p. 9.

55 Cooper to V.Z. de Ferranti, 17 March 1950, Ferranti UK Archives.

56 V.Z. de Ferranti to Cooper, 30 Nov. 1953, Ferranti UK Archives.

Chapter Seven

1 "The Electrical Apparatus and Supply Industry," Canada, Dominion Bureau of Statistics, Census, 1955, 1956, 1957.

2 The demand for distribution transformers is very closely tied to housing starts. In 1960, a 25-per-cent reduction in housing starts cut deeply into the transformer business; "Report Housing Starts Fewer by 25% in 1960," Monetary Times vol. 129, no. 1, Jan. 1961, p. 51. According to a 1961 survey of the electrical industry carried out by the Canadian journal, Monetary Times, "the massive capital expansion projects undertaken by many Canadian industries in the 1950's ... resulted in substantial plant overcapacity – at the current level of business activity – for many of the electrical manufacturing industry's customers. As a consequence in 1960 there was a relatively low level of capital investment carried out by these customers, with a consequent reduction in demand for the products of the electrical manufacturing industry." P. Chisholm, "1961 Report on Canadian Electrical Industry," Monetary Times, 129 no. 3, March 1961, pp. 33–4.

3 For information regarding the value of power transformer shipments, see "The Electrical Apparatus and

Supply Industry," Census, 1955, 1956, 1957.

In 1960, the average profit on sales for the electrical industry was 3 per cent, as compared to 5.1 per cent for the entire manufacturing sector; "Electrical Industry Seeking Protection," *Financial Post*, 15 Oct. 1960, p. 52. The following year, at 2.3 per cent, the average profit on sales for the electrical industry fell to to its lowest point since the depression, "Electrical Companies Face Profit Squeeze," *Financial Post*, 14 Oct. 1961, p. 16. As an aggregated average, this low profit margin concealed even more dramatic drops in the profits in Canada's transformer business.

4 Annual audited statements of Ferranti Ltd, worldwide operations, 1963 F-P.

5 Norton Anderson, "Why Jobs Are Dwindling in Electrical Industry," *Financial Post*, 25 June 1960, pp. 25-6.

6 "In the past a large volume of custom made goods has been imported into Canada as a class or kind not made in Canada free of duty and not subject to anti-dumping provisions simply because the size and specification differed somewhat from that of similar products made in Canada and irrespective of whether such products could be made in Canada or were competitive with products made by Canadian industry." H. Style (president, John Inglis Co. Ltd), "Electrical Industry Leaders' Forecasts for 1961," *Monetary Times* 129, no. 3, March 1961, p. 52.

Herbert Smith, president of CGE wrote: "One of our urgent needs is early stage 'infant industry' tariff protection against European imports." H. Style claimed that Canada "must be given enough protection so that the manufacturers in Canada can capture a larger share of the home market – then we will be able to get export business based on the economies effected by increased Canadian production." And O. Titus, president of Canada Wire and Cable, was unequivocal in his demand that "the Canadian tariff structure needs speedy and serious re-examination." All quotations from Anderson, "Why Jobs Are Dwindling, p. 25.

7 "Electrical Industry Leaders' Forecasts for 1961," pp. 56–7.

8 "'Buy Made-in-Canada' to Protect Own Jobs U-K Industrialist Warns," *Toronto Star*, 8 Jan. 1960, p. 10. The reference to subway cars concerned a controversy surrounding the Toronto Transit Commission's desire to buy the more expensive, but "Made-in-Canada" subway cars. The idea was rejected in favour of cheaper, foreign-made cars.

9 Ibid.

10 Ferranti Minutes, 23 Dec. 1948, p. 2.

11 V.Z. de Ferranti to Cooper, 22 March 1949, Ferranti UK Archives.

12 Cooper to V.Z. de Ferranti, 25 March 1949, Ferranti UK Archives.

13 Ibid.

14 Ferranti Minutes, 25 March 1949, p. 2.

15 V.Z. de Ferranti to Cooper, 29 March 1949, Ferranti UK Archives.

16 R. Rumilly, *Maurice Duplessis et son temps* (Montreal: Fidès, 1978), vol. 1, p. 351.

17 Ibid., p. 556.

18 C. Hogue, A. Bolduc, and D. Larouche, *Québec: un siècle d'électricité* (Montreal: Libre Expression, 1979), p. 234.

19 Ibid.

20 Minutes of the Board of Director's Meeting, Packard Electric, 25 Jan. 1956, p. 1, F-P.

21 Ibid.

22 Ibid.

23 Interview, Charles Begin, Trois-Rivières, 4 April 1989, John Vardalas interviewer, F-P.

24 From a taped radio broadcast made by CHLN-Radio in Trois-Rivières, 18 May 1956, Acc. 9090-0367, Moving Images and Sound Division, National Archives of Canada.

25 Ibid.

26 Ibid.

27 Ibid.

28 Ibid.

29 Ibid.

30 "Brown-Boveri Opens Modern New Plant," *Electrical Digest* 21, Nov. 1952, p. 36.

31 Ibid.

32 Confidential memo, R. Short to T. Edmondson, 16 April 1958, F-P. Short added: "price was not a deciding factor in the placement of the business. Canadian General Electric had a much better offer and we compared very favourably pricewise, with the Brown-Boveri proposal." At a meeting on 25 April 1958, J.-Arthur Savoie explained to Short that he had made promises to Brown-Boveri. Short to D.F. Martin, 25 April 1958, F-P.

33 Notes prepared by, or for, Tom Edmondson on 21 April 1958, F-P.

34 Ibid.

35 R. Short to D.F. Martin, 25 April 1958, F-P.

36 Tom Edmondson to J.-Arthur Savoie, President, Que-

bec Hydro Electric Commission, 22 April, 1958, F-P.

37 Ibid.

38 R. Short to D.F. Martin, 25 April 1958, F-P.

39 R. Sultan, *Pricing in the Electrical Oligopoly*, vol. 1; *Competition or Collusion* (Cambridge, Mass.: Harvard University Press, 1974), p. 81.

40 House of Commons, *Debates: Official Report*, 4th Sess., 24th parl. vol. 2, 1960–61, p. 1798.

41 Ibid., p. 3231.

42 T. Edmondson, untitled, *Monetary Times* 129, no. 3, March 1961, p. 57.

43 T. Edmondson, quoted in "We Live Beyond Our Means," *Financial Post*, 28 Oct. 1961, p. 52.

44 Interview, Ray Taylor, Toronto, 30 Jan. 1988, John Vardalas interviewer, F-P.

45 Ibid.

46 Ibid.

47 Ibid

48 Ibid.

49 Interview, Wordie Hetherington, Toronto, 23 July 1987, John Vardalas interviewer, F-P.

50 Ibid.

51 Videotaped round table discussion, led by John Vardalas, about the history of transformer technology at Ferranti-Packard and in the industry in general. Participants were retired and present design engineers at Ferranti-Packard. 28 Jan. 1988, F-P.

52 Interview, Jack Coopman, 22 July 1989, John Vardalas interviewer, F-P.

53 Ibid.

54 Ibid.

55 Ibid.

56 Ibid.

57 Begin interview, 1989.

58 Ibid.

59 Ibid.

60 Duplessis taped speech, 1956.

Chapter Eight

1 In Michael Bliss, *Northern Enterprise: Five Centuries of Canadian Business* (Toronto: McClelland and Stewart, 1987), p. 448.

2 Desmond Morton, "Strains of Affluence," in C. Brown, ed., *The Illustrated History of Canada* (Toronto: Lester & Orpen Denys, 1987), p. 484.

3 Morton, "Strains," p. 471.

4 Stan Augarten, *Bit By Bit: An Illustrated History of Computers* (New York: Ticknor & Fields, 1984), p. 120.

5 Herman Goldstine, *The Computer: From Pascal to von Neumann* (Princeton, NJ: Princeton University Press, 1972).

6 D.J. Goodspeed, *A History of the Defence Research Board of Canada* (Ottawa: Queen's Printer, 1958), p. 27.

7 The Electronics Industry in Canada, April 1956, a report prepared for the Royal Commission on Canada's Economic Prospects by Canadian Business Service Ltd, p. 37.

8 Captain E.G. Cullwick, Director, Electrical Research Division, for Chairman, Defence Research Board, to Vincent Z. Ferranti, Vice President, Ferranti Electric Co., Defence Research Board Numbering System Canada, DRBS file number 400-640-44, 3 Aug. 1948, Ferranti UK Archives.

9 Commenting on the DRB's first area of applied research, precision servo-systems for computers, including automatic devices for radar systems, Grundy wrote to Sir Vincent: "This is a subject on which we are very well qualified to undertake development. Dr. Prinz is a national authority on theory and practice of servo systems. Both Carter and Nelson have had years of experience on the design and operation of Army and Navy computers. The Admiralty Flyplane, which we have developed and made, embodies electronic computing and regenerative tracking. Remote power control over long distances is a subject which we are studying for the Army, in relation to the early warning system. Prinz is in the States at the moment, studying methods of high speed data transmission about which we know a fair amount (involves Binary Digital Computing machines). We have recently decided to build a machine embodying Professor Williams' storage system". Departmental memo from Eric Grundy to Sir Vincent de Ferranti, 20 Sept. 1948, Ferranti UK Archives.

10 Dr. Ormond Solandt, Chairman of the Defence Research Board, Ottawa, to Sir Vincent Ziani de Ferranti, 7 Jan. 1949, Ferranti UK Archives.

11 A.B. Cooper to Sir Vincent Ziani de Ferranti, 7 Feb. 1949, Ferranti UK Archives.

12 R.H. Davies, Ferranti Electric Inc., New York City, to Sir Vincent Ziani de Ferranti, 14 Feb. 1949, Ferranti UK Archives.

13 A.B. Cooper to Sir Vincent Ziani de Ferranti, 7 Feb. 1949, Ferranti UK Archives.

14 Interview, Jim Belyea, Dec. 1986, Ottawa, John Vardalas interviewer, National Museum of Science and Technology, Ottawa.

15 Kenyon Taylor, Industrial Biography, 1972, p. 18, F-P.

16 Belyea interview, 1986.

17 In 1958, during the merger of Packard Electric and Ferranti Electric, the Research Department was combined with the Ordnance and Electronics departments to form the Electronics Division. All the work in digital computer and communications systems, prior to the merger, had been carried out in the Research Department.

18 Formal approval was given at the 17 June 1950 meeting of the Navy Research Control Committee, composed of Rear Admirals F.L. Houghton, J.G. Knowlton, and W.B. Creery, Dr. C.S. Fields, and M. Johnson. The committee allocated $324,000 "for the present fiscal year." It also set up a project committee to oversee development of DATAR: Dr. Field, Captain Roger (electrical engineer in chief), Stan Knight (EEC), Ord. Lt. Commander P. Henning, (director of fire control), Commander M. Sterling (director of naval communication), Lt. Commander. F. Caldwell (deputy director of weapons and tactics), and J. Johnson (director of scientific services). DATAR was listed under file NSS 7428-16.

19 This anecdote was related to one of the authors in a conversation of 14 April 1988 with Barry Hercus.

20 Letter from Dr. Bowden to Dr. Arthur Porter, 4 Jan. 1951, Ferranti-Packard Archives, Toronto.

21 R. Davies to A. Porter, Ottawa, 30 June 1952, F-P.

22 Ibid.

23 Peter Drucker, Management (New York: Harper & Row, 1973), p. 61.

24 Both quotations from Taylor, Industrial Biography, 1972, pp. 2–3.

25 Interview, Walter Turnbull, Ottawa, 7 July 1988, John Vardalas interviewer, F-P.

26 Louis Rindenour, "A Revolution in Electronics," Scientific American 185, no. 2, Aug. 1951, pp. 13–17.

27 Ernest Braun and Stuart MacDonald, Revolution in Miniature: The History and Impact of Semiconductor Electronics (Cambridge: Cambridge University Press, 1978), p. 60.

28 Dirk Hanson, The New Alchemists (New York: Avon Books, 1982, p. 80).

29 Braun and MacDonald, Revolution in Miniature, p. 60.

30 Interview, Gordon Helwig, Toronto, 23 July 1987, John Vardalas interviewer, F-P. Norman Moody was a talented electronics engineer with remarkable foresight. He saw the immense effect that the transistor would have on civilian and military life. As early as 1953, he convinced the DRB of the strategic importance of establishing a Canadian technological base in transistors. As a result, the Electronics Laboratory (EL) was set up, with Moody at its head, within the Defence Research Telecommunications Establishment (DRTE), in Ottawa. The EL was to explore uses of the transistor in circuit design and to transfer this knowledge to defence industries. The EL started to design a digital computer simply as a vehicle to demonstrate the potential of transistors about the same time that Ferranti Electric started on the Post Office computer.

31 Interview, Don Ritchie, 3 May 1988, John Vardalas interviewer, F-P. D. Ritchie to D. Brown, Lincoln Laboratories, M.I.T., 21 Dec. 1955, F-P.

32 Maurice Levy, "The Electronics Aspects of the Canadian Sorting of Mail System," reprint from Proceedings of the National Electronic Conference, vol. 10, Feb. 1955; Maurice Levy, "Automation in Post Offices," reprint from Proceedings of the National Electronics Conference, Chicago, 3–5 Oct. 1955.

33 J.J. Brown, The Inventors: Great Ideas in Canadian Enterprise (Toronto: McClelland and Stewart, 1967), p. 99.

34 P. Harpur, ed., The Timetable of Technology (New York: Hearst, 1982), p. 168.

35 The system wound up costing $2 million; "Canadian PO Orders Larger Mail Sorter," Electronic News, 17 March 1958.

36 Turnbull interview.

37 Interview, Maurice Levy, 7 July 1988, Ottawa, John Vardalas interviewer, F-P.

38 The Electronics Industry in Canada, p. 44.

39 F-P contains a collection of technical data sheets on all the transistorized digital cards produced by Ferranti Electric, and later by Ferranti-Packard, during the period 1955–64.

40 Helwig interview.

41 Hesitant about embarking on an electronic reservation system, TCA asked an outside consulting firm to assess Richardson's concept. The study was done by L. Casciato, J. Kates, and R. Johnston for Sir Robert Watson-Watt's company, Adelia. Casciato, Kates, and Johnston had tried to build Canada's first computer, UTEC, at the University of Toronto. Their report, Pre-

liminary Report on an Automatic Passenger Service System for Trans-Canada Air Lines, supported Richardson's idea entirely. See John Vardalas, Some Canadian Contributions to Real-Time Data Processing Technology in Transportation, report for the National Museum of Science and Technology, Oct. 1985.

42 Interview, Lyman Richardson, Sept. 1985, Toronto, John Vardalas interviewer, National Museum of Science and Technology, Ottawa.

43 L. Richardson, "RESERVEC: The Electronic Reservation System of Trans-Canada Air Lines," paper presented to the Toronto Section of the Computer and Data Processing Society of Canada, June 1963.

44 Richardson's decision to support Ferranti-Packard did not endear him to IBM, and he recalls: "IBM came in and saw the President of TCA, MacGregor, and told him that they had a high regard for TCA, and it was a major customer and all that. However, they couldn't get along with one guy. MacGregor said: 'That must be Lyman Richardson.' And they said: 'Well, yes, as a matter of fact.' MacGregor entertained the IBM group, and when they left he phoned me and said 'I've had trouble concerning you'. He told me to come in and see him. I figured, 'Uh-oh! I've enjoyed it here anyway.' Then in his office he told me: 'Look, that didn't hit me at all. Those bastards, I hate the sight of them. Keep doing what you're doing. You're doing a good job'. I always got on very well with Mac-Gregor." Richardson interview.

45 Interview, I.P. Sharp, 21 July 1988, Toronto, John Vardalas interviewer, F-P.

46 Ritchie interview.

47 Ibid.

Chapter Nine

1 John Fogarty had discussions with various government representatives in Ottawa through the auspices of the Royal Commission on Government Organization (Glassco Commission). One of the areas investigated was the effect of government R&D spending on industrial development. Two of the project officers of the sub-committee on scientific research and development were Arthur Porter and John Fogarty.

2 Ferranti-Packard Management Meeting Minutes, 18 Aug. 1961, F-P.

3 Interview, I.P. Sharp, Toronto, 13 Aug. 1984, Ted Paull and John Vardalas interviewers, National Museum of Science and Technology, Ottawa.

4 Interview, Les Wood, Gordon Helwig, and Bill Lower, Toronto, 27 Nov. 1987, John Vardalas interviewer. F-P.

5 Ibid.

6 Interview, Gordon Helwig, Toronto, 23 July 1987, John Vardalas interviewer, F-P.

7 Harry Johnson, Involvement of Ferranti Ltd in the Development of the FP-6000 Computer, private communication prepared for Ferranti Ltd, Feb. 1988, p. 4, F-P.

8 Interview, Ted Strain, Gord Lang, Fred Longstaff, and Les Wood, Toronto, 14 Aug. 1984, Ted Paull and John Vardalas interviewers, National Museum of Science and Technology, Ottawa.

9 Johnson, Involvement, p. 4.

10 Robert Sobel, IBM, Colossus in Transition (New York: Bantam, 1983), p. 213.

11 Ibid., p. 212.

12 Kristian Palda, Industrial Innovation: Its Place in the Public Agenda (Vancouver: Fraser Institute, 1984), pp. 130–1.

13 Interview, John Pickin, London, England, 11 May 1989, John Vardalas interviewer, F-P.

14 Interview, Sir Donald MacCallum, London, England, 9 May 1989, John Vardalas interviewer, F-P.

15 Johnson, Involvement, p. 6.

16 Strain, Lang, Longstaff, and Wood interview.

17 Drucker, Management, p. 61.

18 G. Funkhouser and R. Rothberg, The Pursuit of Growth (New York: Tempus, 1987), pp. 157–8.

19 Johnson, Involvement, pp. 6–7.

20 Royal Commission on Government Organization, J. Grant Glassco, Chairman, July 18, 1962, Report, Vol. 4, p. 208.

21 Sharp interview.

22 Lower, Wood, and Helwig interview.

23 Interview, Wordie Hetherington, Toronto, Jan. 1988, John Vardalas interviewer, F-P.

24 Ibid.

25 Ibid.

26 Kenyon Taylor, Industrial Biography, 1972, F-P.

27 Statement prepared by Carle C. Morrill, manager, Fuel Cell Marketing, Pratt and Whitney Aircraft Division, United Aircraft Corp., at hearings before the U.S. Subcommittee on Science, Research, and Development, House Committee on Science and Astronautics, May 1972.

28 Minutes of the Ferranti-Packard Management Meetings, 27 Jan. 1971, F-P.

29 Ferranti-Packard position presented to Gleneagles Conference by Wordie Hetherington, Gleneagles, Scotland, p. 1, F-P.

30 Ibid., p. 2.

31 Ibid.

32 Confidential communication, Wordie Hetherington to Tom Edmondson, 4 Aug. 1970, F-P.

33 Ibid.

34 Ibid.

Chapter Ten

1 Editorial in *F-P Newsletter*, April 1976.

2 On this point Rea writes: "Even the elementary text-books, which normally adopt a positive tone in discussing the limitations of economic analysis, accepted that 'we simply do not know with any degree of confidence the reasons for the drastic deterioration in the productivity performance of the Canadian economy during the 1970's', K.J. Rea, *The Prosperous Years: The Economic History of Ontario, 1939-75* (Toronto: University of Toronto Press, 1985), p. 6.

3 The concept of management by objectives was introduced and discussed in Peter Drucker, *The Practice of Management* (New York: Harper and Row, 1973).

4 "Interview with Sebastian Ziani de Ferranti," *Ferranti News*, Special Supplement, 15 May 1975, p. 2, Ferranti Ltd. Archives.

5 Interview, Sir Donald MacCallum, London, England, 9 May 1989, John Vardalas interviewer, F-P. 1989.

6 Ibid.

7 "Decision Time," *Ferranti News*, 15 May 1975, p. 1, Ferranti Ltd. Archives.

8 Interview, John Pickin, London, England, 11 May 1989, John Vardalas interviewer, F.P.

9 Annual financial audits for Ferranti Ltd. world-wide operations, 1971, F-P.

10 Interview, Barry Hercus, Toronto, 24 March 1988, John Vardalas interviewer, F-P.

11 Interview, Henry Peprnick, Brampton, Ont., 21 July 1989, John Vardalas interviewer, F-P.

12 Ibid.

13 Peprnick interview.

14 Interview, Barry Hercus, Toronto, 14 April 1988, John Vardalas interviewer, F-P.

15 Hercus interview, 24 March 1988.

16 Hercus interview, 14 April 1988.

17 Report on the Financial Position of Ferranti-Packard Limited Based on the Accounts for the Four Years Ended 31 March 1977, prepared for the Board of Directors of Ferranti Ltd by Price-Waterhouse & Co., London, England, and Thornton Baker, Chartered Accountants, London, England, 3 April 1978; F-P.

18 Interview, Don Smart, Toronto, 29 June 1988, John Vardalas interviewer, F-P.

19 Ibid.

20 Ibid.

21 Ibid.

22 Ibid.

23 Ibid.

24 Ibid.

25 Interview, Barry Hercus, Toronto, 24 April 1988, John Vardalas interviewer, F-P.

26 Unidentified preprint, erroneously identified in archives as "Automation", F-P.

27 "$1,500,000 U.S. Electronic Order for Canada," Ferranti-Packard News Release, 25 May 1961, F-P.

28 Hercus interview, 24 April 1988.

29 Ibid.

30 Report for Ferranti Ltd, 3 April 1978.

31 Hercus interview, 24 April 1988.

32 Ibid.

33 Ibid.

34 Ibid.

35 An open letter from J. Pickin to W. Hetherington, to be read into the Ferranti-Packard's Fall 1977 Briars Conference, F-P.

36 Ibid.

37 Ibid.

38 Interview, Jack Coopman, 22 July 1989, John Vardalas interviewer, F-P.

39 Bob MacKimmie, untitled article on postwar meter developments at Packard Electric and Ferranti-Packard, c. 1979, p. 50, F-P.

40 Ibid., 52.

41 MacCallum interview.

42 Pickin interview.

43 Interview, Wordie Hetherington, Toronto, 28 June 1989, John Vardalas interviewer, F-P.

44 W. Hetherington to The Hon. Michael Wilson, Minister of Finance, 18 Oct. 1979, F-P.

Index